ASCENDANCE OF A BOOKWORM
I'll do anything to become a librarian!

Part 1 If there aren't any books,
I'll just have to make some!

Volume 6

Author: **Miya Kazuki** / Artist: **Suzuka**
Character Designer: **You Shiina**

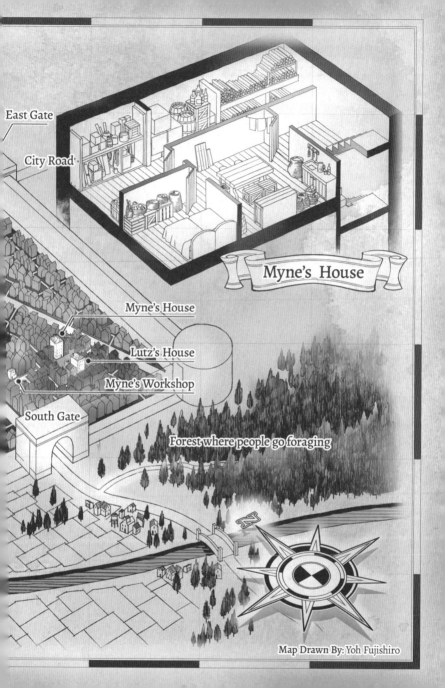

East Gate

City Road

Myne's_House

Myne's House

Lutz's House

Myne's Workshop

South Gate

Forest where people go foraging

Map Drawn By: Yoh Fujishiro

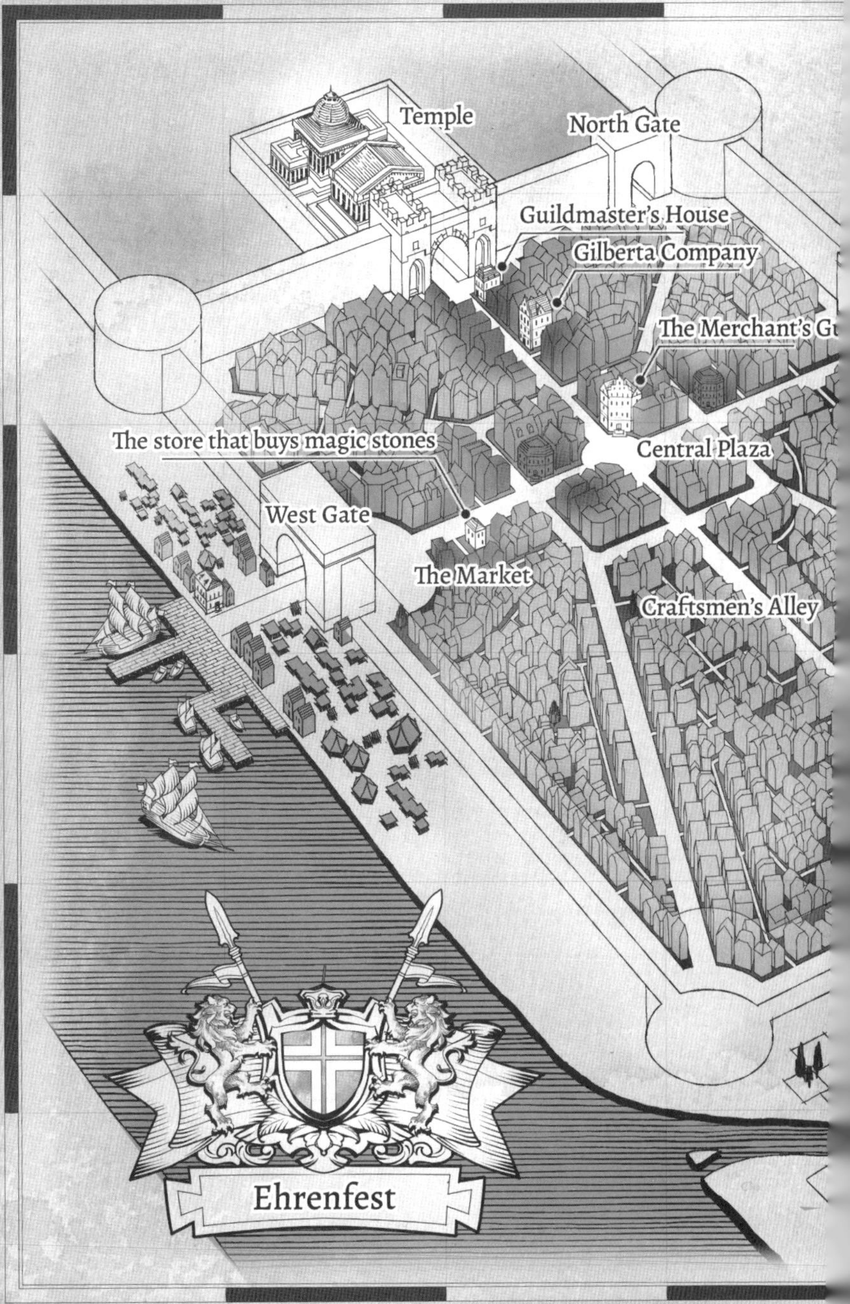
Temple
North Gate
Guildmaster's House
Gilberta Company
The Merchant's Gu
The store that buys magic stones
Central Plaza
West Gate
The Market
Craftsmen's Alley
Ehrenfest

ASCENDANCE OF A BOOKWORM
I'll do anything to become a librarian!
Part 1 If there aren't any books, I'll just have to make some! Volume VI

Chapter 25: **Freida and Myne** 005

Chapter 26: **The Beginning of Winter** 053

Chapter 27: **Family Meeting** 087

Chapter 28: **Resuming Paper-Making** 111

Chapter 29: **Vested Interests** 135

Extra: **Some Time in the Woods** 171

Story: **A Long-Awaited Reunion** 181

Afterword: **Artist's** 190

Afterword: **Author's** 191

Ch.25 Freida and Myne

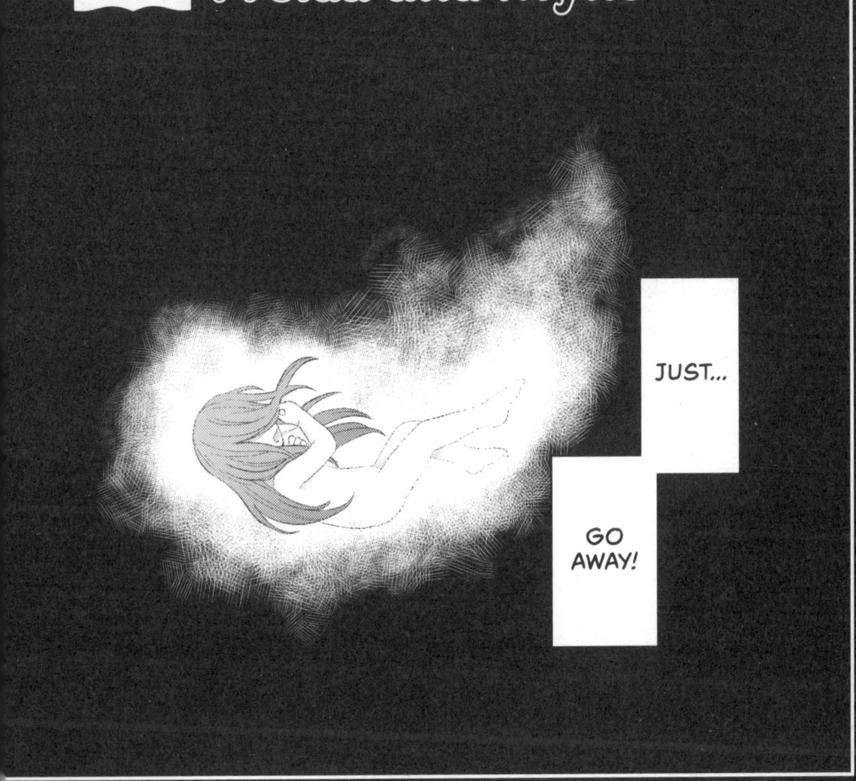
JUST...
GO AWAY!

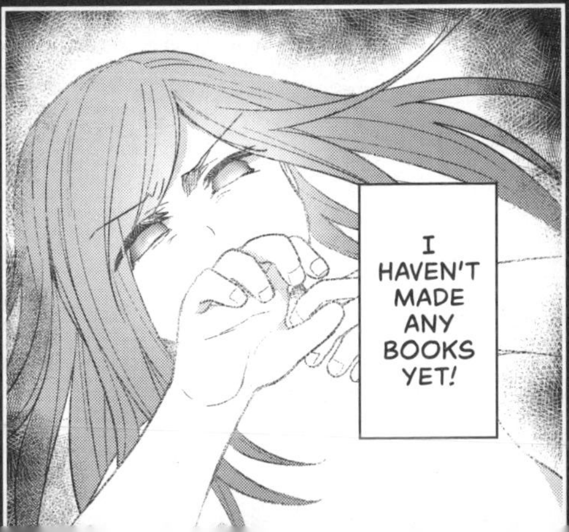
I HAVEN'T MADE ANY BOOKS YET!

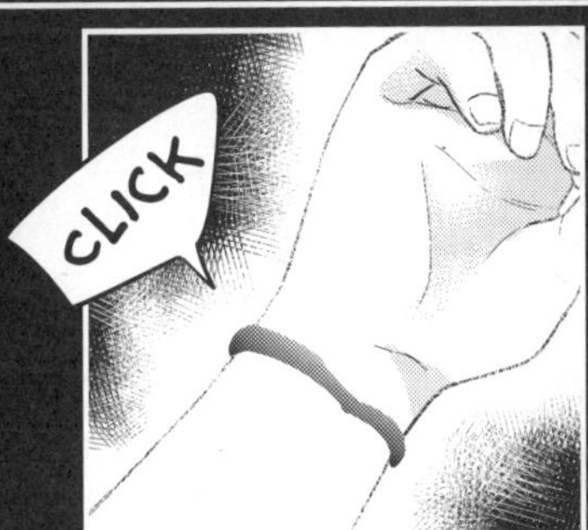
CLICK

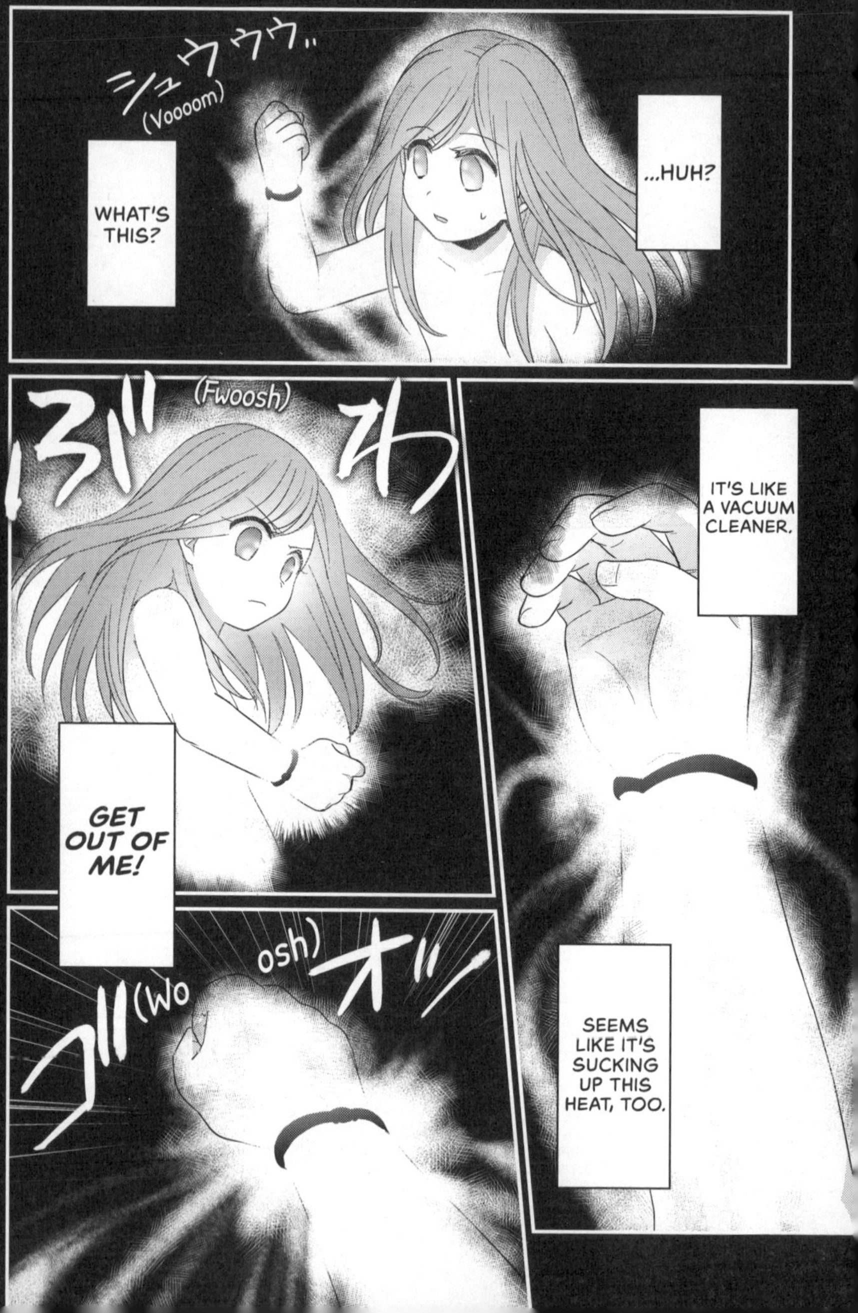
...HUH?
シュウウウ
(Voooom)
WHAT'S THIS?
IT'S LIKE A VACUUM CLEANER.
SEEMS LIKE IT'S SUCKING UP THIS HEAT, TOO.
ぶわっ
(Fwoosh)
GET OUT OF ME!
ゴオッ
(Woosh)

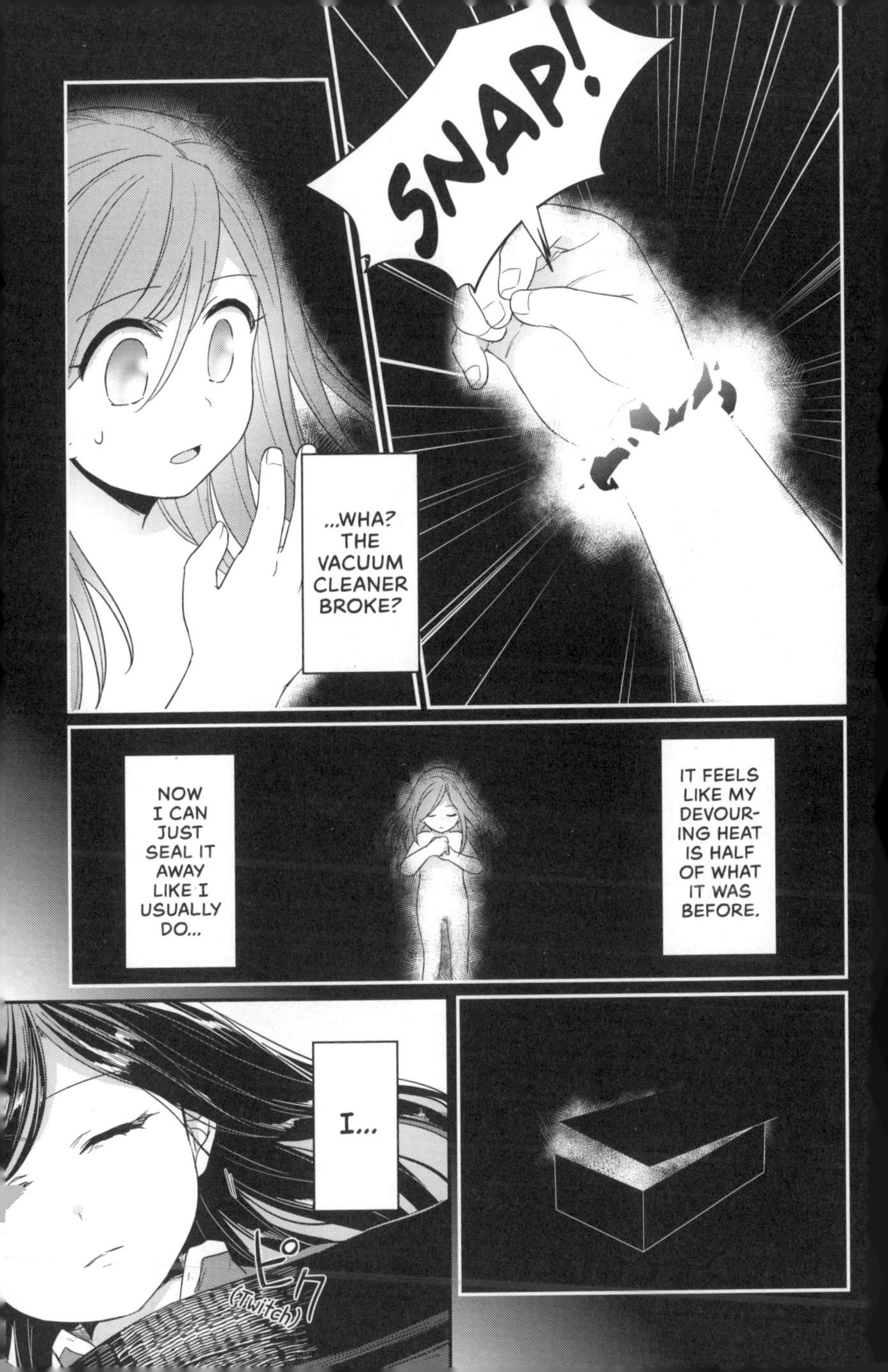
SNAP!
...WHA? THE VACUUM CLEANER BROKE?
IT FEELS LIKE MY DEVOUR-ING HEAT IS HALF OF WHAT IT WAS BEFORE.
NOW I CAN JUST SEAL IT AWAY LIKE I USUALLY DO...
I...
ピク
(Twitch)

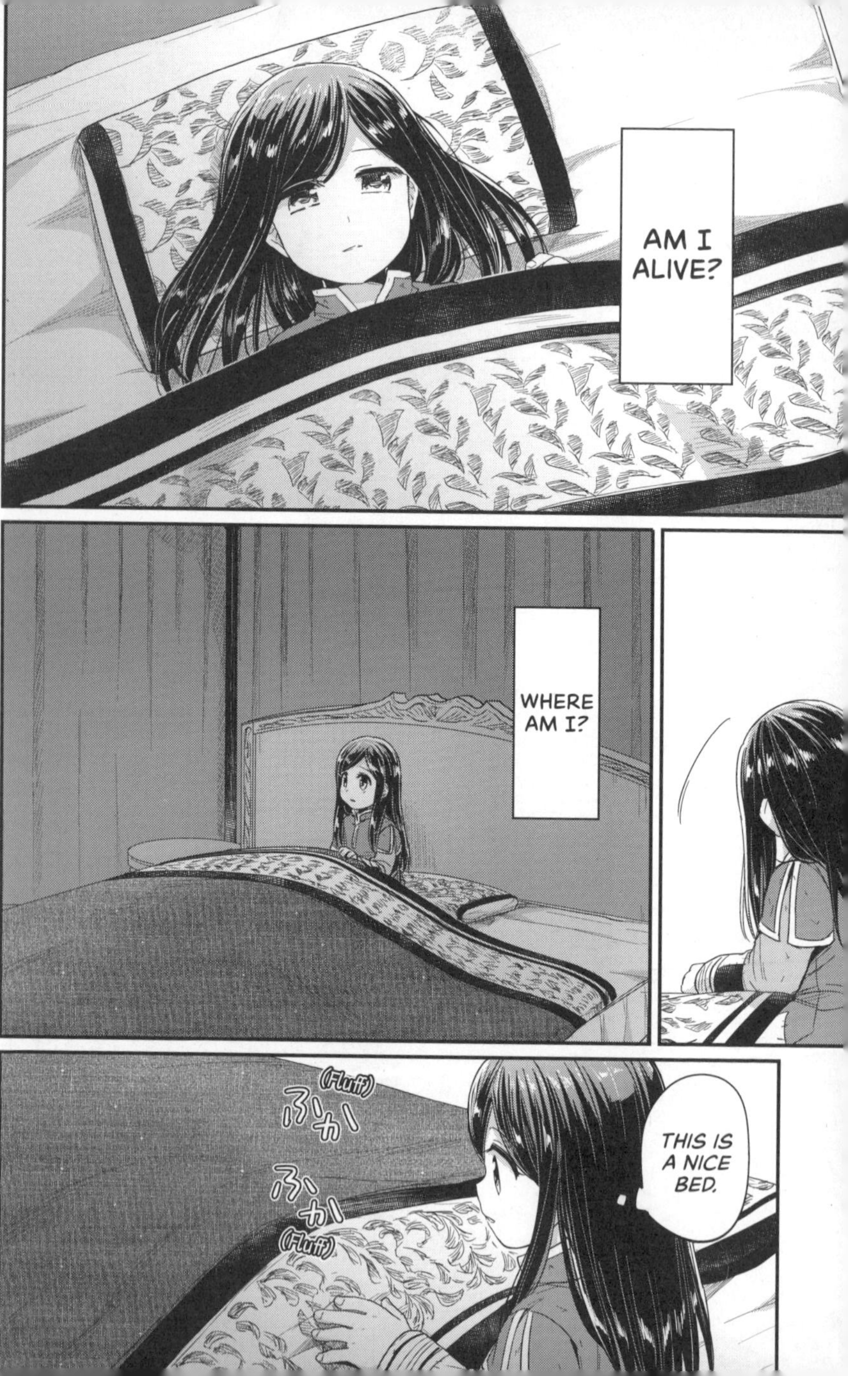
AM I ALIVE?
WHERE AM I?
THIS IS A NICE BED.
(Fluff) ふか
ふか (Fluff)

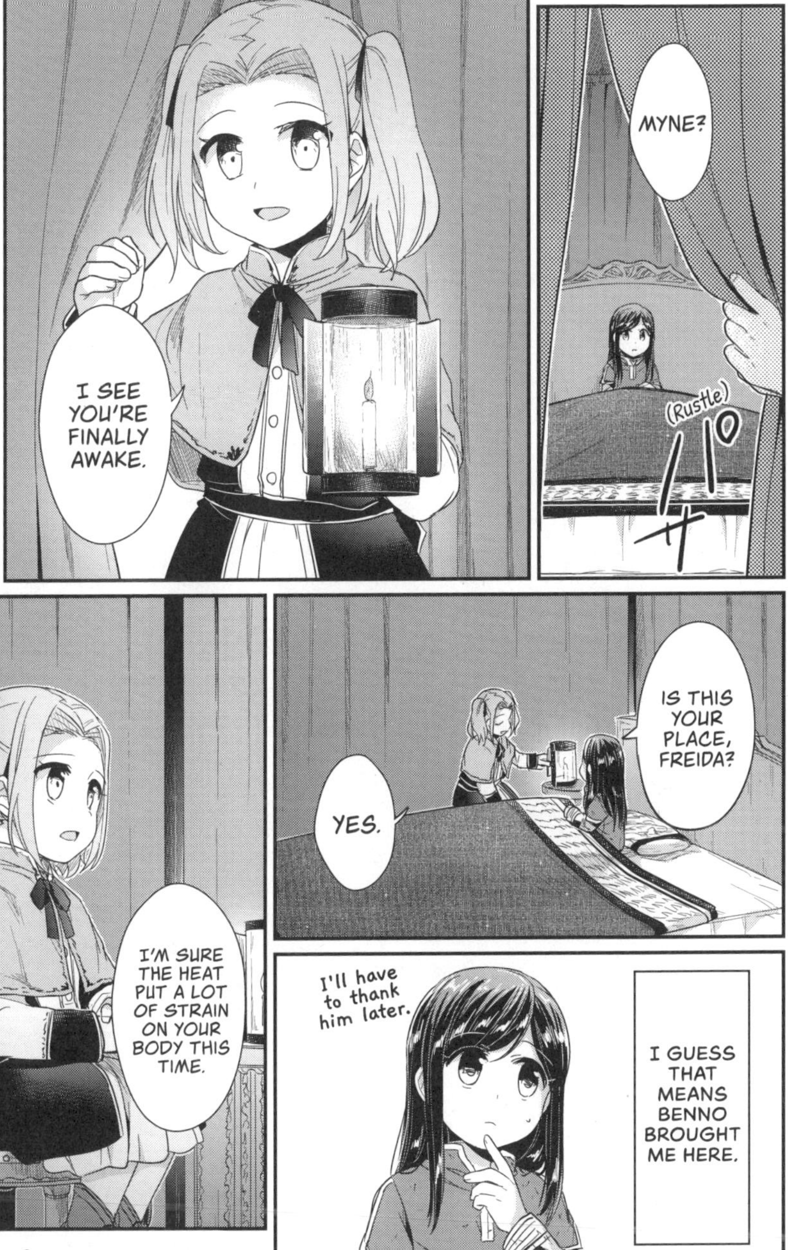
MYNE?
(Rustle)
I SEE YOU'RE FINALLY AWAKE.
IS THIS YOUR PLACE, FREIDA?
YES.
I GUESS THAT MEANS BENNO BROUGHT ME HERE.
I'll have to thank him later.
I'M SURE THE HEAT PUT A LOT OF STRAIN ON YOUR BODY THIS TIME.

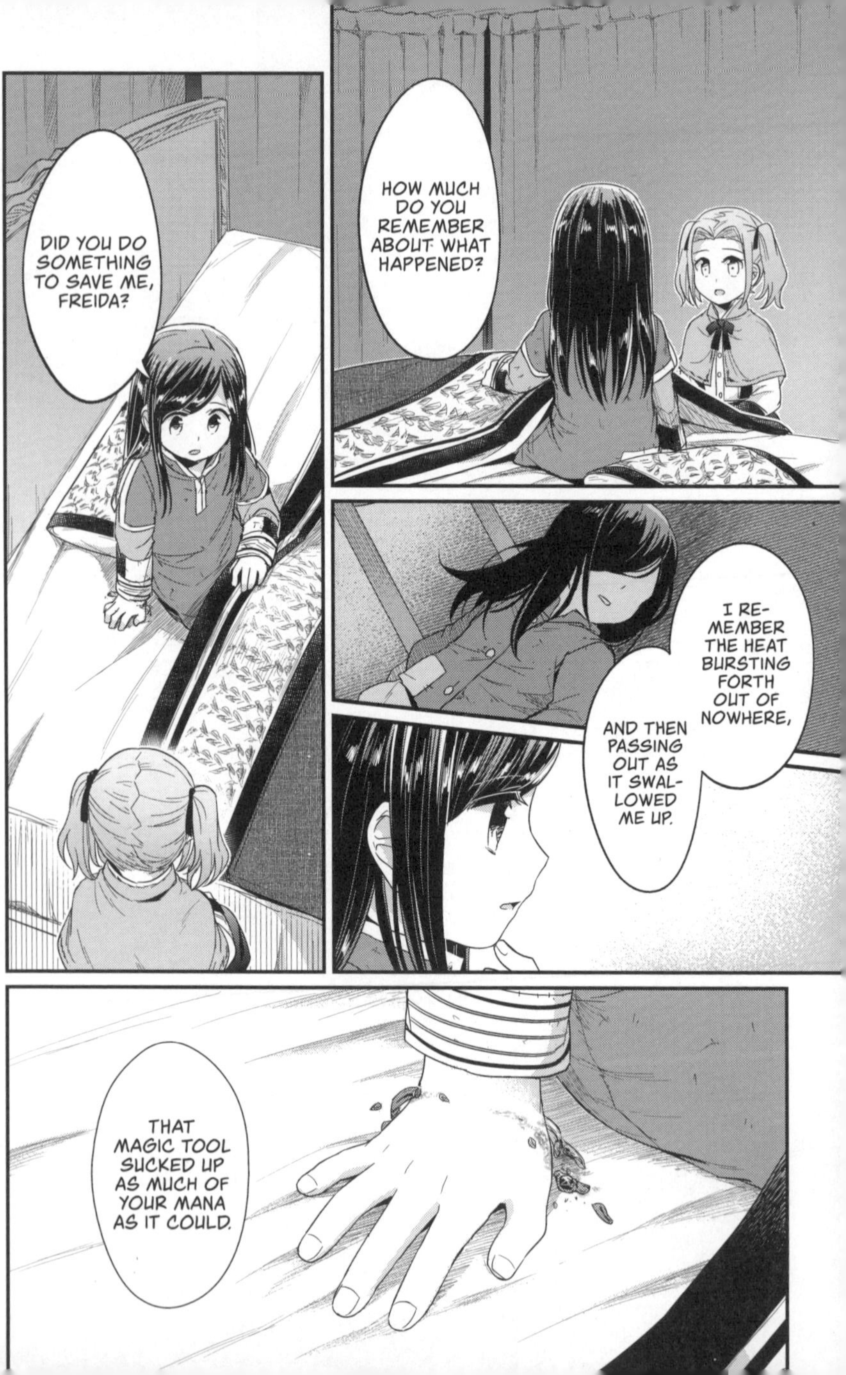
HOW MUCH DO YOU REMEMBER ABOUT WHAT HAPPENED?
I RE-MEMBER THE HEAT BURSTING FORTH OUT OF NOWHERE,
AND THEN PASSING OUT AS IT SWAL-LOWED ME UP.
DID YOU DO SOMETHING TO SAVE ME, FREIDA?
THAT MAGIC TOOL SUCKED UP AS MUCH OF YOUR MANA AS IT COULD.

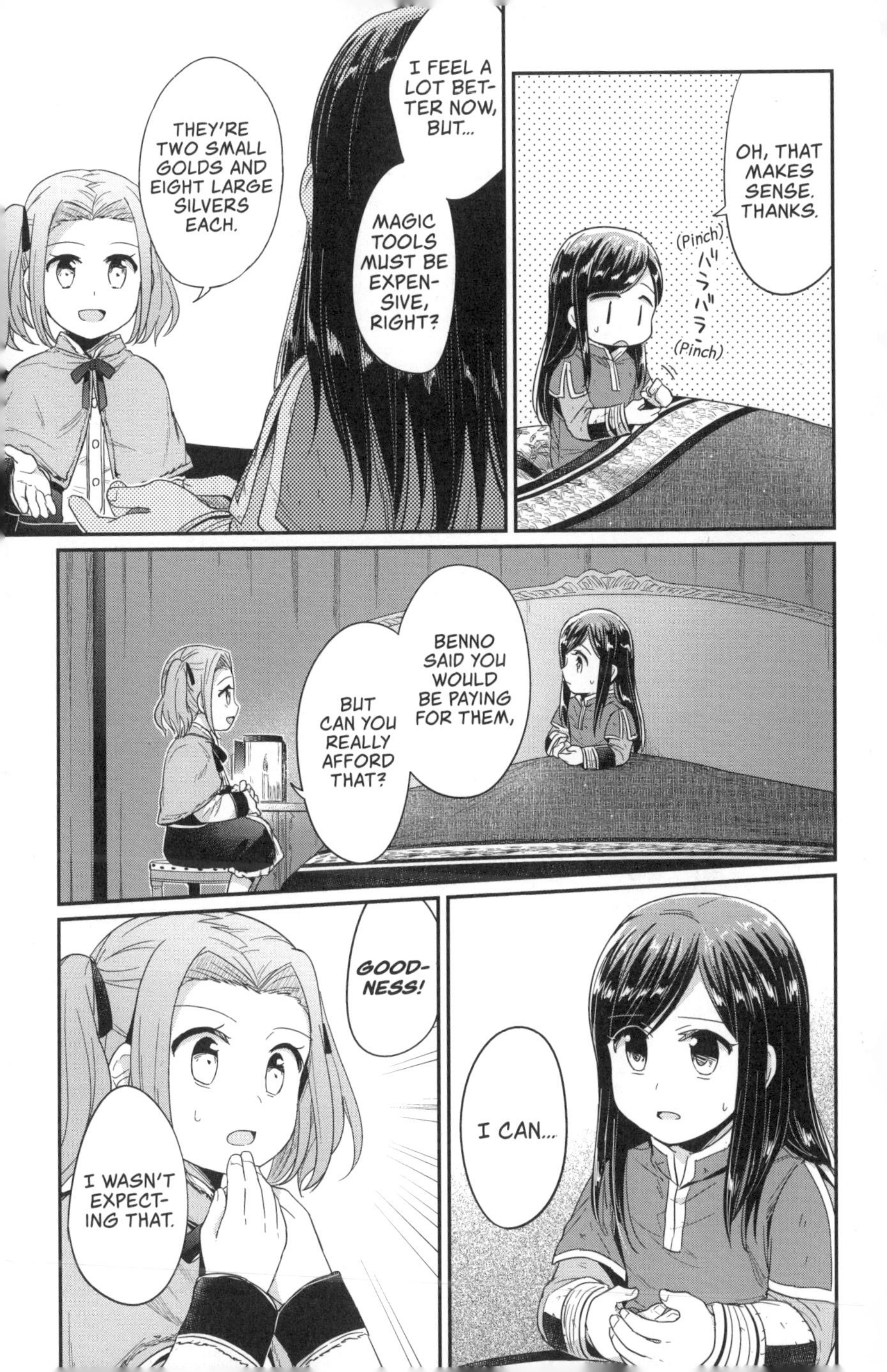
OH, THAT MAKES SENSE. THANKS.
(Pinch)
バラバラ
(Pinch)
I FEEL A LOT BETTER NOW, BUT...
MAGIC TOOLS MUST BE EXPENSIVE, RIGHT?
THEY'RE TWO SMALL GOLDS AND EIGHT LARGE SILVERS EACH.
BENNO SAID YOU WOULD BE PAYING FOR THEM,
BUT CAN YOU REALLY AFFORD THAT?
I CAN...
GOODNESS!
I WASN'T EXPECTING THAT.

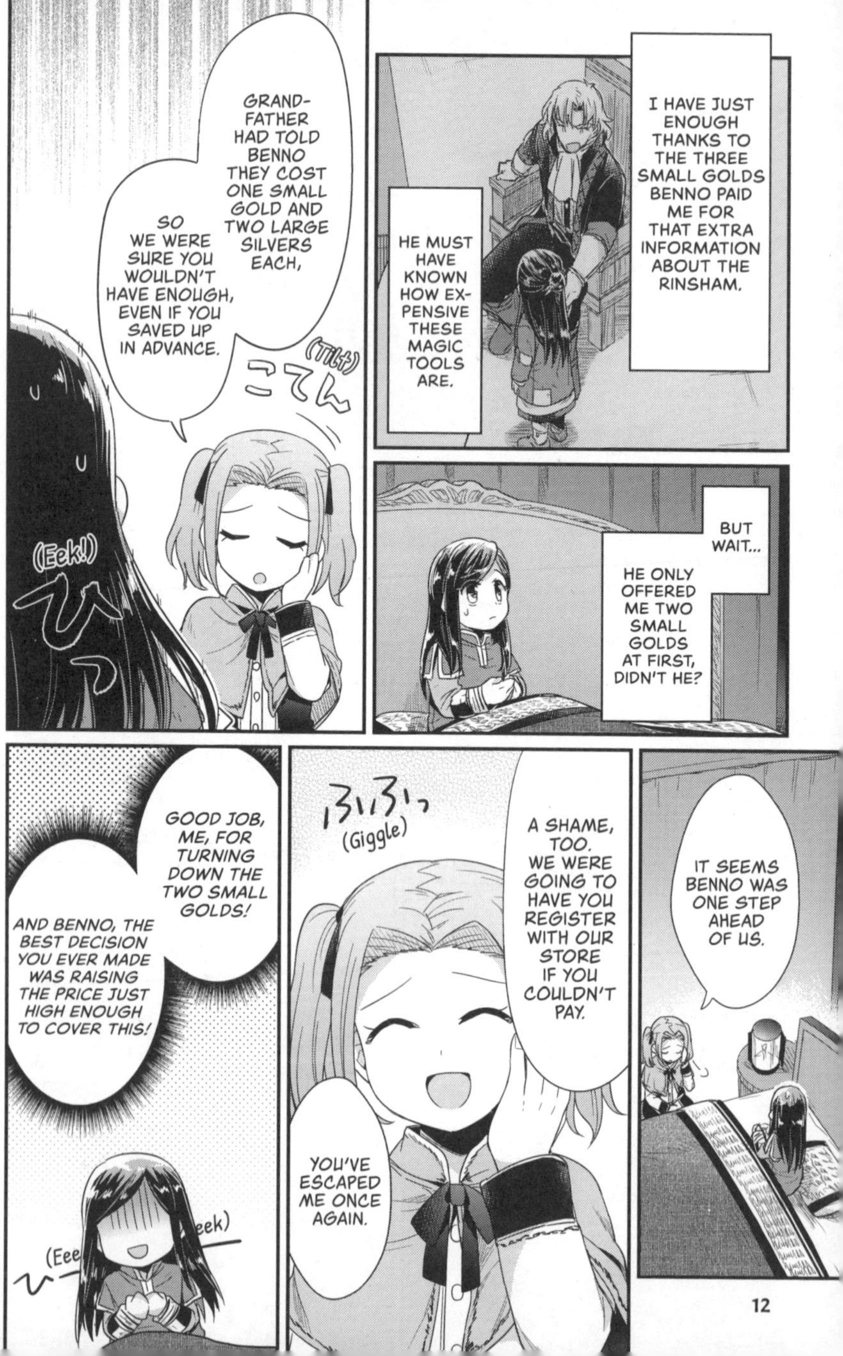

I HAVE JUST ENOUGH THANKS TO THE THREE SMALL GOLDS BENNO PAID ME FOR THAT EXTRA INFORMATION ABOUT THE RINSHAM.
HE MUST HAVE KNOWN HOW EXPENSIVE THESE MAGIC TOOLS ARE.
BUT WAIT...
HE ONLY OFFERED ME TWO SMALL GOLDS AT FIRST, DIDN'T HE?
GRANDFATHER HAD TOLD BENNO THEY COST ONE SMALL GOLD AND TWO LARGE SILVERS EACH,
SO WE WERE SURE YOU WOULDN'T HAVE ENOUGH, EVEN IF YOU SAVED UP IN ADVANCE.
こてん
(Tilt)
ひっ
(Eek!)
IT SEEMS BENNO WAS ONE STEP AHEAD OF US.
ふふっ
(Giggle)
A SHAME, TOO. WE WERE GOING TO HAVE YOU REGISTER WITH OUR STORE IF YOU COULDN'T PAY.
YOU'VE ESCAPED ME ONCE AGAIN.
GOOD JOB, ME, FOR TURNING DOWN THE TWO SMALL GOLDS!
AND BENNO, THE BEST DECISION YOU EVER MADE WAS RAISING THE PRICE JUST HIGH ENOUGH TO COVER THIS!
ひー
(Eee eek)

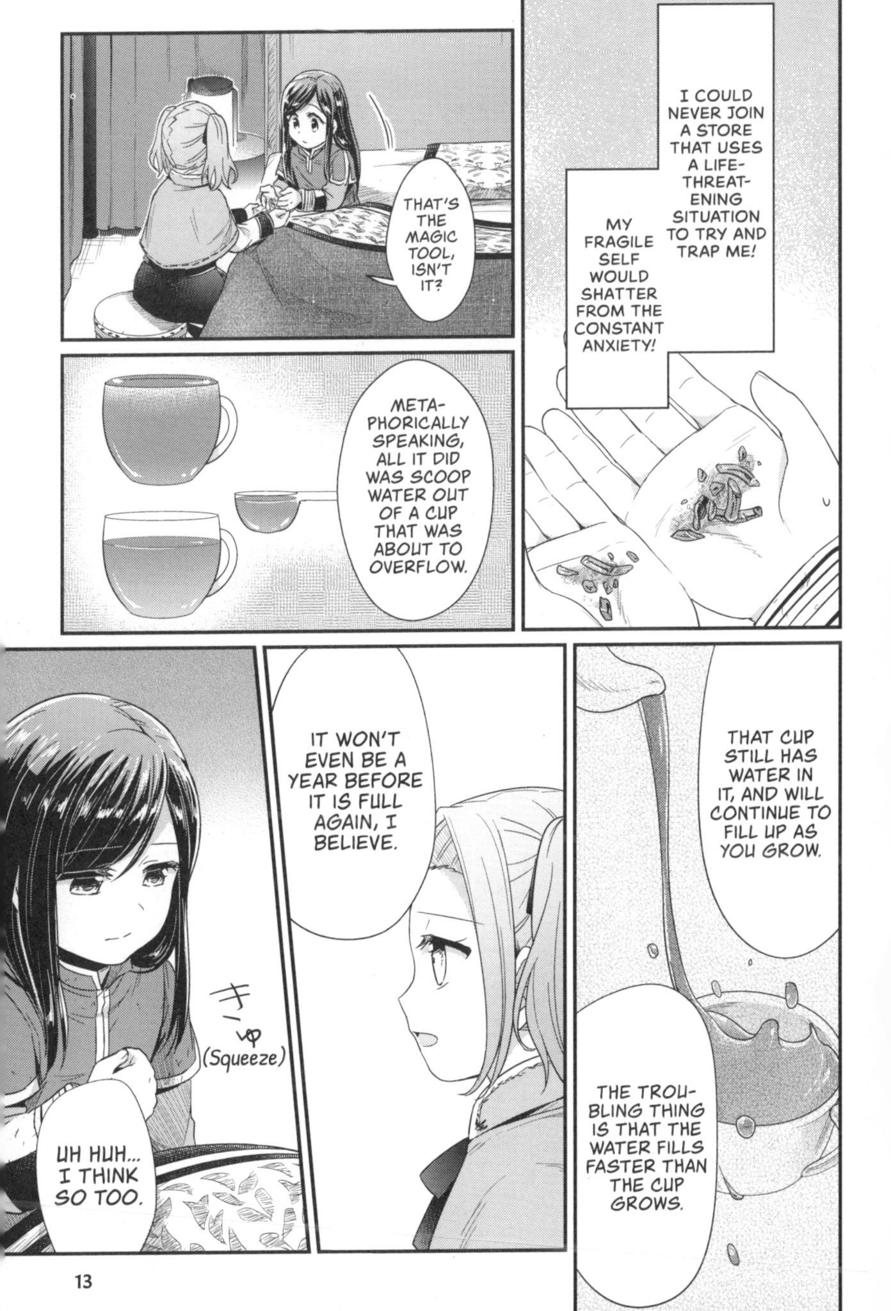
I COULD NEVER JOIN A STORE THAT USES A LIFE-THREATENING SITUATION TO TRY AND TRAP ME!
MY FRAGILE SELF WOULD SHATTER FROM THE CONSTANT ANXIETY!
THAT'S THE MAGIC TOOL, ISN'T IT?
METAPHORICALLY SPEAKING, ALL IT DID WAS SCOOP WATER OUT OF A CUP THAT WAS ABOUT TO OVERFLOW.
THAT CUP STILL HAS WATER IN IT, AND WILL CONTINUE TO FILL UP AS YOU GROW.
THE TROUBLING THING IS THAT THE WATER FILLS FASTER THAN THE CUP GROWS.
IT WON'T EVEN BE A YEAR BEFORE IT IS FULL AGAIN, I BELIEVE.
きゅ
(Squeeze)
UH HUH... I THINK SO TOO.

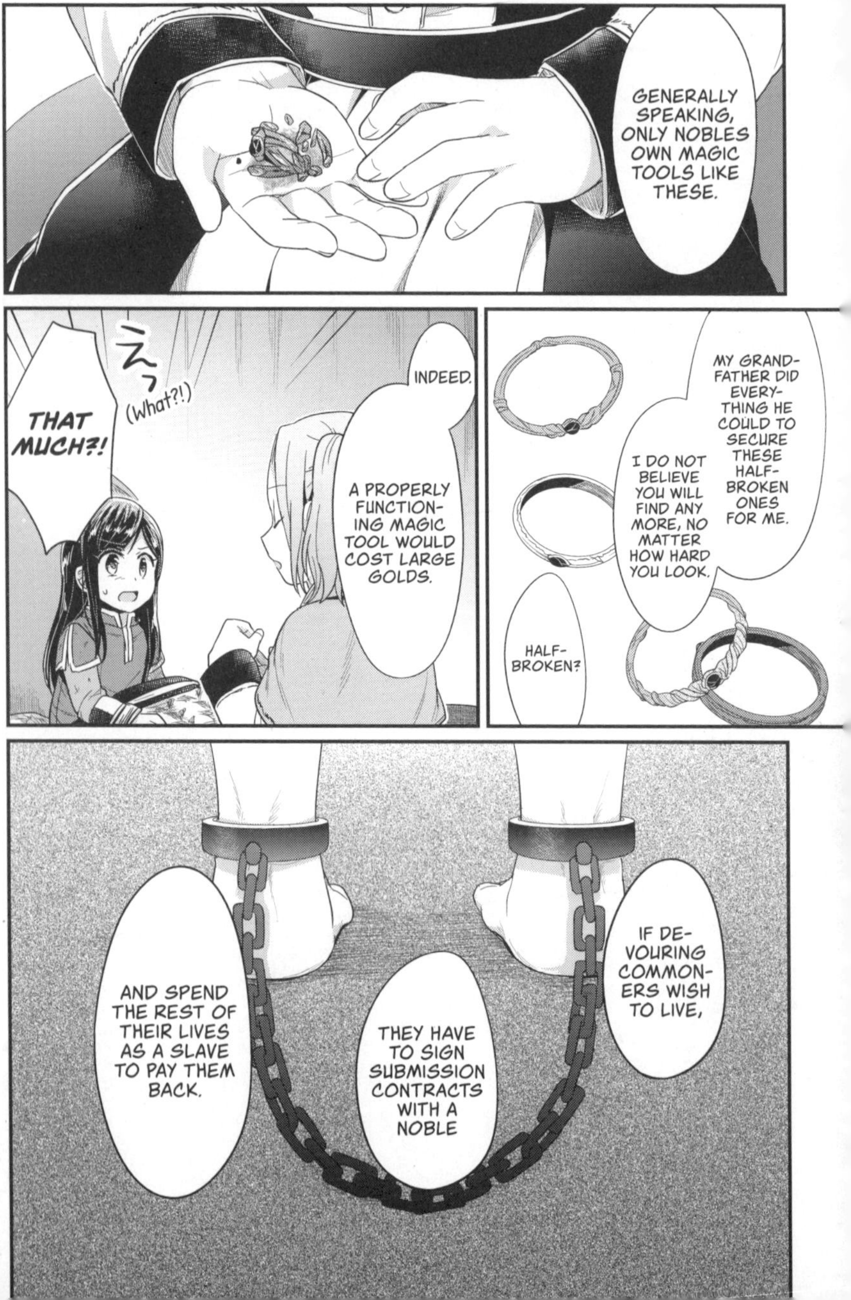
GENERALLY SPEAKING, ONLY NOBLES OWN MAGIC TOOLS LIKE THESE.
MY GRAND-FATHER DID EVERY-THING HE COULD TO SECURE THESE HALF-BROKEN ONES FOR ME.
I DO NOT BELIEVE YOU WILL FIND ANY MORE, NO MATTER HOW HARD YOU LOOK.
HALF-BROKEN?
INDEED.
えっ
(What?!)
THAT MUCH?!
A PROPERLY FUNCTION-ING MAGIC TOOL WOULD COST LARGE GOLDS.
IF DE-VOURING COMMON-ERS WISH TO LIVE,
THEY HAVE TO SIGN SUBMISSION CONTRACTS WITH A NOBLE
AND SPEND THE REST OF THEIR LIVES AS A SLAVE TO PAY THEM BACK.

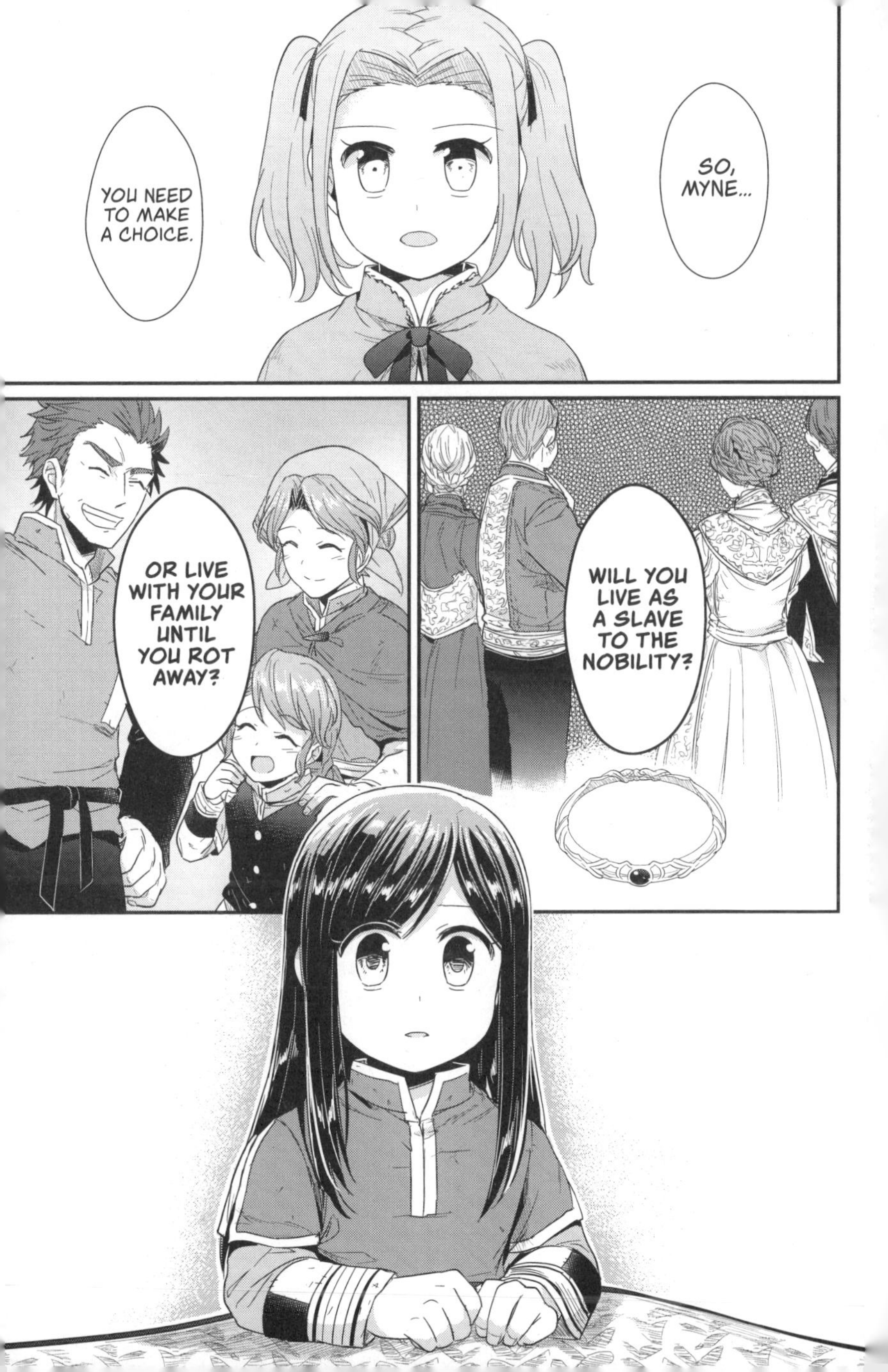
SO, MYNE...
YOU NEED TO MAKE A CHOICE.
WILL YOU LIVE AS A SLAVE TO THE NOBILITY?
OR LIVE WITH YOUR FAMILY UNTIL YOU ROT AWAY?

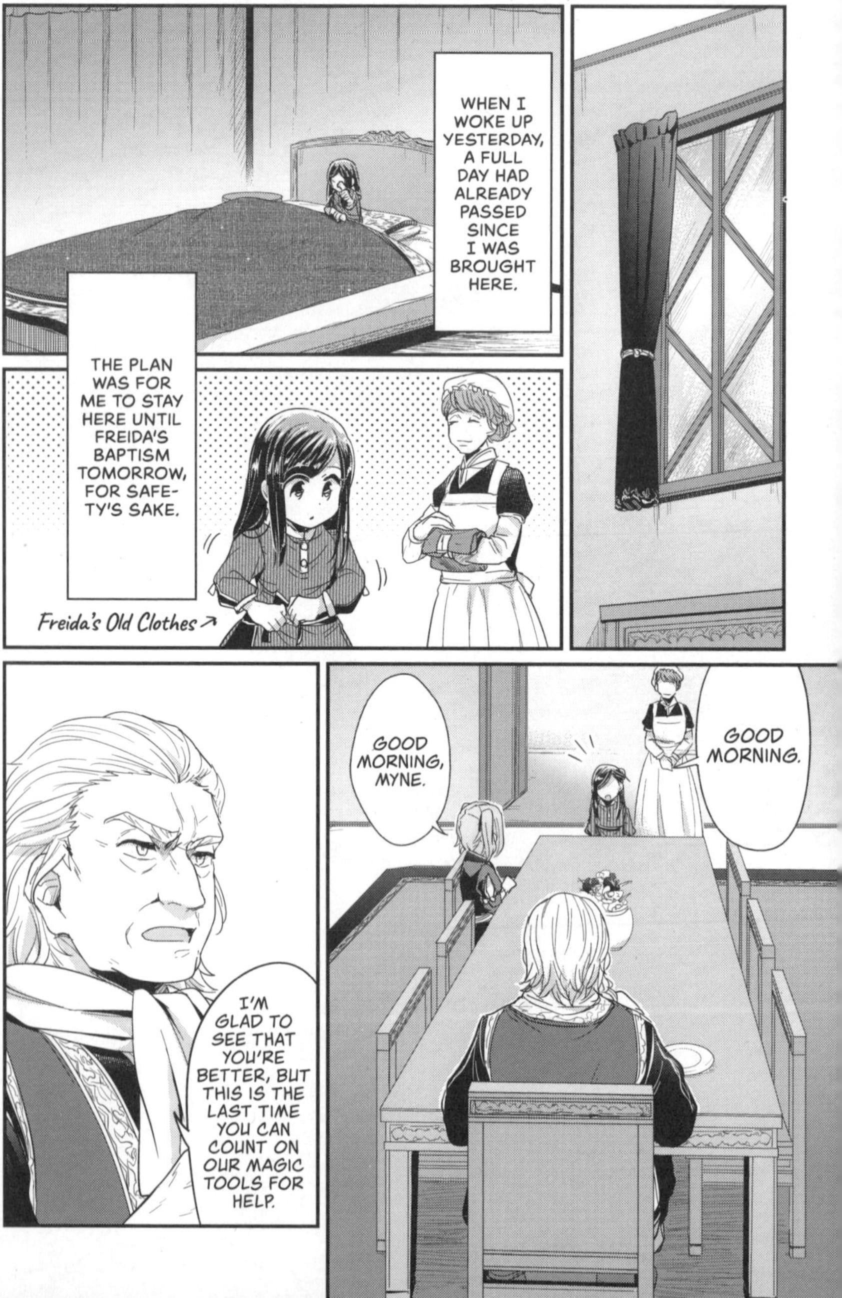
WHEN I WOKE UP YESTERDAY, A FULL DAY HAD ALREADY PASSED SINCE I WAS BROUGHT HERE.
THE PLAN WAS FOR ME TO STAY HERE UNTIL FREIDA'S BAPTISM TOMORROW, FOR SAFETY'S SAKE.
Freida's Old Clothes
GOOD MORNING.
GOOD MORNING, MYNE.
I'M GLAD TO SEE THAT YOU'RE BETTER, BUT THIS IS THE LAST TIME YOU CAN COUNT ON OUR MAGIC TOOLS FOR HELP.

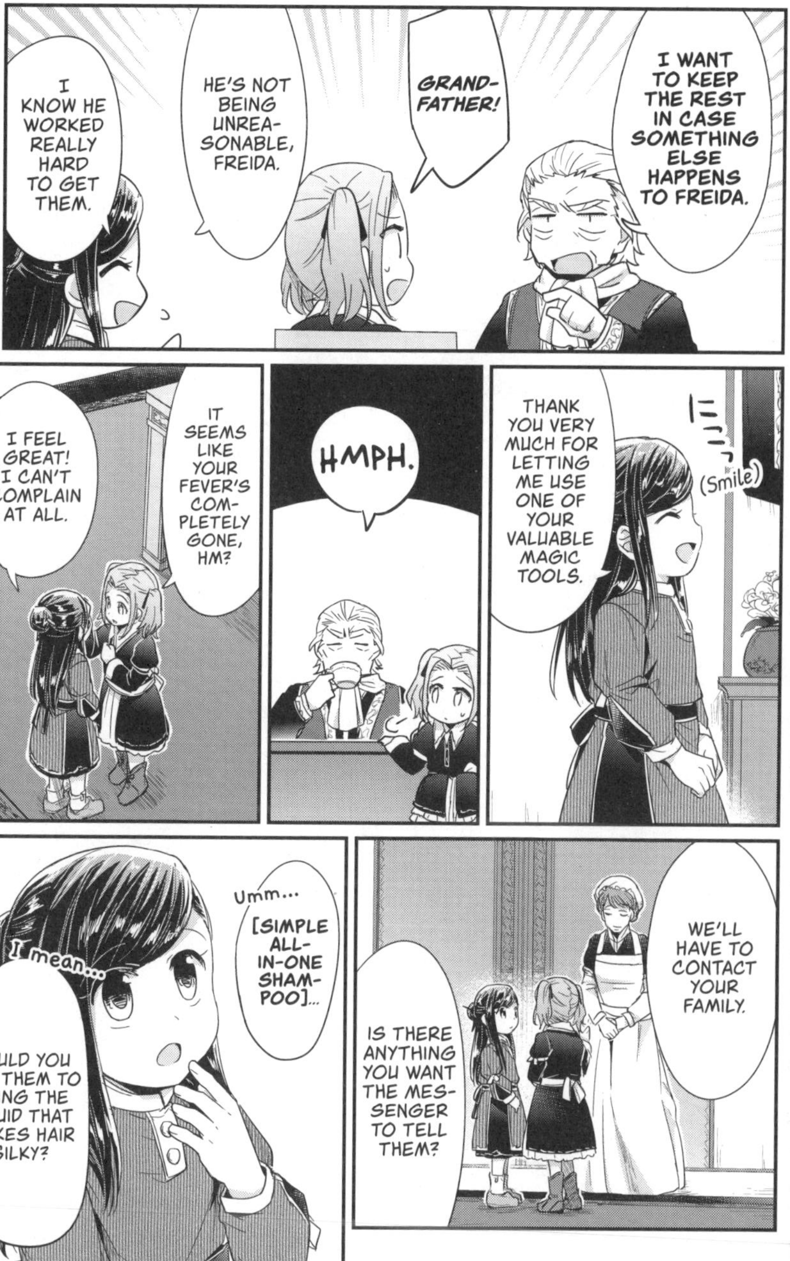
I WANT TO KEEP THE REST IN CASE SOMETHING ELSE HAPPENS TO FREIDA.
GRAND-FATHER!
HE'S NOT BEING UNREA-SONABLE, FREIDA.
I KNOW HE WORKED REALLY HARD TO GET THEM.
(Smile)
THANK YOU VERY MUCH FOR LETTING ME USE ONE OF YOUR VALUABLE MAGIC TOOLS.
HMPH.
IT SEEMS LIKE YOUR FEVER'S COM-PLETELY GONE, HM?
I FEEL GREAT! I CAN'T COMPLAIN AT ALL.
WE'LL HAVE TO CONTACT YOUR FAMILY.
IS THERE ANYTHING YOU WANT THE MES-SENGER TO TELL THEM?
Umm...
[SIMPLE ALL-IN-ONE SHAM-POO]...
I mean...
COULD YOU ASK THEM TO BRING THE LIQUID THAT MAKES HAIR SILKY?

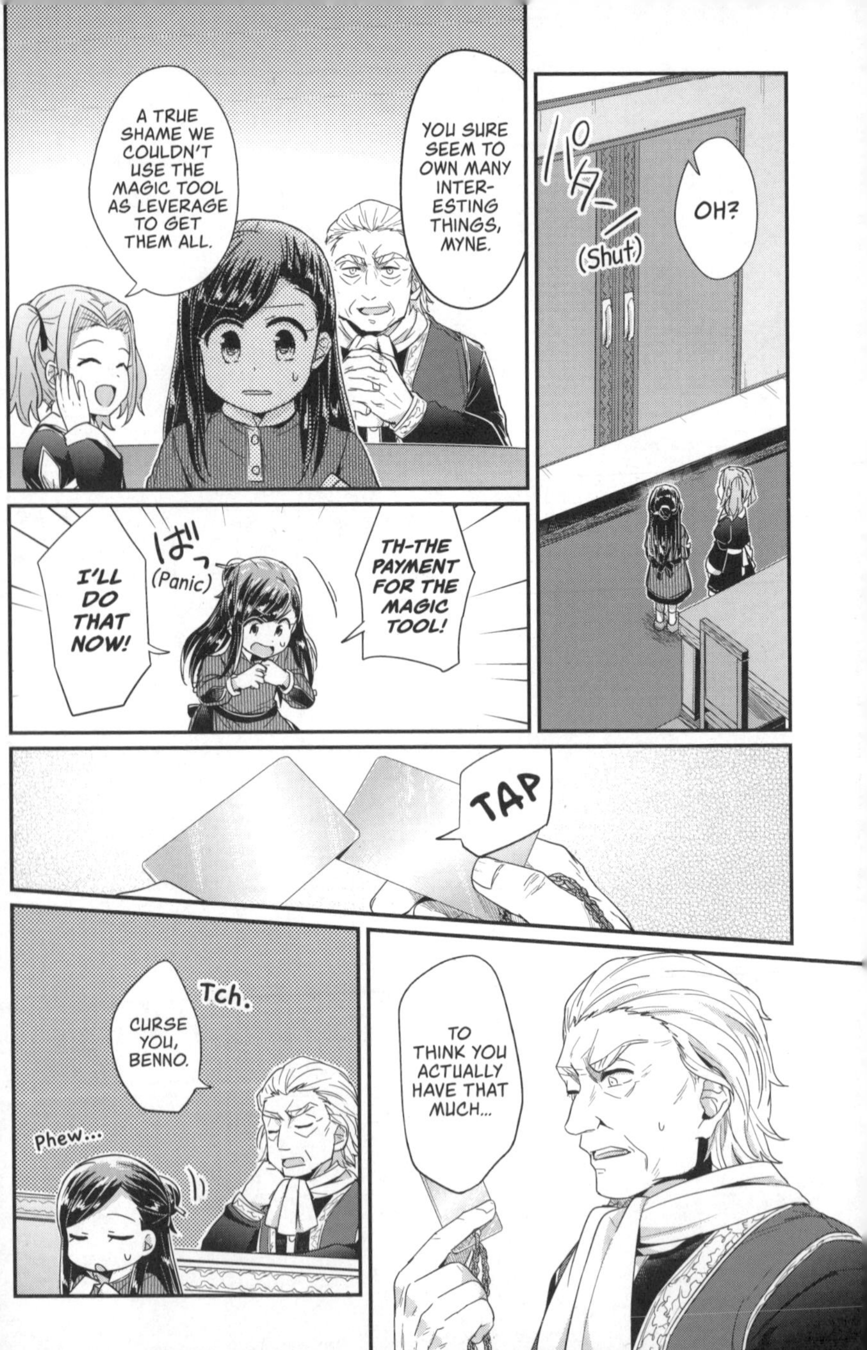

パター
(Shut)
OH?
YOU SURE SEEM TO OWN MANY INTER-ESTING THINGS, MYNE.
A TRUE SHAME WE COULDN'T USE THE MAGIC TOOL AS LEVERAGE TO GET THEM ALL.
TH-THE PAYMENT FOR THE MAGIC TOOL!
ばっ
(Panic)
I'LL DO THAT NOW!
TAP
TO THINK YOU ACTUALLY HAVE THAT MUCH...
Tch.
CURSE YOU, BENNO.
Phew...

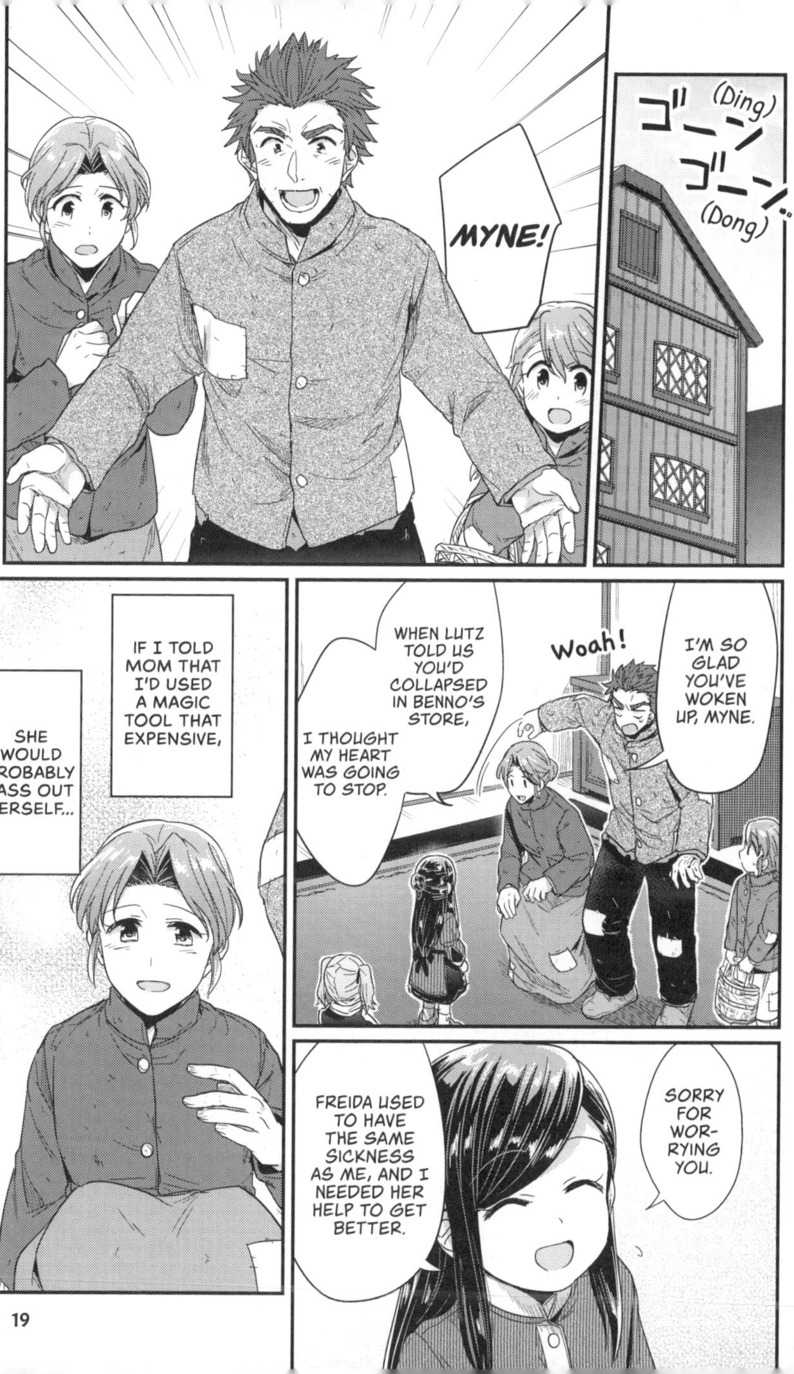
ゴーン ゴーン
(Ding)
(Dong)
MYNE!
I'M SO GLAD YOU'VE WOKEN UP, MYNE.
Woah!
WHEN LUTZ TOLD US YOU'D COLLAPSED IN BENNO'S STORE,
I THOUGHT MY HEART WAS GOING TO STOP.
SORRY FOR WOR-RYING YOU.
FREIDA USED TO HAVE THE SAME SICKNESS AS ME, AND I NEEDED HER HELP TO GET BETTER.
IF I TOLD MOM THAT I'D USED A MAGIC TOOL THAT EXPENSIVE,
SHE WOULD PROBABLY PASS OUT HERSELF...

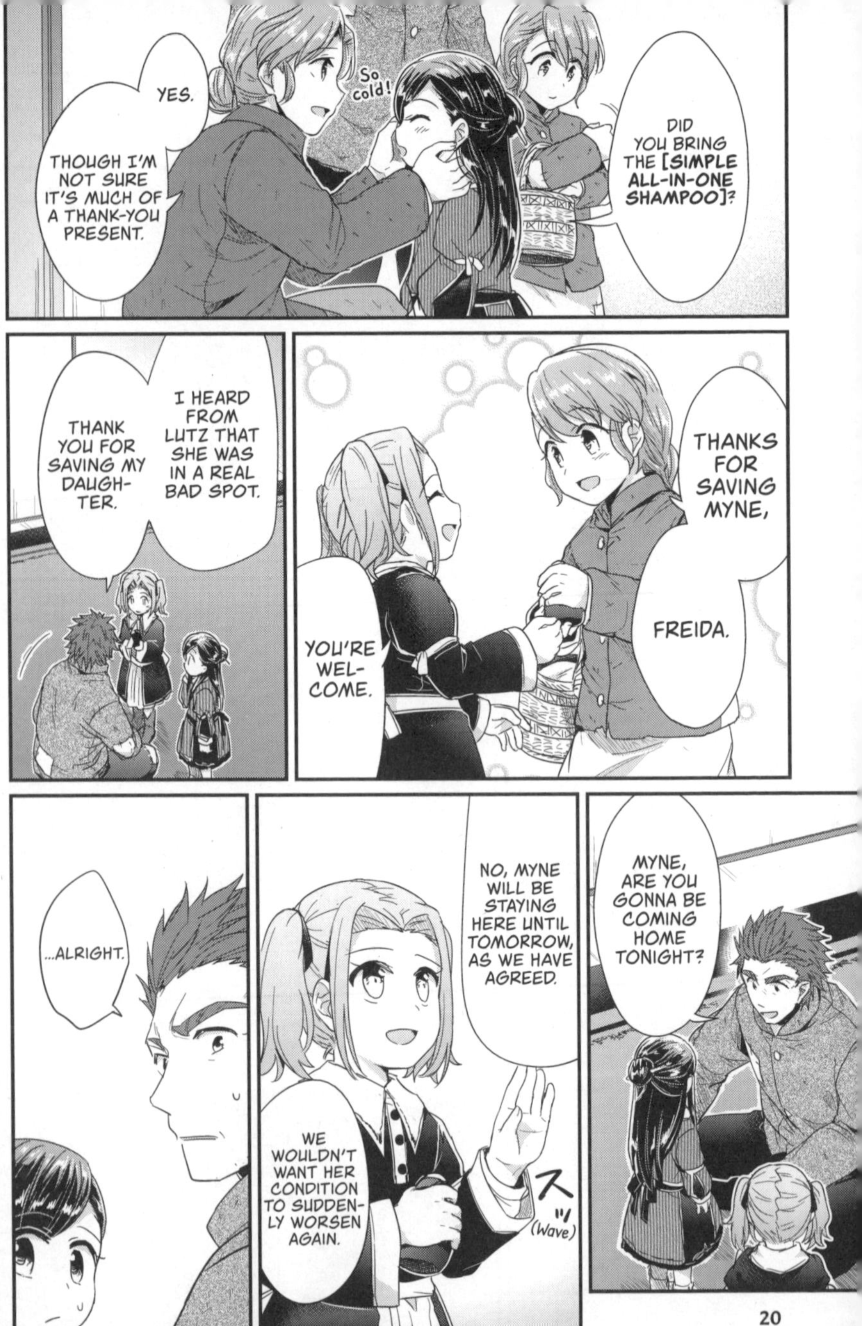
DID YOU BRING THE [SIMPLE ALL-IN-ONE SHAMPOO]?
So cold!
YES.
THOUGH I'M NOT SURE IT'S MUCH OF A THANK-YOU PRESENT.
THANKS FOR SAVING MYNE,
FREIDA.
YOU'RE WEL-COME.
I HEARD FROM LUTZ THAT SHE WAS IN A REAL BAD SPOT.
THANK YOU FOR SAVING MY DAUGH-TER.
MYNE, ARE YOU GONNA BE COMING HOME TONIGHT?
NO, MYNE WILL BE STAYING HERE UNTIL TOMORROW, AS WE HAVE AGREED.
スッ
(Wave)
WE WOULDN'T WANT HER CONDITION TO SUDDEN-LY WORSEN AGAIN.
...ALRIGHT.

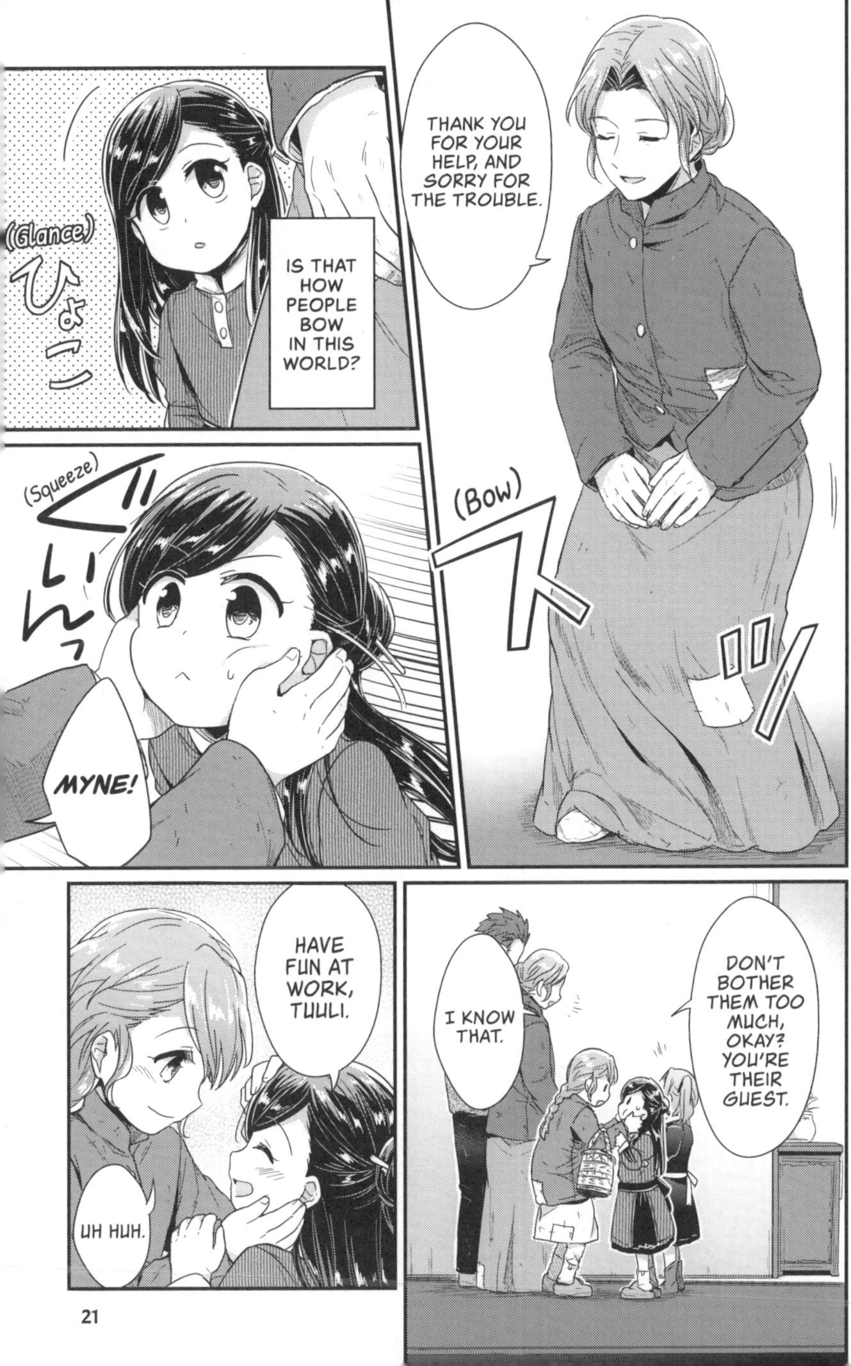
THANK YOU FOR YOUR HELP, AND SORRY FOR THE TROUBLE.
(Bow)
(Glance)
IS THAT HOW PEOPLE BOW IN THIS WORLD?
(Squeeze)
MYNE!
DON'T BOTHER THEM TOO MUCH, OKAY? YOU'RE THEIR GUEST.
I KNOW THAT.
HAVE FUN AT WORK, TUULI.
UH HUH.

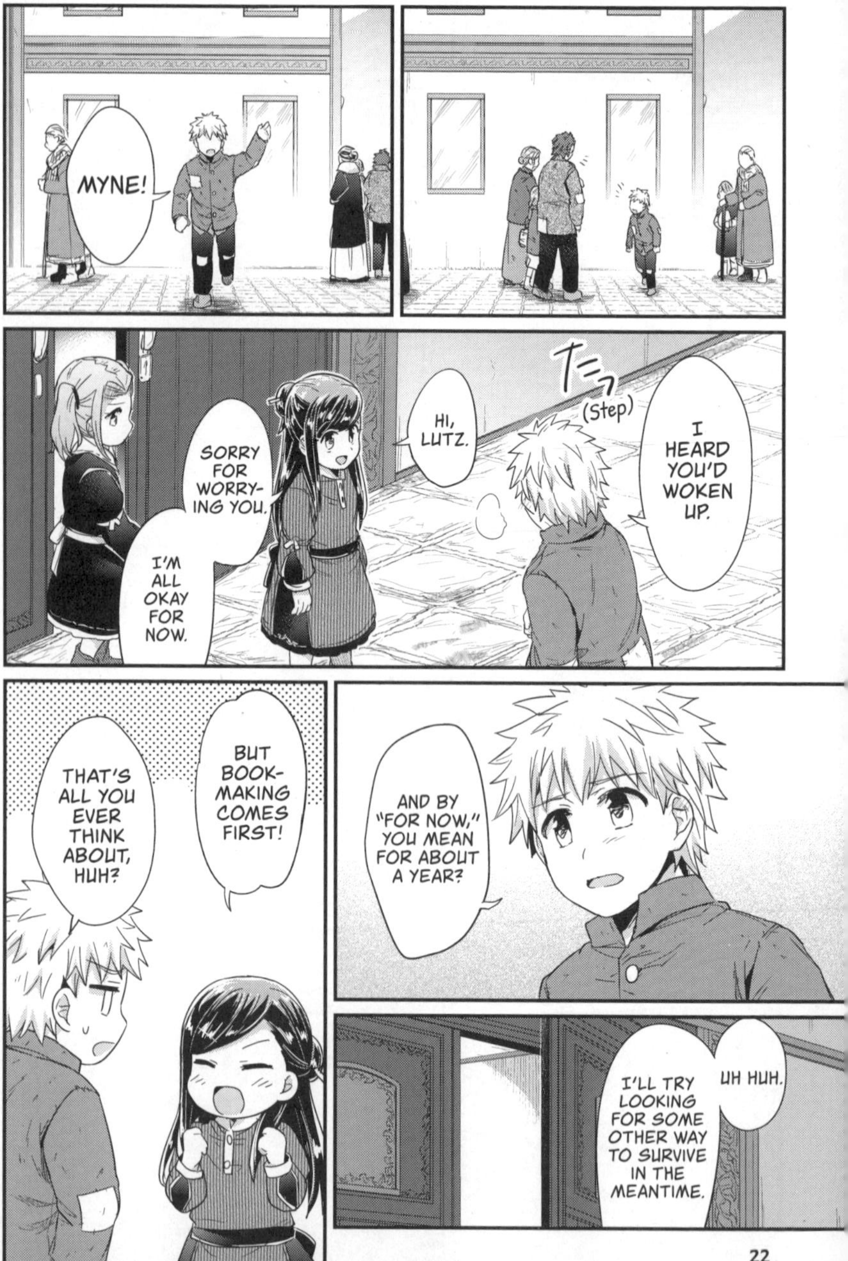
MYNE!
(Step)
I HEARD YOU'D WOKEN UP.
HI, LUTZ.
SORRY FOR WORRYING YOU.
I'M ALL OKAY FOR NOW.
AND BY "FOR NOW," YOU MEAN FOR ABOUT A YEAR?
UH HUH.
I'LL TRY LOOKING FOR SOME OTHER WAY TO SURVIVE IN THE MEANTIME.
BUT BOOK-MAKING COMES FIRST!
THAT'S ALL YOU EVER THINK ABOUT, HUH?

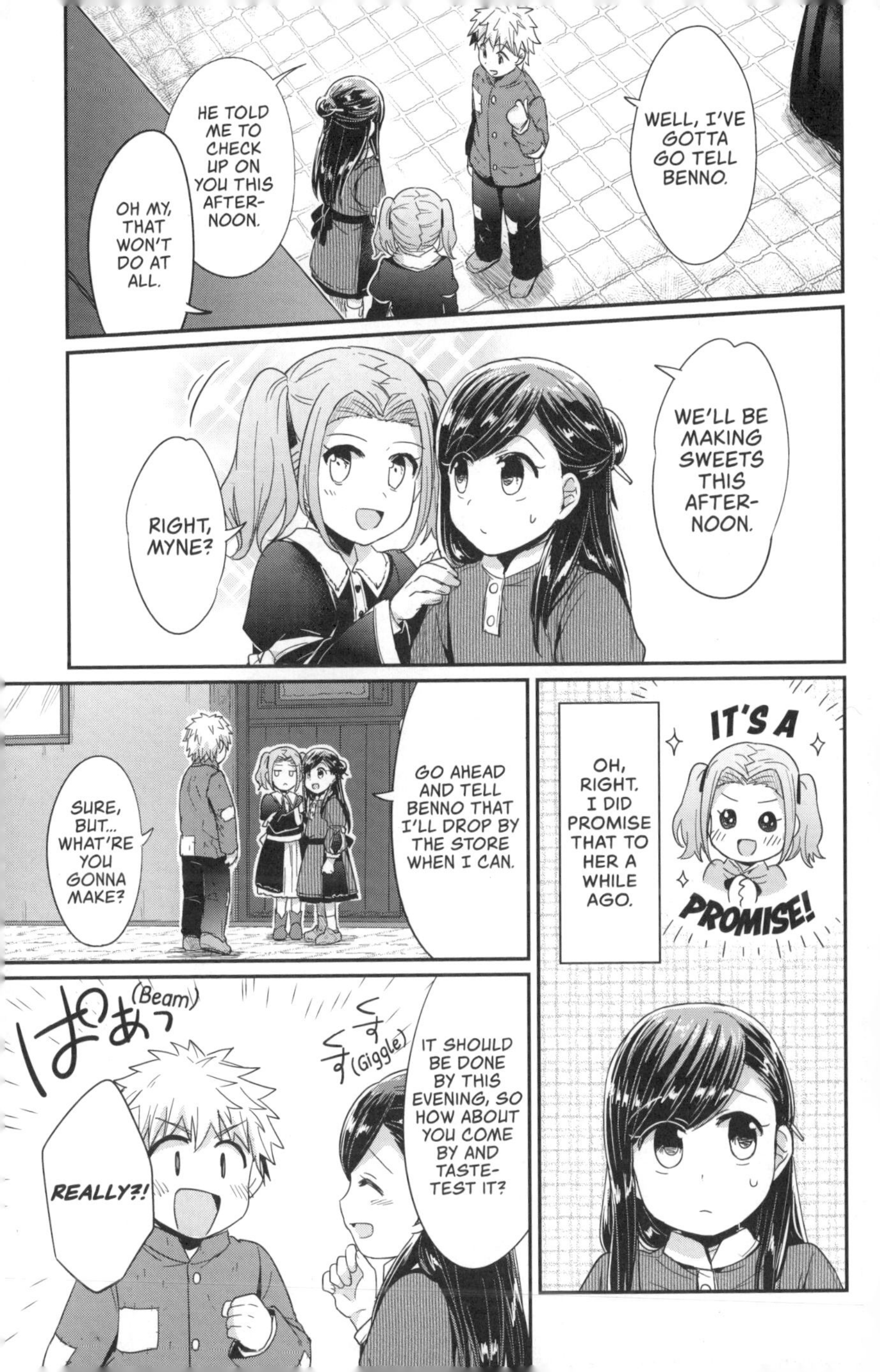
WELL, I'VE GOTTA GO TELL BENNO.
HE TOLD ME TO CHECK UP ON YOU THIS AFTERNOON.
OH MY, THAT WON'T DO AT ALL.
WE'LL BE MAKING SWEETS THIS AFTERNOON.
RIGHT, MYNE?
IT'S A PROMISE!
OH, RIGHT. I DID PROMISE THAT TO HER A WHILE AGO.
GO AHEAD AND TELL BENNO THAT I'LL DROP BY THE STORE WHEN I CAN.
SURE, BUT... WHAT'RE YOU GONNA MAKE?
くすくす (Giggle)
IT SHOULD BE DONE BY THIS EVENING, SO HOW ABOUT YOU COME BY AND TASTE-TEST IT?
ぱあっ (Beam)
REALLY?!

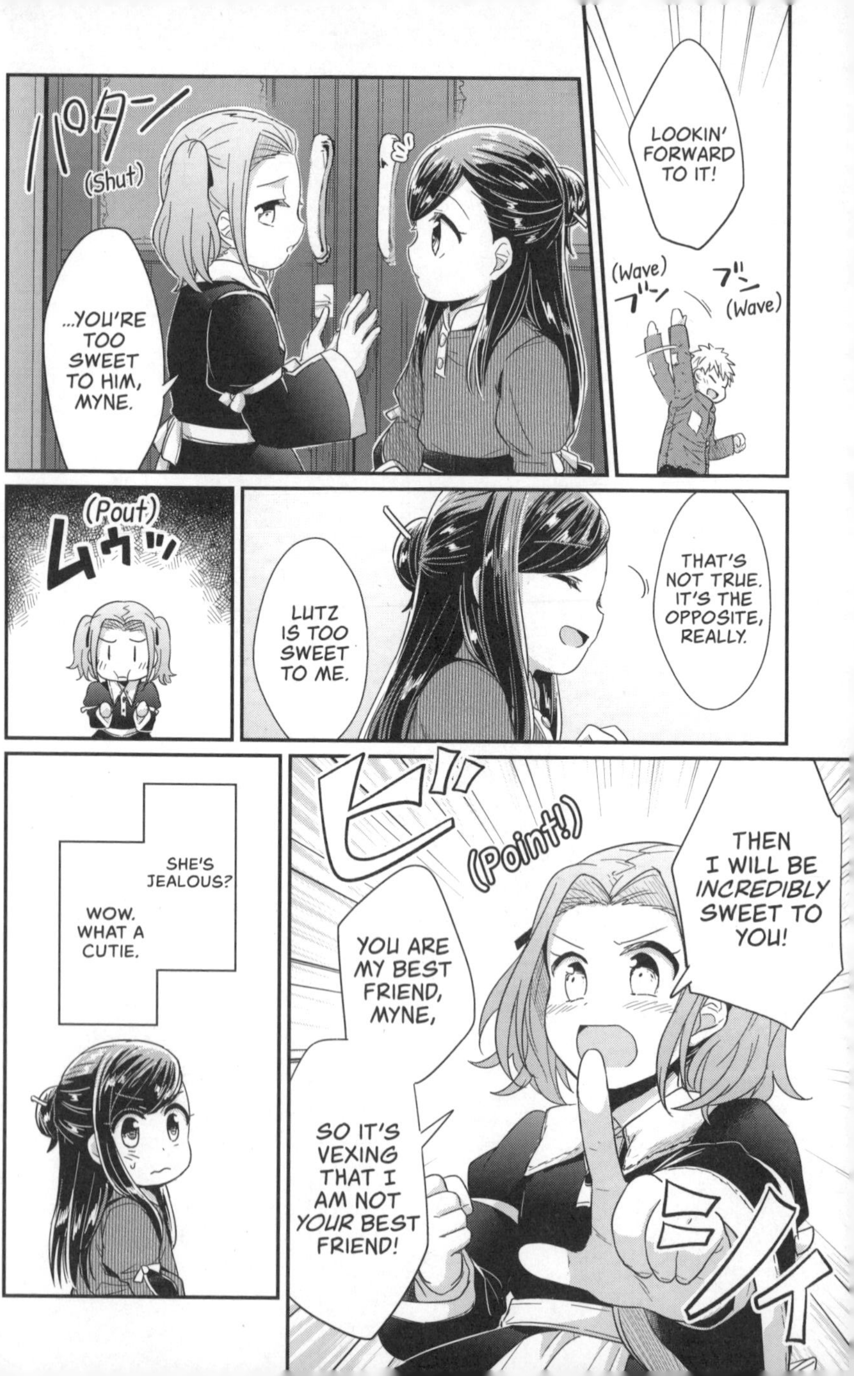

LOOKIN' FORWARD TO IT!
(Wave)
ブンブン
(Wave)
パターン
(Shut)
...YOU'RE TOO SWEET TO HIM, MYNE.
THAT'S NOT TRUE. IT'S THE OPPOSITE, REALLY.
LUTZ IS TOO SWEET TO ME.
(Pout)
ムウッ
ビシッ
(Point!)
THEN I WILL BE *INCREDIBLY* SWEET TO YOU!
YOU ARE MY BEST FRIEND, MYNE,
SO IT'S VEXING THAT I AM NOT *YOUR* BEST FRIEND!
SHE'S JEALOUS?
WOW. WHAT A CUTIE.

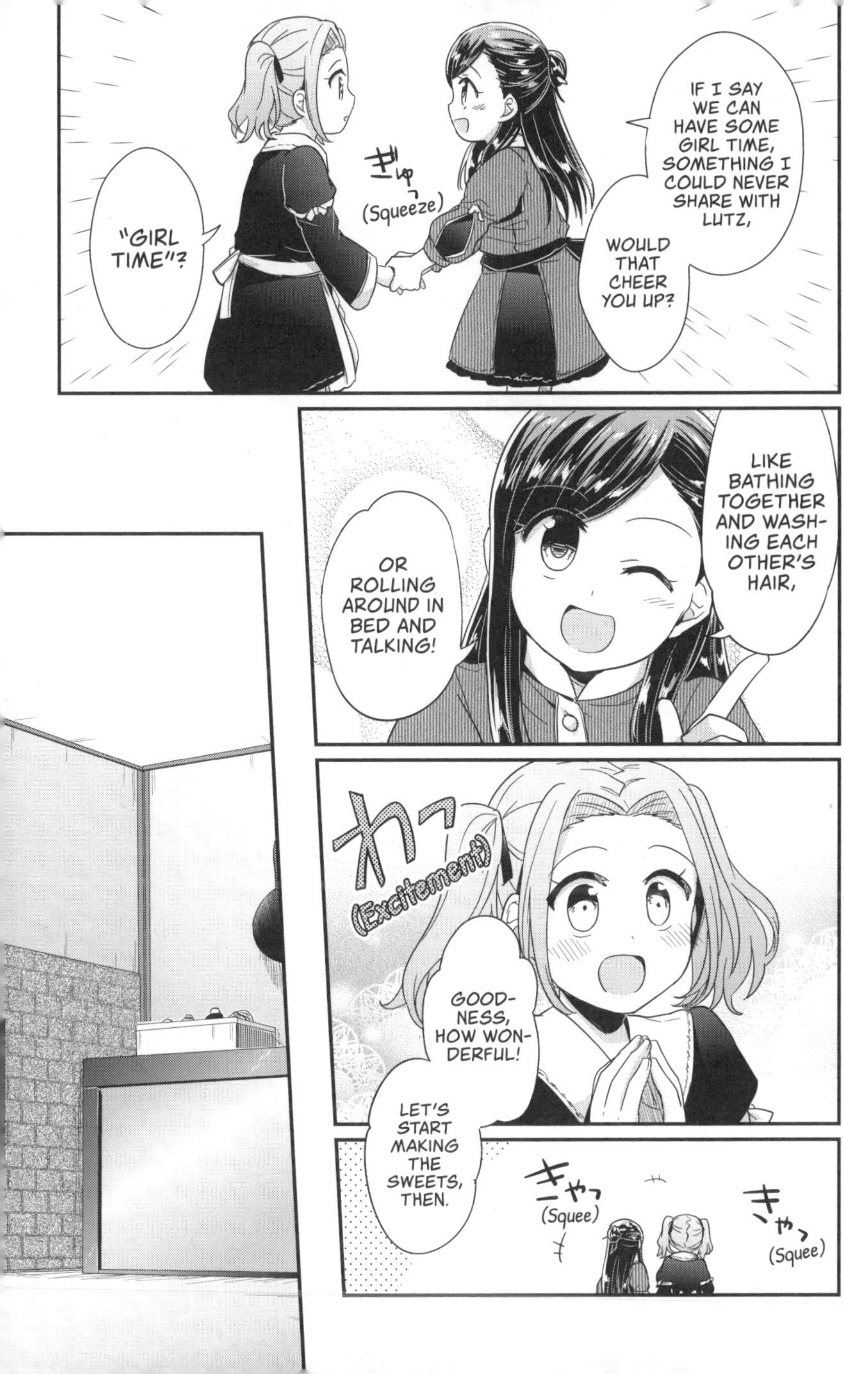
IF I SAY WE CAN HAVE SOME GIRL TIME, SOMETHING I COULD NEVER SHARE WITH LUTZ,
WOULD THAT CHEER YOU UP?
ぎゅっ
(Squeeze)
"GIRL TIME"?
LIKE BATHING TOGETHER AND WASH-ING EACH OTHER'S HAIR,
OR ROLLING AROUND IN BED AND TALKING!
わっ
(Excitement)
GOOD-NESS, HOW WON-DERFUL!
LET'S START MAKING THE SWEETS, THEN.
きゃっ
(Squee)
きゃっ
(Squee)

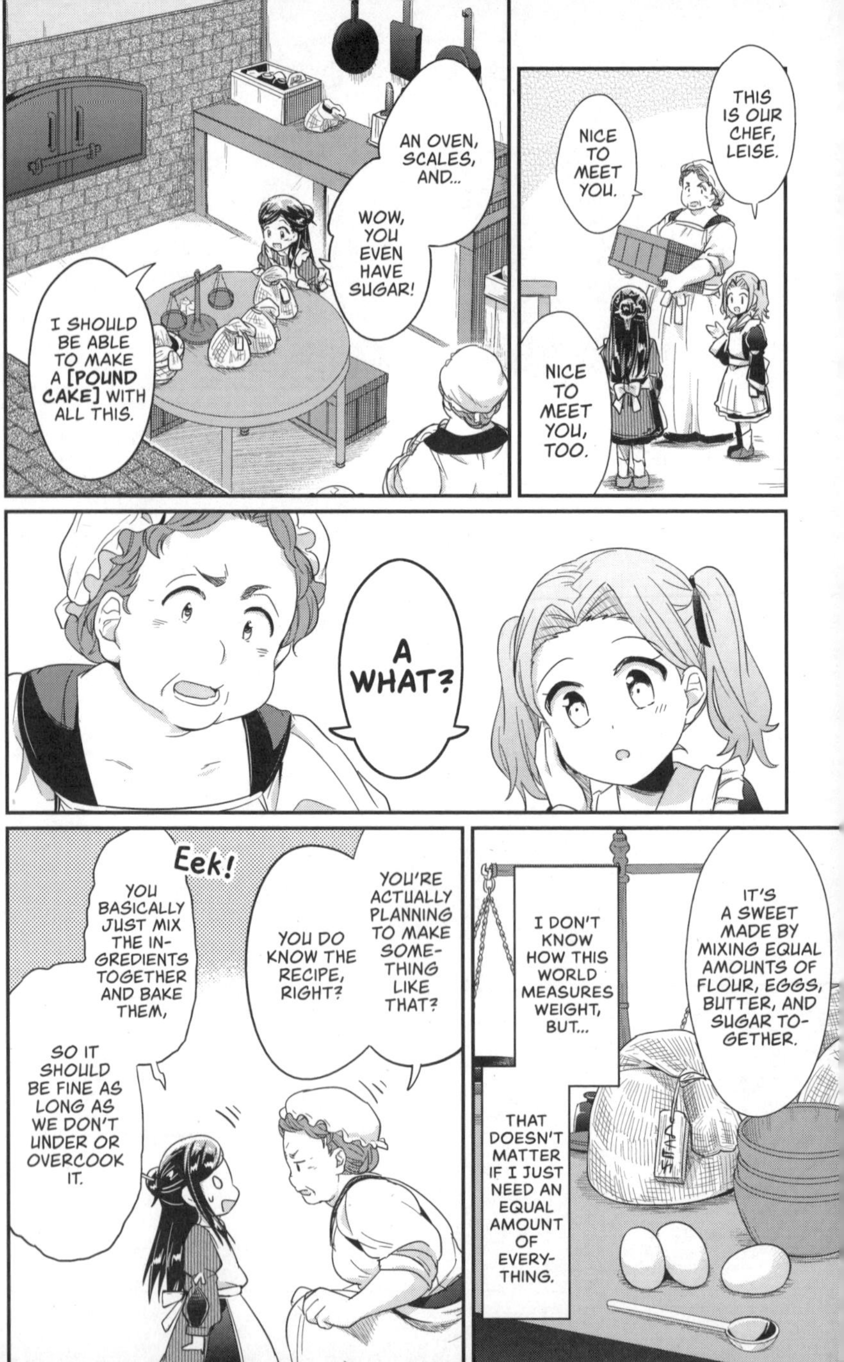
THIS IS OUR CHEF, LEISE.
NICE TO MEET YOU.
NICE TO MEET YOU, TOO.
AN OVEN, SCALES, AND...
WOW, YOU EVEN HAVE SUGAR!
I SHOULD BE ABLE TO MAKE A **[POUND CAKE]** WITH ALL THIS.
A WHAT?
IT'S A SWEET MADE BY MIXING EQUAL AMOUNTS OF FLOUR, EGGS, BUTTER, AND SUGAR TO-GETHER.
I DON'T KNOW HOW THIS WORLD MEASURES WEIGHT, BUT...
THAT DOESN'T MATTER IF I JUST NEED AN EQUAL AMOUNT OF EVERY-THING.
YOU'RE ACTUALLY PLANNING TO MAKE SOME-THING LIKE THAT?
YOU DO KNOW THE RECIPE, RIGHT?
Eek!
YOU BASICALLY JUST MIX THE IN-GREDIENTS TOGETHER AND BAKE THEM,
SO IT SHOULD BE FINE AS LONG AS WE DON'T UNDER OR OVERCOOK IT.

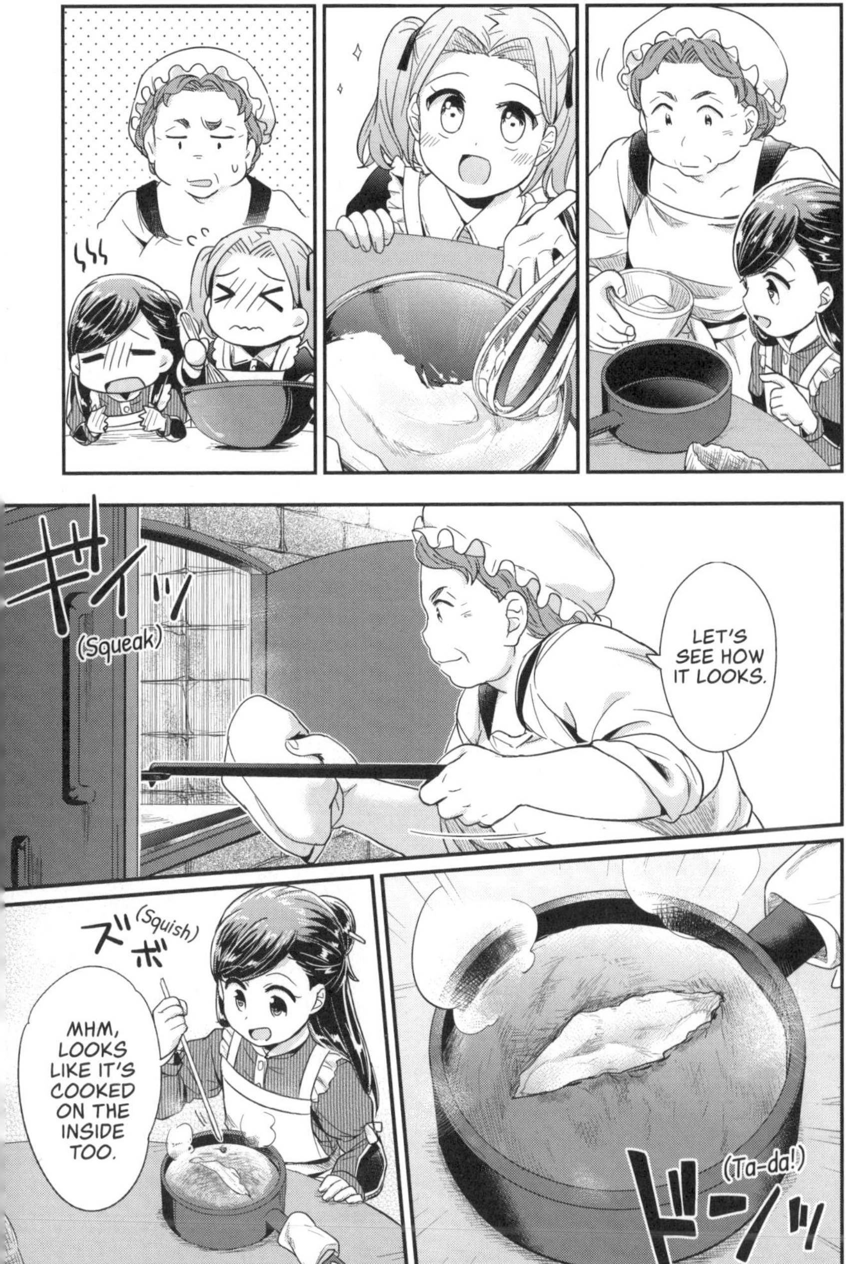
LET'S SEE HOW IT LOOKS.
ギイッ
(Squeak)
ドーンッ
(Ta-da!)
ズボ
(Squish)
MHM, LOOKS LIKE IT'S COOKED ON THE INSIDE TOO.

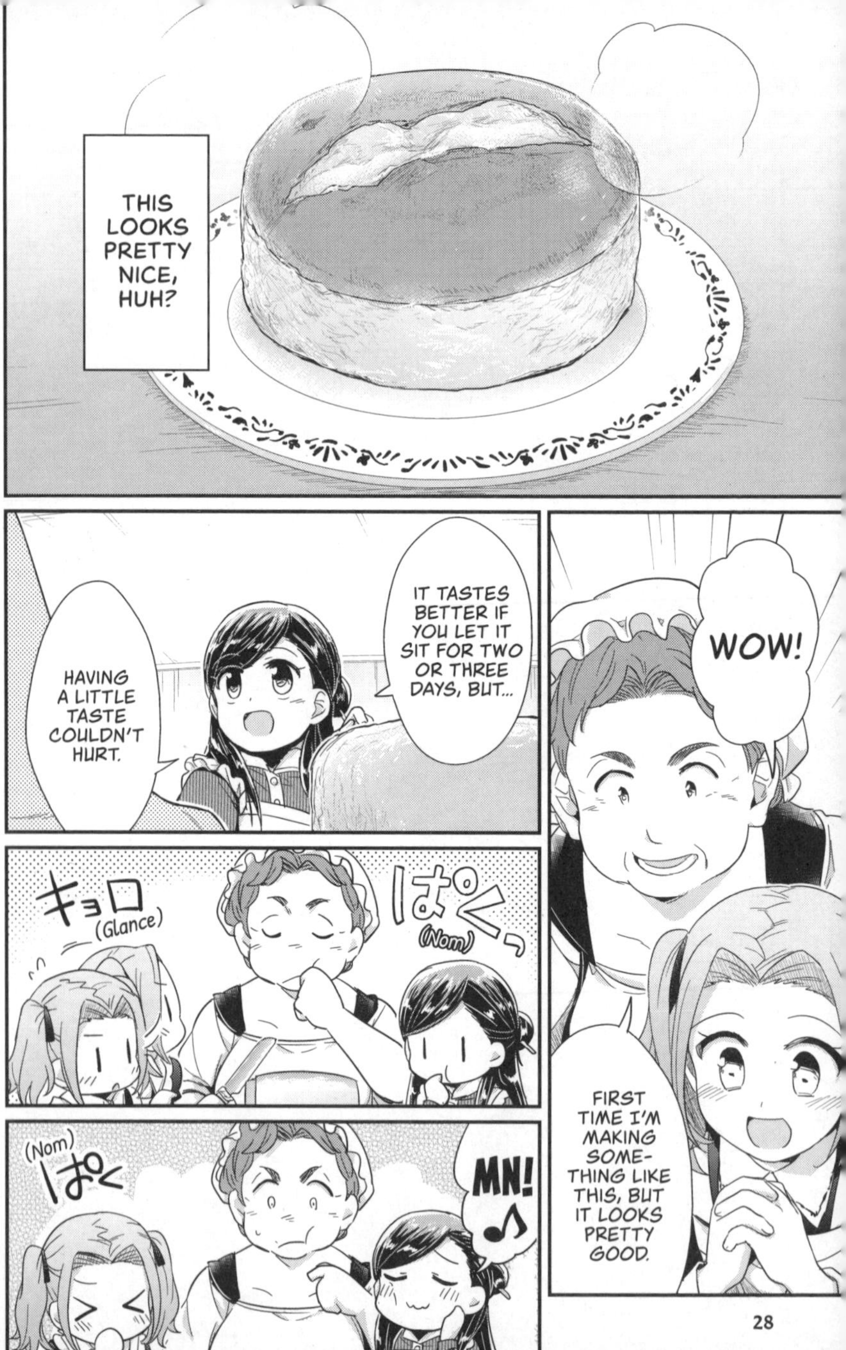
THIS LOOKS PRETTY NICE, HUH?
WOW!
FIRST TIME I'M MAKING SOME-THING LIKE THIS, BUT IT LOOKS PRETTY GOOD.
IT TASTES BETTER IF YOU LET IT SIT FOR TWO OR THREE DAYS, BUT...
HAVING A LITTLE TASTE COULDN'T HURT.
ぱくっ
(Nom)
キョロ
(Glance)
MN! ♪
ぱく
(Nom)

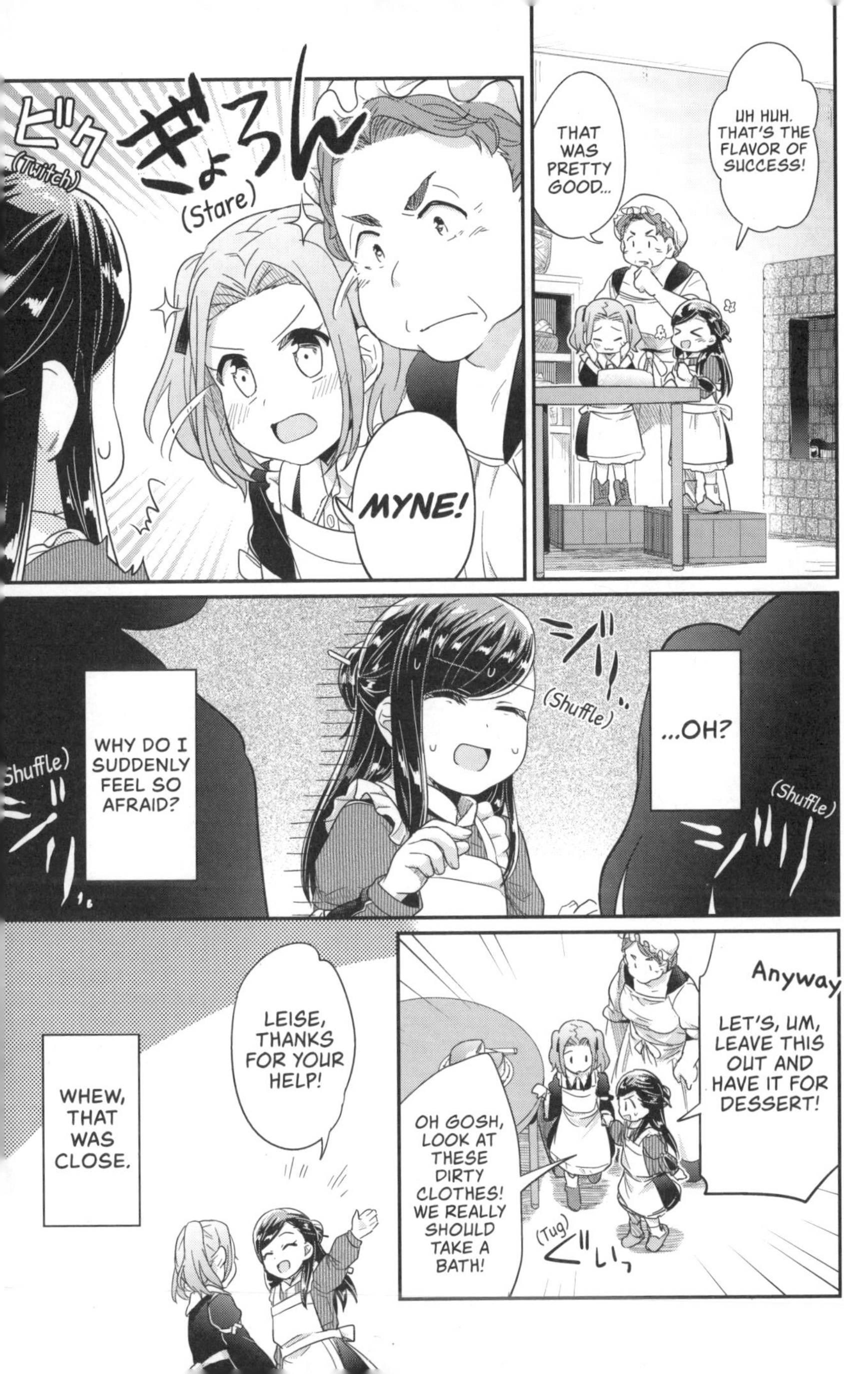
UH HUH. THAT'S THE FLAVOR OF SUCCESS!
THAT WAS PRETTY GOOD...
ぎょろん
(Stare)
ビク
(Twitch)
MYNE!
(Shuffle)
...OH?
(Shuffle)
WHY DO I SUDDENLY FEEL SO AFRAID?
(Shuffle)
Anyway!
LET'S, UM, LEAVE THIS OUT AND HAVE IT FOR DESSERT!
OH GOSH, LOOK AT THESE DIRTY CLOTHES! WE REALLY SHOULD TAKE A BATH!
(Tug)
ぐいっ
LEISE, THANKS FOR YOUR HELP!
WHEW, THAT WAS CLOSE.

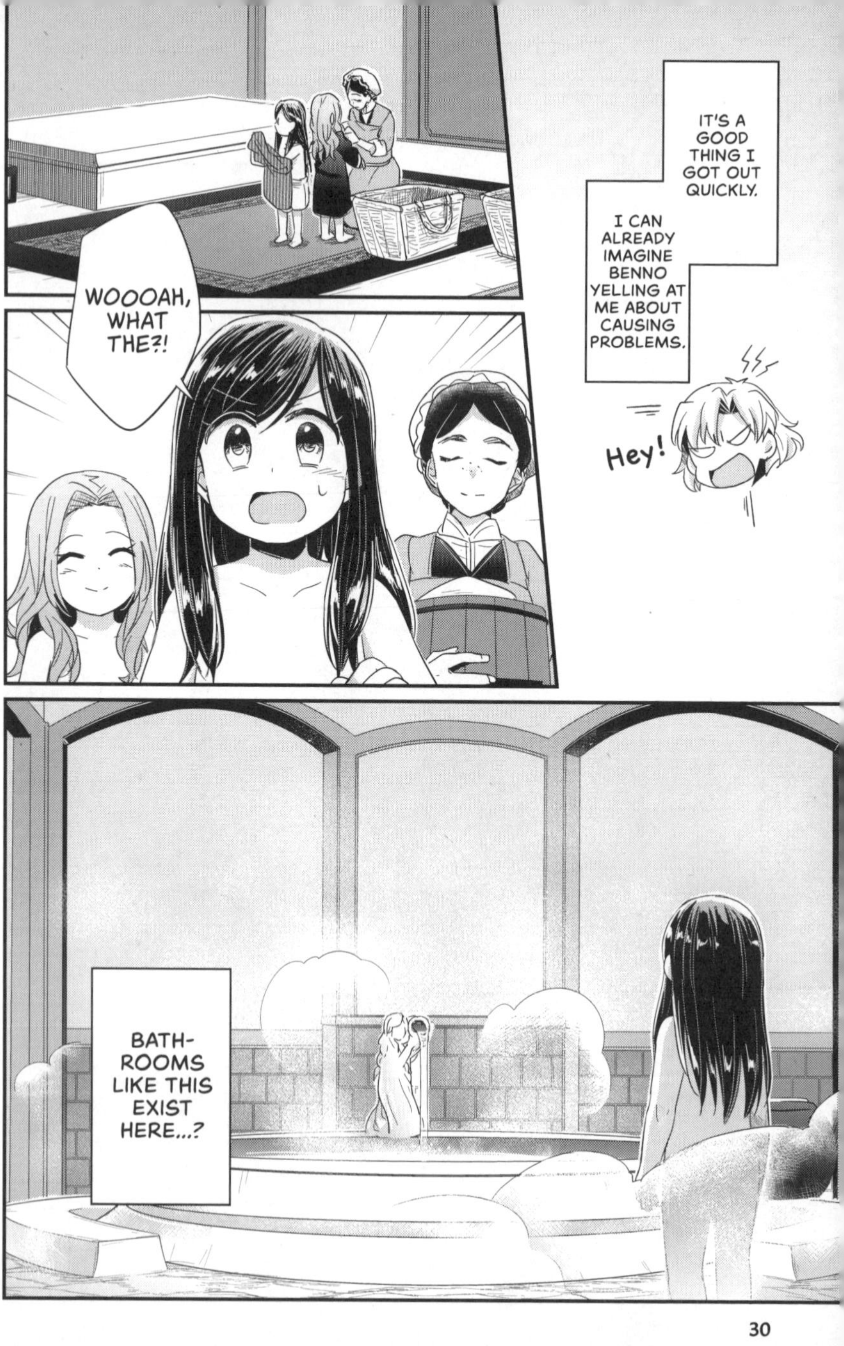
IT'S A GOOD THING I GOT OUT QUICKLY.
I CAN ALREADY IMAGINE BENNO YELLING AT ME ABOUT CAUSING PROBLEMS.
Hey!
WOOOAH, WHAT THE?!
BATH-ROOMS LIKE THIS EXIST HERE...?

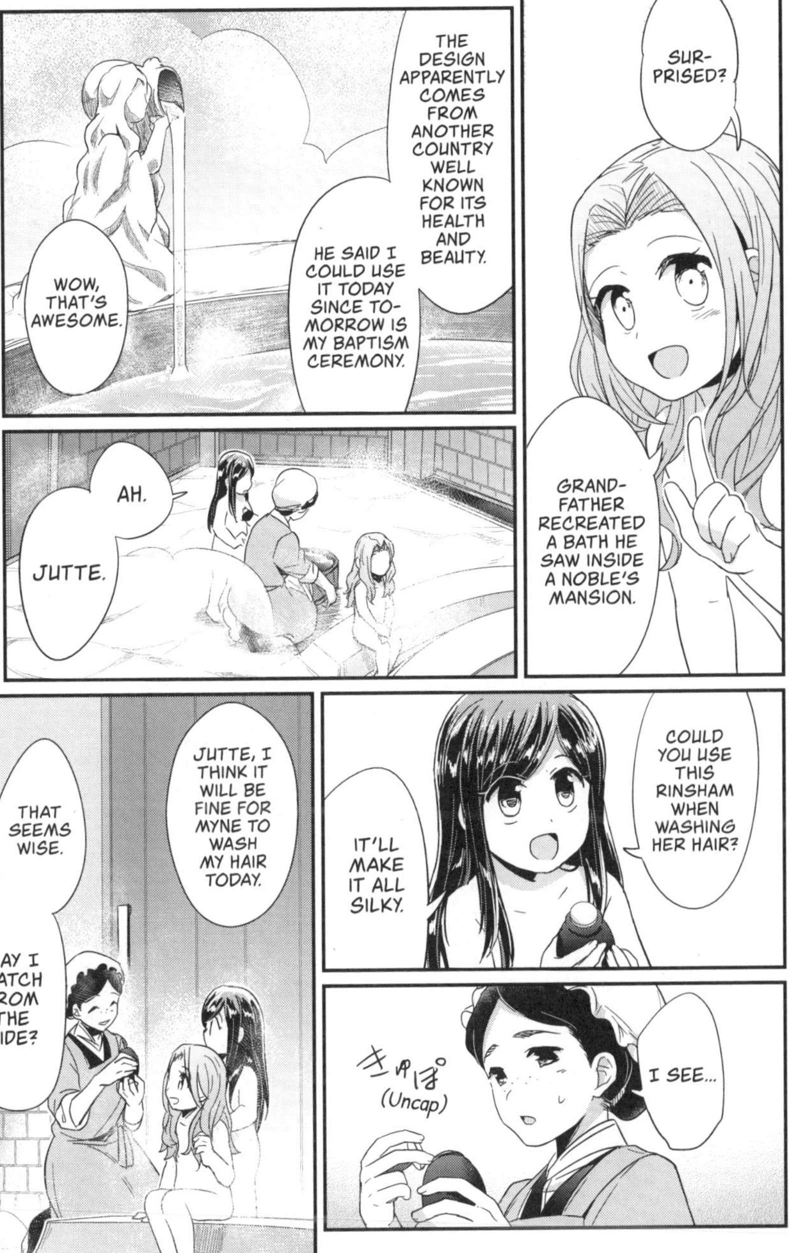
SUR-PRISED?
GRAND-FATHER RECREATED A BATH HE SAW INSIDE A NOBLE'S MANSION.
THE DESIGN APPARENTLY COMES FROM ANOTHER COUNTRY WELL KNOWN FOR ITS HEALTH AND BEAUTY.
HE SAID I COULD USE IT TODAY SINCE TO-MORROW IS MY BAPTISM CEREMONY.
WOW, THAT'S AWESOME.
AH.
JUTTE.
COULD YOU USE THIS RINSHAM WHEN WASHING HER HAIR?
IT'LL MAKE IT ALL SILKY.
I SEE...
きゅぽ
(Uncap)
JUTTE, I THINK IT WILL BE FINE FOR MYNE TO WASH MY HAIR TODAY.
THAT SEEMS WISE.
MAY I WATCH FROM THE SIDE?

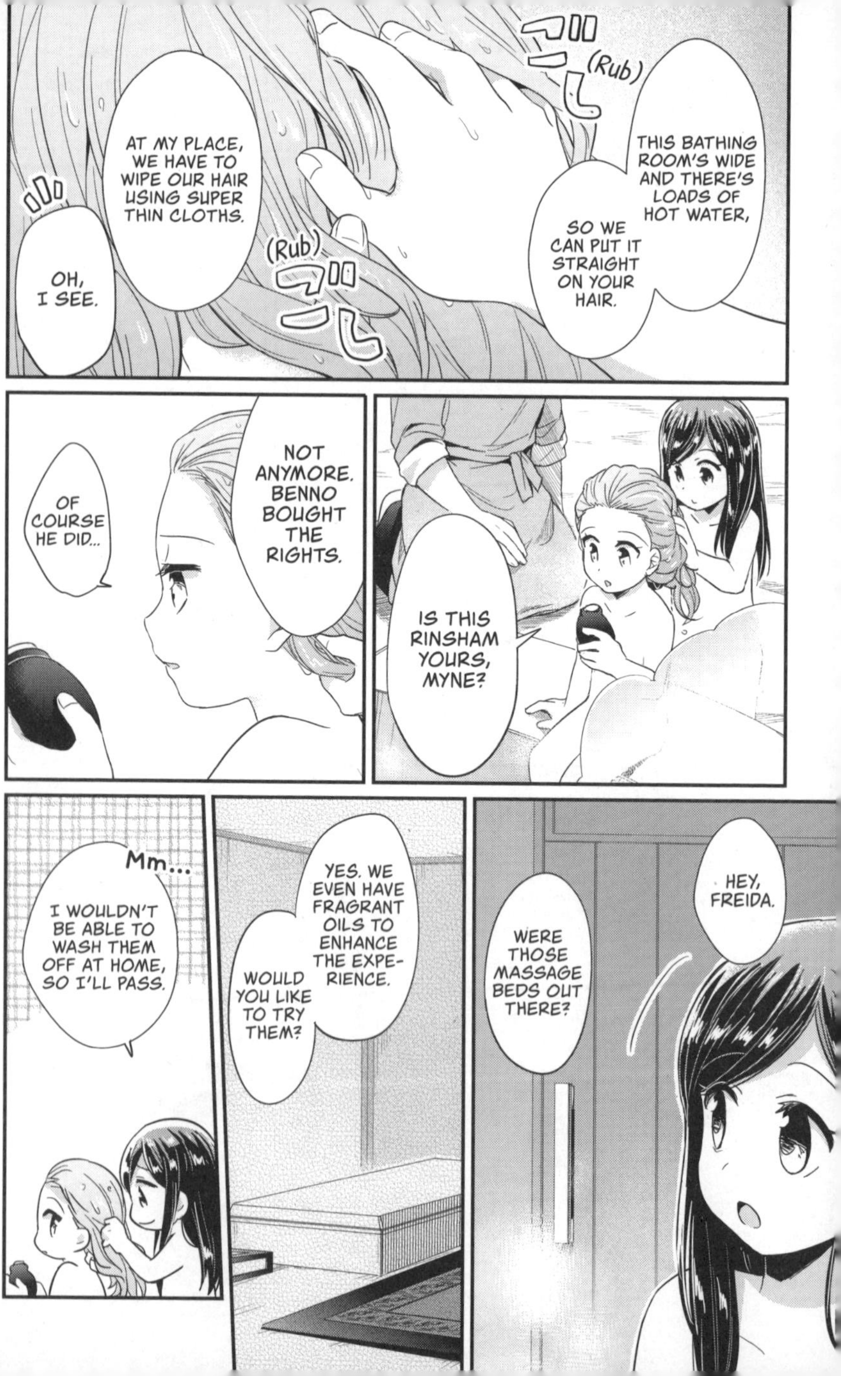
(Rub)
THIS BATHING ROOM'S WIDE AND THERE'S LOADS OF HOT WATER,
SO WE CAN PUT IT STRAIGHT ON YOUR HAIR.
(Rub)
AT MY PLACE, WE HAVE TO WIPE OUR HAIR USING SUPER THIN CLOTHS.
OH, I SEE.
IS THIS RINSHAM YOURS, MYNE?
NOT ANYMORE. BENNO BOUGHT THE RIGHTS.
OF COURSE HE DID...
HEY, FREIDA.
WERE THOSE MASSAGE BEDS OUT THERE?
YES. WE EVEN HAVE FRAGRANT OILS TO ENHANCE THE EXPE-RIENCE.
WOULD YOU LIKE TO TRY THEM?
Mm...
I WOULDN'T BE ABLE TO WASH THEM OFF AT HOME, SO I'LL PASS.

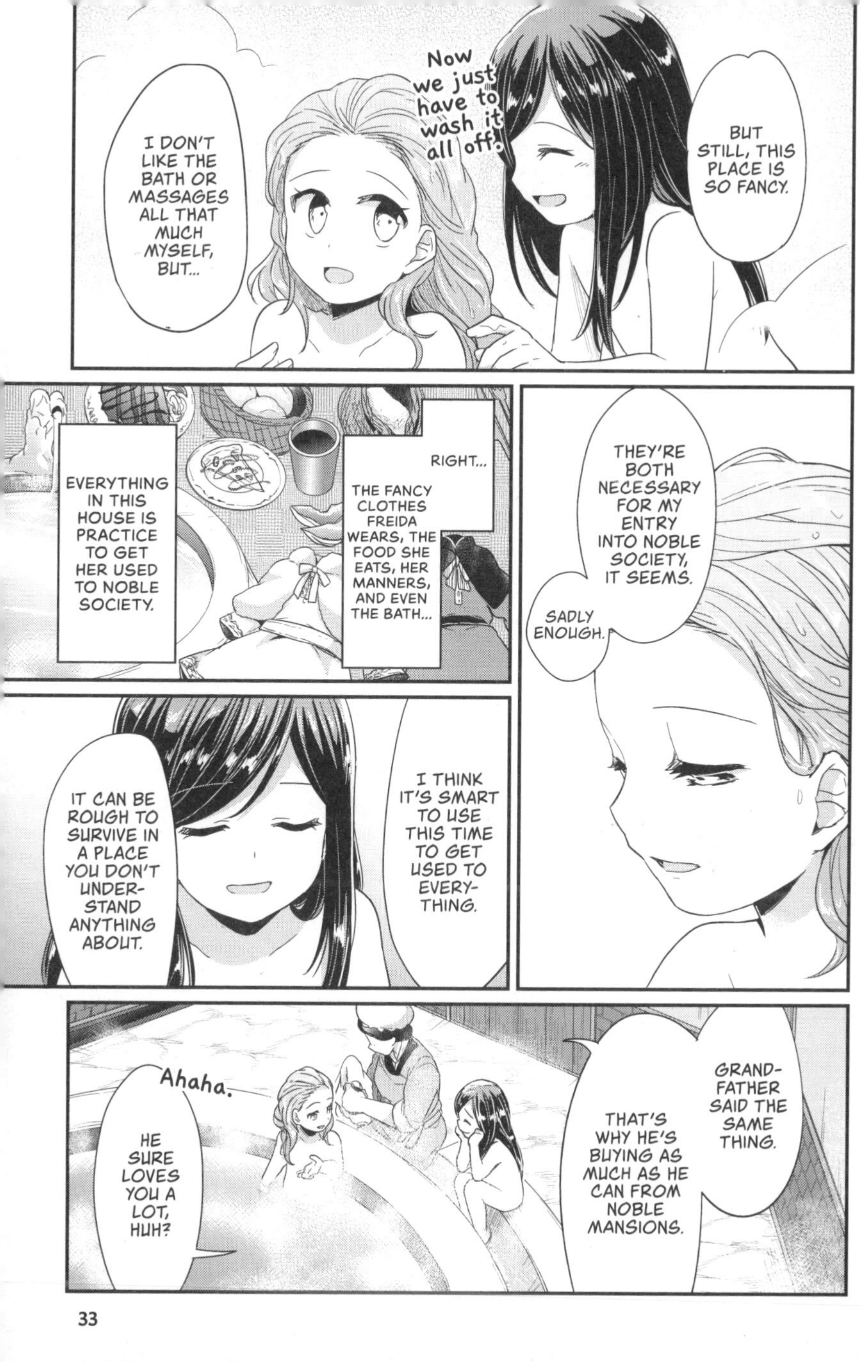
BUT STILL, THIS PLACE IS SO FANCY.
Now we just have to wash it all off.
I DON'T LIKE THE BATH OR MASSAGES ALL THAT MUCH MYSELF, BUT...
THEY'RE BOTH NECESSARY FOR MY ENTRY INTO NOBLE SOCIETY, IT SEEMS.
SADLY ENOUGH.
RIGHT...
THE FANCY CLOTHES FREIDA WEARS, THE FOOD SHE EATS, HER MANNERS, AND EVEN THE BATH...
EVERYTHING IN THIS HOUSE IS PRACTICE TO GET HER USED TO NOBLE SOCIETY.
I THINK IT'S SMART TO USE THIS TIME TO GET USED TO EVERYTHING.
IT CAN BE ROUGH TO SURVIVE IN A PLACE YOU DON'T UNDERSTAND ANYTHING ABOUT.
GRANDFATHER SAID THE SAME THING.
THAT'S WHY HE'S BUYING AS MUCH AS HE CAN FROM NOBLE MANSIONS.
Ahaha.
HE SURE LOVES YOU A LOT, HUH?

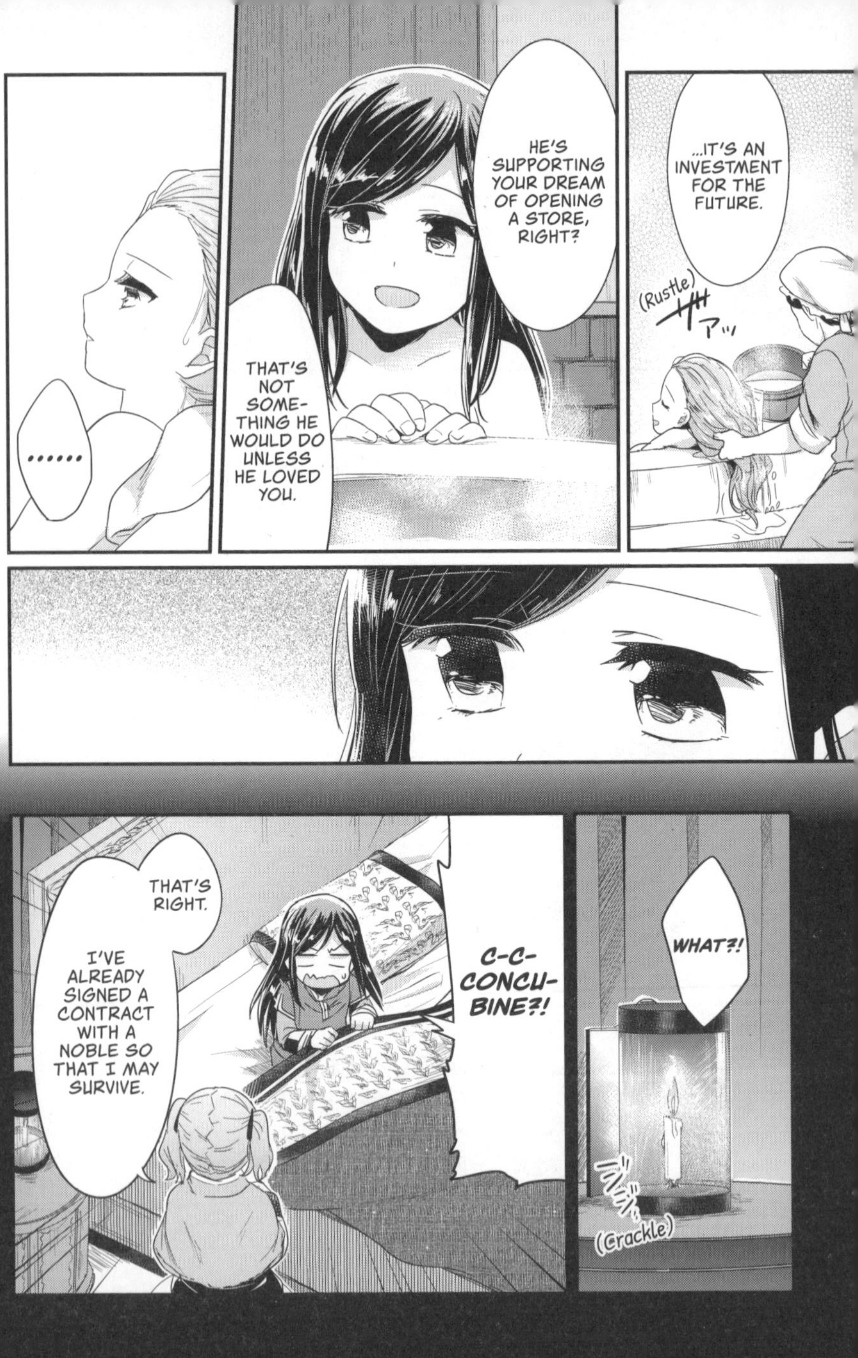
...IT'S AN INVESTMENT FOR THE FUTURE.
(Rustle)
HE'S SUPPORTING YOUR DREAM OF OPENING A STORE, RIGHT?
THAT'S NOT SOMETHING HE WOULD DO UNLESS HE LOVED YOU.
......
WHAT?!
(Crackle)
C-C-CONCUBINE?!
THAT'S RIGHT.
I'VE ALREADY SIGNED A CONTRACT WITH A NOBLE SO THAT I MAY SURVIVE.

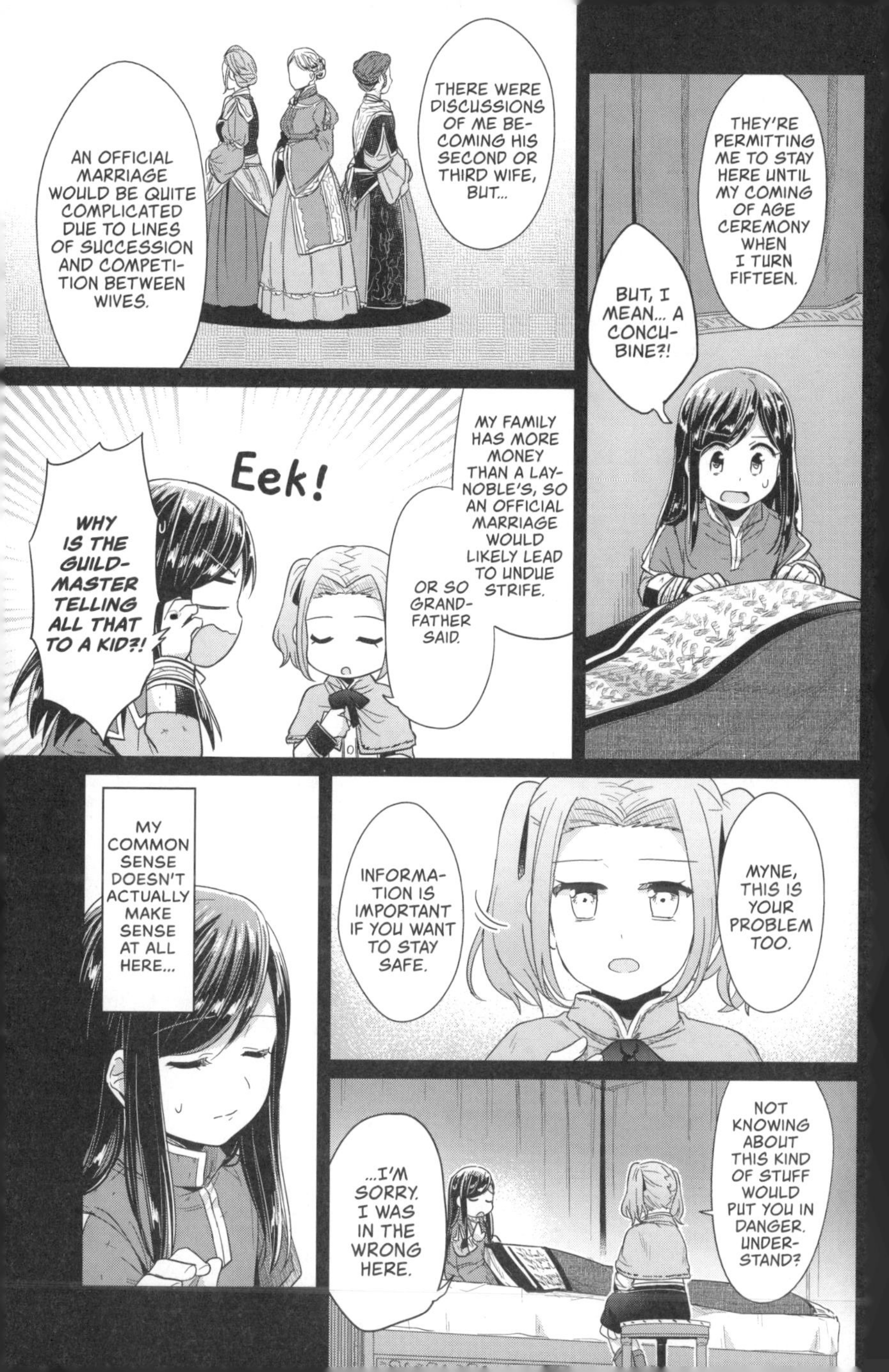
THEY'RE PERMITTING ME TO STAY HERE UNTIL MY COMING OF AGE CEREMONY WHEN I TURN FIFTEEN.
BUT, I MEAN... A CONCUBINE?!
THERE WERE DISCUSSIONS OF ME BE-COMING HIS SECOND OR THIRD WIFE, BUT...
AN OFFICIAL MARRIAGE WOULD BE QUITE COMPLICATED DUE TO LINES OF SUCCESSION AND COMPETI-TION BETWEEN WIVES.
MY FAMILY HAS MORE MONEY THAN A LAY-NOBLE'S, SO AN OFFICIAL MARRIAGE WOULD LIKELY LEAD TO UNDUE STRIFE.
OR SO GRAND-FATHER SAID.
Eek!
WHY IS THE GUILD-MASTER TELLING ALL THAT TO A KID?!
MYNE, THIS IS YOUR PROBLEM TOO.
INFORMA-TION IS IMPORTANT IF YOU WANT TO STAY SAFE.
NOT KNOWING ABOUT THIS KIND OF STUFF WOULD PUT YOU IN DANGER. UNDER-STAND?
...I'M SORRY. I WAS IN THE WRONG HERE.
MY COMMON SENSE DOESN'T ACTUALLY MAKE SENSE AT ALL HERE...

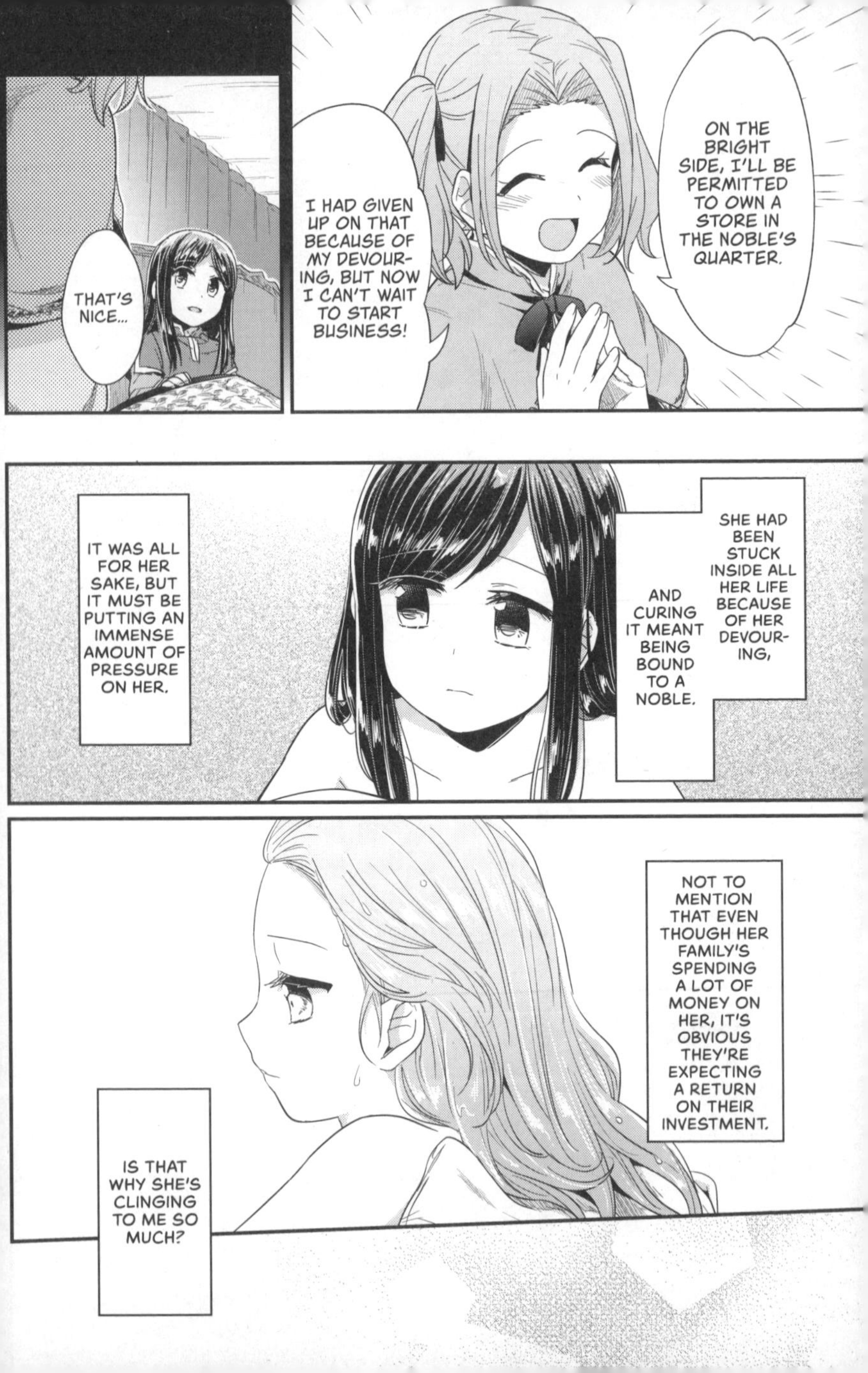
ON THE BRIGHT SIDE, I'LL BE PERMITTED TO OWN A STORE IN THE NOBLE'S QUARTER.
I HAD GIVEN UP ON THAT BECAUSE OF MY DEVOURING, BUT NOW I CAN'T WAIT TO START BUSINESS!
THAT'S NICE...
SHE HAD BEEN STUCK INSIDE ALL HER LIFE BECAUSE OF HER DEVOURING,
AND CURING IT MEANT BEING BOUND TO A NOBLE.
IT WAS ALL FOR HER SAKE, BUT IT MUST BE PUTTING AN IMMENSE AMOUNT OF PRESSURE ON HER.
NOT TO MENTION THAT EVEN THOUGH HER FAMILY'S SPENDING A LOT OF MONEY ON HER, IT'S OBVIOUS THEY'RE EXPECTING A RETURN ON THEIR INVESTMENT.
IS THAT WHY SHE'S CLINGING TO ME SO MUCH?

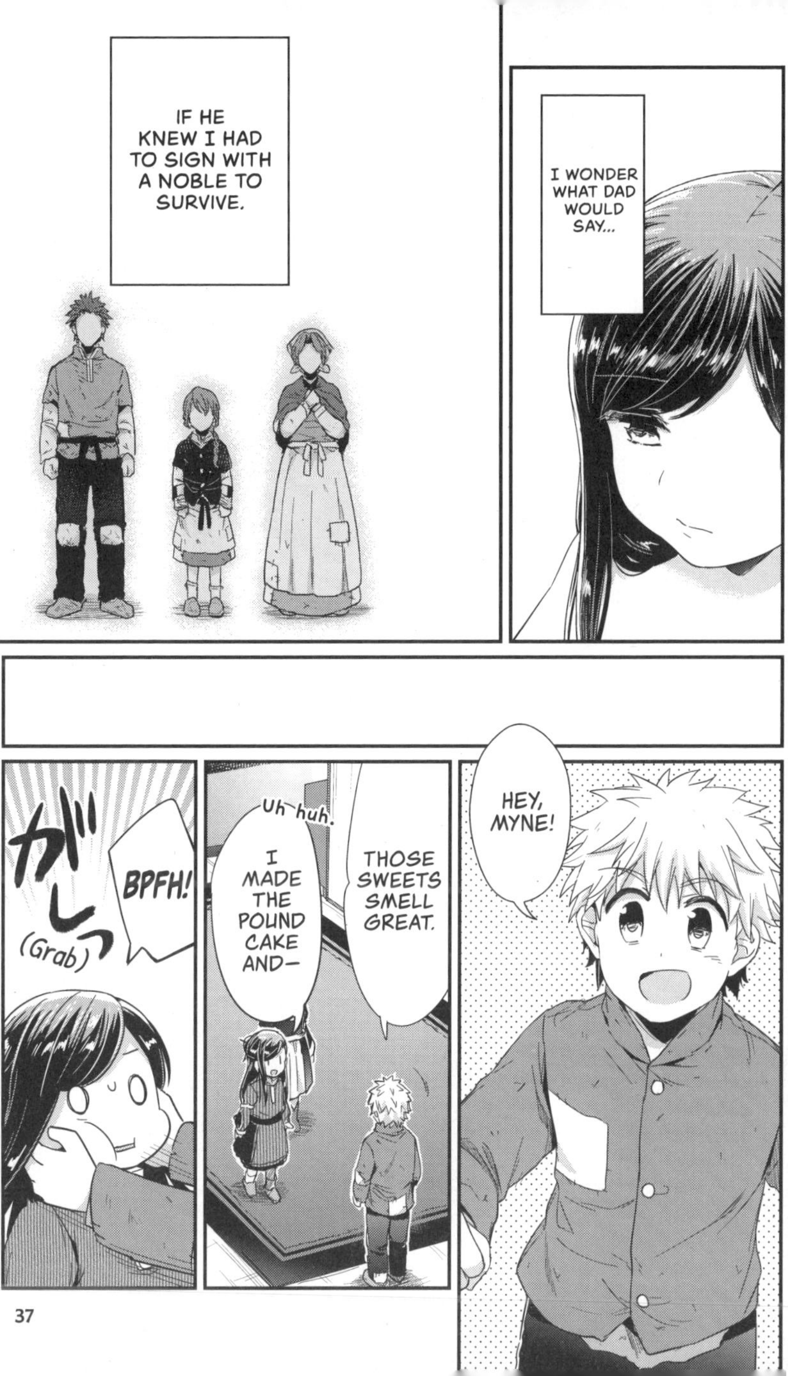
I WONDER WHAT DAD WOULD SAY...
IF HE KNEW I HAD TO SIGN WITH A NOBLE TO SURVIVE.
HEY, MYNE!
THOSE SWEETS SMELL GREAT.
Uh huh.
I MADE THE POUND CAKE AND—
BPFH!
がしっ
(Grab)

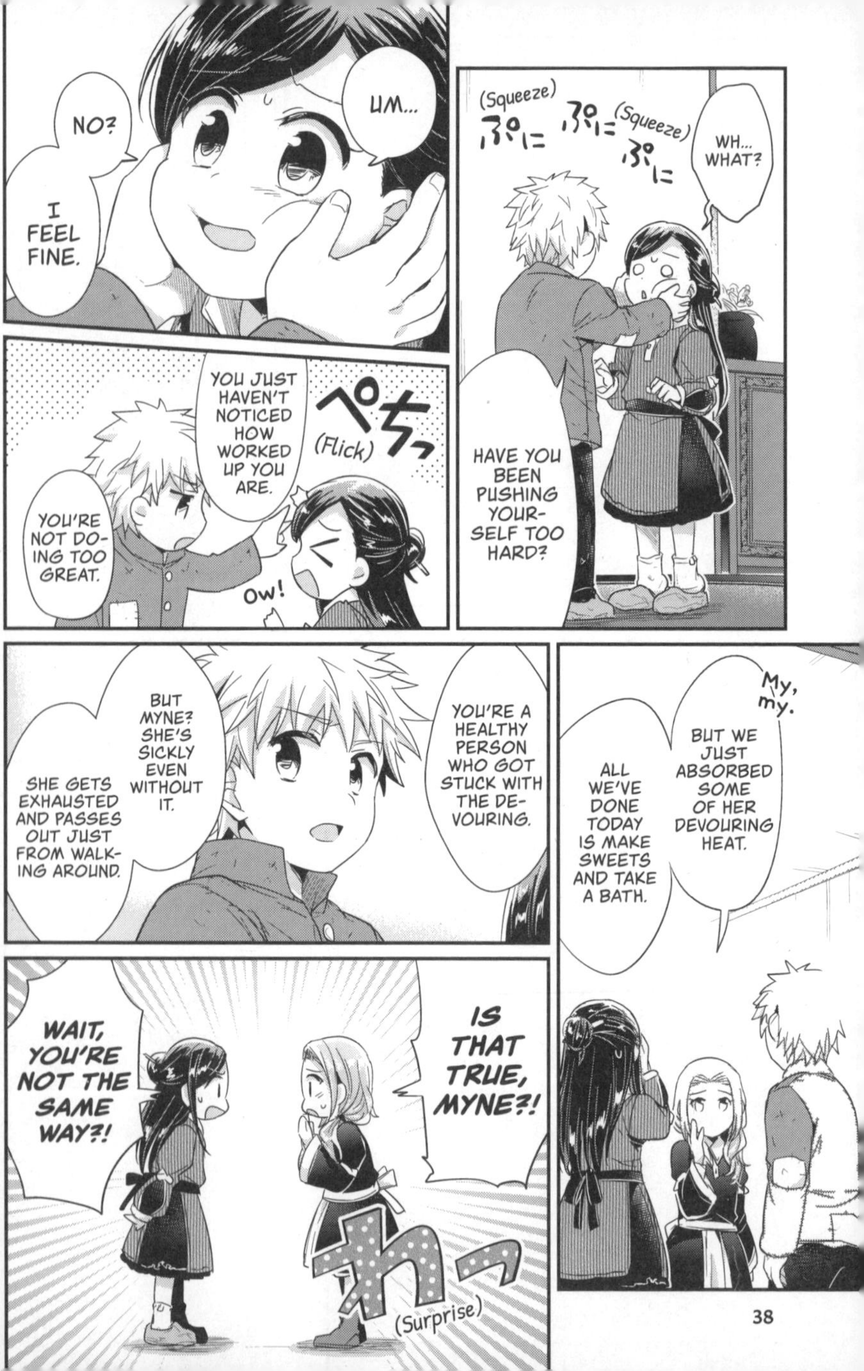
(Squeeze)
ぷに
ぷに (Squeeze)
ぷに
WH... WHAT?
HAVE YOU BEEN PUSHING YOUR-SELF TOO HARD?
UM...
NO?
I FEEL FINE.
YOU JUST HAVEN'T NOTICED HOW WORKED UP YOU ARE.
ぺちっ
(Flick)
YOU'RE NOT DO-ING TOO GREAT.
Ow!
My, my.
BUT WE JUST ABSORBED SOME OF HER DEVOURING HEAT.
ALL WE'VE DONE TODAY IS MAKE SWEETS AND TAKE A BATH.
YOU'RE A HEALTHY PERSON WHO GOT STUCK WITH THE DE-VOURING.
BUT MYNE? SHE'S SICKLY EVEN WITHOUT IT.
SHE GETS EXHAUSTED AND PASSES OUT JUST FROM WALK-ING AROUND.
IS THAT TRUE, MYNE?!
WAIT, YOU'RE NOT THE SAME WAY?!
わっ
(Surprise)

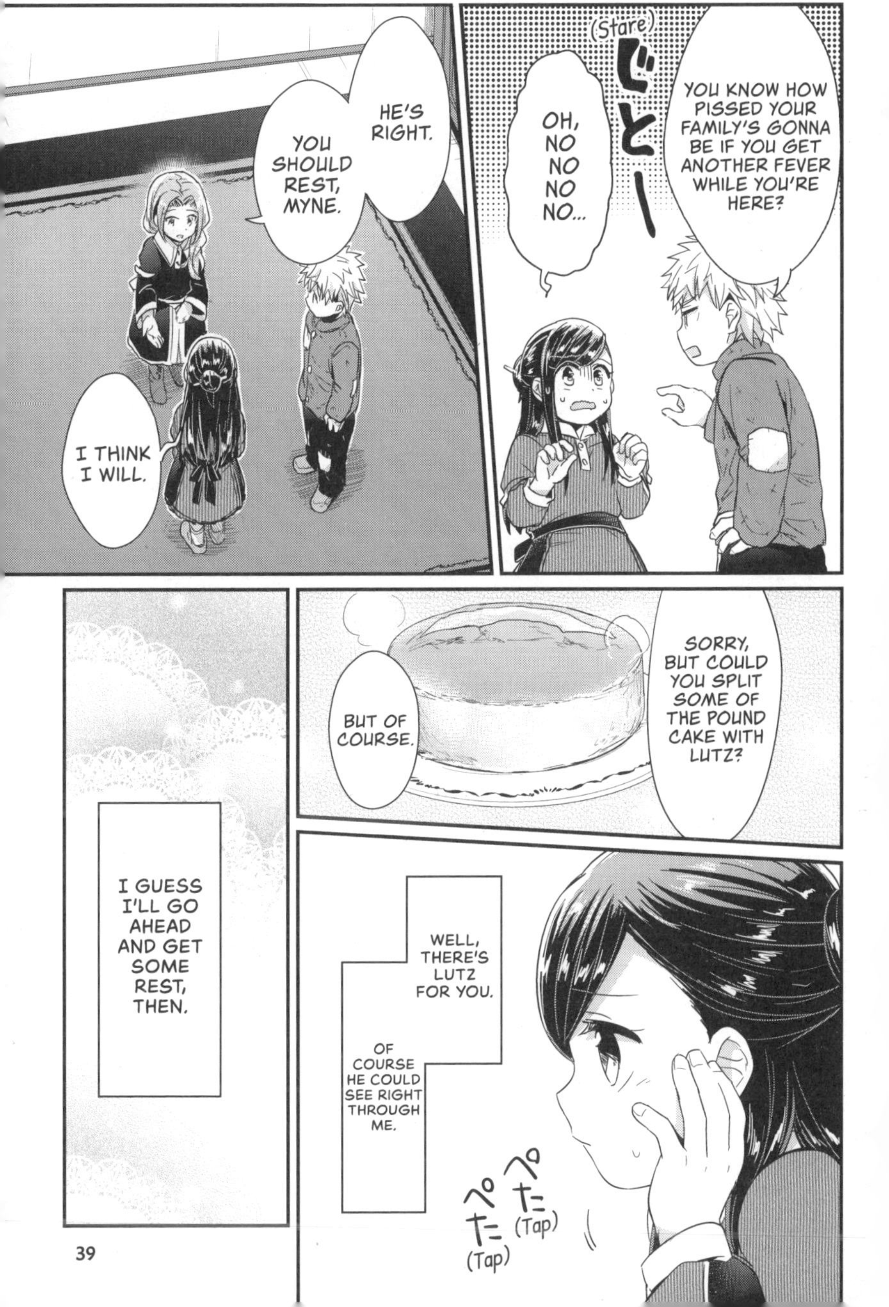
YOU KNOW HOW PISSED YOUR FAMILY'S GONNA BE IF YOU GET ANOTHER FEVER WHILE YOU'RE HERE?
じとー (Stare)
OH, NO NO NO NO...
HE'S RIGHT.
YOU SHOULD REST, MYNE.
I THINK I WILL.
SORRY, BUT COULD YOU SPLIT SOME OF THE POUND CAKE WITH LUTZ?
BUT OF COURSE.
WELL, THERE'S LUTZ FOR YOU.
OF COURSE HE COULD SEE RIGHT THROUGH ME.
ぺた (Tap)
ぺた (Tap)
I GUESS I'LL GO AHEAD AND GET SOME REST, THEN.

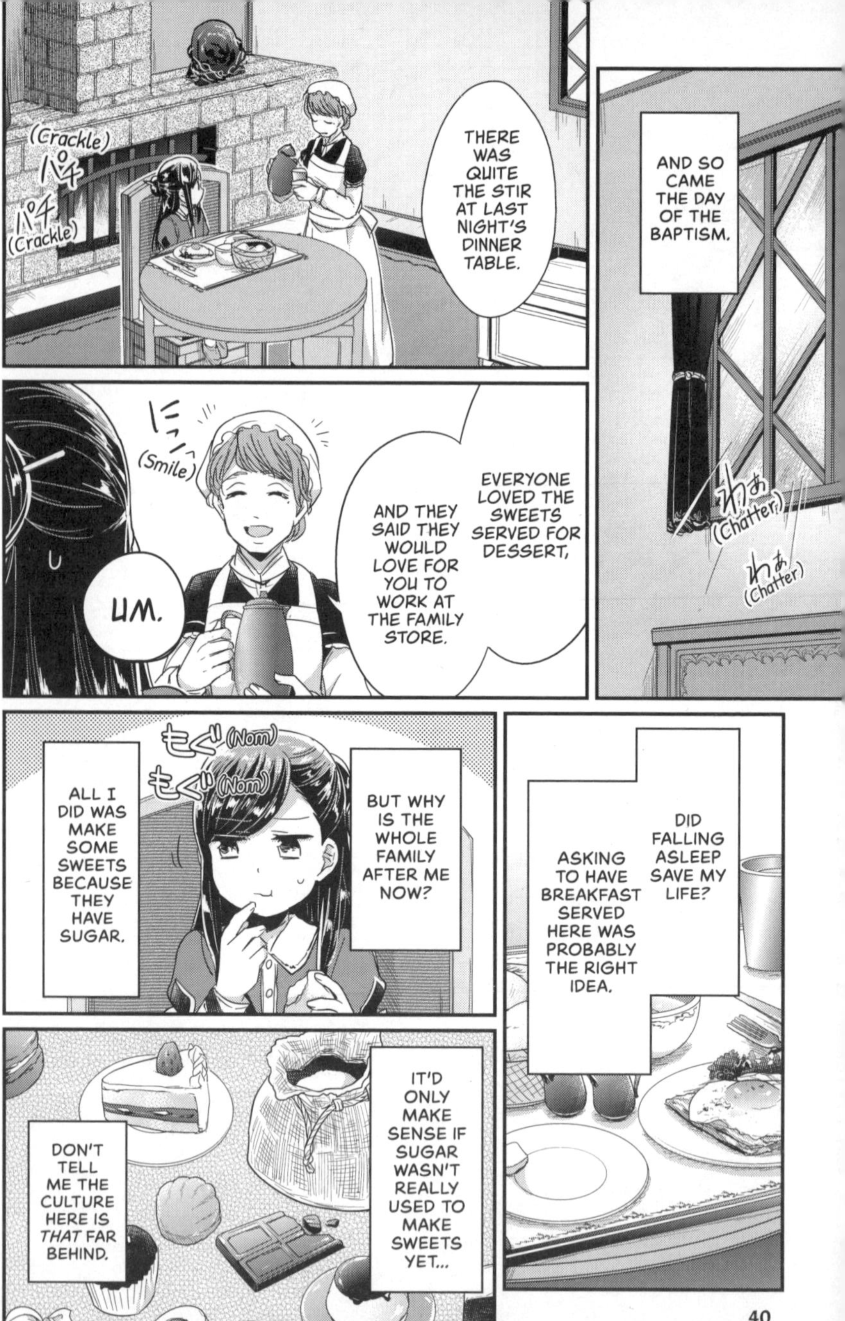
AND SO CAME THE DAY OF THE BAPTISM.
わぁ (Chatter)
わぁ (Chatter)
THERE WAS QUITE THE STIR AT LAST NIGHT'S DINNER TABLE.
パチ (Crackle)
パチ (Crackle)
EVERYONE LOVED THE SWEETS SERVED FOR DESSERT,
AND THEY SAID THEY WOULD LOVE FOR YOU TO WORK AT THE FAMILY STORE.
(Smile)
UM.
DID FALLING ASLEEP SAVE MY LIFE?
ASKING TO HAVE BREAKFAST SERVED HERE WAS PROBABLY THE RIGHT IDEA.
BUT WHY IS THE WHOLE FAMILY AFTER ME NOW?
もぐ (Nom)
もぐ (Nom)
ALL I DID WAS MAKE SOME SWEETS BECAUSE THEY HAVE SUGAR.
IT'D ONLY MAKE SENSE IF SUGAR WASN'T REALLY USED TO MAKE SWEETS YET...
DON'T TELL ME THE CULTURE HERE IS *THAT* FAR BEHIND.

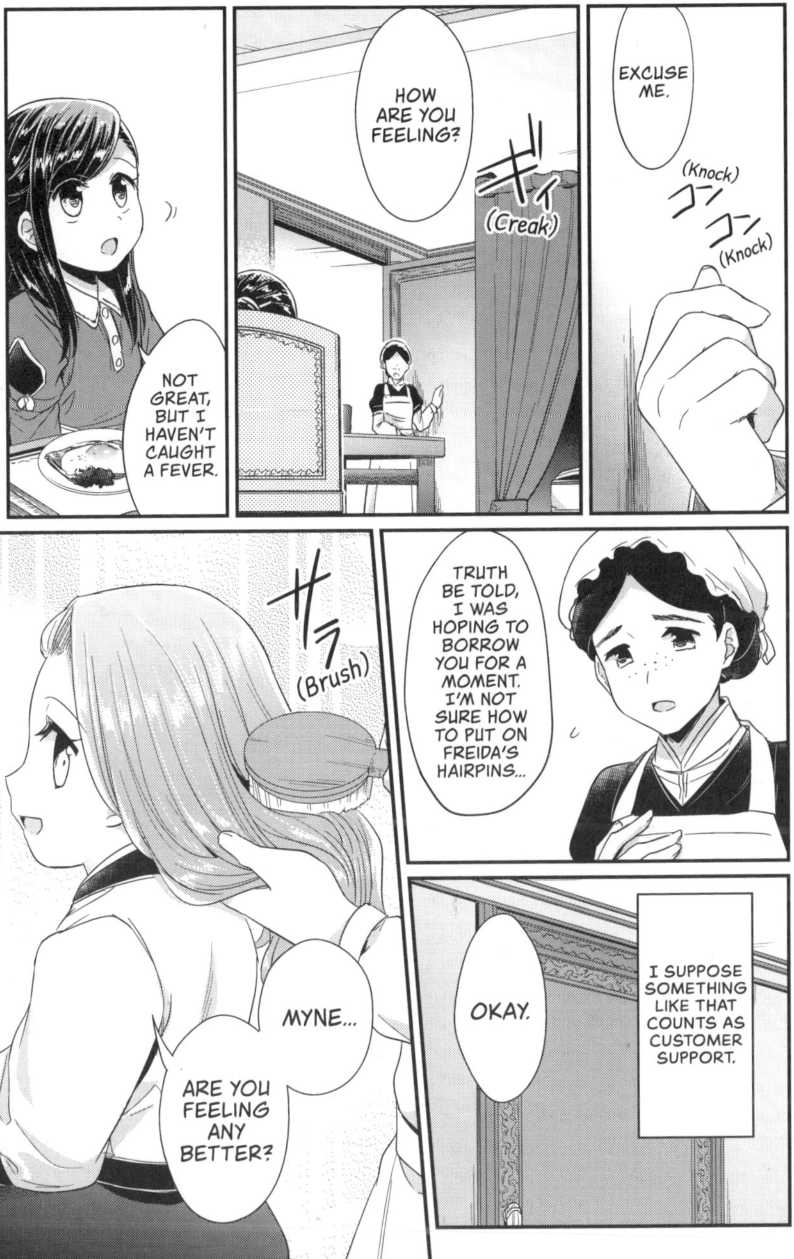
EXCUSE ME.
(Knock)
コン
コン
(Knock)
HOW ARE YOU FEELING?
ギィ
(Creak)
NOT GREAT, BUT I HAVEN'T CAUGHT A FEVER.
TRUTH BE TOLD, I WAS HOPING TO BORROW YOU FOR A MOMENT. I'M NOT SURE HOW TO PUT ON FREIDA'S HAIRPINS...
OKAY.
I SUPPOSE SOMETHING LIKE THAT COUNTS AS CUSTOMER SUPPORT.
サラ
(Brush)
MYNE...
ARE YOU FEELING ANY BETTER?

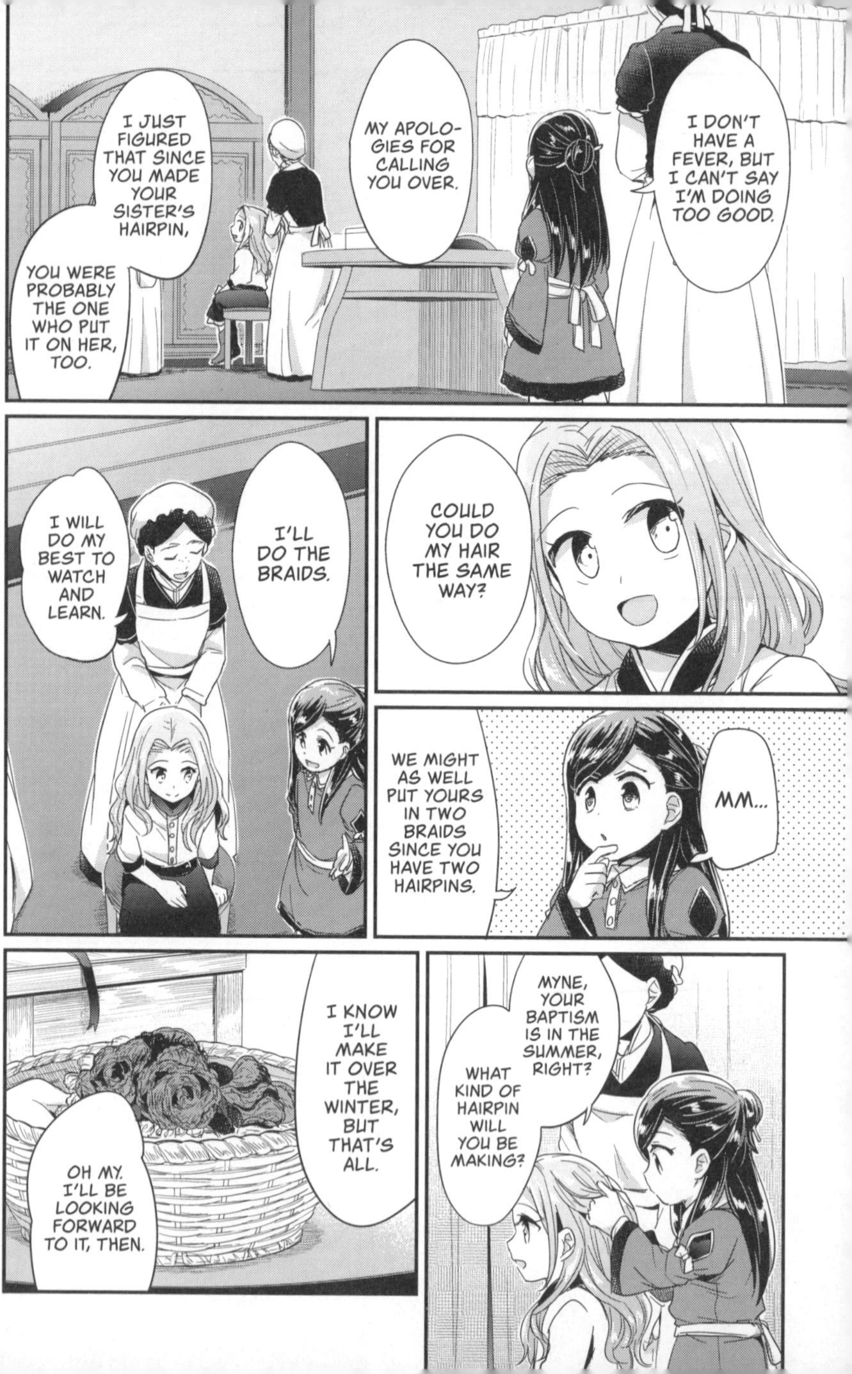
I DON'T HAVE A FEVER, BUT I CAN'T SAY I'M DOING TOO GOOD.
MY APOLOGIES FOR CALLING YOU OVER.
I JUST FIGURED THAT SINCE YOU MADE YOUR SISTER'S HAIRPIN,
YOU WERE PROBABLY THE ONE WHO PUT IT ON HER, TOO.
COULD YOU DO MY HAIR THE SAME WAY?
MM...
WE MIGHT AS WELL PUT YOURS IN TWO BRAIDS SINCE YOU HAVE TWO HAIRPINS.
I'LL DO THE BRAIDS.
I WILL DO MY BEST TO WATCH AND LEARN.
MYNE, YOUR BAPTISM IS IN THE SUMMER, RIGHT?
WHAT KIND OF HAIRPIN WILL YOU BE MAKING?
I KNOW I'LL MAKE IT OVER THE WINTER, BUT THAT'S ALL.
OH MY. I'LL BE LOOKING FORWARD TO IT, THEN.

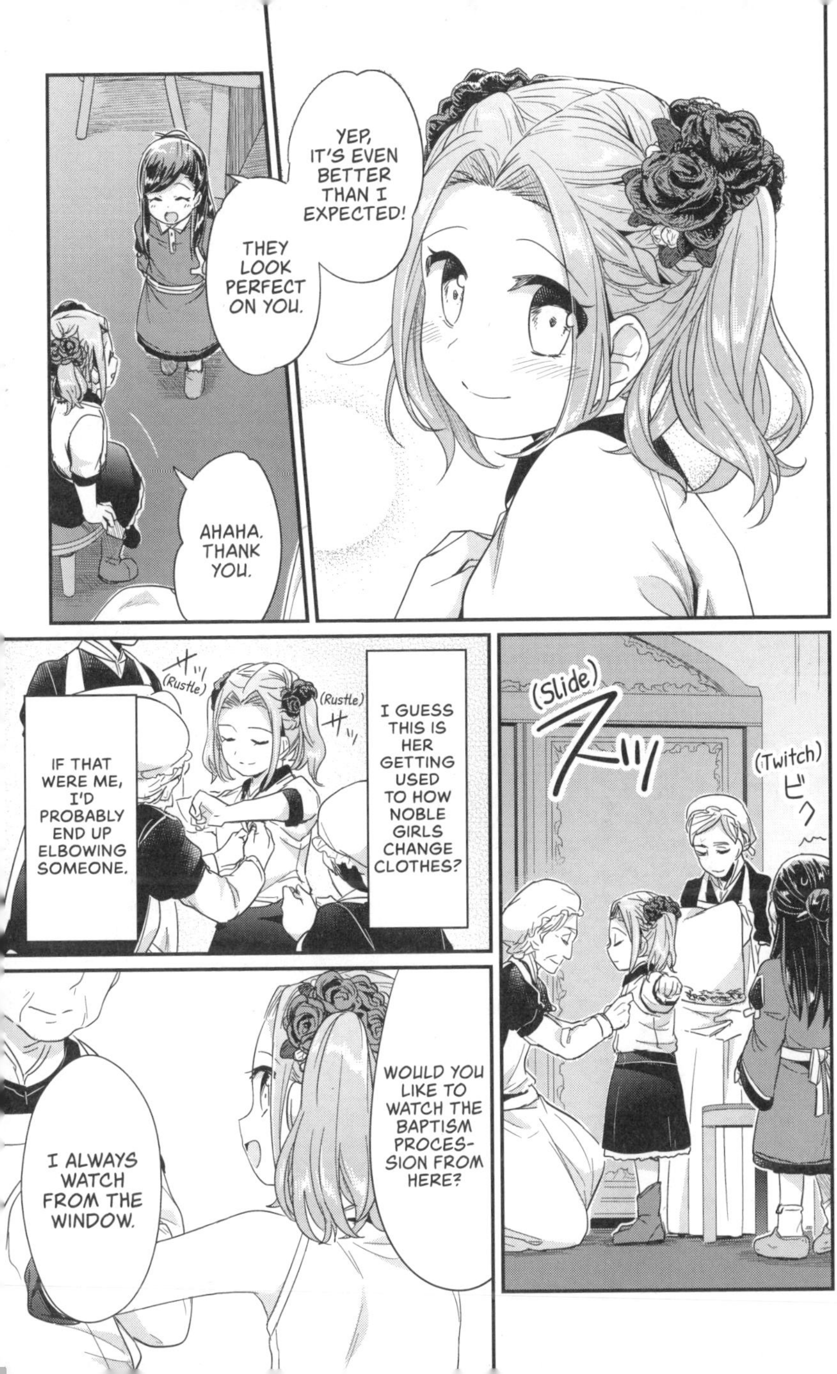
YEP, IT'S EVEN BETTER THAN I EXPECTED!
THEY LOOK PERFECT ON YOU.
AHAHA. THANK YOU.
(Slide) スッ
(Twitch) ビク
I GUESS THIS IS HER GETTING USED TO HOW NOBLE GIRLS CHANGE CLOTHES?
(Rustle) サッ
(Rustle) サッ
IF THAT WERE ME, I'D PROBABLY END UP ELBOWING SOMEONE.
WOULD YOU LIKE TO WATCH THE BAPTISM PROCES-SION FROM HERE?
I ALWAYS WATCH FROM THE WINDOW.

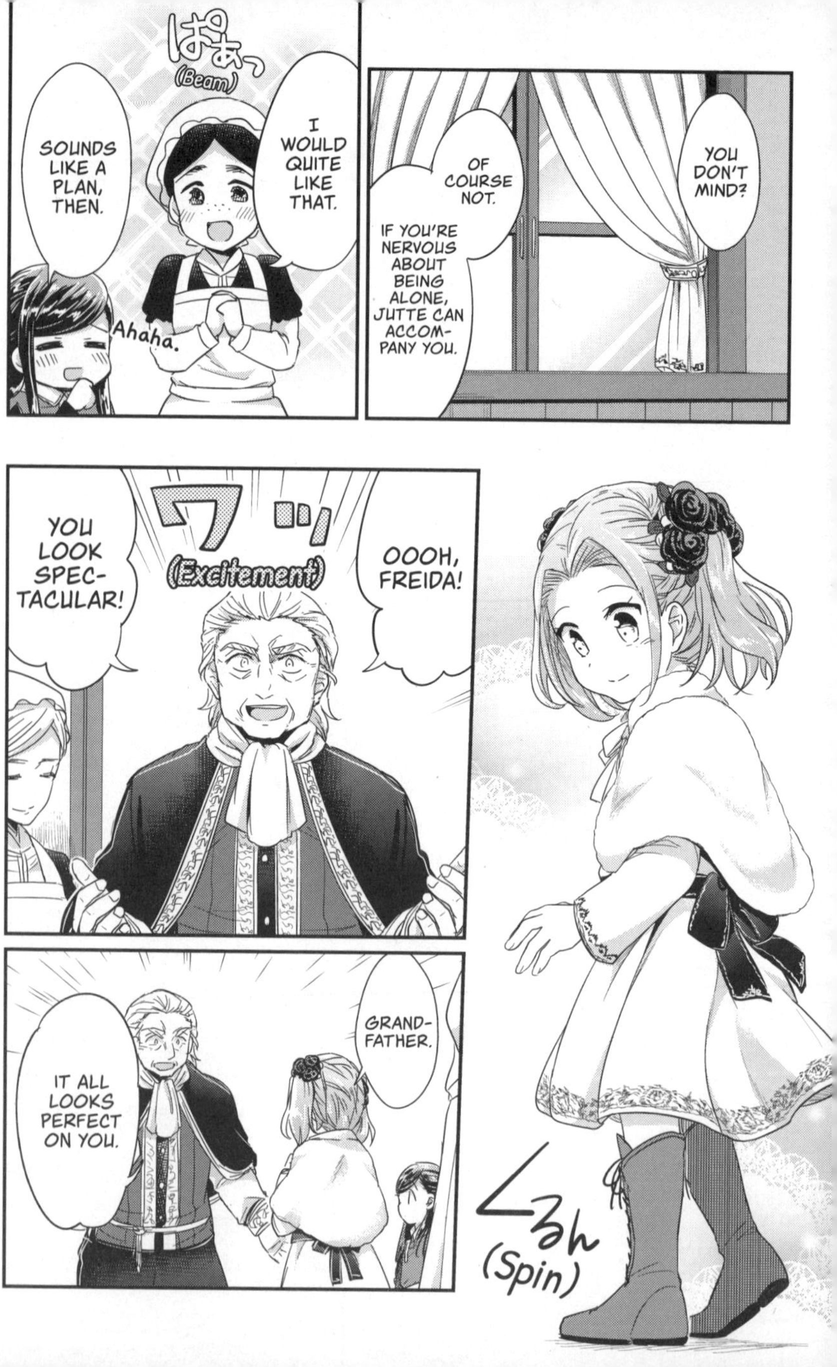
YOU DON'T MIND?
OF COURSE NOT.
IF YOU'RE NERVOUS ABOUT BEING ALONE, JUTTE CAN ACCOMPANY YOU.
ぱあっ
(Beam)
I WOULD QUITE LIKE THAT.
SOUNDS LIKE A PLAN, THEN.
Ahaha.
くるん
(Spin)
ワッ
(Excitement)
OOOH, FREIDA!
YOU LOOK SPECTACULAR!
GRAND-FATHER.
IT ALL LOOKS PERFECT ON YOU.

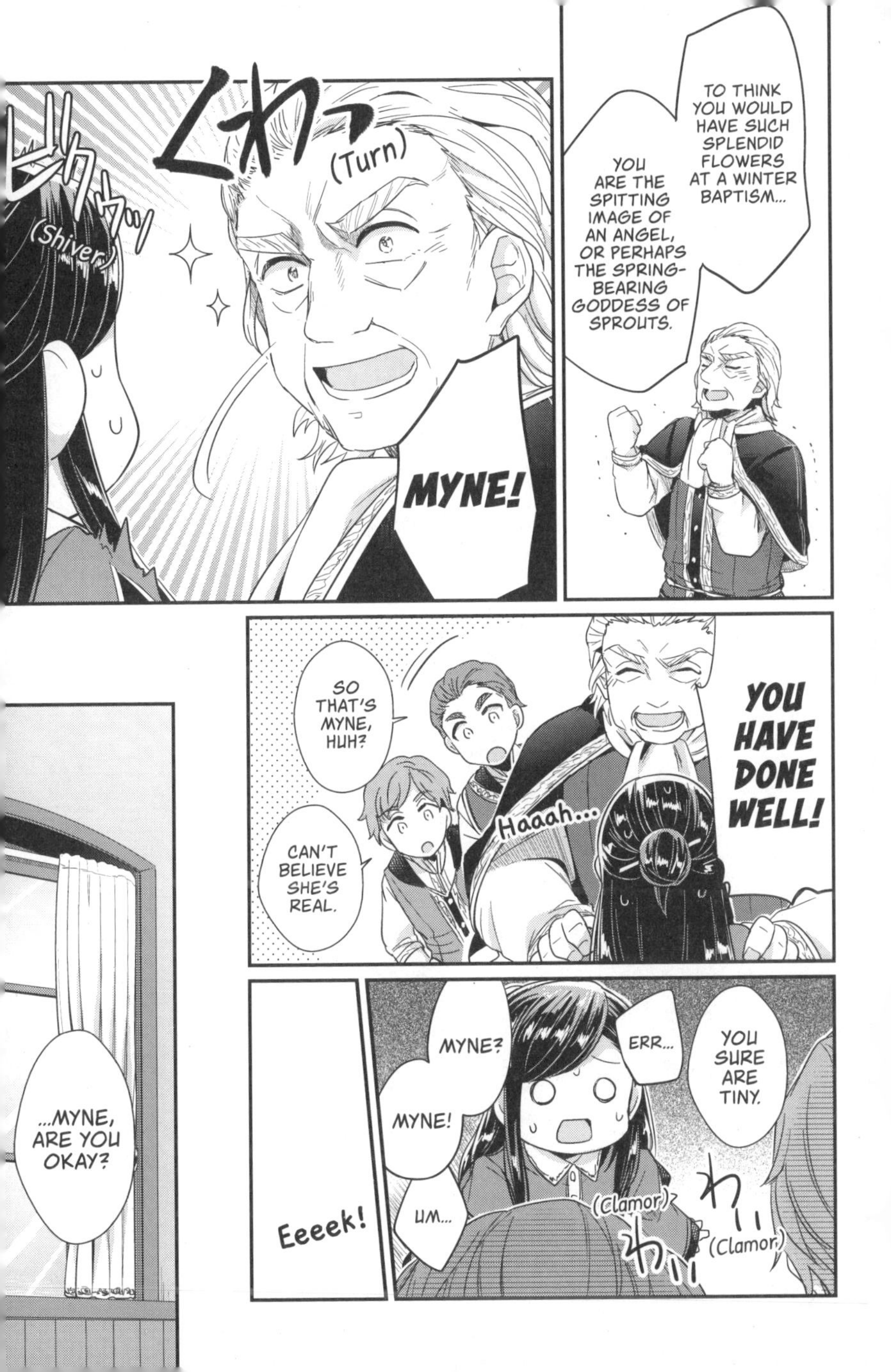

TO THINK YOU WOULD HAVE SUCH SPLENDID FLOWERS AT A WINTER BAPTISM...
YOU ARE THE SPITTING IMAGE OF AN ANGEL, OR PERHAPS THE SPRING-BEARING GODDESS OF SPROUTS.
くわっ
(Turn)
(Shiver)
MYNE!
YOU HAVE DONE WELL!
Haaah...
SO THAT'S MYNE, HUH?
CAN'T BELIEVE SHE'S REAL.
YOU SURE ARE TINY.
ERR...
MYNE?
MYNE!
UM...
(Clamor)
(Clamor)
Eeeek!
...MYNE, ARE YOU OKAY?

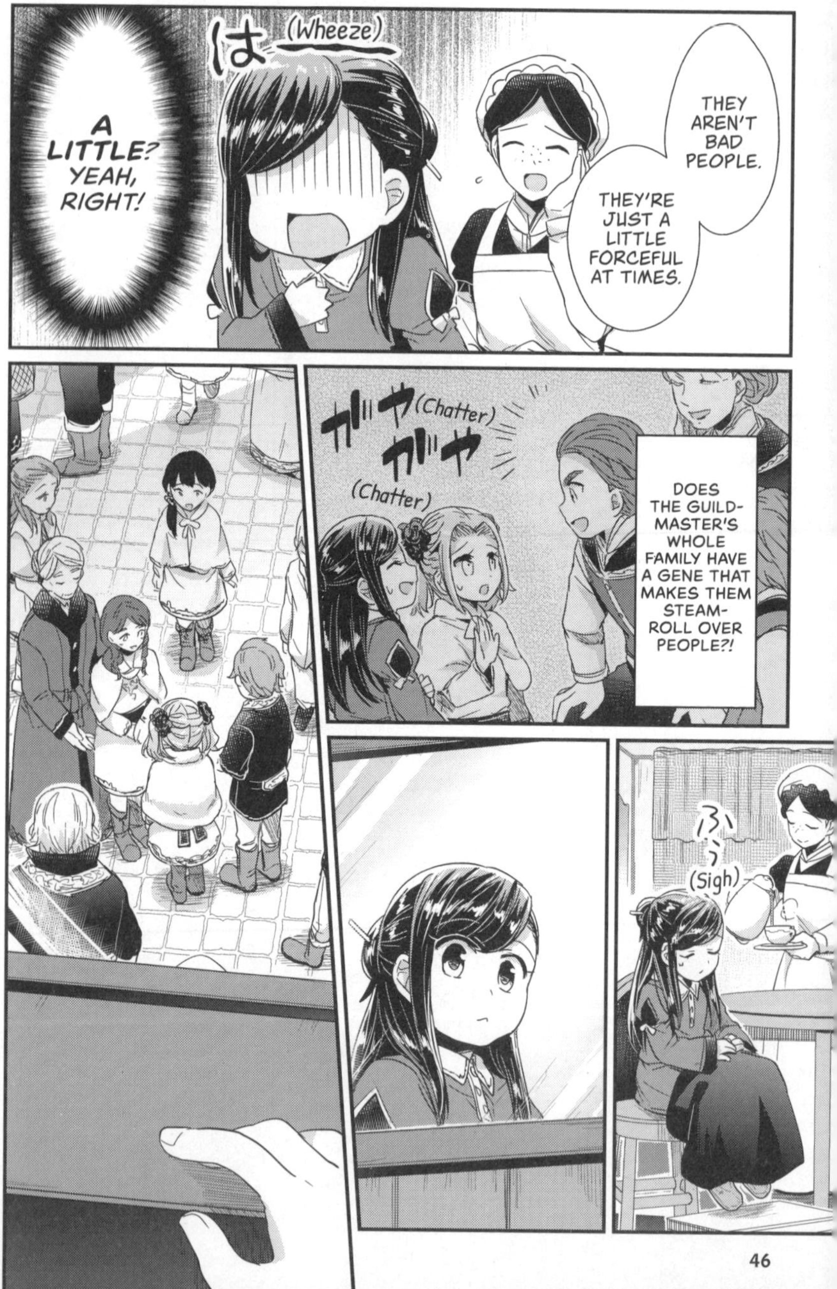
THEY AREN'T BAD PEOPLE.
THEY'RE JUST A LITTLE FORCEFUL AT TIMES.
は (Wheeze)
A LITTLE? YEAH, RIGHT!
ガヤ (Chatter)
ガヤ (Chatter)
DOES THE GUILD-MASTER'S WHOLE FAMILY HAVE A GENE THAT MAKES THEM STEAM-ROLL OVER PEOPLE?!
ふぅ (Sigh)

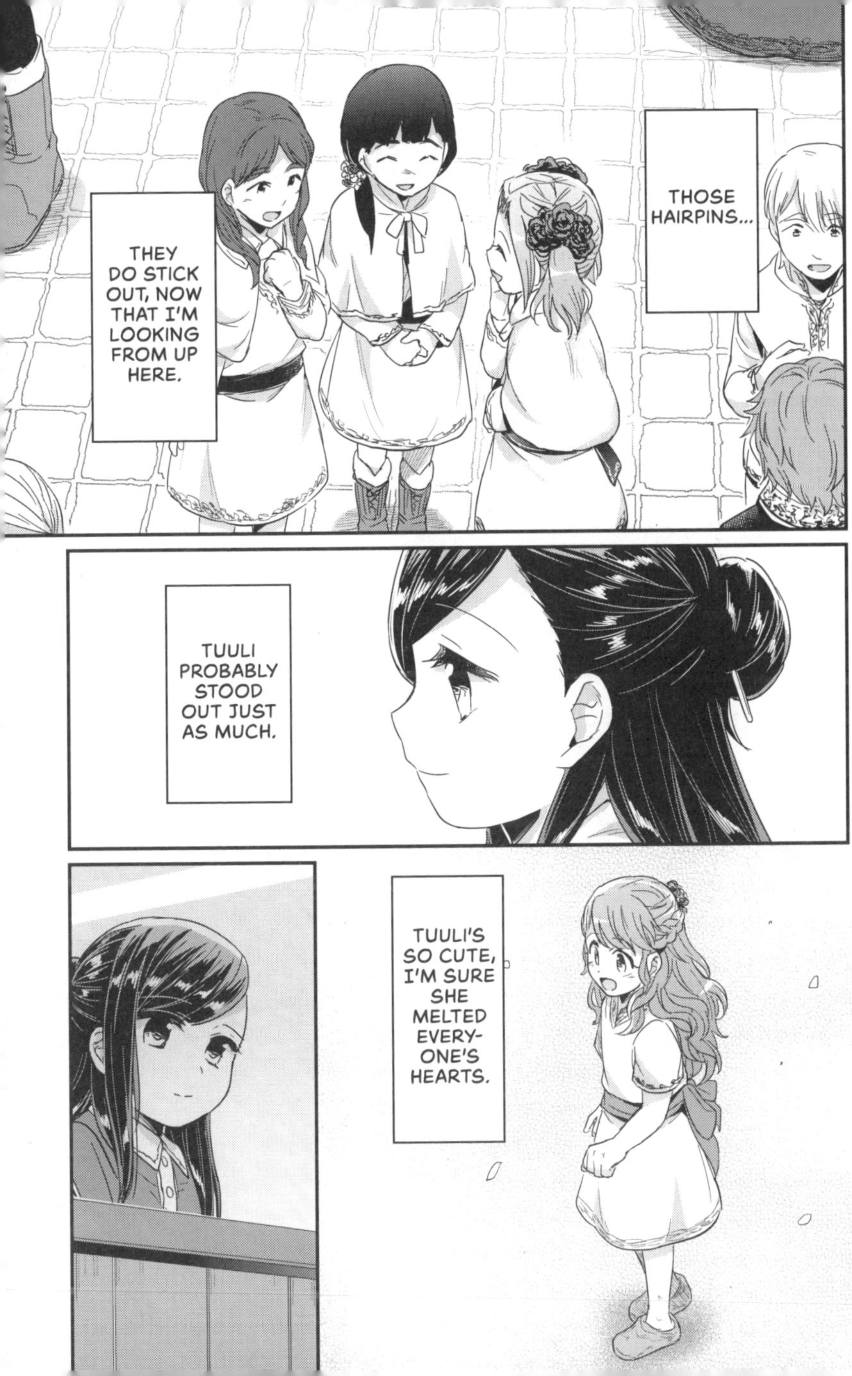
THOSE HAIRPINS...
THEY DO STICK OUT, NOW THAT I'M LOOKING FROM UP HERE.
TUULI PROBABLY STOOD OUT JUST AS MUCH.
TUULI'S SO CUTE, I'M SURE SHE MELTED EVERY-ONE'S HEARTS.

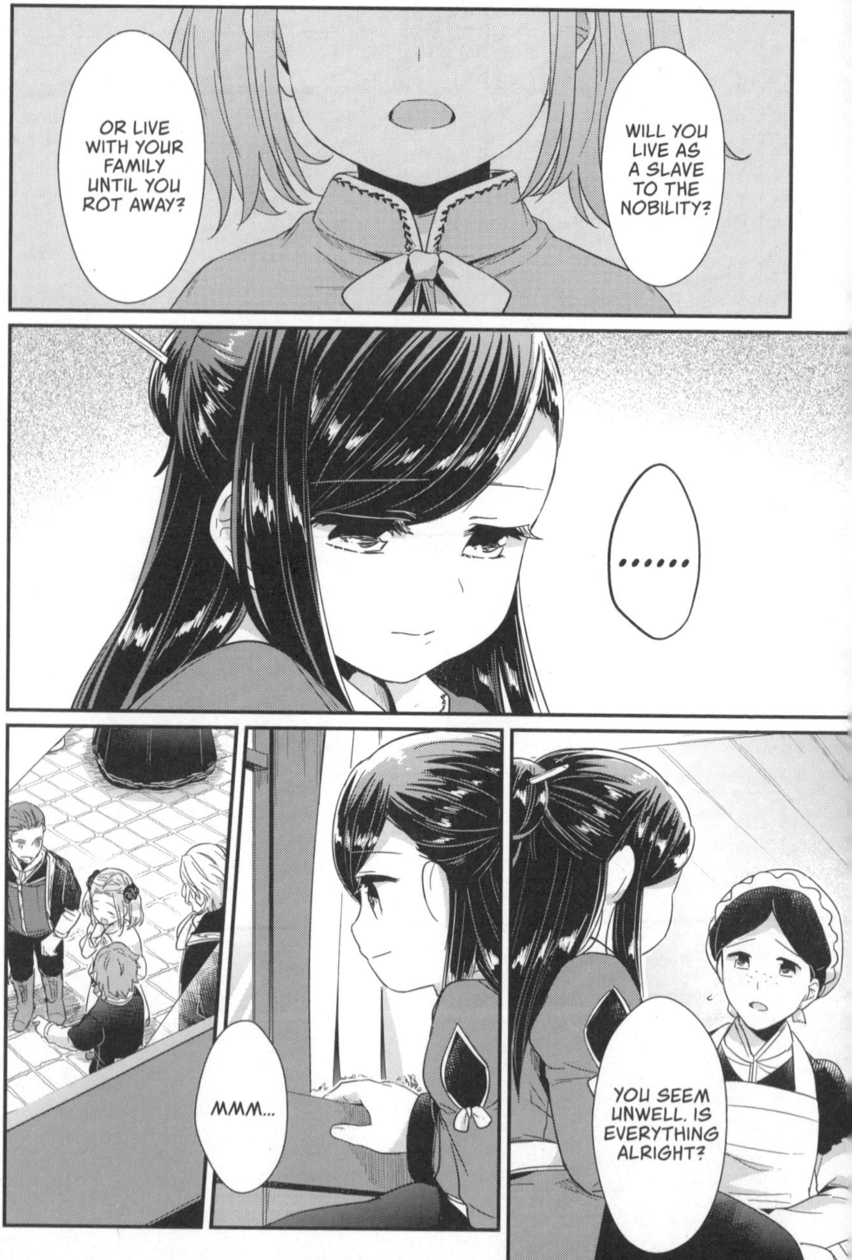
WILL YOU LIVE AS A SLAVE TO THE NOBILITY?
OR LIVE WITH YOUR FAMILY UNTIL YOU ROT AWAY?
......
YOU SEEM UNWELL, IS EVERYTHING ALRIGHT?
MMM...

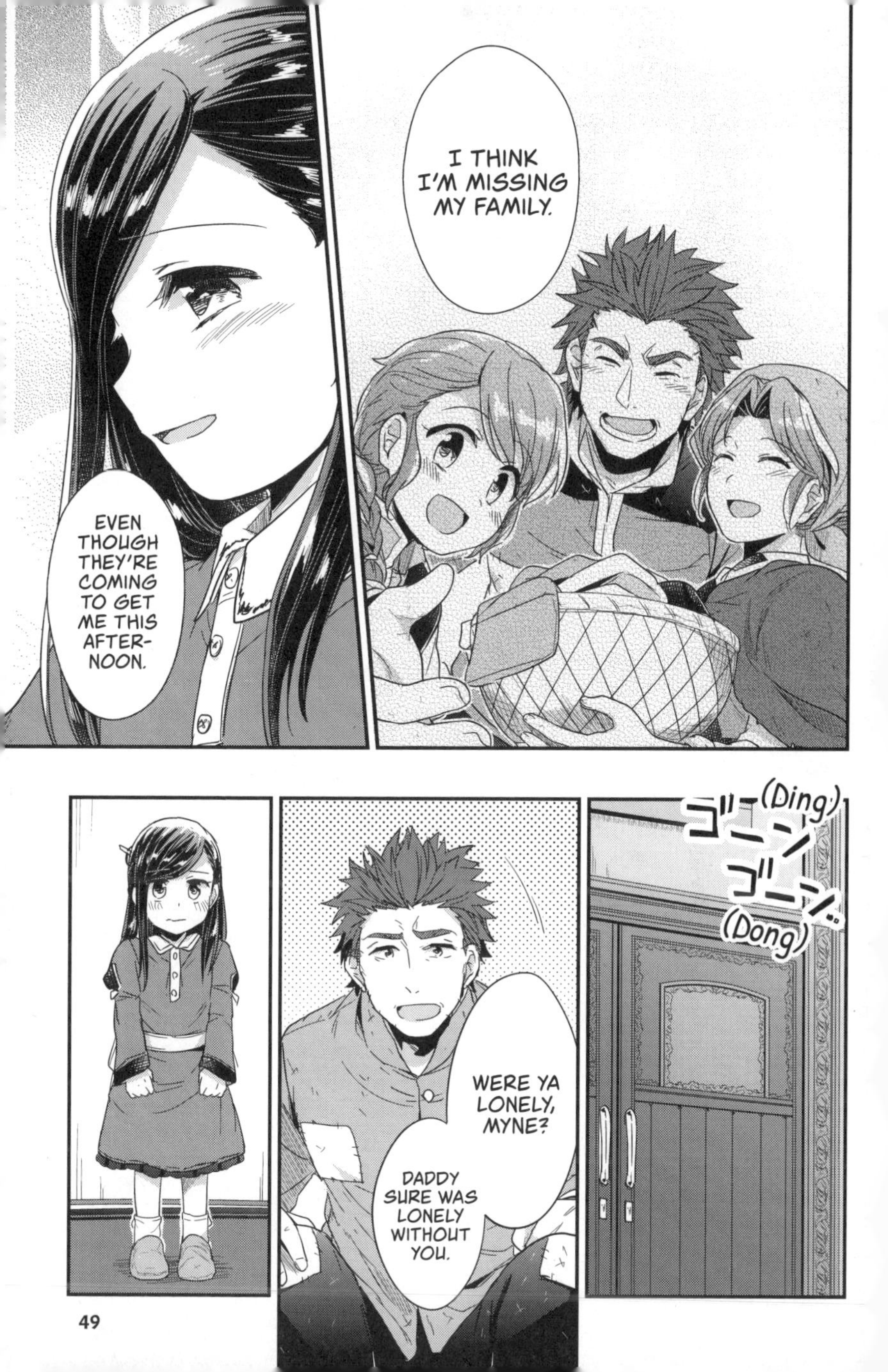
I THINK I'M MISSING MY FAMILY.
EVEN THOUGH THEY'RE COMING TO GET ME THIS AFTER-NOON.
ゴーン (Ding)
ゴーン (Dong)
WERE YA LONELY, MYNE?
DADDY SURE WAS LONELY WITHOUT YOU.

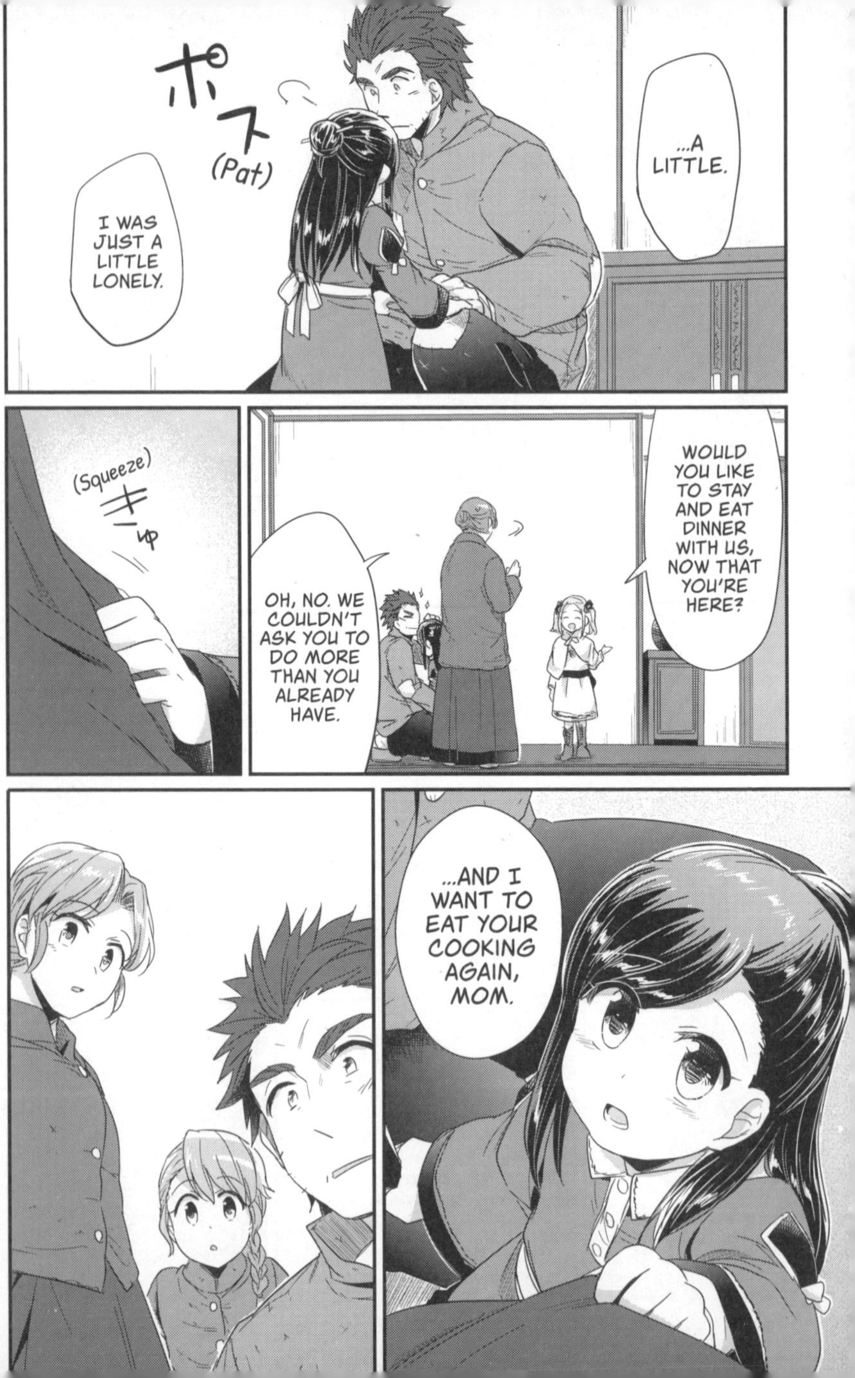
...A LITTLE.
ポス
(Pat)
I WAS JUST A LITTLE LONELY.
WOULD YOU LIKE TO STAY AND EAT DINNER WITH US, NOW THAT YOU'RE HERE?
OH, NO. WE COULDN'T ASK YOU TO DO MORE THAN YOU ALREADY HAVE.
(Squeeze)
キーゅ
...AND I WANT TO EAT YOUR COOKING AGAIN, MOM.

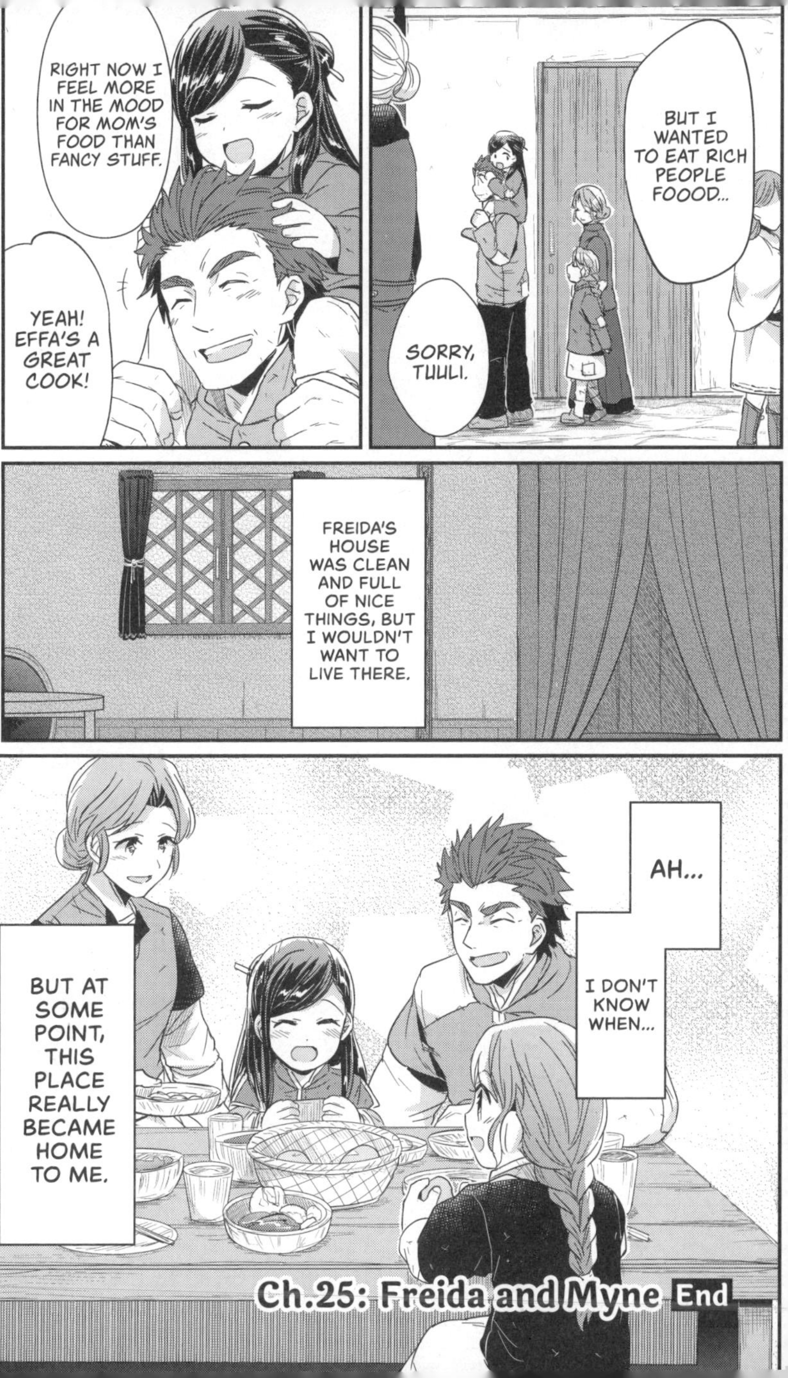
BUT I WANTED TO EAT RICH PEOPLE FOOOD...
SORRY, TUULI.
RIGHT NOW I FEEL MORE IN THE MOOD FOR MOM'S FOOD THAN FANCY STUFF.
YEAH! EFFA'S A GREAT COOK!
FREIDA'S HOUSE WAS CLEAN AND FULL OF NICE THINGS, BUT I WOULDN'T WANT TO LIVE THERE.
AH...
I DON'T KNOW WHEN...
BUT AT SOME POINT, THIS PLACE REALLY BECAME HOME TO ME.
Ch.25: Freida and Myne End

Ch.26 The Beginning of Winter

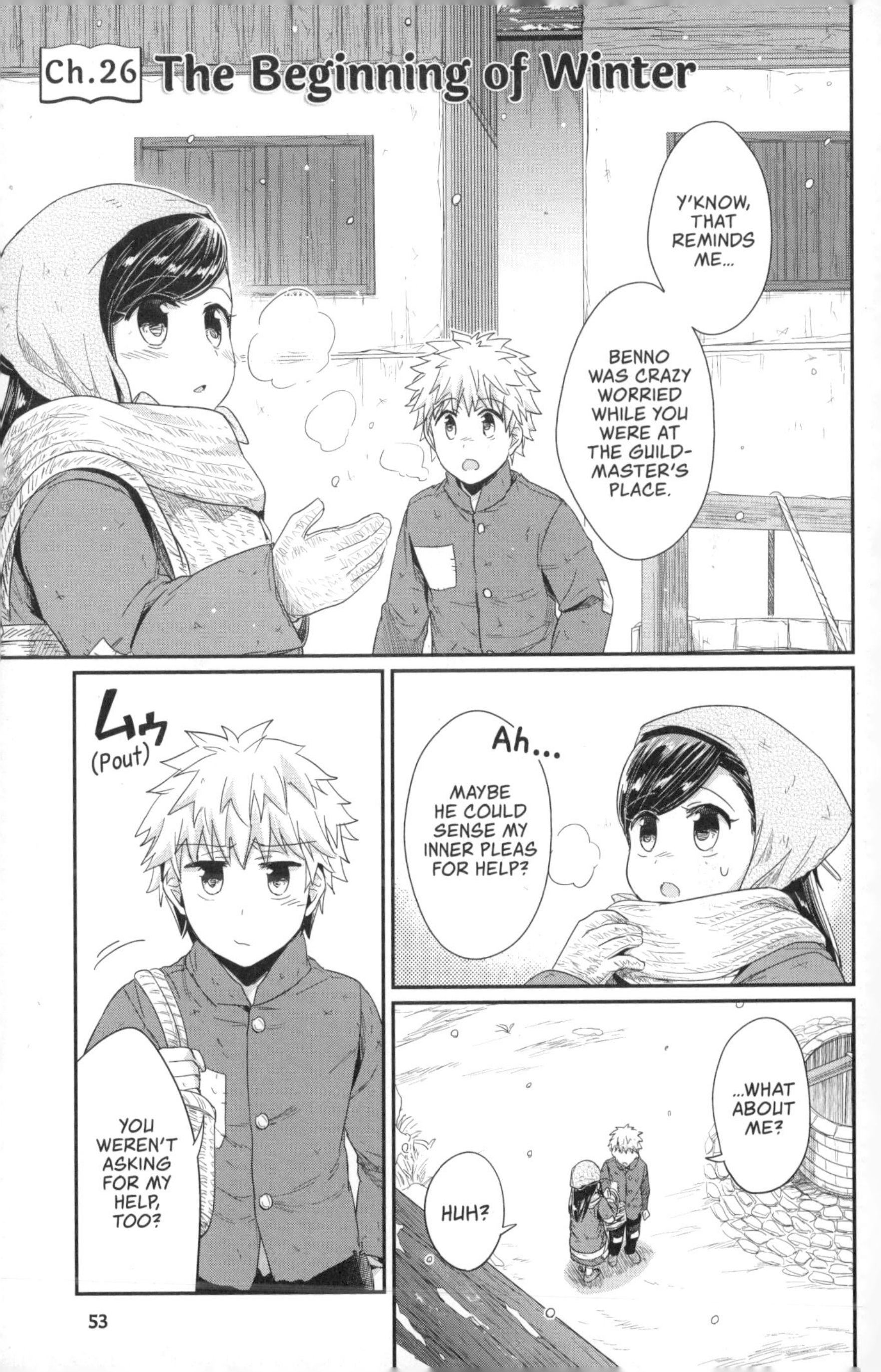

Y'KNOW, THAT REMINDS ME...
BENNO WAS CRAZY WORRIED WHILE YOU WERE AT THE GUILD-MASTER'S PLACE.
Ah...
MAYBE HE COULD SENSE MY INNER PLEAS FOR HELP?
...WHAT ABOUT ME?
HUH?
ムッ
(Pout)
YOU WEREN'T ASKING FOR MY HELP, TOO?

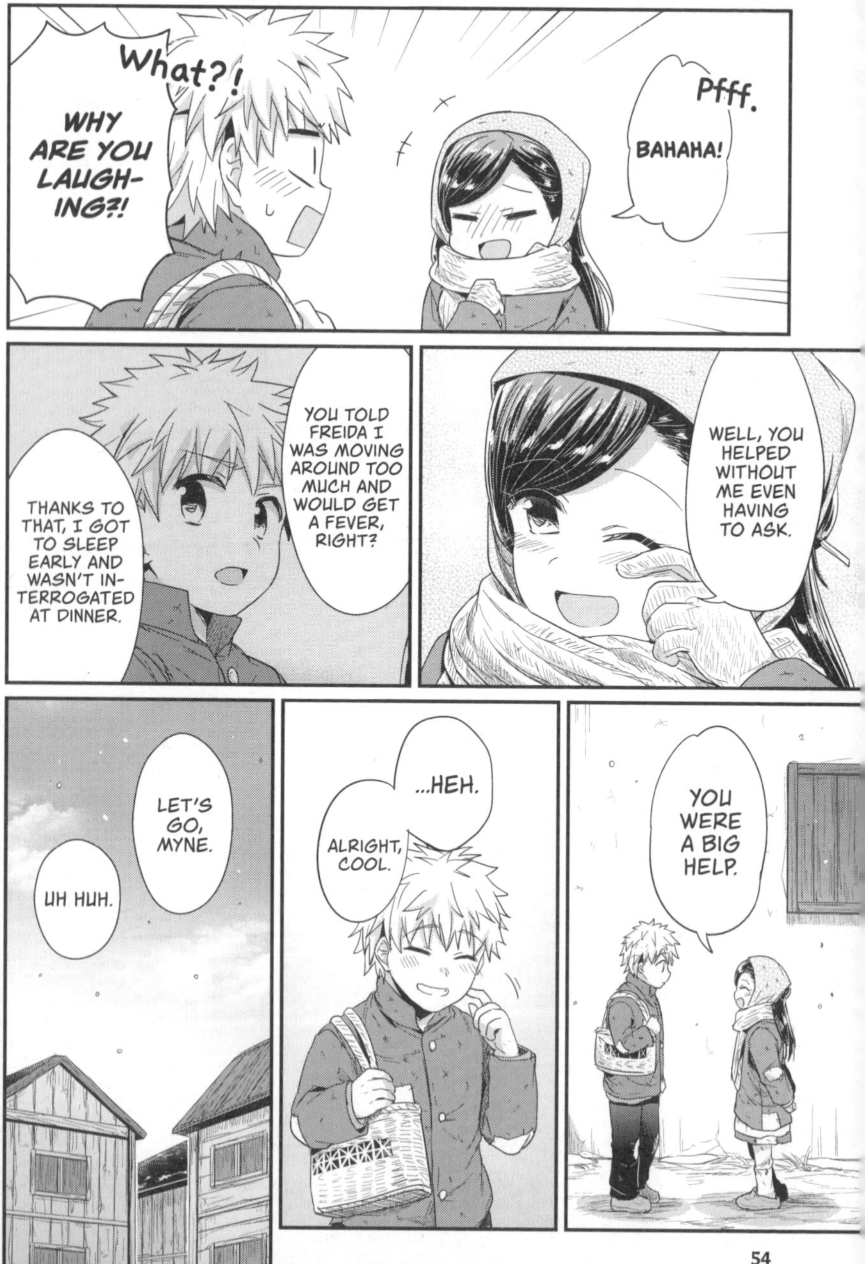
Pfff.
BAHAHA!
What?!
WHY ARE YOU LAUGHING?!
WELL, YOU HELPED WITHOUT ME EVEN HAVING TO ASK.
YOU TOLD FREIDA I WAS MOVING AROUND TOO MUCH AND WOULD GET A FEVER, RIGHT?
THANKS TO THAT, I GOT TO SLEEP EARLY AND WASN'T INTERROGATED AT DINNER.
YOU WERE A BIG HELP.
...HEH.
ALRIGHT, COOL.
LET'S GO, MYNE.
UH HUH.

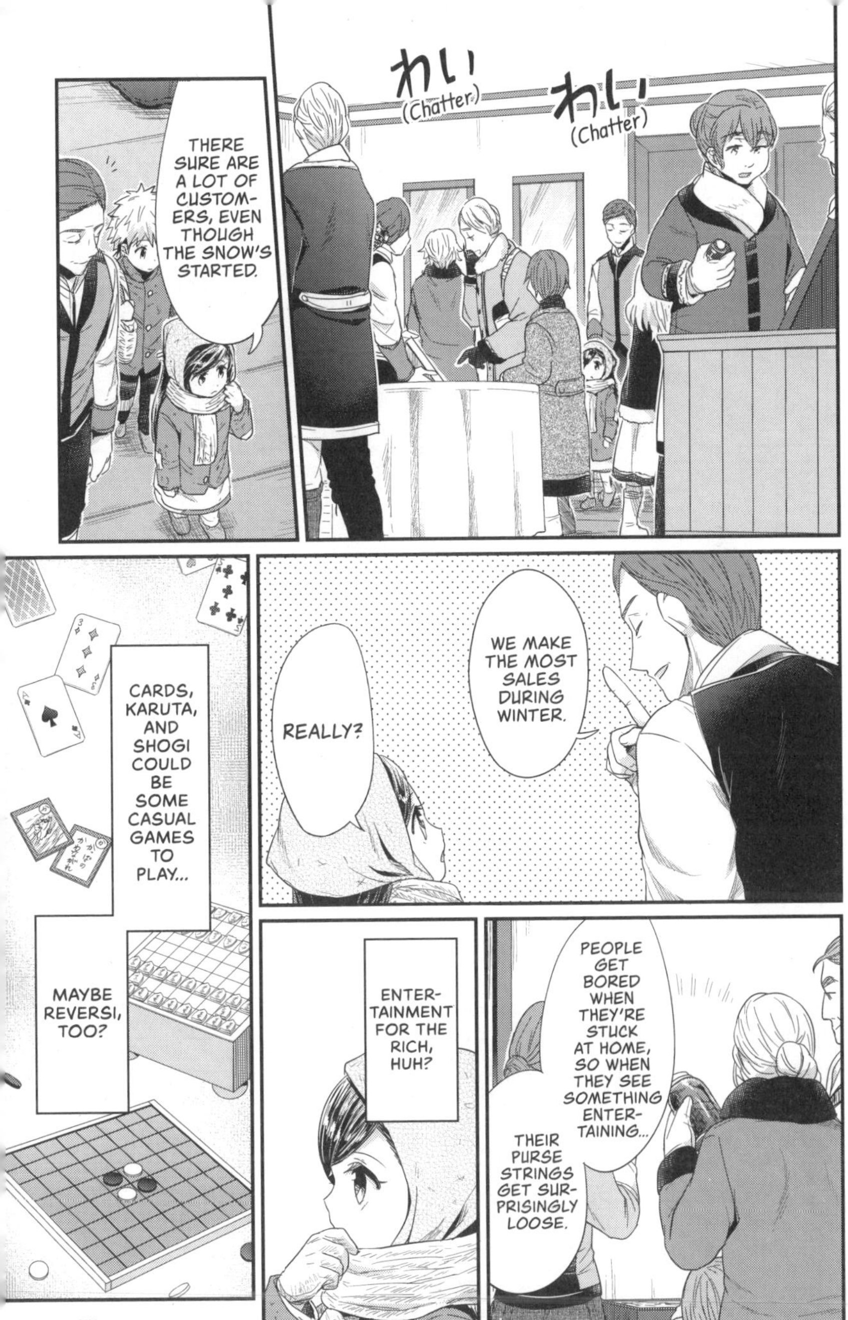
わい
(Chatter)
わい
(Chatter)
THERE SURE ARE A LOT OF CUSTOMERS, EVEN THOUGH THE SNOW'S STARTED.
WE MAKE THE MOST SALES DURING WINTER.
REALLY?
PEOPLE GET BORED WHEN THEY'RE STUCK AT HOME, SO WHEN THEY SEE SOMETHING ENTERTAINING...
THEIR PURSE STRINGS GET SURPRISINGLY LOOSE.
ENTERTAINMENT FOR THE RICH, HUH?
CARDS, KARUTA, AND SHOGI COULD BE SOME CASUAL GAMES TO PLAY...
MAYBE REVERSI, TOO?

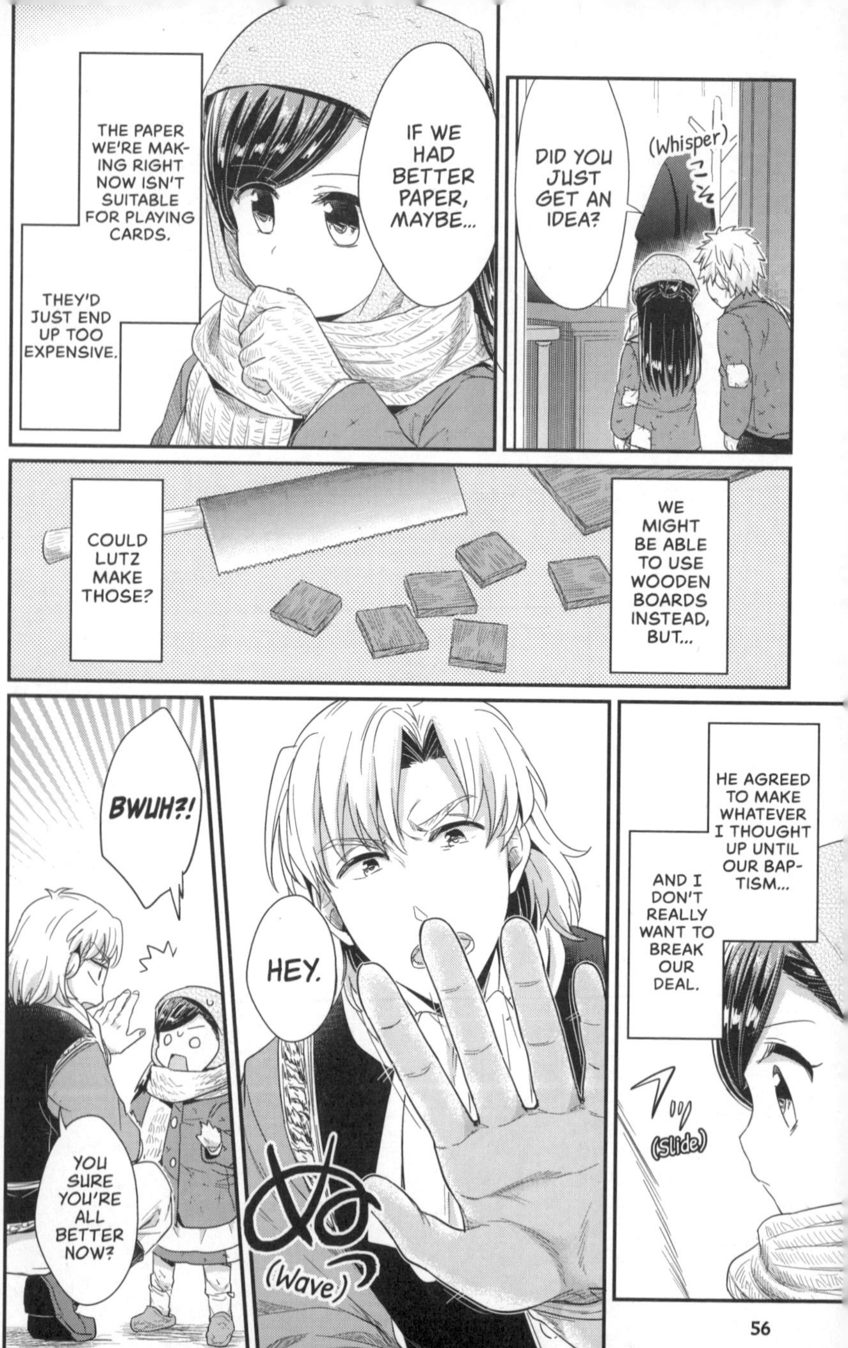
(Whisper)
DID YOU JUST GET AN IDEA?
IF WE HAD BETTER PAPER, MAYBE...
THE PAPER WE'RE MAKING RIGHT NOW ISN'T SUITABLE FOR PLAYING CARDS.
THEY'D JUST END UP TOO EXPENSIVE.
WE MIGHT BE ABLE TO USE WOODEN BOARDS INSTEAD, BUT...
COULD LUTZ MAKE THOSE?
HE AGREED TO MAKE WHATEVER I THOUGHT UP UNTIL OUR BAPTISM...
AND I DON'T REALLY WANT TO BREAK OUR DEAL.
(Slide)
HEY.
(Wave)
BWUH?!
YOU SURE YOU'RE ALL BETTER NOW?

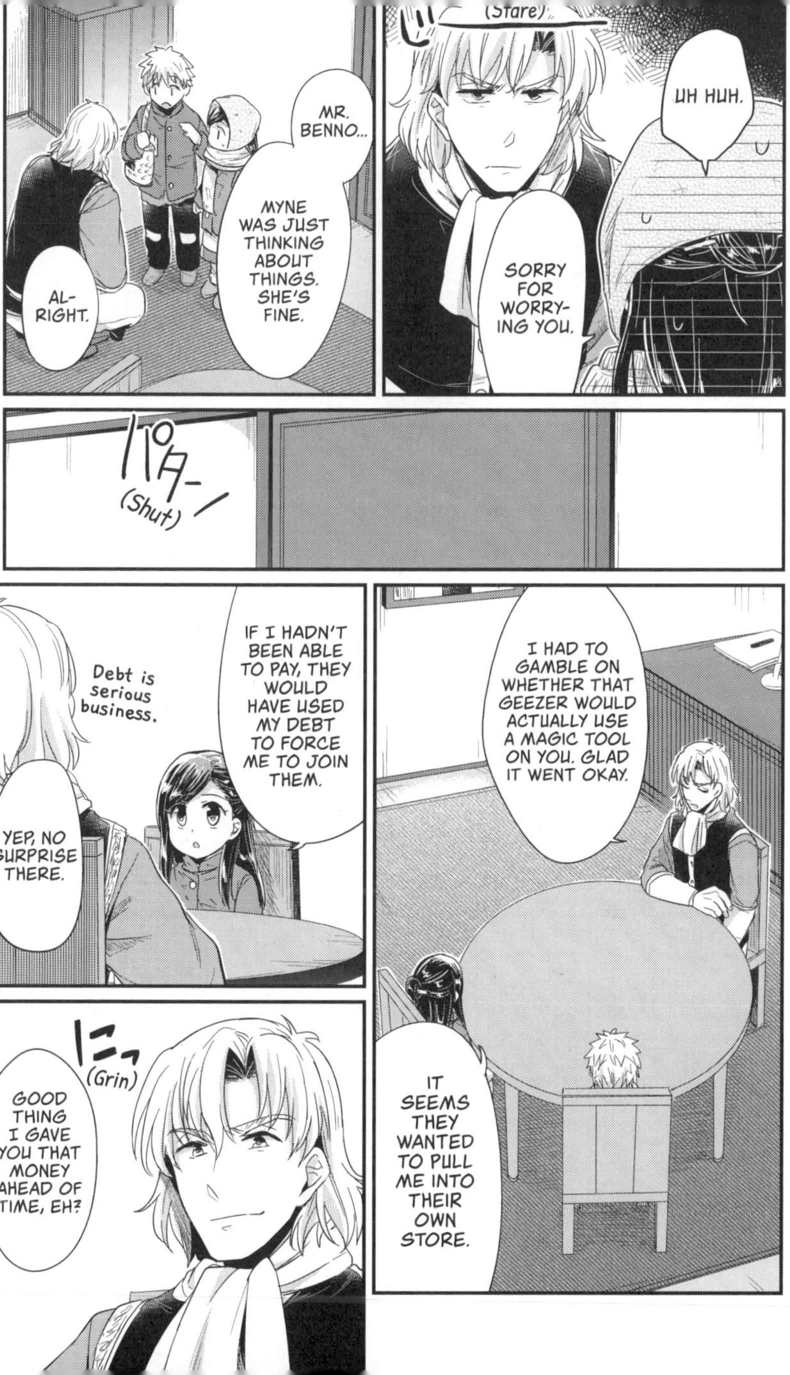
(Stare)
UH HUH.
SORRY FOR WORRYING YOU.
MR. BENNO...
MYNE WAS JUST THINKING ABOUT THINGS. SHE'S FINE.
AL-RIGHT.
(Shut)
I HAD TO GAMBLE ON WHETHER THAT GEEZER WOULD ACTUALLY USE A MAGIC TOOL ON YOU. GLAD IT WENT OKAY.
IT SEEMS THEY WANTED TO PULL ME INTO THEIR OWN STORE.
IF I HADN'T BEEN ABLE TO PAY, THEY WOULD HAVE USED MY DEBT TO FORCE ME TO JOIN THEM.
Debt is serious business.
YEP, NO SURPRISE THERE.
ニッ
(Grin)
GOOD THING I GAVE YOU THAT MONEY AHEAD OF TIME, EH?

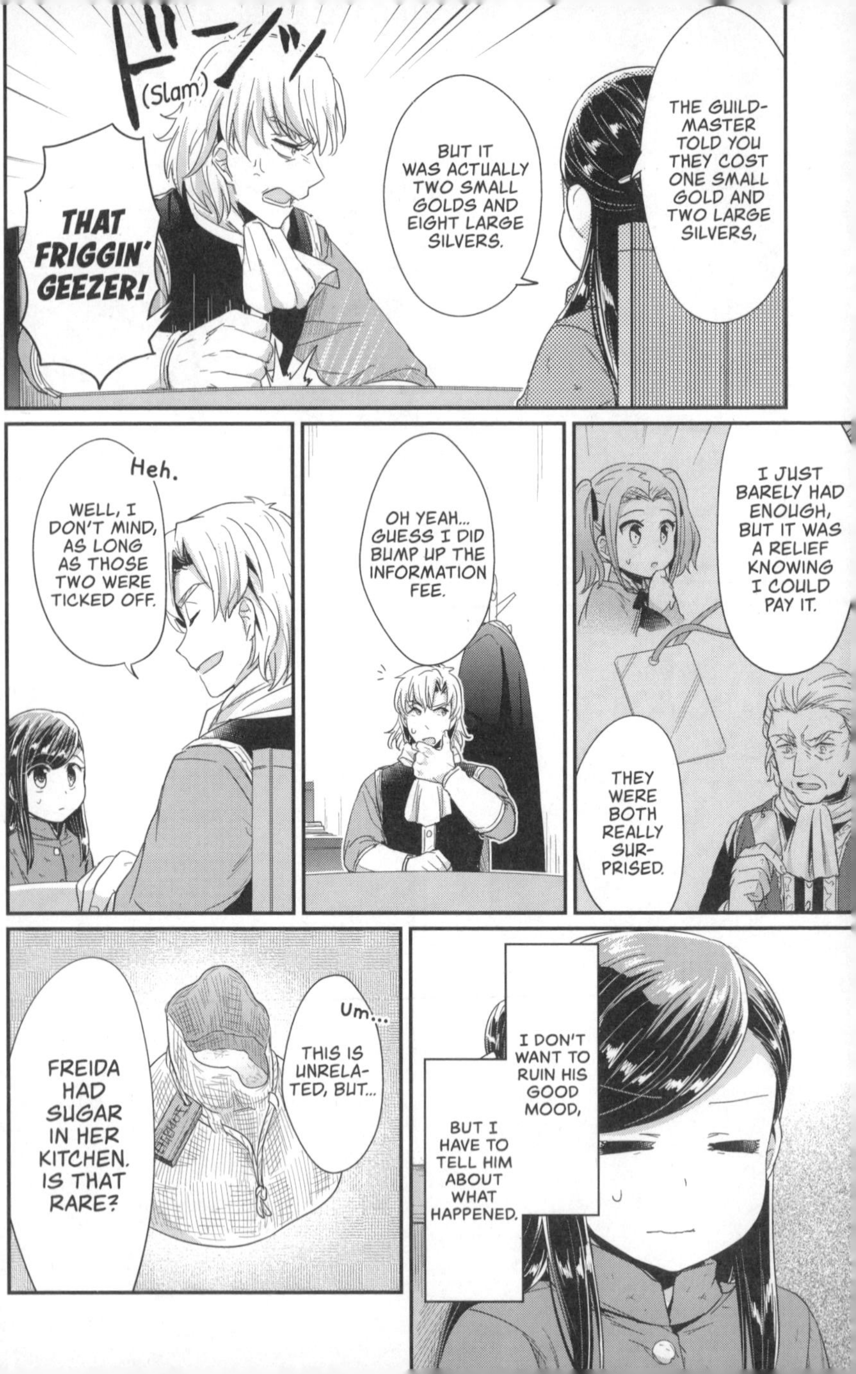
THE GUILD-MASTER TOLD YOU THEY COST ONE SMALL GOLD AND TWO LARGE SILVERS,
BUT IT WAS ACTUALLY TWO SMALL GOLDS AND EIGHT LARGE SILVERS.
(Slam)
THAT FRIGGIN' GEEZER!
I JUST BARELY HAD ENOUGH, BUT IT WAS A RELIEF KNOWING I COULD PAY IT.
THEY WERE BOTH REALLY SUR-PRISED.
OH YEAH... GUESS I DID BUMP UP THE INFORMATION FEE.
Heh.
WELL, I DON'T MIND, AS LONG AS THOSE TWO WERE TICKED OFF.
I DON'T WANT TO RUIN HIS GOOD MOOD,
BUT I HAVE TO TELL HIM ABOUT WHAT HAPPENED.
Um...
THIS IS UNRELA-TED, BUT...
FREIDA HAD SUGAR IN HER KITCHEN. IS THAT RARE?

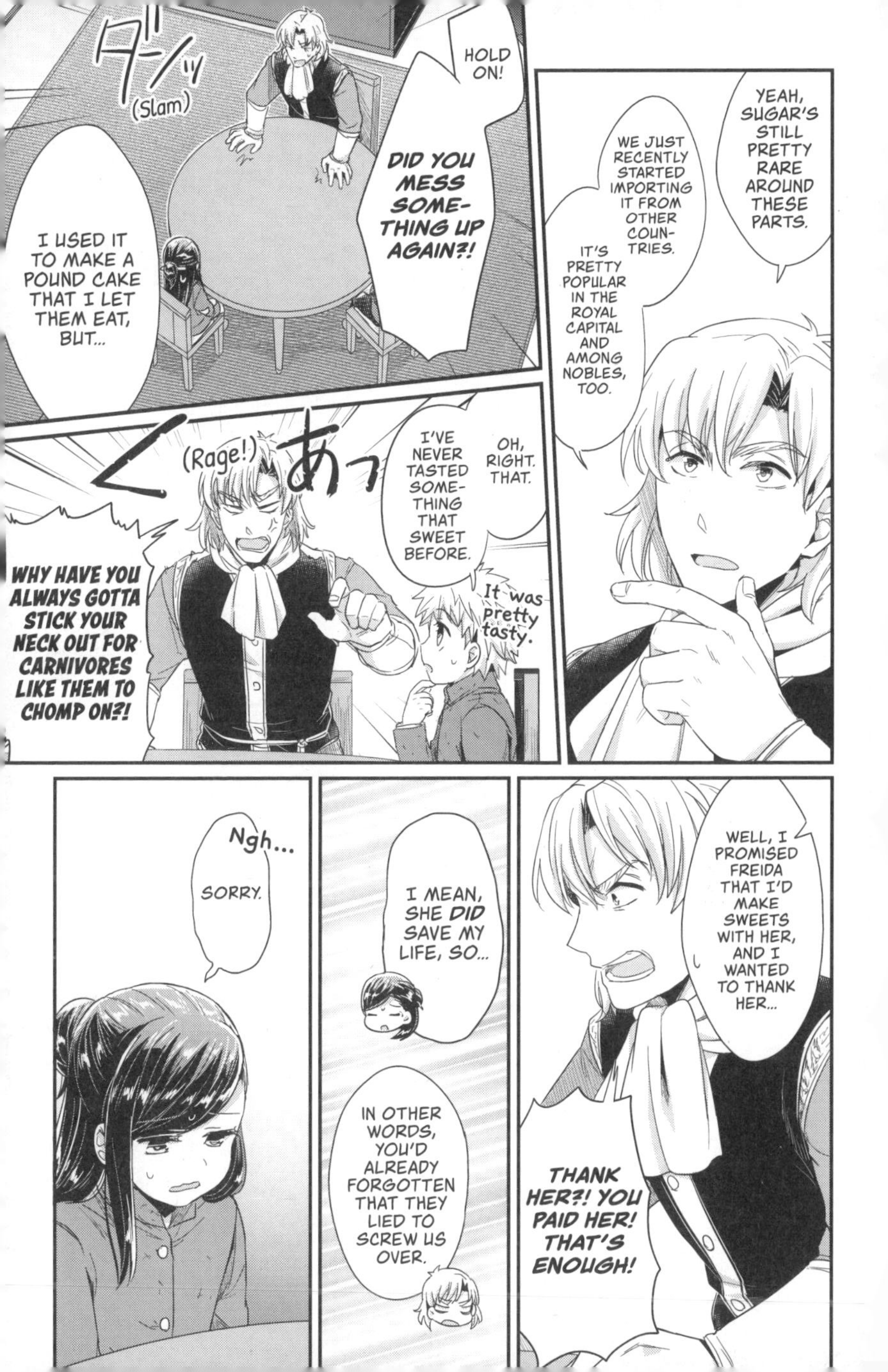
YEAH, SUGAR'S STILL PRETTY RARE AROUND THESE PARTS.
WE JUST RECENTLY STARTED IMPORTING IT FROM OTHER COUNTRIES.
IT'S PRETTY POPULAR IN THE ROYAL CAPITAL AND AMONG NOBLES, TOO.
HOLD ON!
DID YOU MESS SOMETHING UP AGAIN?!
ダーンッ
(Slam)
I USED IT TO MAKE A POUND CAKE THAT I LET THEM EAT, BUT...
OH, RIGHT. THAT.
I'VE NEVER TASTED SOMETHING THAT SWEET BEFORE.
It was pretty tasty.
くあっ
(Rage!)
WHY HAVE YOU ALWAYS GOTTA STICK YOUR NECK OUT FOR CARNIVORES LIKE THEM TO CHOMP ON?!
WELL, I PROMISED FREIDA THAT I'D MAKE SWEETS WITH HER, AND I WANTED TO THANK HER...
THANK HER?! YOU PAID HER! THAT'S ENOUGH!
I MEAN, SHE DID SAVE MY LIFE, SO...
IN OTHER WORDS, YOU'D ALREADY FORGOTTEN THAT THEY LIED TO SCREW US OVER.
Ngh...
SORRY.

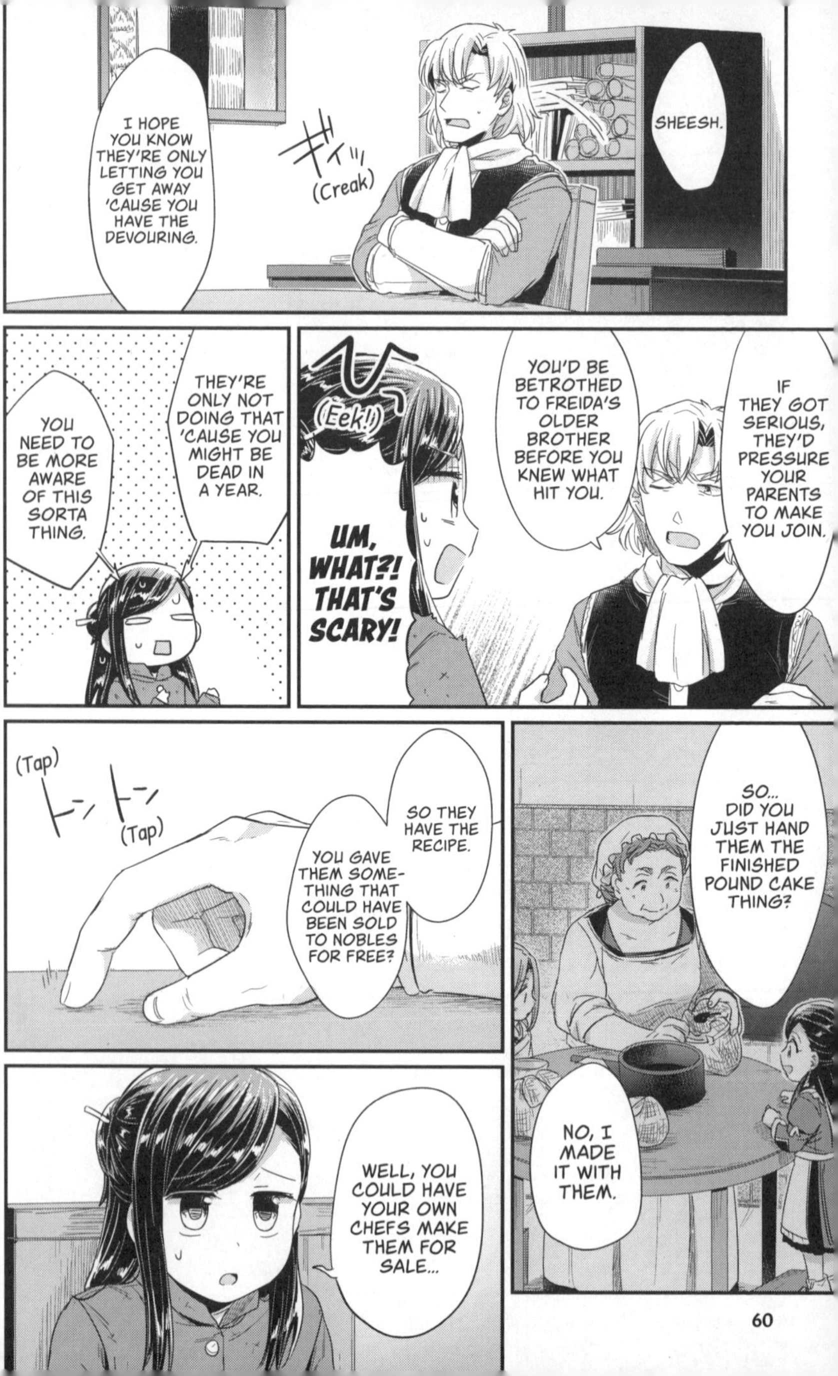
SHEESH.
(Creak)
I HOPE YOU KNOW THEY'RE ONLY LETTING YOU GET AWAY 'CAUSE YOU HAVE THE DEVOURING.
IF THEY GOT SERIOUS, THEY'D PRESSURE YOUR PARENTS TO MAKE YOU JOIN.
YOU'D BE BETROTHED TO FREIDA'S OLDER BROTHER BEFORE YOU KNEW WHAT HIT YOU.
(Eek!)
UM, WHAT?! THAT'S SCARY!
THEY'RE ONLY NOT DOING THAT 'CAUSE YOU MIGHT BE DEAD IN A YEAR.
YOU NEED TO BE MORE AWARE OF THIS SORTA THING.
SO... DID YOU JUST HAND THEM THE FINISHED POUND CAKE THING?
NO, I MADE IT WITH THEM.
(Tap)
(Tap)
SO THEY HAVE THE RECIPE.
YOU GAVE THEM SOME-THING THAT COULD HAVE BEEN SOLD TO NOBLES FOR FREE?
WELL, YOU COULD HAVE YOUR OWN CHEFS MAKE THEM FOR SALE...

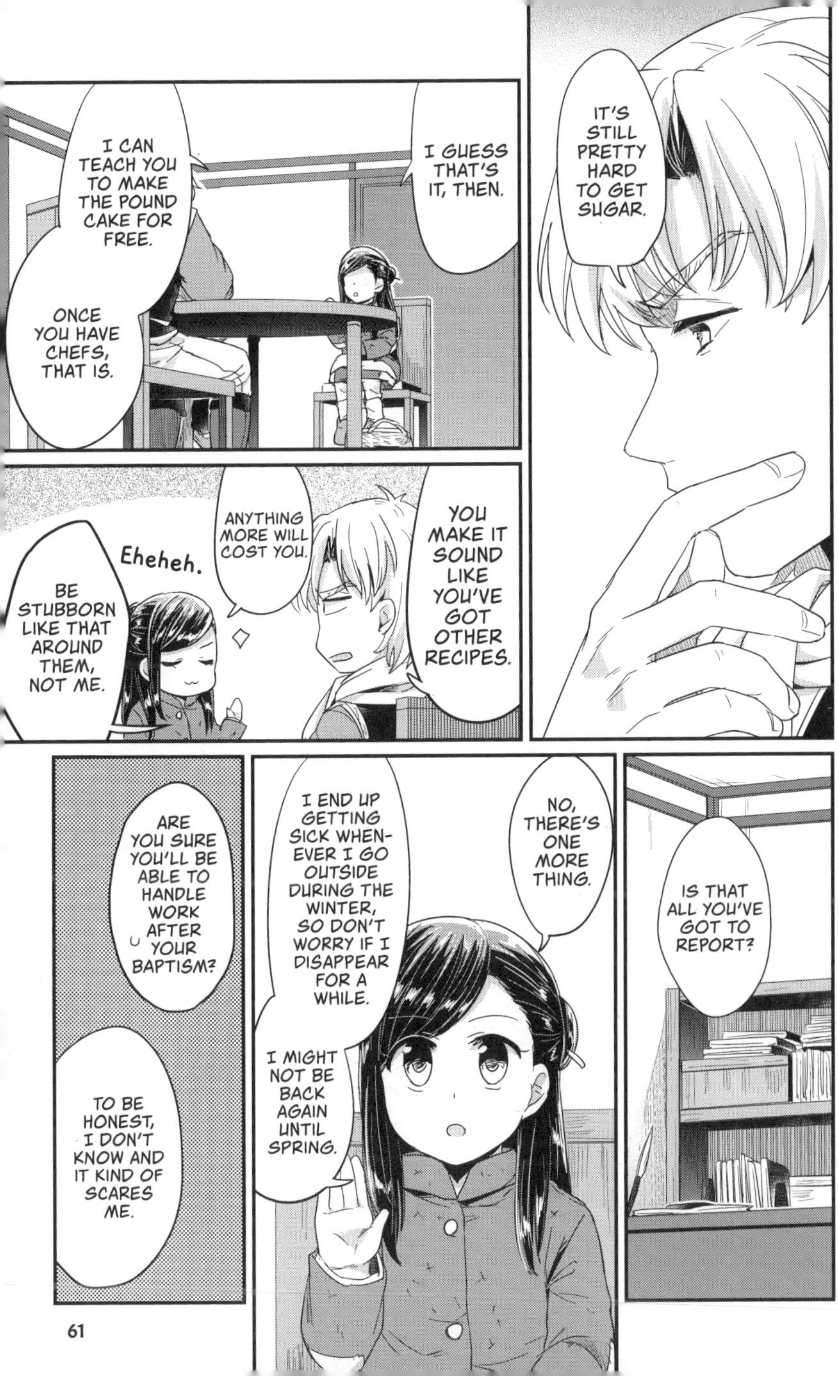
IT'S STILL PRETTY HARD TO GET SUGAR.
I GUESS THAT'S IT, THEN.
I CAN TEACH YOU TO MAKE THE POUND CAKE FOR FREE.
ONCE YOU HAVE CHEFS, THAT IS.
YOU MAKE IT SOUND LIKE YOU'VE GOT OTHER RECIPES.
ANYTHING MORE WILL COST YOU.
Eheheh.
BE STUBBORN LIKE THAT AROUND THEM, NOT ME.
IS THAT ALL YOU'VE GOT TO REPORT?
NO, THERE'S ONE MORE THING.
I END UP GETTING SICK WHEN-EVER I GO OUTSIDE DURING THE WINTER, SO DON'T WORRY IF I DISAPPEAR FOR A WHILE.
I MIGHT NOT BE BACK AGAIN UNTIL SPRING.
ARE YOU SURE YOU'LL BE ABLE TO HANDLE WORK AFTER YOUR BAPTISM?
TO BE HONEST, I DON'T KNOW AND IT KIND OF SCARES ME.

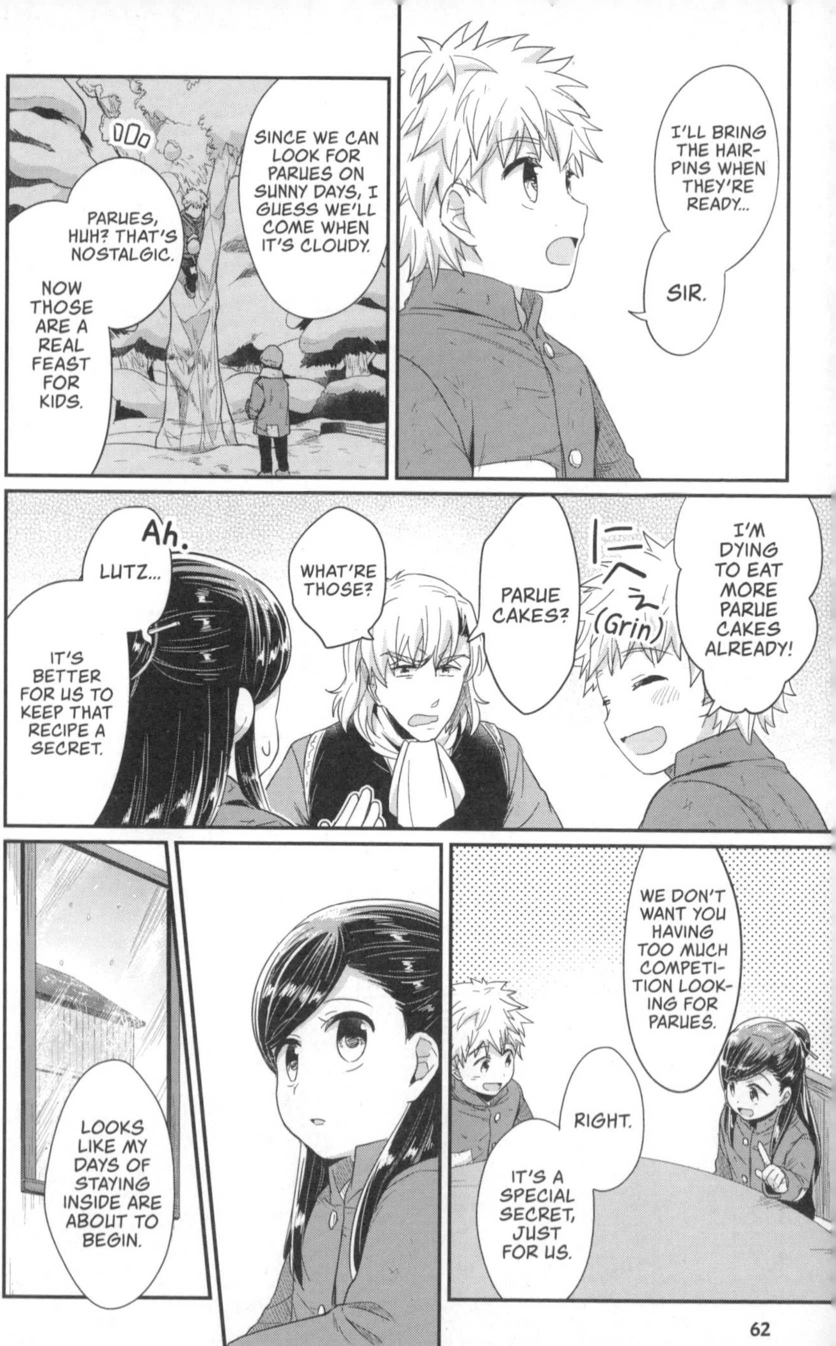
I'LL BRING THE HAIRPINS WHEN THEY'RE READY...
SIR.
SINCE WE CAN LOOK FOR PARUES ON SUNNY DAYS, I GUESS WE'LL COME WHEN IT'S CLOUDY.
PARUES, HUH? THAT'S NOSTALGIC.
NOW THOSE ARE A REAL FEAST FOR KIDS.
I'M DYING TO EAT MORE PARUE CAKES ALREADY!
(Grin)
PARUE CAKES?
WHAT'RE THOSE?
Ah.
LUTZ...
IT'S BETTER FOR US TO KEEP THAT RECIPE A SECRET.
WE DON'T WANT YOU HAVING TOO MUCH COMPETITION LOOKING FOR PARUES.
RIGHT.
IT'S A SPECIAL SECRET, JUST FOR US.
LOOKS LIKE MY DAYS OF STAYING INSIDE ARE ABOUT TO BEGIN.

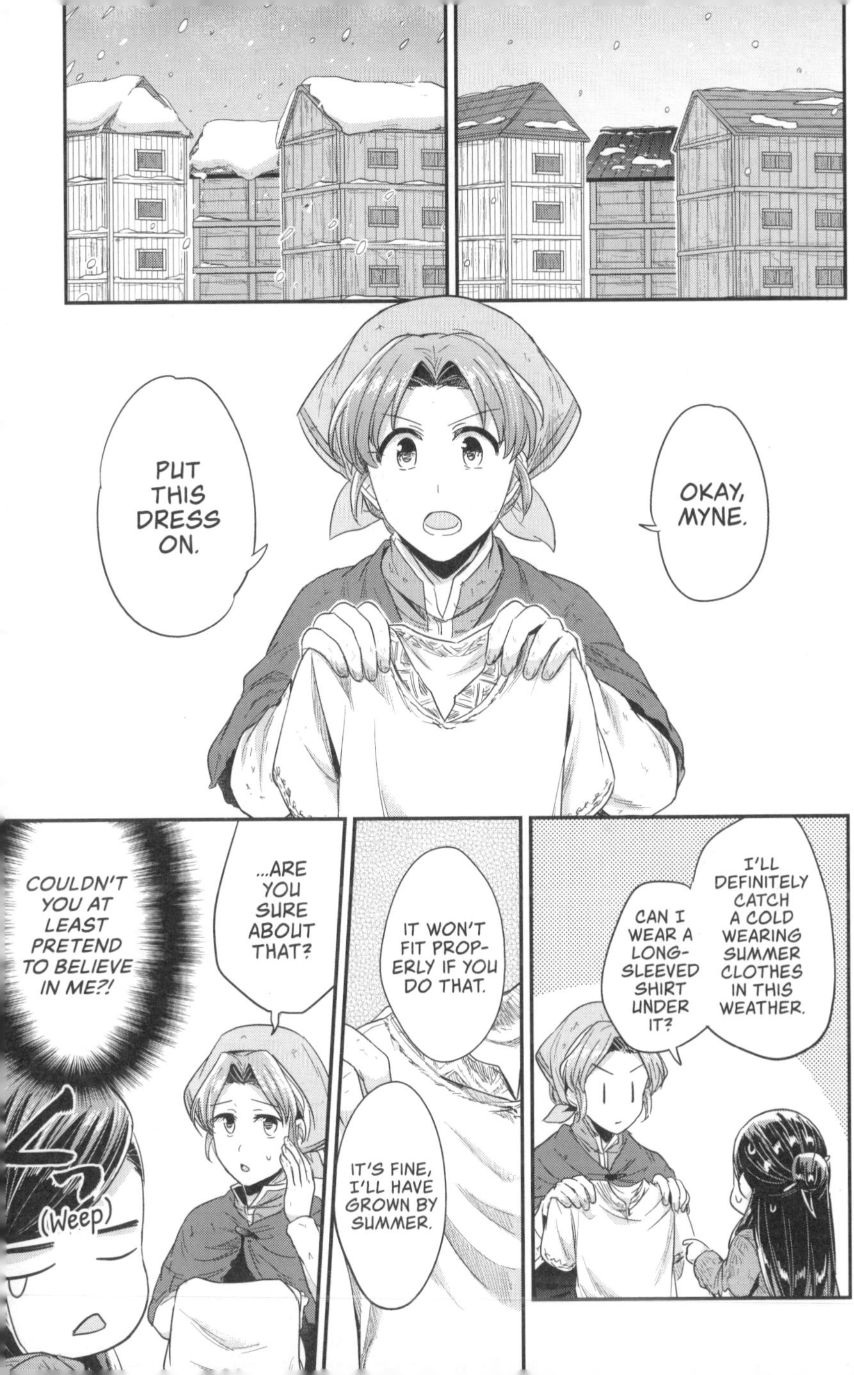
OKAY, MYNE.
PUT THIS DRESS ON.
I'LL DEFINITELY CATCH A COLD WEARING SUMMER CLOTHES IN THIS WEATHER.
CAN I WEAR A LONG-SLEEVED SHIRT UNDER IT?
IT WON'T FIT PROPERLY IF YOU DO THAT.
IT'S FINE, I'LL HAVE GROWN BY SUMMER.
...ARE YOU SURE ABOUT THAT?
COULDN'T YOU AT LEAST PRETEND TO BELIEVE IN ME?!
(Weep)

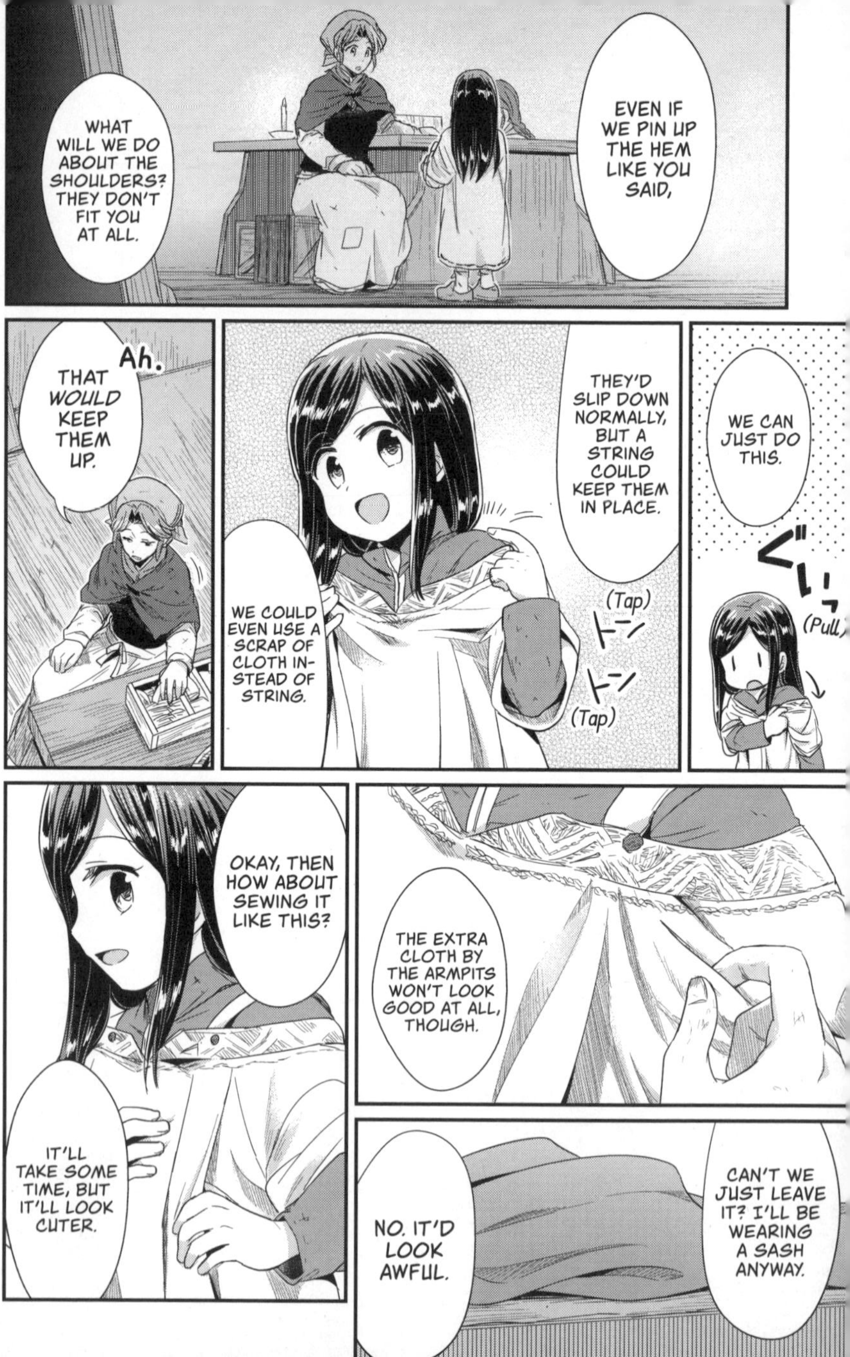
EVEN IF WE PIN UP THE HEM LIKE YOU SAID,
WHAT WILL WE DO ABOUT THE SHOULDERS? THEY DON'T FIT YOU AT ALL.
WE CAN JUST DO THIS.
ぐいっ
(Pull)
THEY'D SLIP DOWN NORMALLY, BUT A STRING COULD KEEP THEM IN PLACE.
(Tap)
トン
トン
(Tap)
WE COULD EVEN USE A SCRAP OF CLOTH IN-STEAD OF STRING.
Ah.
THAT *WOULD* KEEP THEM UP.
THE EXTRA CLOTH BY THE ARMPITS WON'T LOOK GOOD AT ALL, THOUGH.
CAN'T WE JUST LEAVE IT? I'LL BE WEARING A SASH ANYWAY.
NO. IT'D LOOK AWFUL.
OKAY, THEN HOW ABOUT SEWING IT LIKE THIS?
IT'LL TAKE SOME TIME, BUT IT'LL LOOK CUTER.

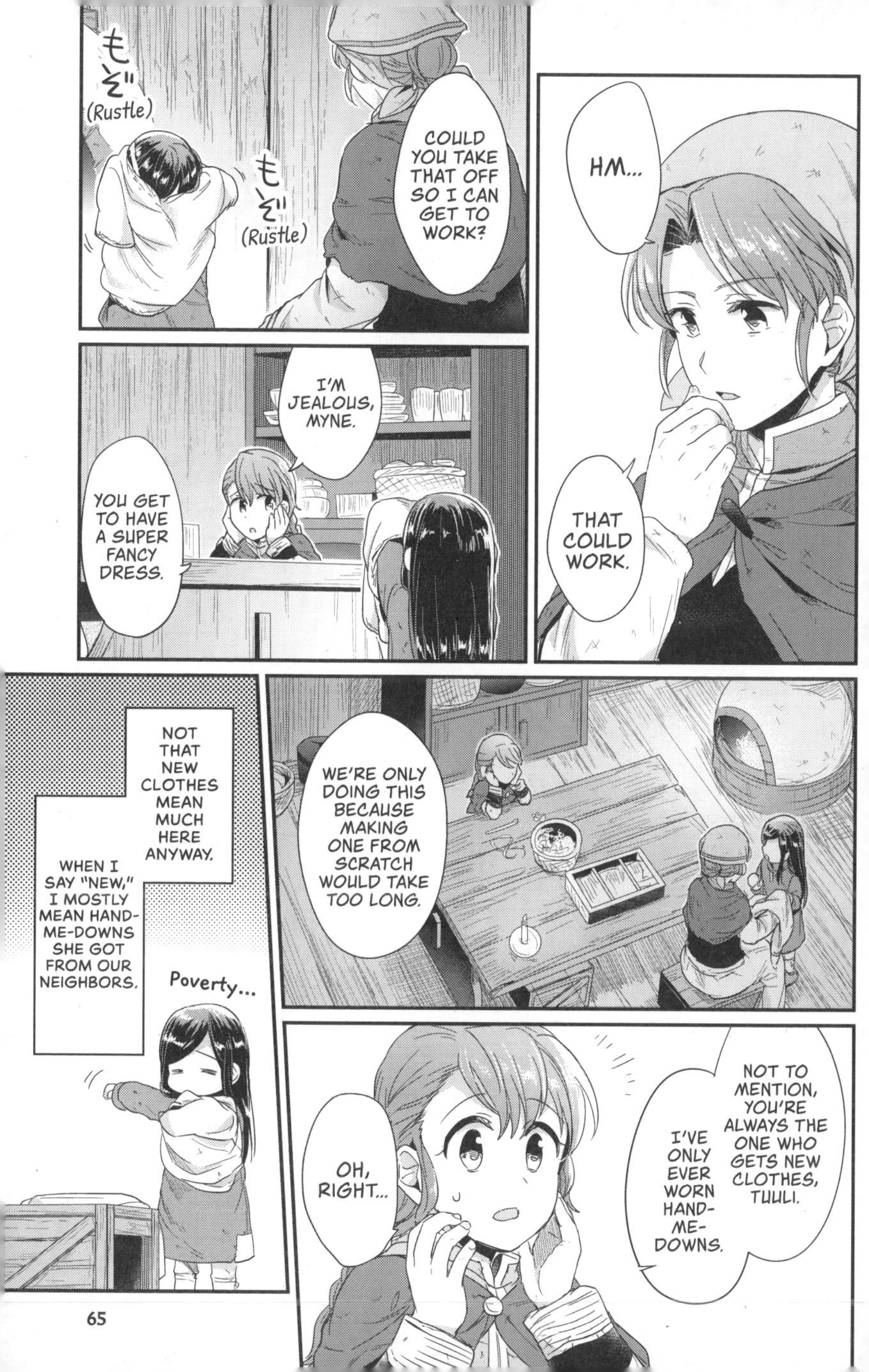
HM...
THAT COULD WORK.
COULD YOU TAKE THAT OFF SO I CAN GET TO WORK?
もぞ (Rustle)
もぞ (Rustle)
I'M JEALOUS, MYNE.
YOU GET TO HAVE A SUPER FANCY DRESS.
WE'RE ONLY DOING THIS BECAUSE MAKING ONE FROM SCRATCH WOULD TAKE TOO LONG.
NOT THAT NEW CLOTHES MEAN MUCH HERE ANYWAY.
WHEN I SAY "NEW," I MOSTLY MEAN HAND-ME-DOWNS SHE GOT FROM OUR NEIGHBORS.
Poverty...
NOT TO MENTION, YOU'RE ALWAYS THE ONE WHO GETS NEW CLOTHES, TUULI.
I'VE ONLY EVER WORN HAND-ME-DOWNS.
OH, RIGHT...

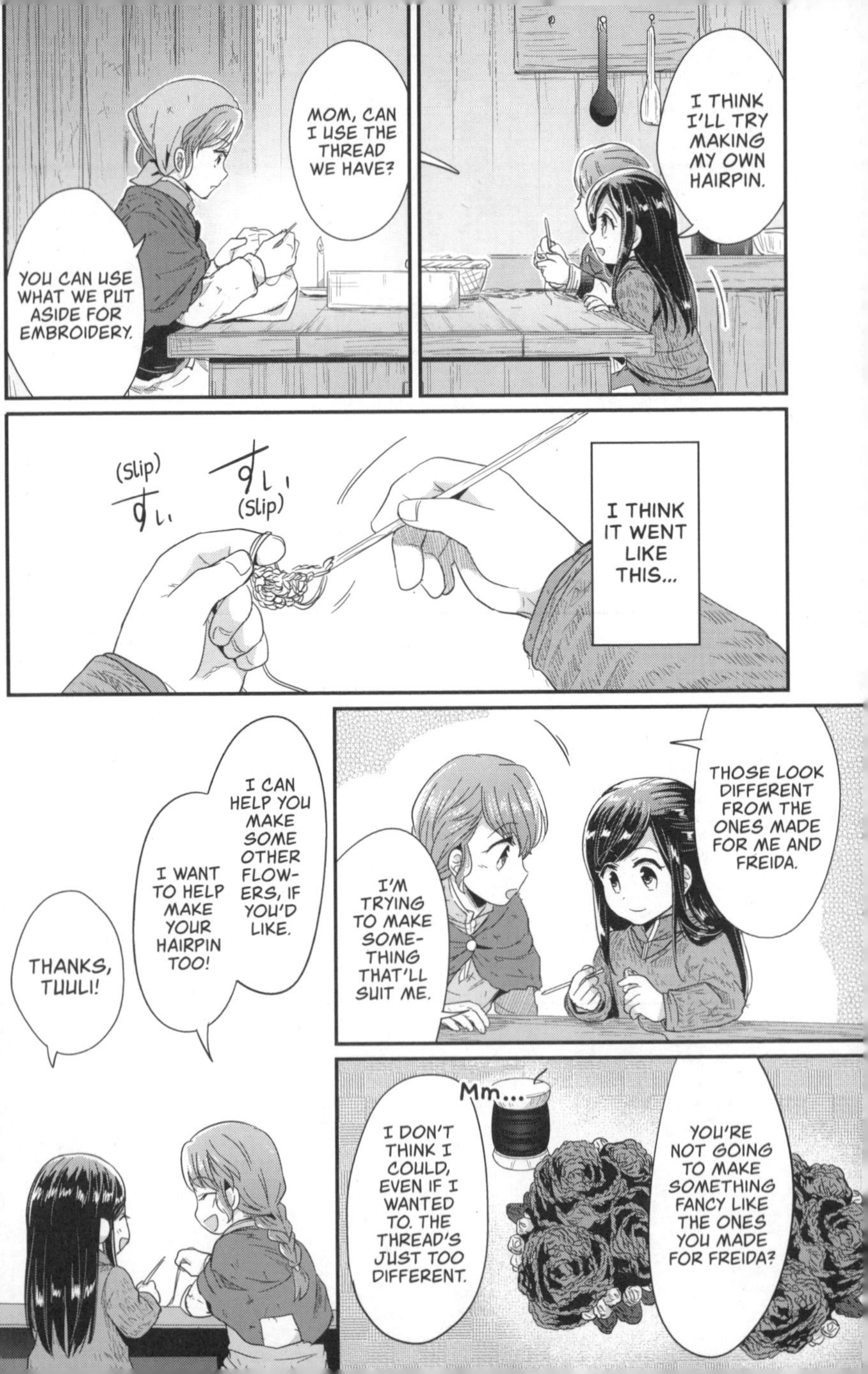
I THINK I'LL TRY MAKING MY OWN HAIRPIN.
MOM, CAN I USE THE THREAD WE HAVE?
YOU CAN USE WHAT WE PUT ASIDE FOR EMBROIDERY.
I THINK IT WENT LIKE THIS...
すい (Slip)
(Slip) すい
THOSE LOOK DIFFERENT FROM THE ONES MADE FOR ME AND FREIDA.
I'M TRYING TO MAKE SOMETHING THAT'LL SUIT ME.
I CAN HELP YOU MAKE SOME OTHER FLOWERS, IF YOU'D LIKE.
I WANT TO HELP MAKE YOUR HAIRPIN TOO!
THANKS, TUULI!
YOU'RE NOT GOING TO MAKE SOMETHING FANCY LIKE THE ONES YOU MADE FOR FREIDA?
Mm...
I DON'T THINK I COULD, EVEN IF I WANTED TO. THE THREAD'S JUST TOO DIFFERENT.

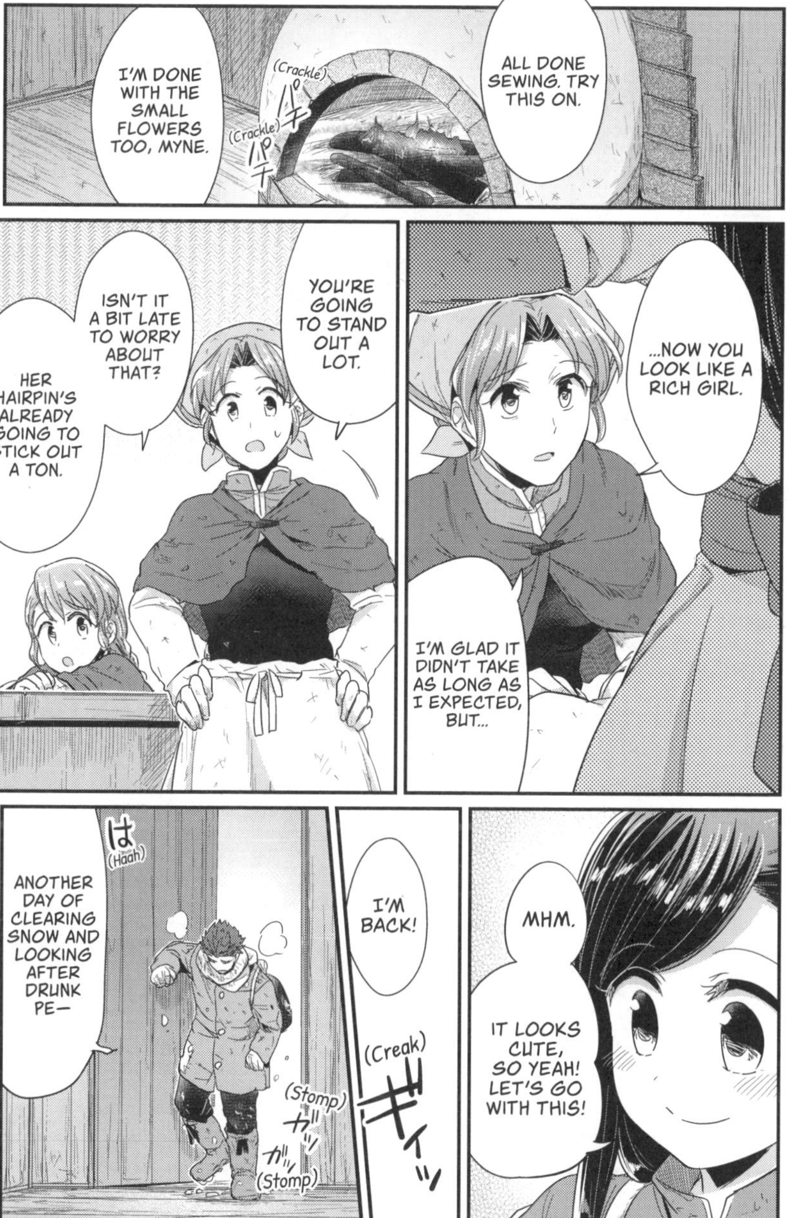

ALL DONE SEWING. TRY THIS ON.
(Crackle) パチ
(Crackle) パチ
I'M DONE WITH THE SMALL FLOWERS TOO, MYNE.
...NOW YOU LOOK LIKE A RICH GIRL.
I'M GLAD IT DIDN'T TAKE AS LONG AS I EXPECTED, BUT...
YOU'RE GOING TO STAND OUT A LOT.
ISN'T IT A BIT LATE TO WORRY ABOUT THAT?
HER HAIRPIN'S ALREADY GOING TO STICK OUT A TON.
MHM.
IT LOOKS CUTE, SO YEAH! LET'S GO WITH THIS!
I'M BACK!
(Creak)
ギイッ
は
(Haah)
ANOTHER DAY OF CLEARING SNOW AND LOOKING AFTER DRUNK PE—
(Stomp)
ガッ
ガッ
(Stomp)

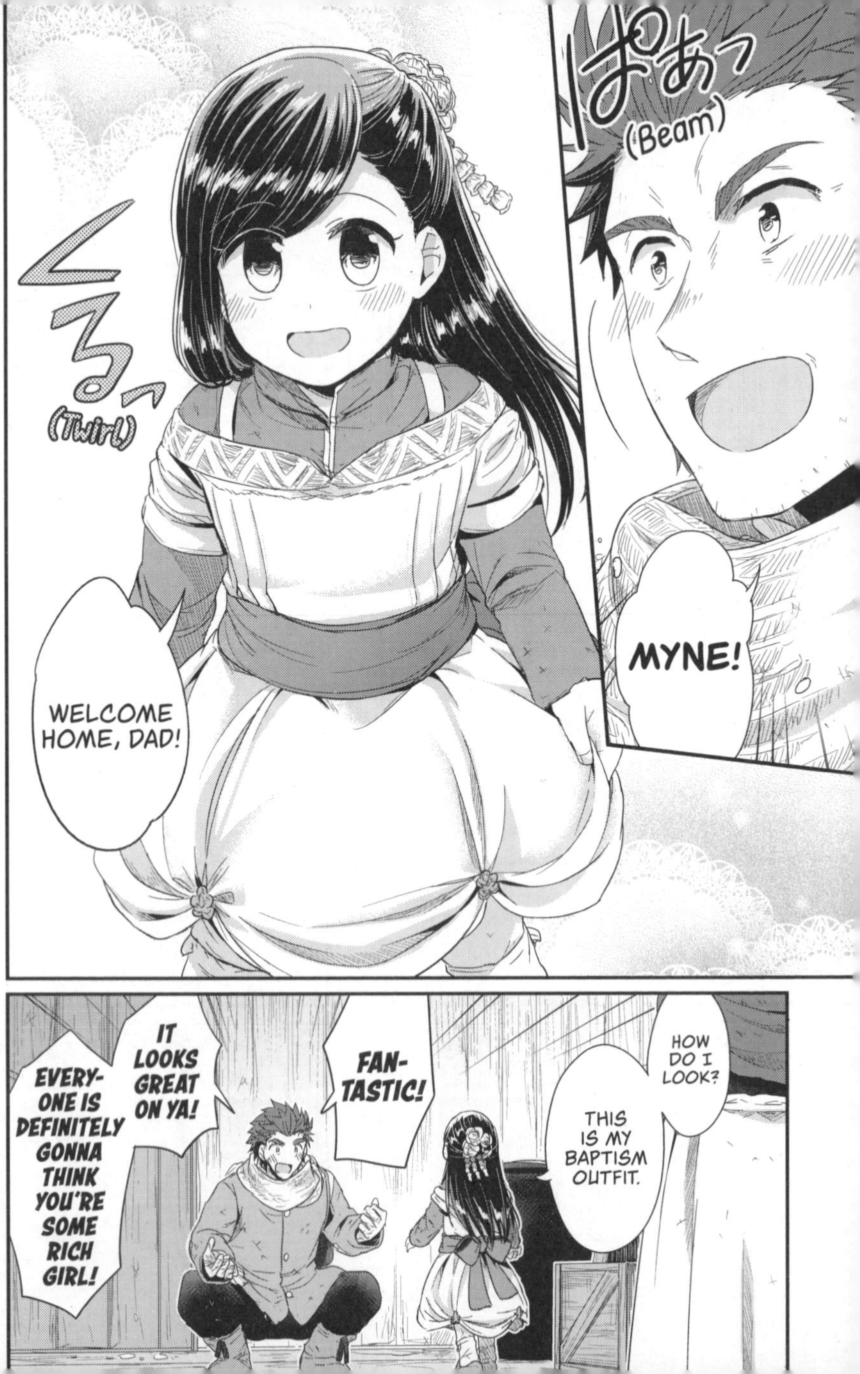
ぱあっ
(Beam)
MYNE!
くるっ
(Twirl)
WELCOME HOME, DAD!
HOW DO I LOOK?
THIS IS MY BAPTISM OUTFIT.
FAN-TASTIC!
IT LOOKS GREAT ON YA!
EVERY-ONE IS DEFINITELY GONNA THINK YOU'RE SOME RICH GIRL!

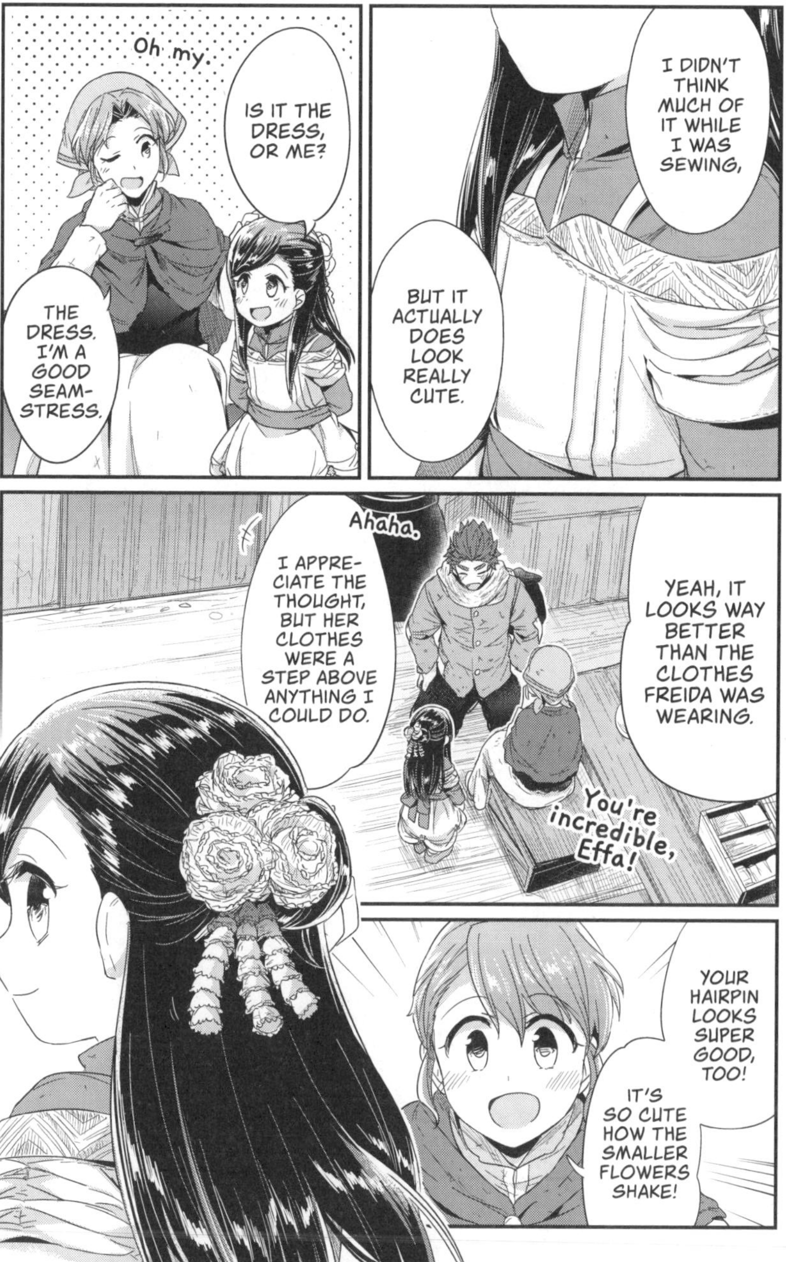
I DIDN'T THINK MUCH OF IT WHILE I WAS SEWING,
BUT IT ACTUALLY DOES LOOK REALLY CUTE.
Oh my.
IS IT THE DRESS, OR ME?
THE DRESS. I'M A GOOD SEAM-STRESS.
YEAH, IT LOOKS WAY BETTER THAN THE CLOTHES FREIDA WAS WEARING.
You're incredible, Effa!
Ahaha.
I APPRE-CIATE THE THOUGHT, BUT HER CLOTHES WERE A STEP ABOVE ANYTHING I COULD DO.
YOUR HAIRPIN LOOKS SUPER GOOD, TOO!
IT'S SO CUTE HOW THE SMALLER FLOWERS SHAKE!

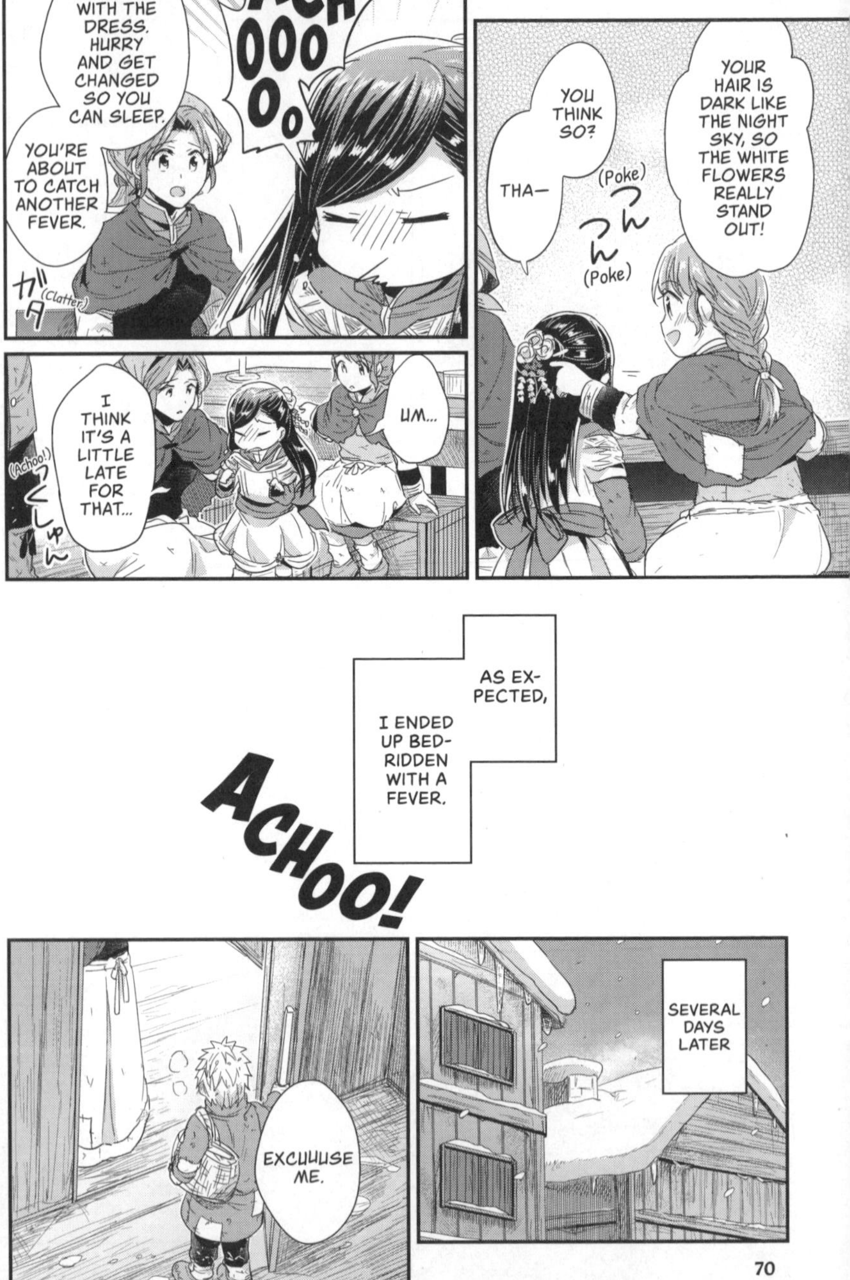
YOUR HAIR IS DARK LIKE THE NIGHT SKY, SO THE WHITE FLOWERS REALLY STAND OUT!
YOU THINK SO?
THA—
つん (Poke)
つん (Poke)
ACHOOOOOo
THAT'S ENOUGH WITH THE DRESS. HURRY AND GET CHANGED SO YOU CAN SLEEP.
YOU'RE ABOUT TO CATCH ANOTHER FEVER.
ガタ (Clatter)
UM...
I THINK IT'S A LITTLE LATE FOR THAT...
っくしゅん (Achoo!)
AS EXPECTED,
I ENDED UP BED-RIDDEN WITH A FEVER.
ACHOO!
SEVERAL DAYS LATER
EXCUUUSE ME.

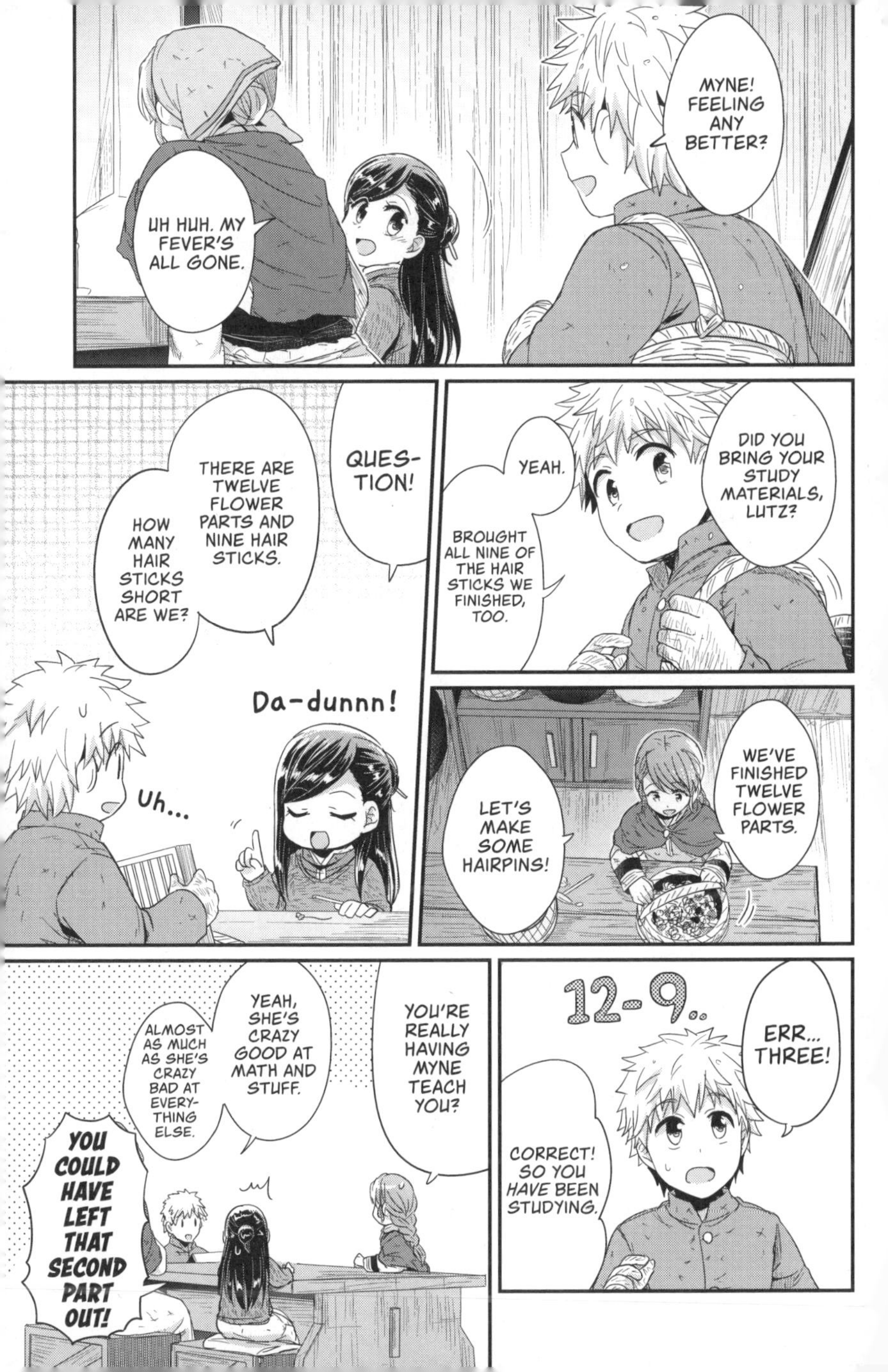
MYNE! FEELING ANY BETTER?
UH HUH. MY FEVER'S ALL GONE.
DID YOU BRING YOUR STUDY MATERIALS, LUTZ?
YEAH.
BROUGHT ALL NINE OF THE HAIR STICKS WE FINISHED, TOO.
WE'VE FINISHED TWELVE FLOWER PARTS.
LET'S MAKE SOME HAIRPINS!
QUES-TION!
THERE ARE TWELVE FLOWER PARTS AND NINE HAIR STICKS.
HOW MANY HAIR STICKS SHORT ARE WE?
Da-dunnn!
Uh...
12-9..
ERR... THREE!
CORRECT! SO YOU HAVE BEEN STUDYING.
YOU'RE REALLY HAVING MYNE TEACH YOU?
YEAH, SHE'S CRAZY GOOD AT MATH AND STUFF.
ALMOST AS MUCH AS SHE'S CRAZY BAD AT EVERY-THING ELSE.
YOU COULD HAVE LEFT THAT SECOND PART OUT!

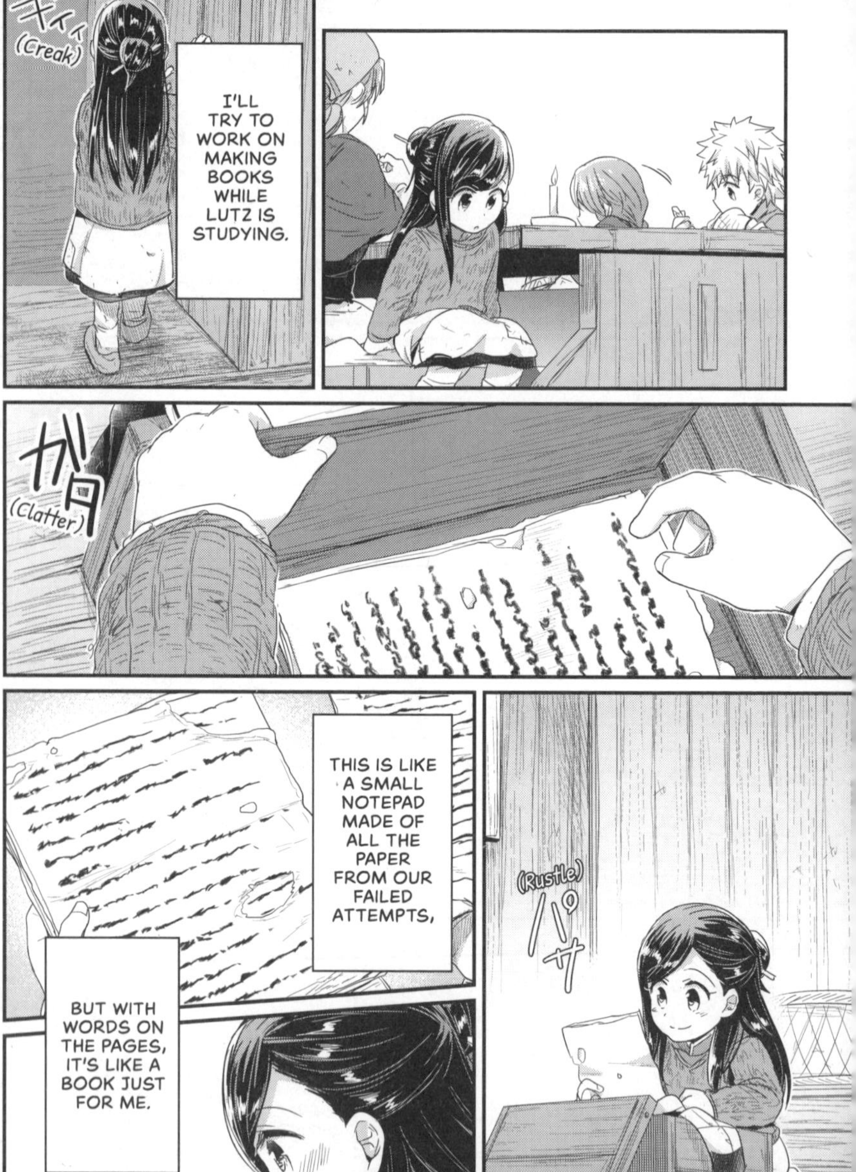
ギィィ
(Creak)
I'LL TRY TO WORK ON MAKING BOOKS WHILE LUTZ IS STUDYING.
ガタ
(Clatter)
(Rustle)
パサ
THIS IS LIKE A SMALL NOTEPAD MADE OF ALL THE PAPER FROM OUR FAILED ATTEMPTS,
BUT WITH WORDS ON THE PAGES, IT'S LIKE A BOOK JUST FOR ME.
Eheheh~

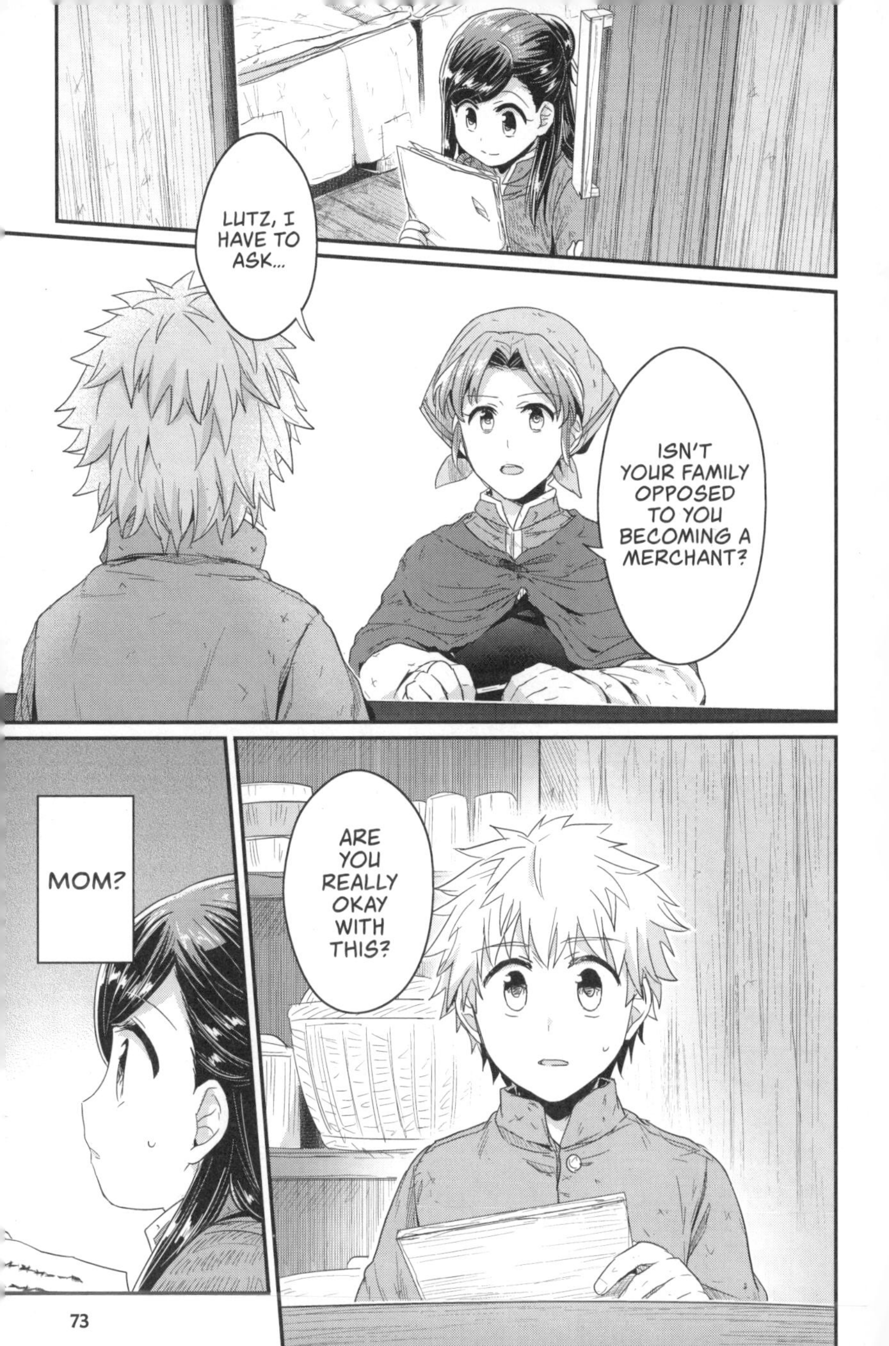
LUTZ, I HAVE TO ASK...
ISN'T YOUR FAMILY OPPOSED TO YOU BECOMING A MERCHANT?
ARE YOU REALLY OKAY WITH THIS?
MOM?

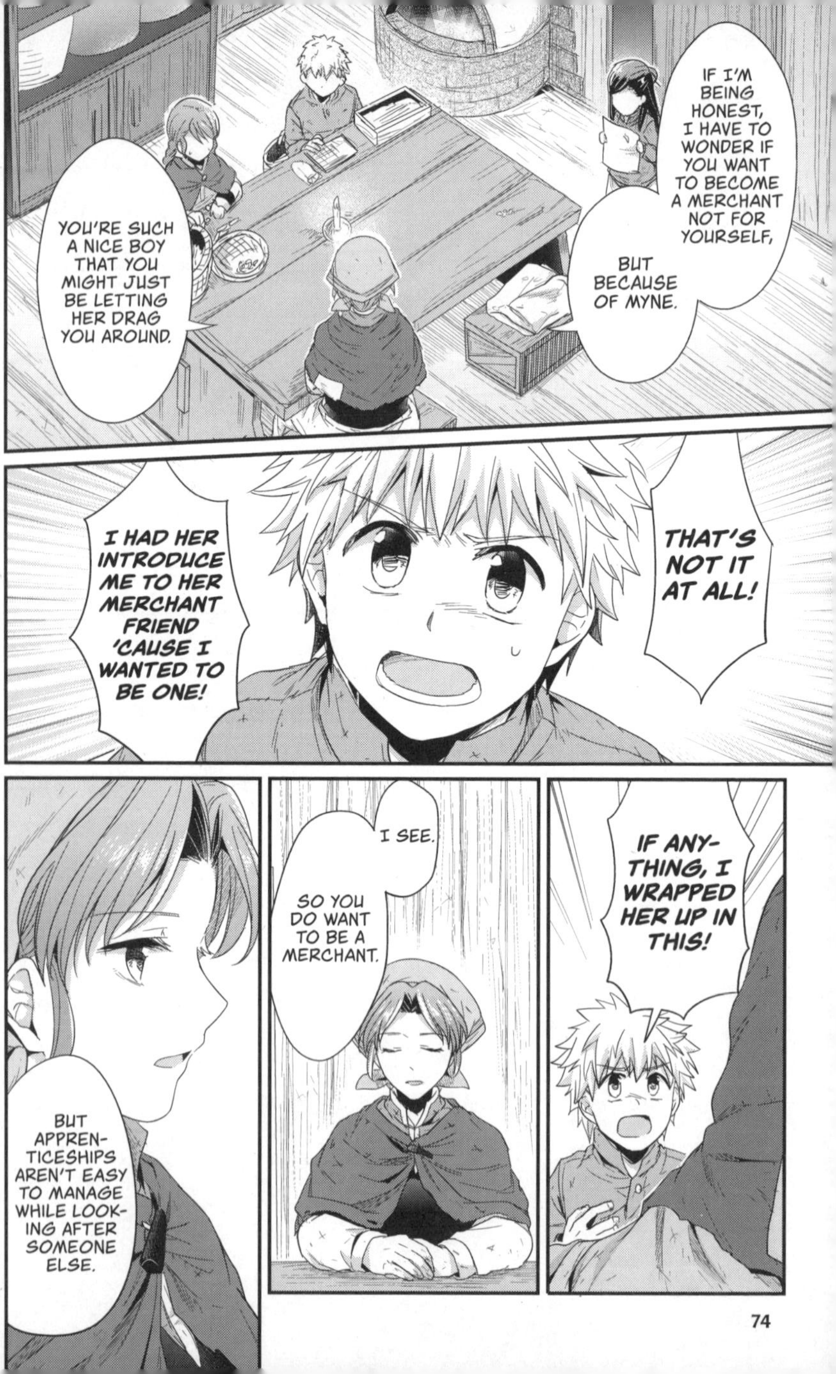
IF I'M BEING HONEST, I HAVE TO WONDER IF YOU WANT TO BECOME A MERCHANT NOT FOR YOURSELF,
BUT BECAUSE OF MYNE.
YOU'RE SUCH A NICE BOY THAT YOU MIGHT JUST BE LETTING HER DRAG YOU AROUND.
THAT'S NOT IT AT ALL!
I HAD HER INTRODUCE ME TO HER MERCHANT FRIEND 'CAUSE I WANTED TO BE ONE!
IF ANY-THING, I WRAPPED HER UP IN THIS!
I SEE.
SO YOU DO WANT TO BE A MERCHANT.
BUT APPREN-TICESHIPS AREN'T EASY TO MANAGE WHILE LOOK-ING AFTER SOMEONE ELSE.

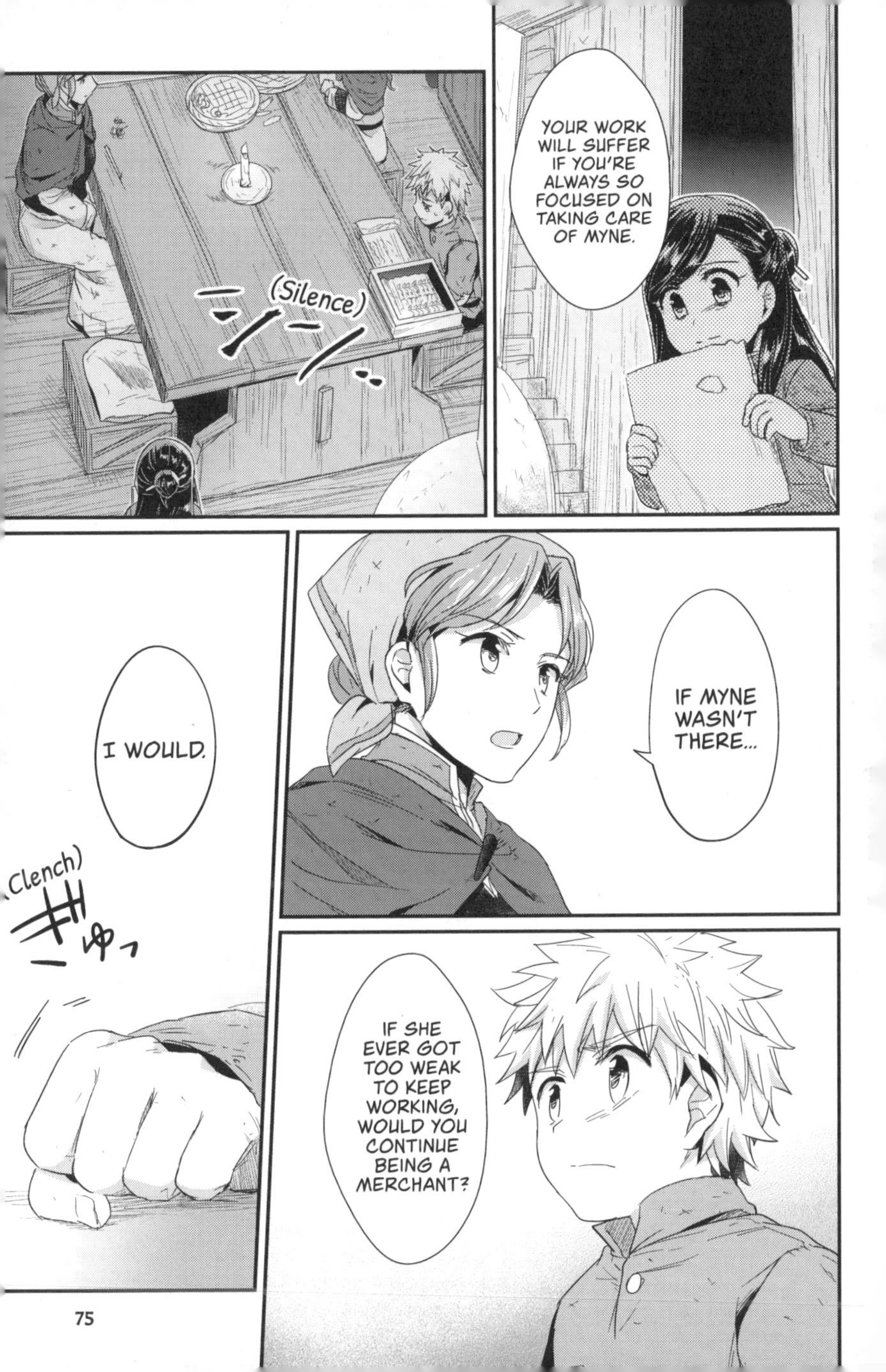
YOUR WORK WILL SUFFER IF YOU'RE ALWAYS SO FOCUSED ON TAKING CARE OF MYNE.
(Silence)
IF MYNE WASN'T THERE...
IF SHE EVER GOT TOO WEAK TO KEEP WORKING, WOULD YOU CONTINUE BEING A MERCHANT?
I WOULD.
(Clench)

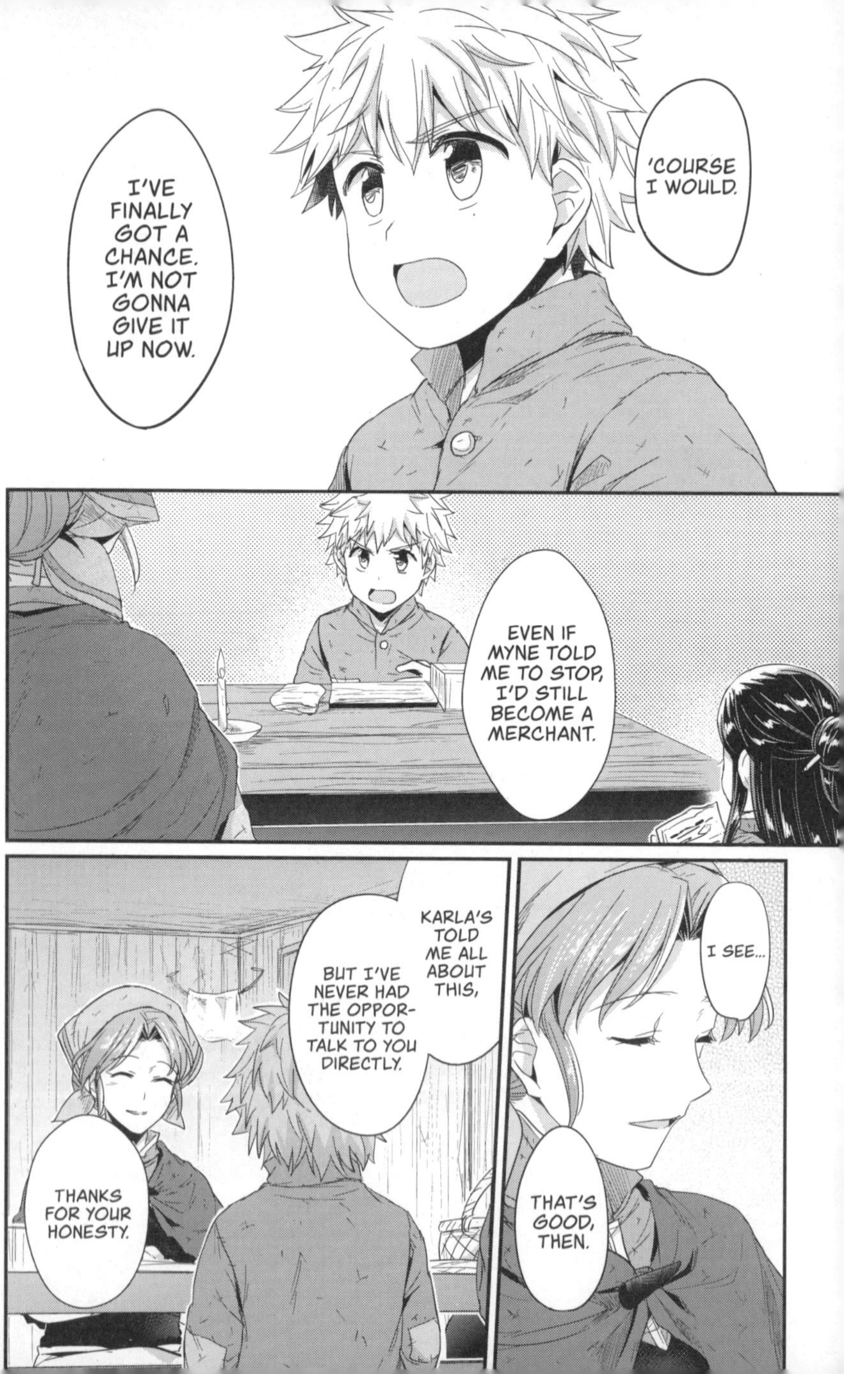
'COURSE I WOULD.
I'VE FINALLY GOT A CHANCE. I'M NOT GONNA GIVE IT UP NOW.
EVEN IF MYNE TOLD ME TO STOP, I'D STILL BECOME A MERCHANT.
I SEE...
THAT'S GOOD, THEN.
KARLA'S TOLD ME ALL ABOUT THIS,
BUT I'VE NEVER HAD THE OPPOR-TUNITY TO TALK TO YOU DIRECTLY.
THANKS FOR YOUR HONESTY.

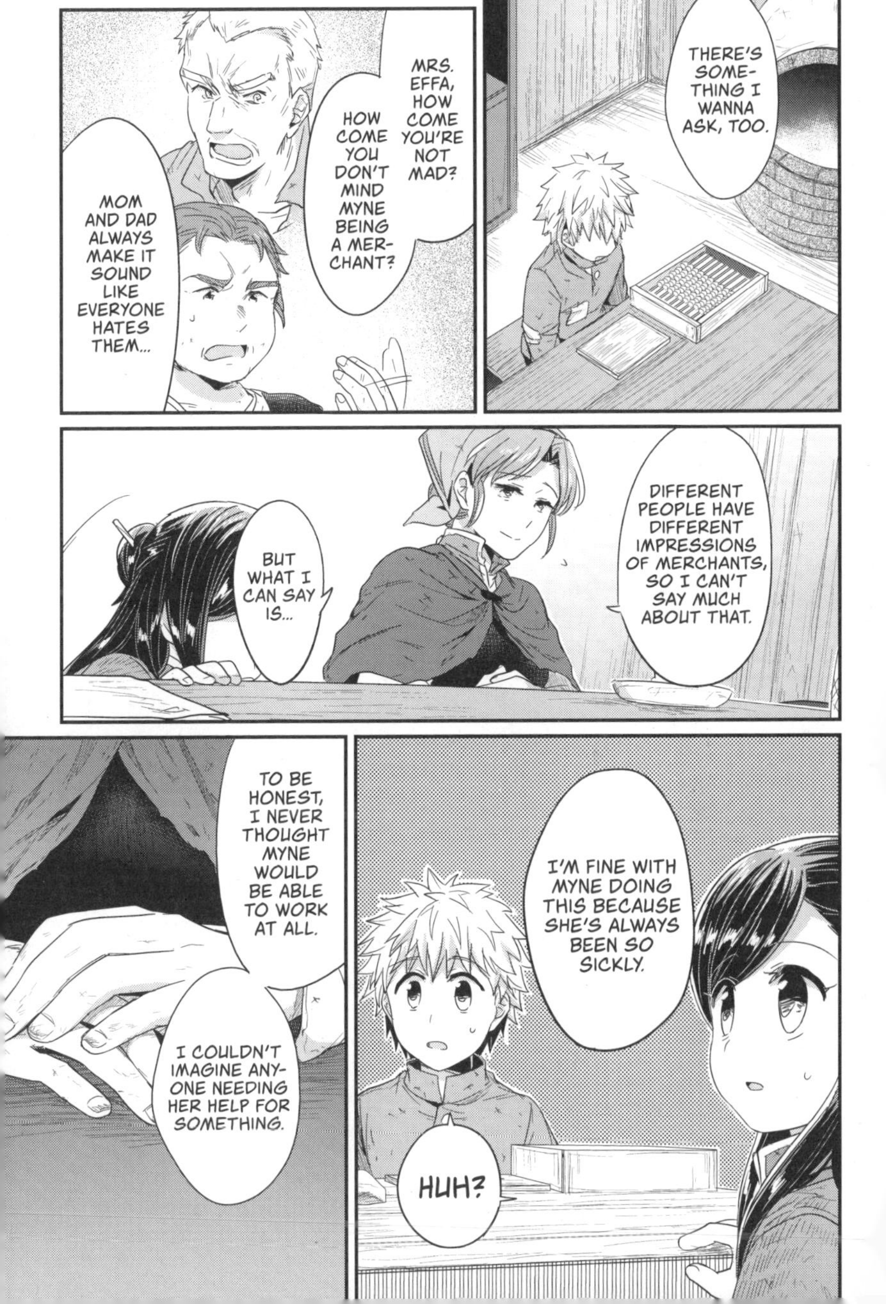
THERE'S SOME-THING I WANNA ASK, TOO.
MRS. EFFA, HOW COME YOU'RE NOT MAD?
HOW COME YOU DON'T MIND MYNE BEING A MER-CHANT?
MOM AND DAD ALWAYS MAKE IT SOUND LIKE EVERYONE HATES THEM...
DIFFERENT PEOPLE HAVE DIFFERENT IMPRESSIONS OF MERCHANTS, SO I CAN'T SAY MUCH ABOUT THAT.
BUT WHAT I CAN SAY IS...
I'M FINE WITH MYNE DOING THIS BECAUSE SHE'S ALWAYS BEEN SO SICKLY.
HUH?
TO BE HONEST, I NEVER THOUGHT MYNE WOULD BE ABLE TO WORK AT ALL.
I COULDN'T IMAGINE ANY-ONE NEEDING HER HELP FOR SOMETHING.

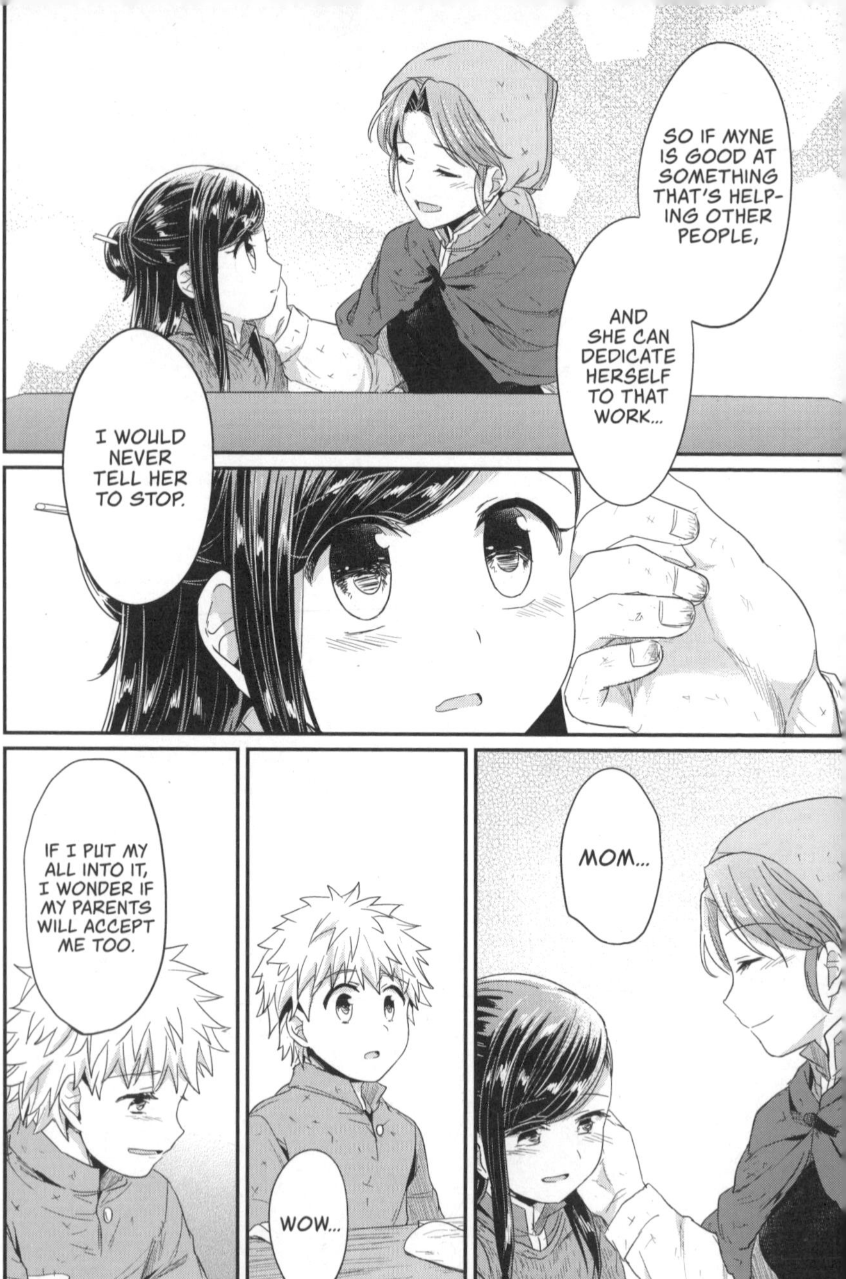
SO IF MYNE IS GOOD AT SOMETHING THAT'S HELPING OTHER PEOPLE,
AND SHE CAN DEDICATE HERSELF TO THAT WORK...
I WOULD NEVER TELL HER TO STOP.
MOM...
WOW...
IF I PUT MY ALL INTO IT, I WONDER IF MY PARENTS WILL ACCEPT ME TOO.

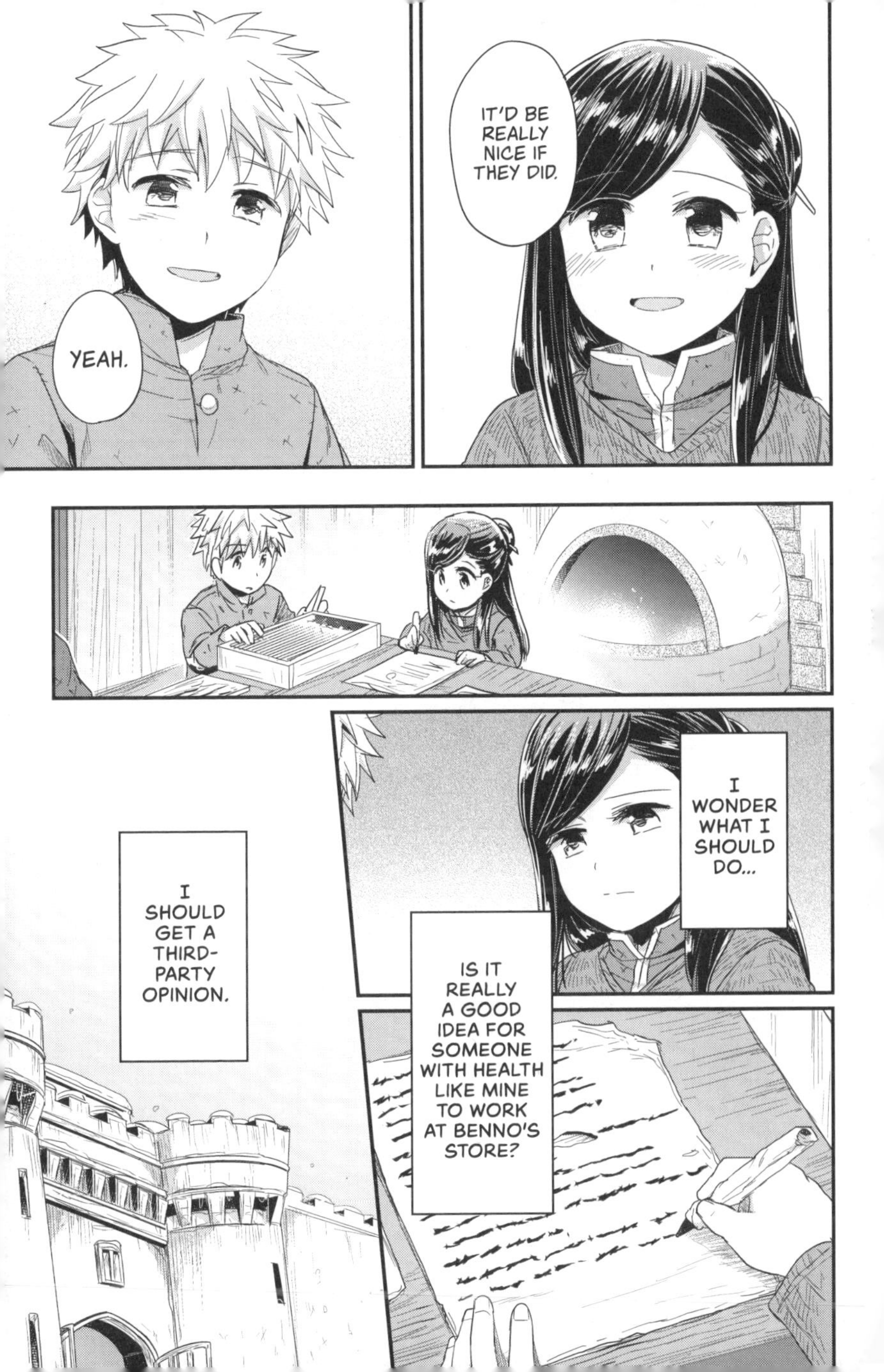
IT'D BE REALLY NICE IF THEY DID.
YEAH.
I WONDER WHAT I SHOULD DO...
IS IT REALLY A GOOD IDEA FOR SOMEONE WITH HEALTH LIKE MINE TO WORK AT BENNO'S STORE?
I SHOULD GET A THIRD-PARTY OPINION.

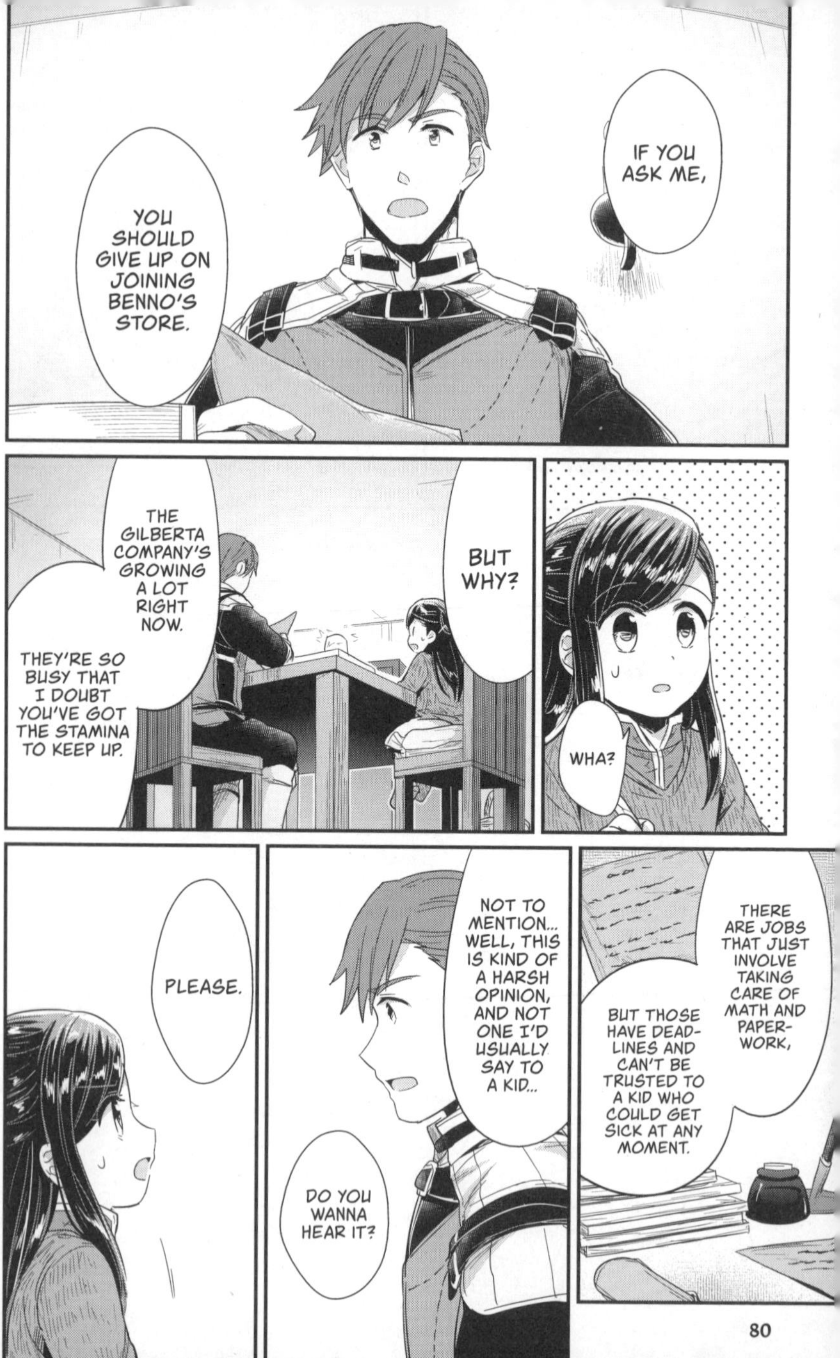
IF YOU ASK ME,
YOU SHOULD GIVE UP ON JOINING BENNO'S STORE.
WHA?
BUT WHY?
THE GILBERTA COMPANY'S GROWING A LOT RIGHT NOW.
THEY'RE SO BUSY THAT I DOUBT YOU'VE GOT THE STAMINA TO KEEP UP.
THERE ARE JOBS THAT JUST INVOLVE TAKING CARE OF MATH AND PAPER-WORK,
BUT THOSE HAVE DEAD-LINES AND CAN'T BE TRUSTED TO A KID WHO COULD GET SICK AT ANY MOMENT.
NOT TO MENTION... WELL, THIS IS KIND OF A HARSH OPINION, AND NOT ONE I'D USUALLY SAY TO A KID...
DO YOU WANNA HEAR IT?
PLEASE.

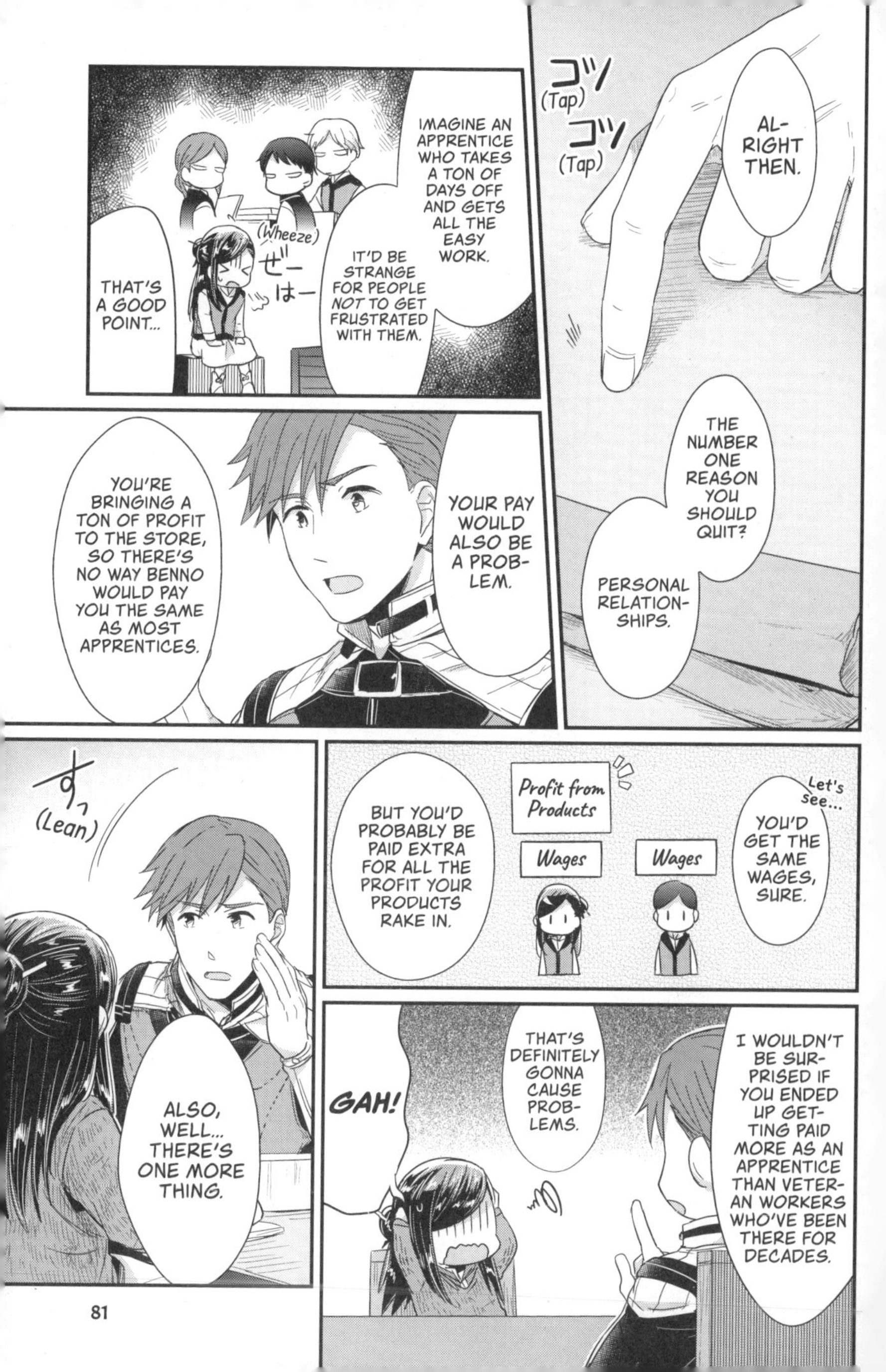
ゴツ
(Tap)
ゴツ
(Tap)
AL-RIGHT THEN.
THE NUMBER ONE REASON YOU SHOULD QUIT?
PERSONAL RELATION-SHIPS.
IMAGINE AN APPRENTICE WHO TAKES A TON OF DAYS OFF AND GETS ALL THE EASY WORK.
IT'D BE STRANGE FOR PEOPLE NOT TO GET FRUSTRATED WITH THEM.
(Wheeze)
ぜーはー
THAT'S A GOOD POINT...
YOUR PAY WOULD ALSO BE A PROB-LEM.
YOU'RE BRINGING A TON OF PROFIT TO THE STORE, SO THERE'S NO WAY BENNO WOULD PAY YOU THE SAME AS MOST APPRENTICES.
Let's see...
YOU'D GET THE SAME WAGES, SURE.
Profit from Products
Wages
Wages
BUT YOU'D PROBABLY BE PAID EXTRA FOR ALL THE PROFIT YOUR PRODUCTS RAKE IN.
I WOULDN'T BE SUR-PRISED IF YOU ENDED UP GET-TING PAID MORE AS AN APPRENTICE THAN VETER-AN WORKERS WHO'VE BEEN THERE FOR DECADES.
THAT'S DEFINITELY GONNA CAUSE PROB-LEMS.
GAH!
すっ
(Lean)
ALSO, WELL... THERE'S ONE MORE THING.

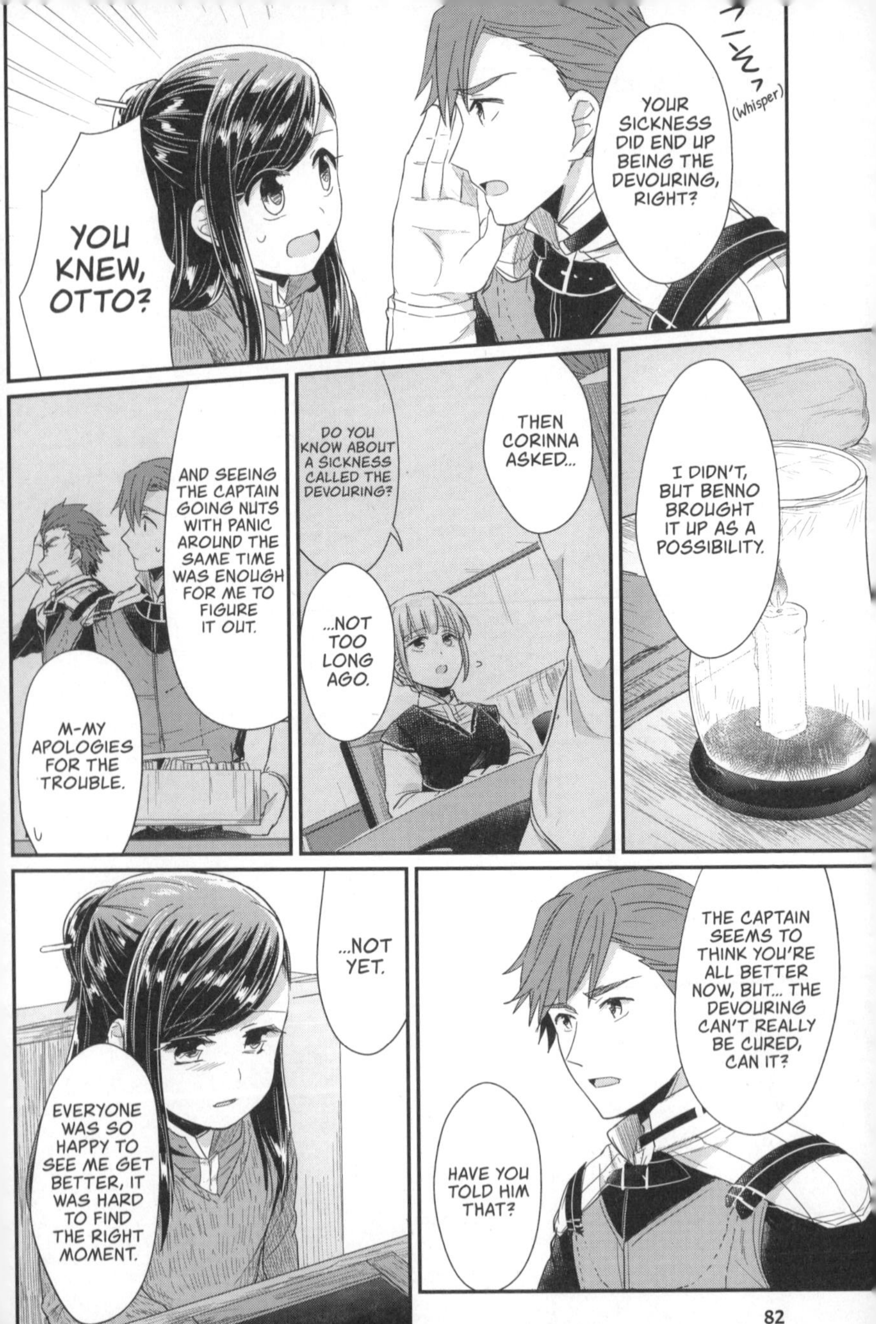
(Whisper)
YOUR SICKNESS DID END UP BEING THE DEVOURING, RIGHT?
YOU KNEW, OTTO?
I DIDN'T, BUT BENNO BROUGHT IT UP AS A POSSIBILITY.
THEN CORINNA ASKED...
DO YOU KNOW ABOUT A SICKNESS CALLED THE DEVOURING?
...NOT TOO LONG AGO.
AND SEEING THE CAPTAIN GOING NUTS WITH PANIC AROUND THE SAME TIME WAS ENOUGH FOR ME TO FIGURE IT OUT.
M-MY APOLOGIES FOR THE TROUBLE.
THE CAPTAIN SEEMS TO THINK YOU'RE ALL BETTER NOW, BUT... THE DEVOURING CAN'T REALLY BE CURED, CAN IT?
HAVE YOU TOLD HIM THAT?
...NOT YET.
EVERYONE WAS SO HAPPY TO SEE ME GET BETTER, IT WAS HARD TO FIND THE RIGHT MOMENT.

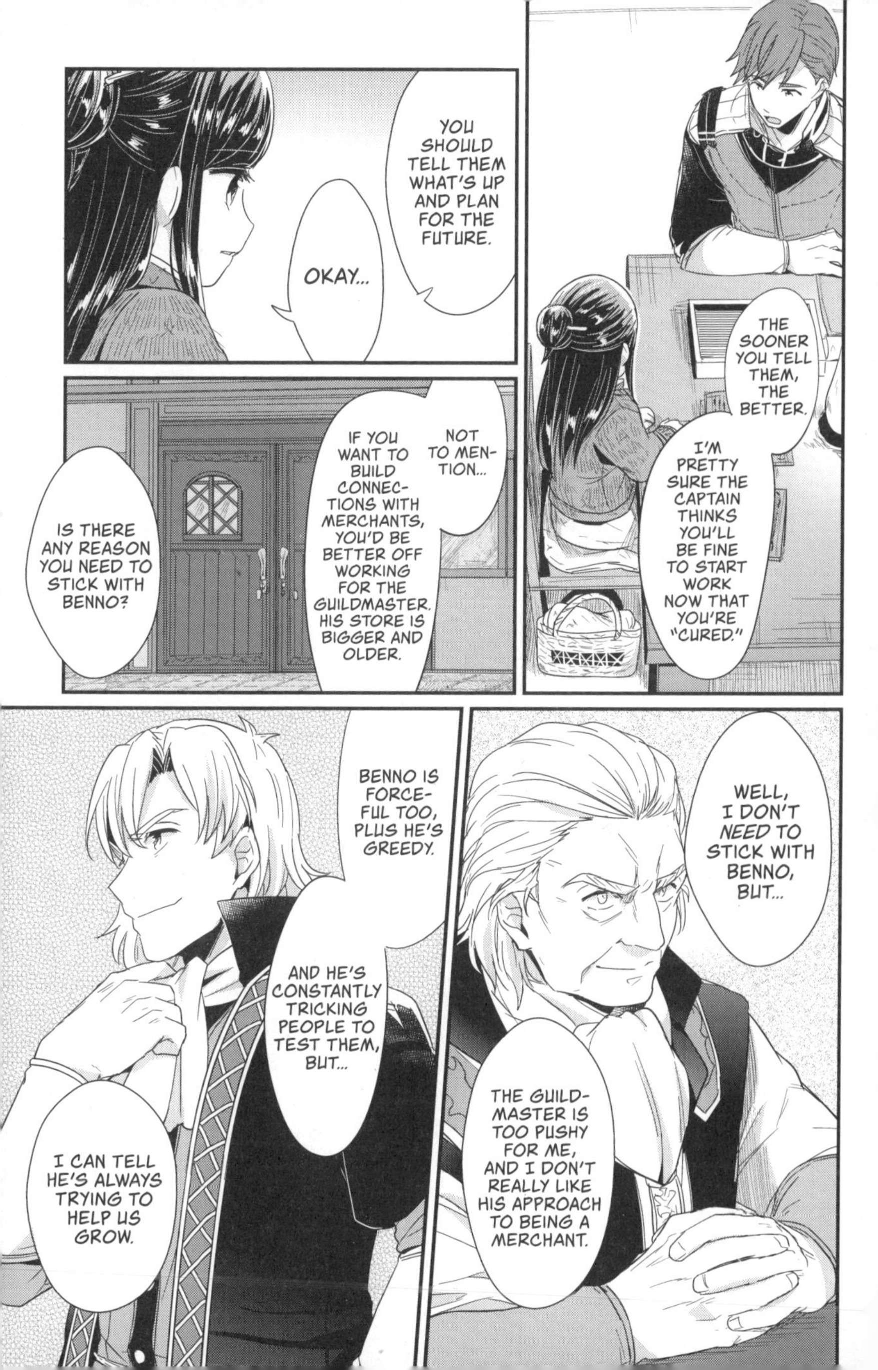
THE SOONER YOU TELL THEM, THE BETTER.
I'M PRETTY SURE THE CAPTAIN THINKS YOU'LL BE FINE TO START WORK NOW THAT YOU'RE "CURED."
YOU SHOULD TELL THEM WHAT'S UP AND PLAN FOR THE FUTURE.
OKAY...
NOT TO MENTION...
IF YOU WANT TO BUILD CONNECTIONS WITH MERCHANTS, YOU'D BE BETTER OFF WORKING FOR THE GUILDMASTER. HIS STORE IS BIGGER AND OLDER.
IS THERE ANY REASON YOU NEED TO STICK WITH BENNO?
WELL, I DON'T *NEED* TO STICK WITH BENNO, BUT...
THE GUILDMASTER IS TOO PUSHY FOR ME, AND I DON'T REALLY LIKE HIS APPROACH TO BEING A MERCHANT.
BENNO IS FORCEFUL TOO, PLUS HE'S GREEDY.
AND HE'S CONSTANTLY TRICKING PEOPLE TO TEST THEM, BUT...
I CAN TELL HE'S ALWAYS TRYING TO HELP US GROW.

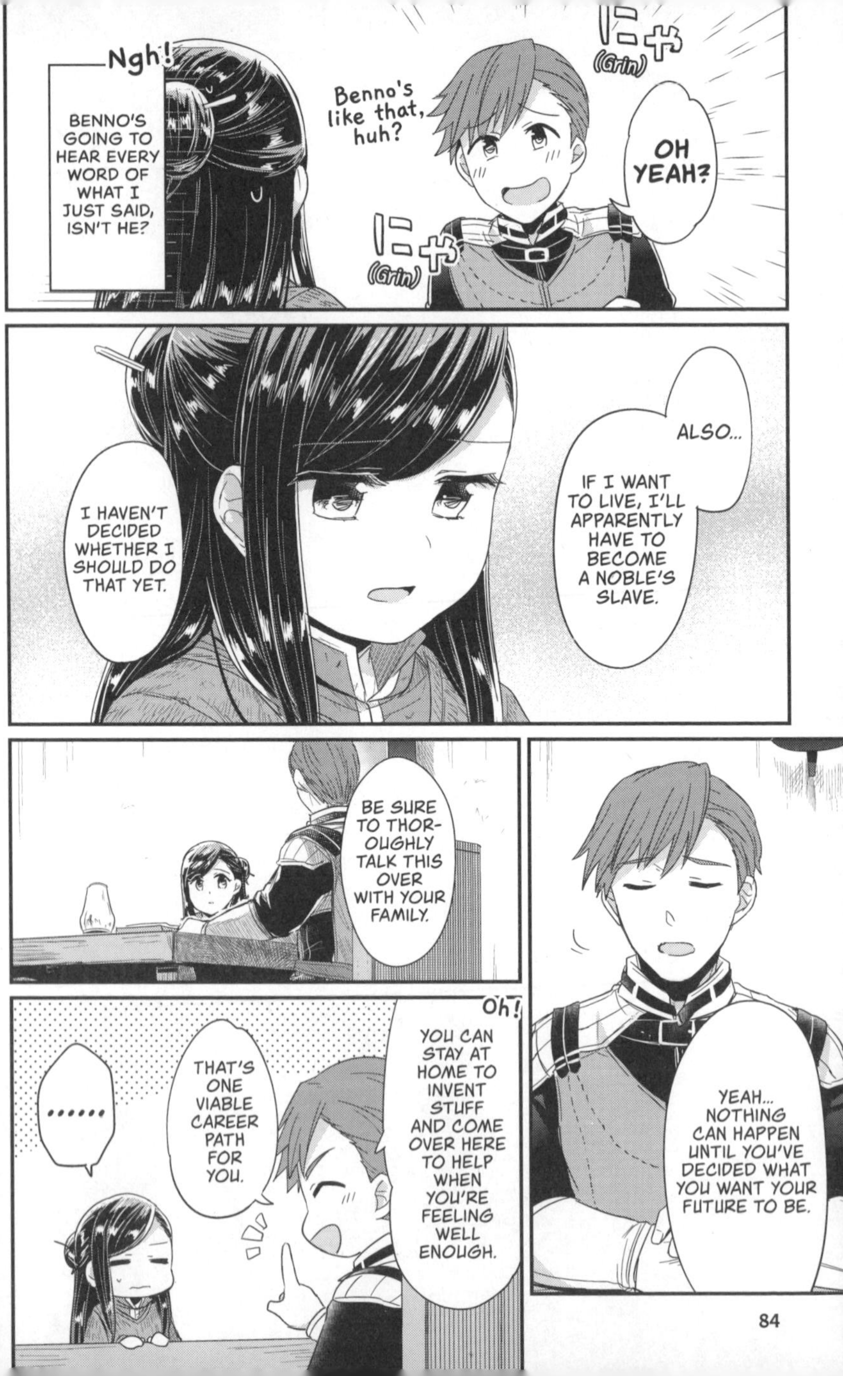
にや
(Grin)
OH YEAH?
Benno's like that, huh?
にや
(Grin)
Ngh!
BENNO'S GOING TO HEAR EVERY WORD OF WHAT I JUST SAID, ISN'T HE?
ALSO...
IF I WANT TO LIVE, I'LL APPARENTLY HAVE TO BECOME A NOBLE'S SLAVE.
I HAVEN'T DECIDED WHETHER I SHOULD DO THAT YET.
YEAH... NOTHING CAN HAPPEN UNTIL YOU'VE DECIDED WHAT YOU WANT YOUR FUTURE TO BE.
BE SURE TO THOR-OUGHLY TALK THIS OVER WITH YOUR FAMILY.
Oh!
YOU CAN STAY AT HOME TO INVENT STUFF AND COME OVER HERE TO HELP WHEN YOU'RE FEELING WELL ENOUGH.
THAT'S ONE VIABLE CAREER PATH FOR YOU.
......

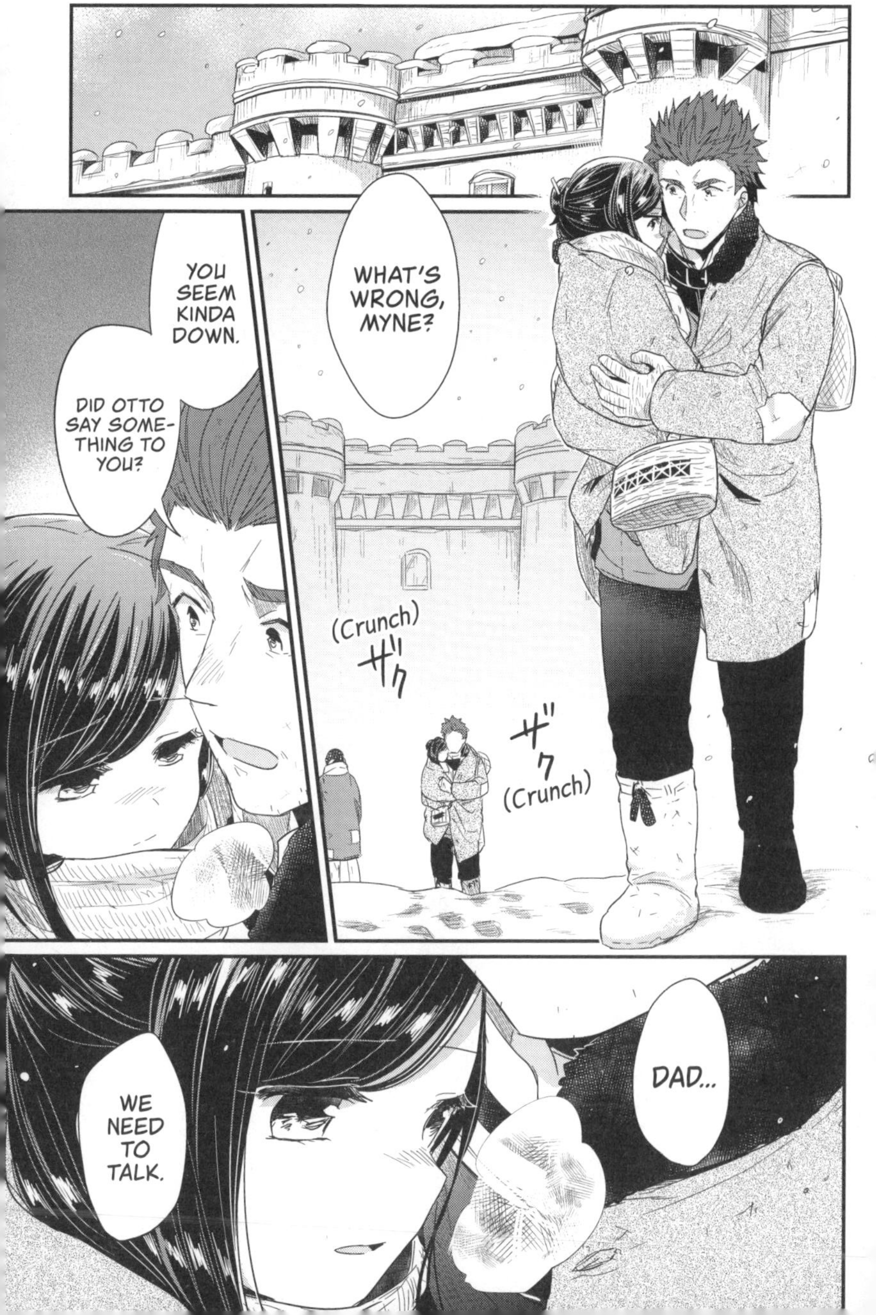
WHAT'S WRONG, MYNE?
(Crunch)
ザク
ザク
(Crunch)
YOU SEEM KINDA DOWN.
DID OTTO SAY SOME-THING TO YOU?
DAD...
WE NEED TO TALK.

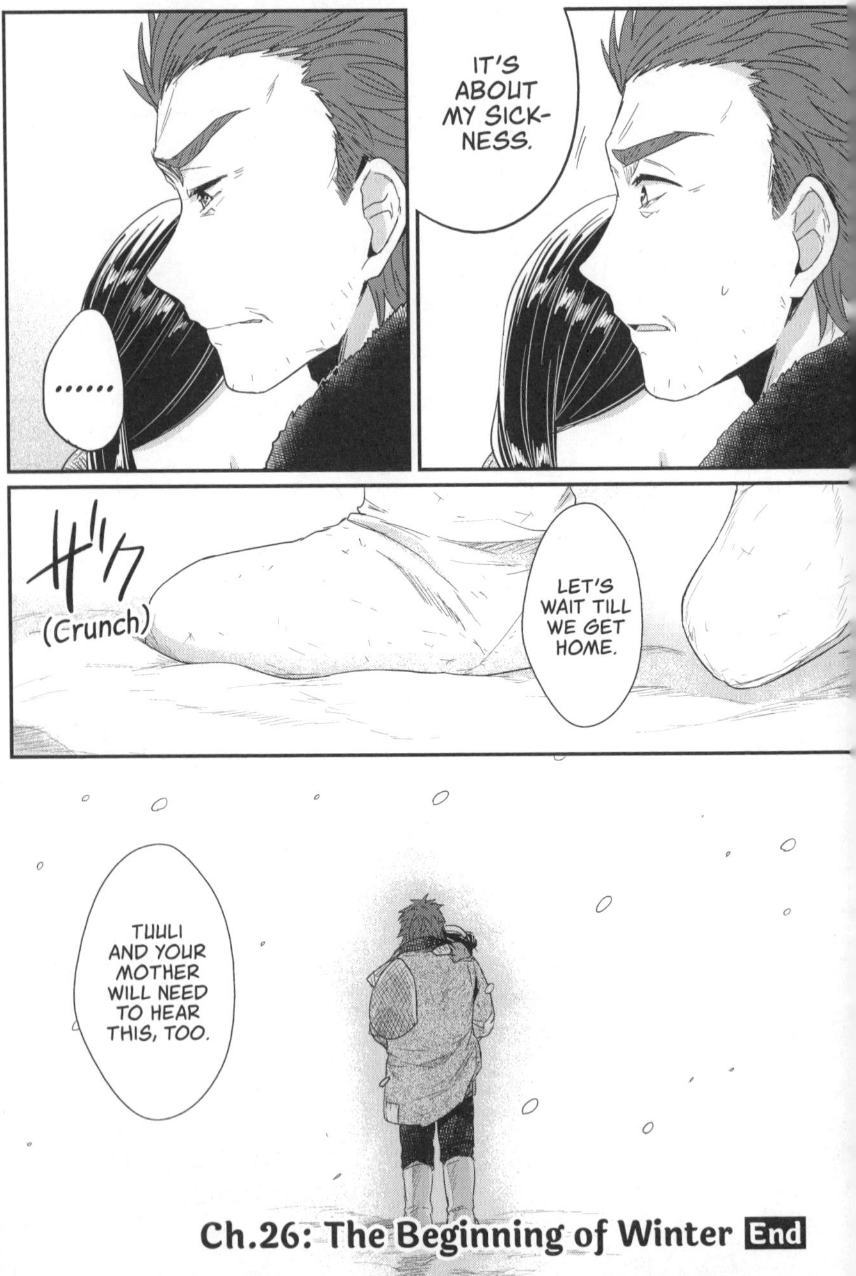
IT'S ABOUT MY SICKNESS.
......
LET'S WAIT TILL WE GET HOME.
ザク
(Crunch)
TUULI AND YOUR MOTHER WILL NEED TO HEAR THIS, TOO.
Ch.26: The Beginning of Winter End

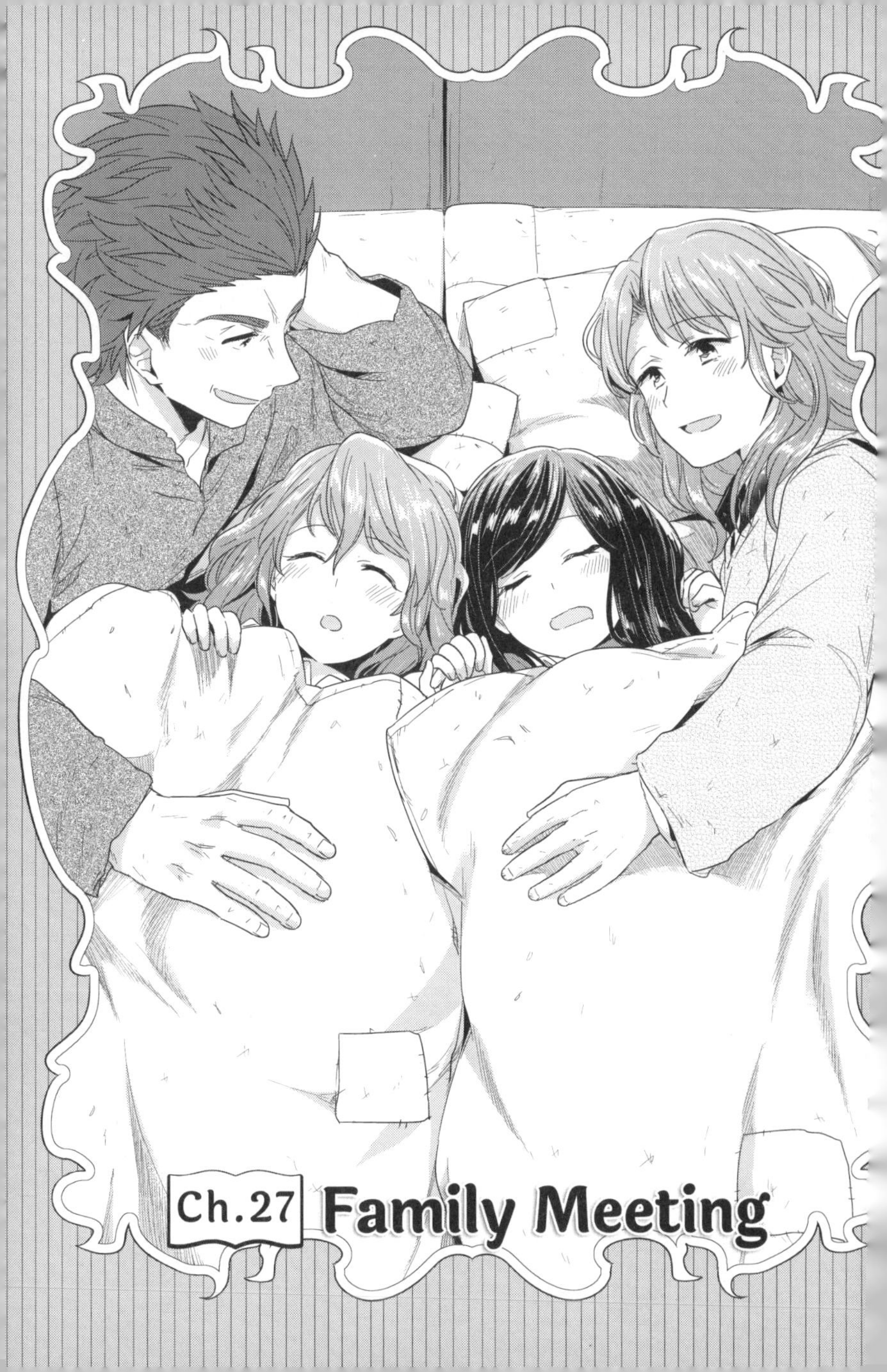
Ch. 27
Family Meeting

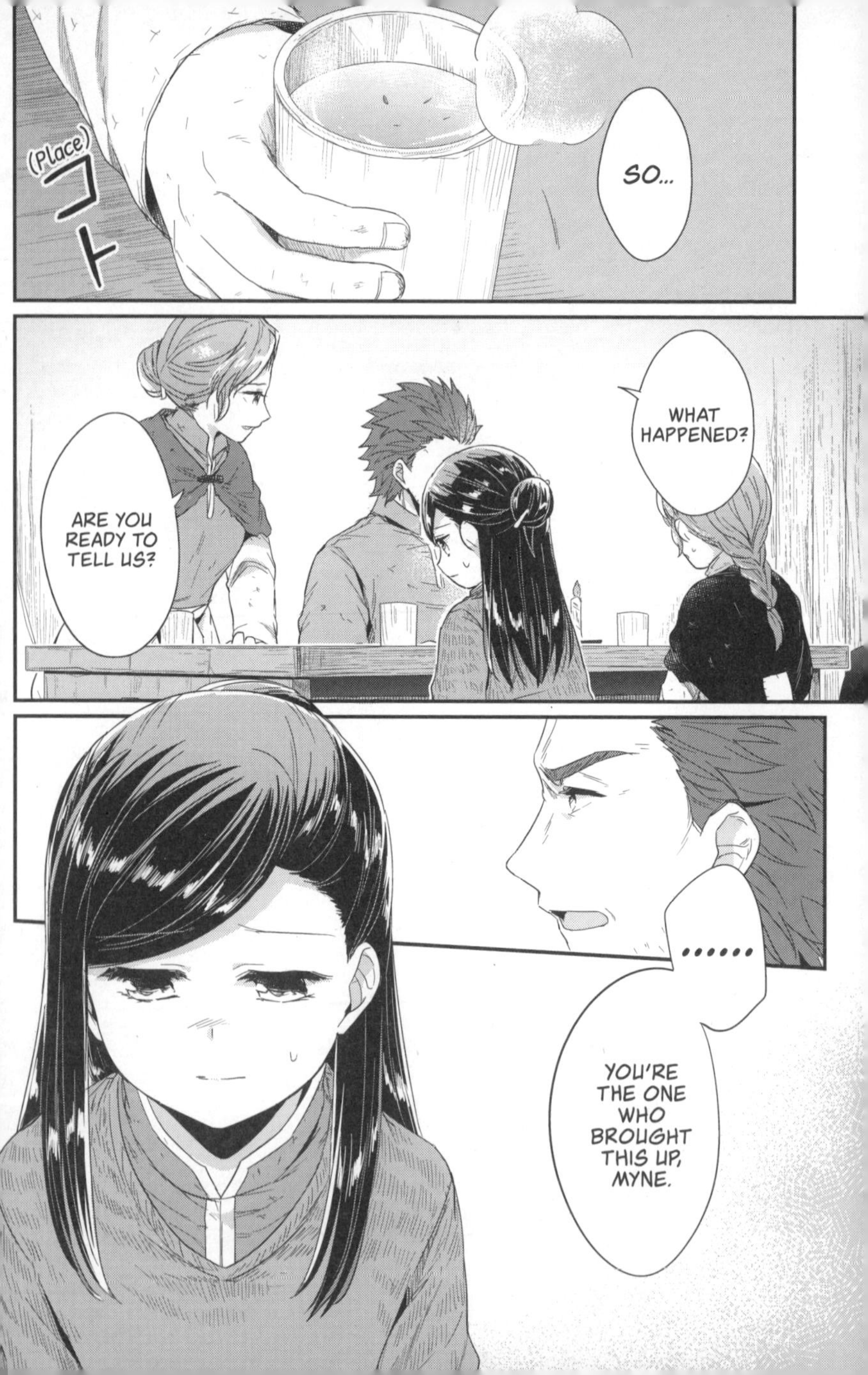
SO...
(Place)
コト
WHAT HAPPENED?
ARE YOU READY TO TELL US?
......
YOU'RE THE ONE WHO BROUGHT THIS UP, MYNE.

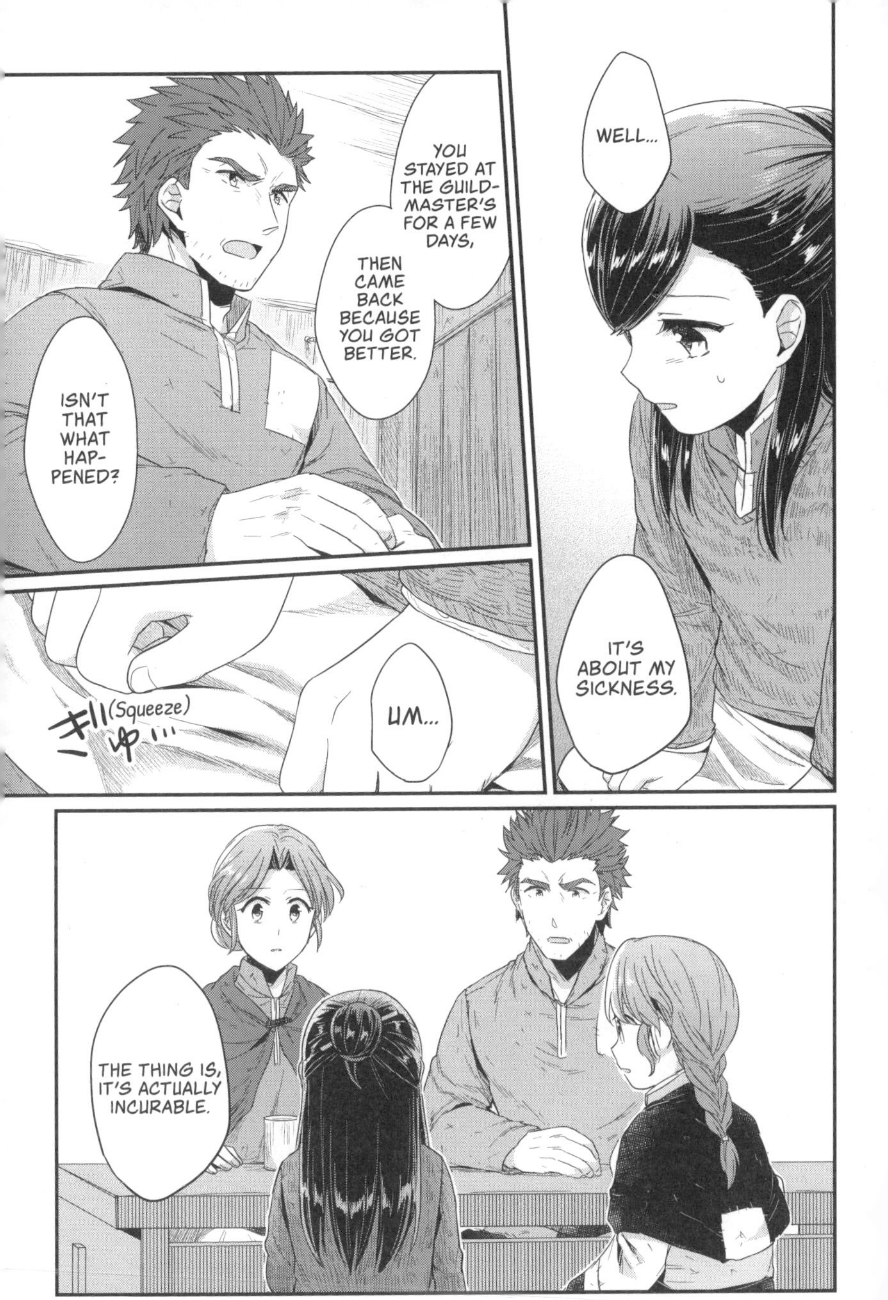
WELL...
IT'S ABOUT MY SICKNESS.
YOU STAYED AT THE GUILD-MASTER'S FOR A FEW DAYS,
THEN CAME BACK BECAUSE YOU GOT BETTER.
ISN'T THAT WHAT HAPPENED?
(Squeeze)
UM...
THE THING IS, IT'S ACTUALLY INCURABLE.

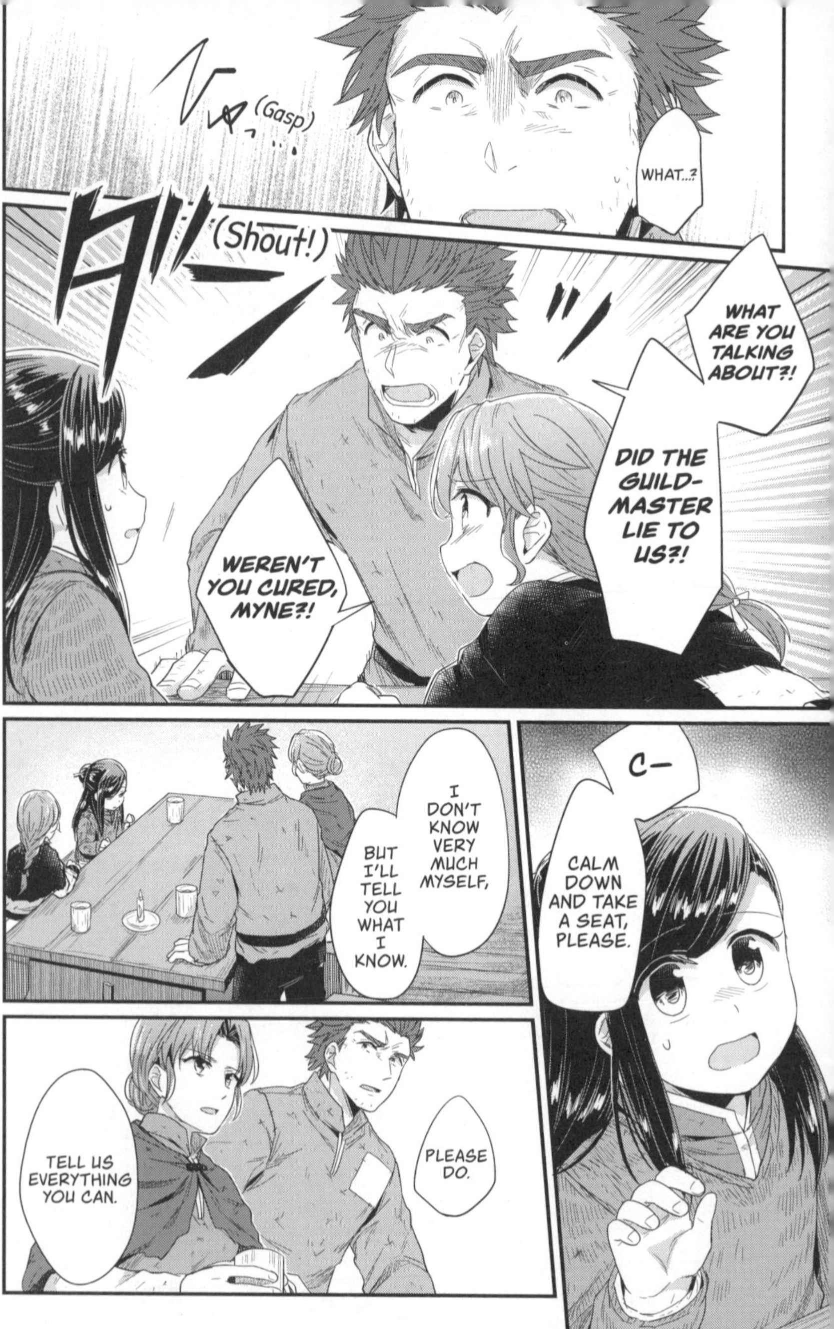
(Gasp)
WHAT...?
(Shout!)
WHAT ARE YOU TALKING ABOUT?!
DID THE GUILD-MASTER LIE TO US?!
WEREN'T YOU CURED, MYNE?!
C—
CALM DOWN AND TAKE A SEAT, PLEASE.
I DON'T KNOW VERY MUCH MYSELF,
BUT I'LL TELL YOU WHAT I KNOW.
PLEASE DO.
TELL US EVERYTHING YOU CAN.

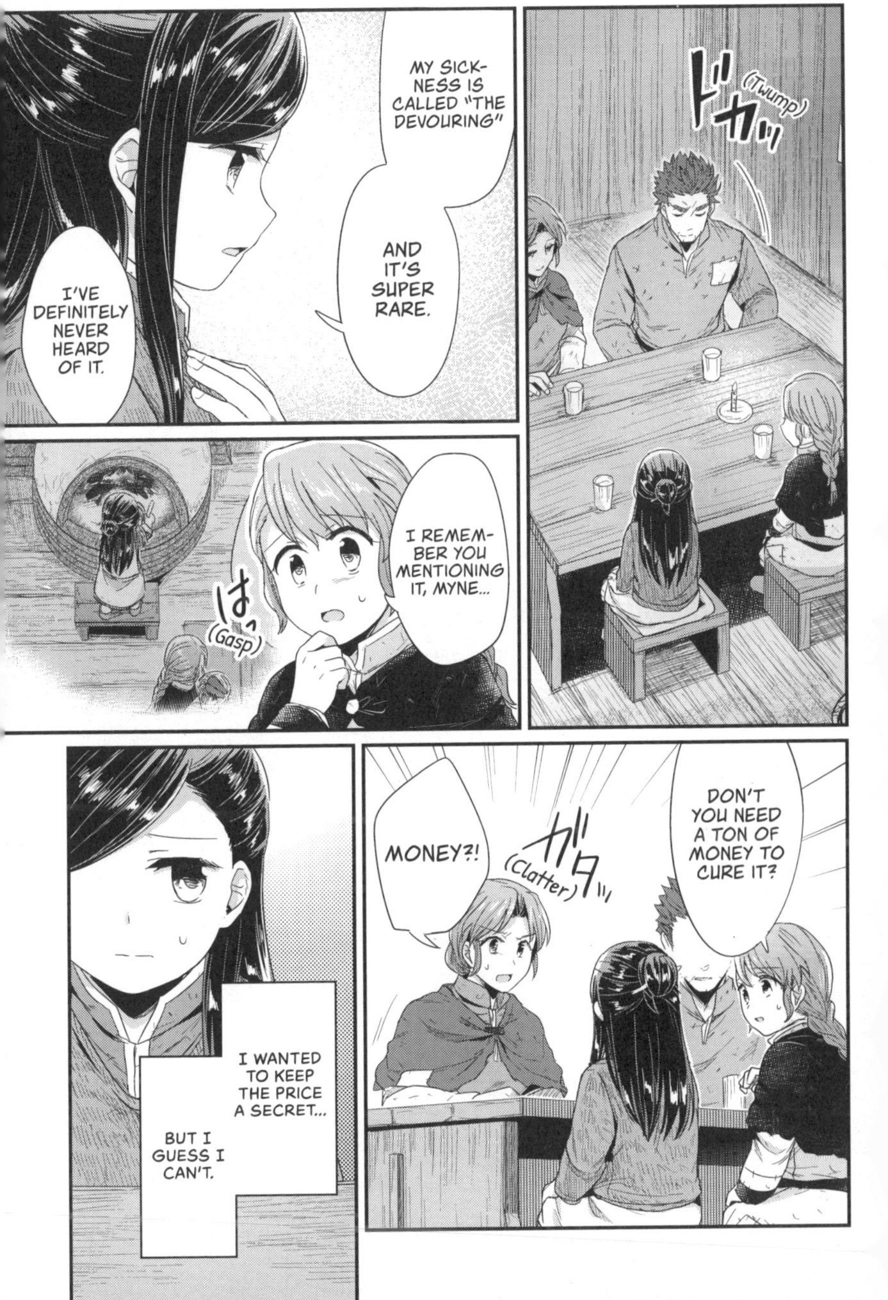
ドカッ
(Twump)
MY SICK-NESS IS CALLED "THE DEVOURING"
AND IT'S SUPER RARE.
I'VE DEFINITELY NEVER HEARD OF IT.
I REMEM-BER YOU MENTIONING IT, MYNE...
はっ
(Gasp)
DON'T YOU NEED A TON OF MONEY TO CURE IT?
ガタッ
(Clatter)
MONEY?!
I WANTED TO KEEP THE PRICE A SECRET...
BUT I GUESS I CAN'T.

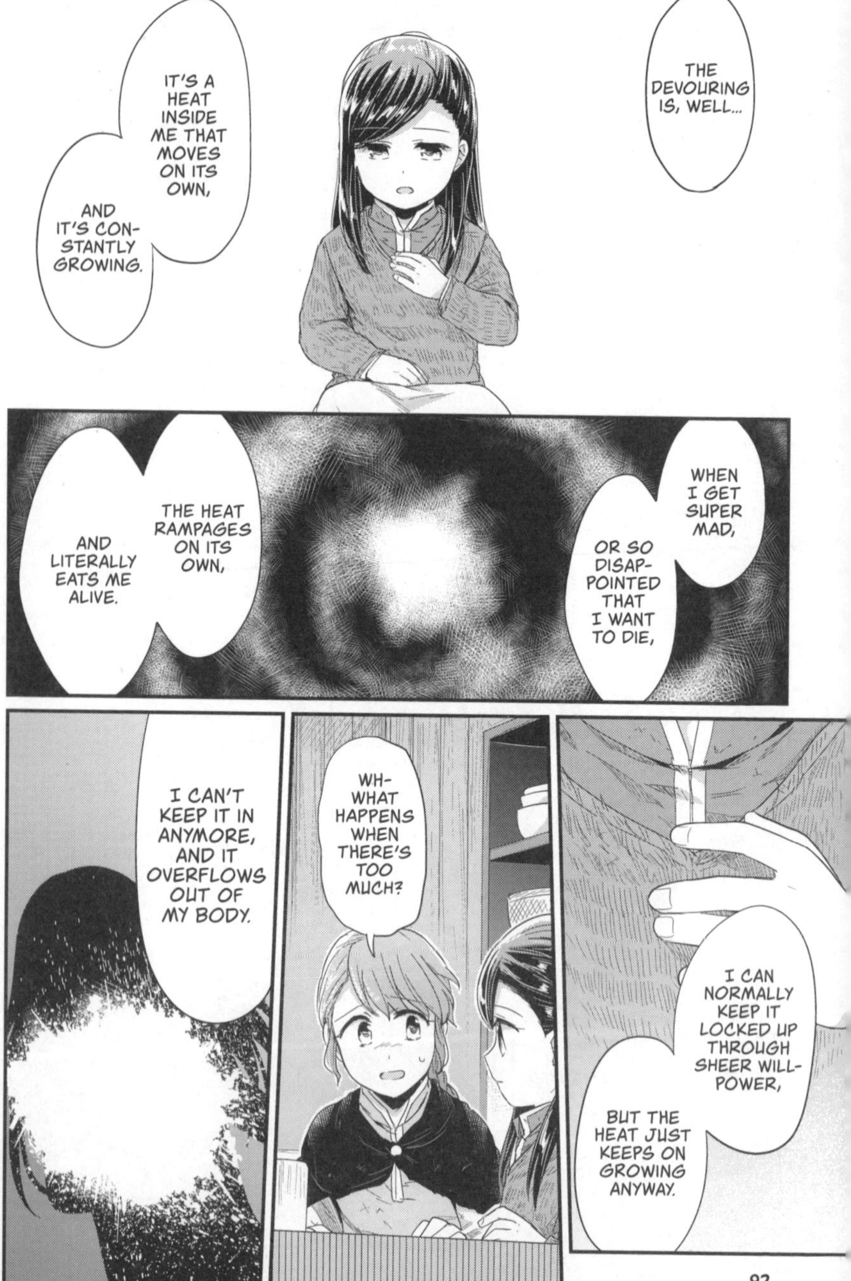
THE DEVOURING IS, WELL...
IT'S A HEAT INSIDE ME THAT MOVES ON ITS OWN,
AND IT'S CONSTANTLY GROWING.
WHEN I GET SUPER MAD,
OR SO DISAPPOINTED THAT I WANT TO DIE,
THE HEAT RAMPAGES ON ITS OWN,
AND LITERALLY EATS ME ALIVE.
I CAN NORMALLY KEEP IT LOCKED UP THROUGH SHEER WILLPOWER,
BUT THE HEAT JUST KEEPS ON GROWING ANYWAY.
WH-WHAT HAPPENS WHEN THERE'S TOO MUCH?
I CAN'T KEEP IT IN ANYMORE, AND IT OVERFLOWS OUT OF MY BODY.

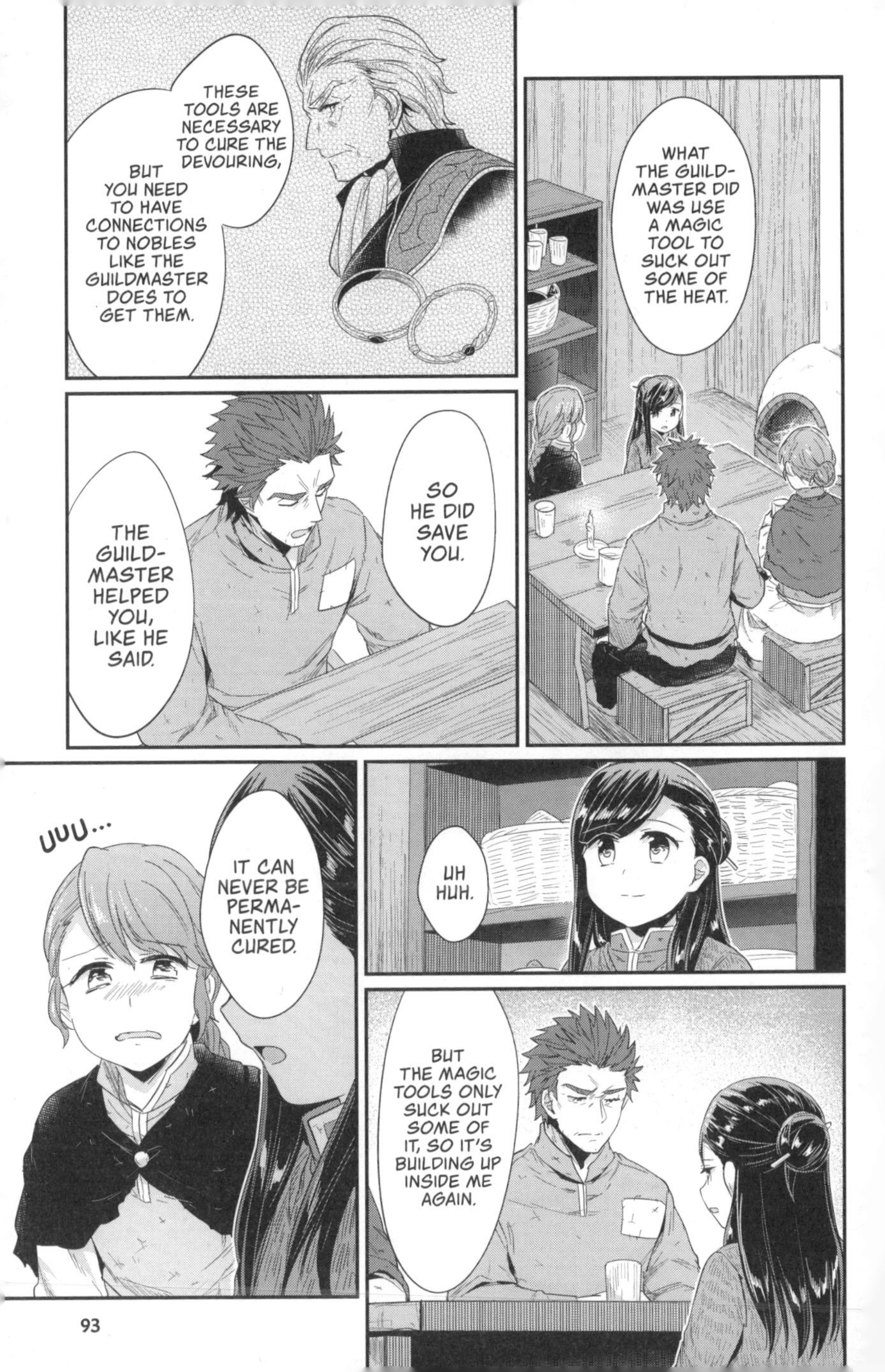
WHAT THE GUILD-MASTER DID WAS USE A MAGIC TOOL TO SUCK OUT SOME OF THE HEAT.
THESE TOOLS ARE NECESSARY TO CURE THE DEVOURING,
BUT YOU NEED TO HAVE CONNECTIONS TO NOBLES LIKE THE GUILDMASTER DOES TO GET THEM.
SO HE DID SAVE YOU.
THE GUILD-MASTER HELPED YOU, LIKE HE SAID.
UH HUH.
BUT THE MAGIC TOOLS ONLY SUCK OUT SOME OF IT, SO IT'S BUILDING UP INSIDE ME AGAIN.
IT CAN NEVER BE PERMA-NENTLY CURED.
UUU...

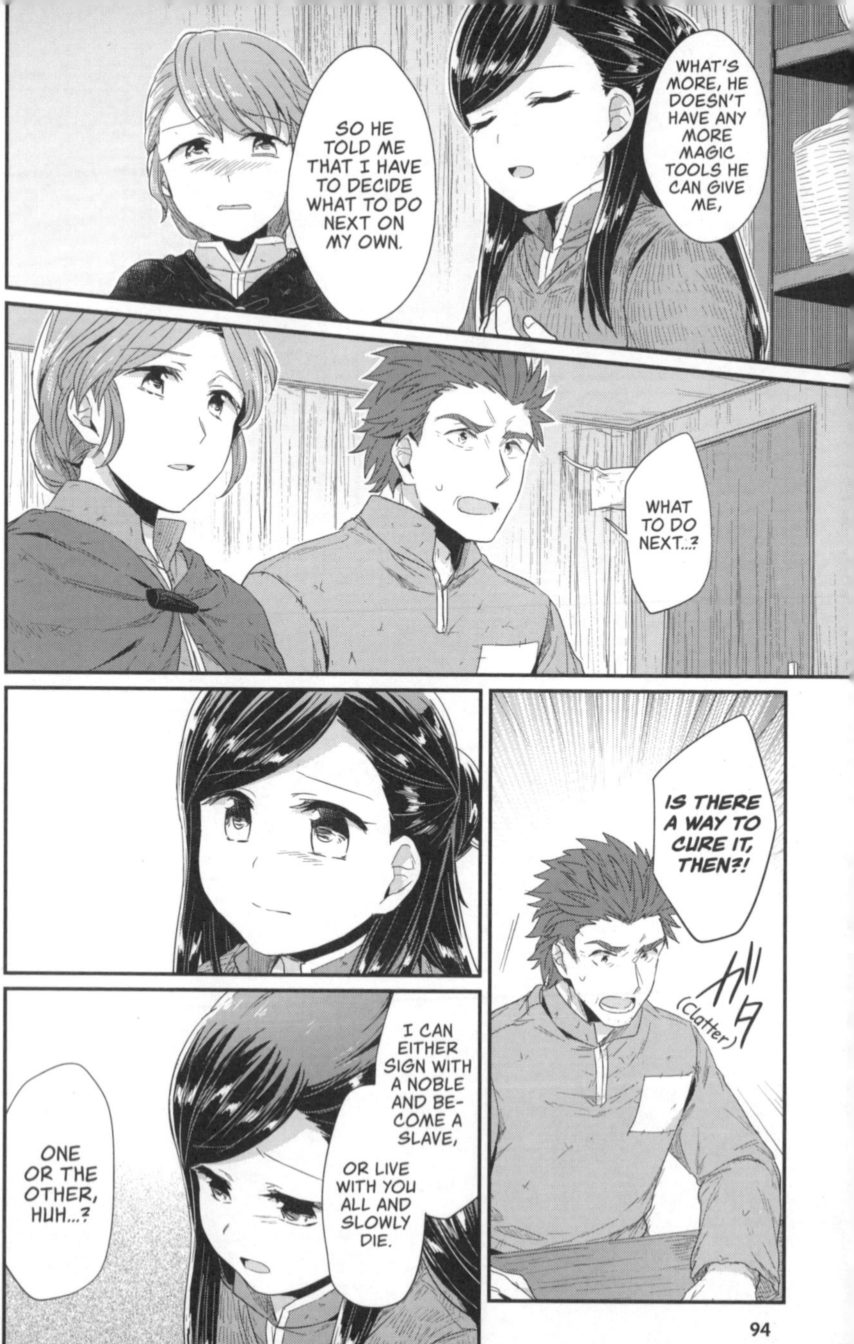
WHAT'S MORE, HE DOESN'T HAVE ANY MORE MAGIC TOOLS HE CAN GIVE ME,
SO HE TOLD ME THAT I HAVE TO DECIDE WHAT TO DO NEXT ON MY OWN.
WHAT TO DO NEXT...?
IS THERE A WAY TO CURE IT, THEN?!
(Clatter)
I CAN EITHER SIGN WITH A NOBLE AND BE-COME A SLAVE,
OR LIVE WITH YOU ALL AND SLOWLY DIE.
ONE OR THE OTHER, HUH...?

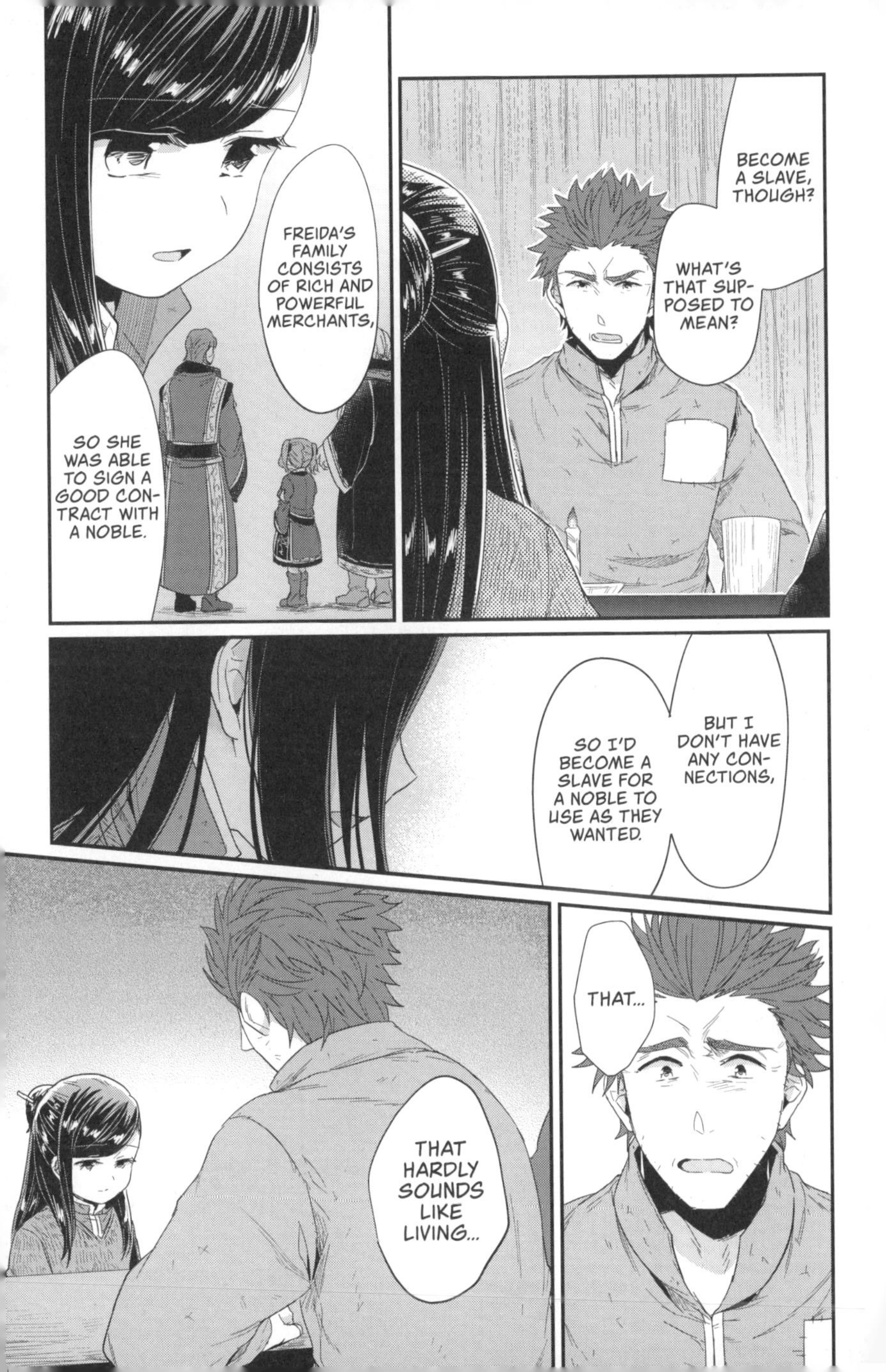
BECOME A SLAVE, THOUGH?
WHAT'S THAT SUPPOSED TO MEAN?
FREIDA'S FAMILY CONSISTS OF RICH AND POWERFUL MERCHANTS,
SO SHE WAS ABLE TO SIGN A GOOD CONTRACT WITH A NOBLE.
BUT I DON'T HAVE ANY CONNECTIONS,
SO I'D BECOME A SLAVE FOR A NOBLE TO USE AS THEY WANTED.
THAT...
THAT HARDLY SOUNDS LIKE LIVING...

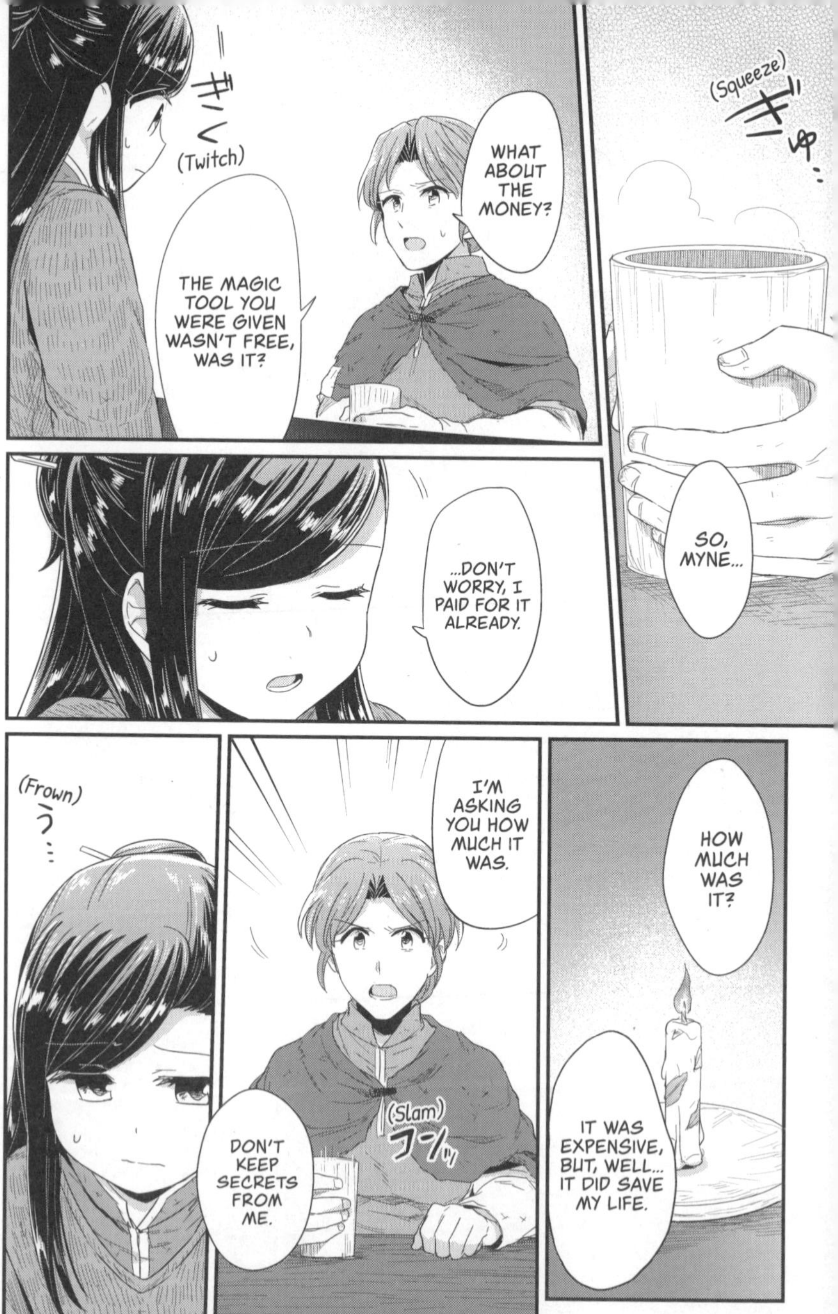
(Squeeze)
ぎゅ
SO, MYNE...
WHAT ABOUT THE MONEY?
ぎく
(Twitch)
THE MAGIC TOOL YOU WERE GIVEN WASN'T FREE, WAS IT?
...DON'T WORRY, I PAID FOR IT ALREADY.
HOW MUCH WAS IT?
IT WAS EXPENSIVE, BUT, WELL... IT DID SAVE MY LIFE.
I'M ASKING YOU HOW MUCH IT WAS.
(Slam)
DON'T KEEP SECRETS FROM ME.
(Frown)
う

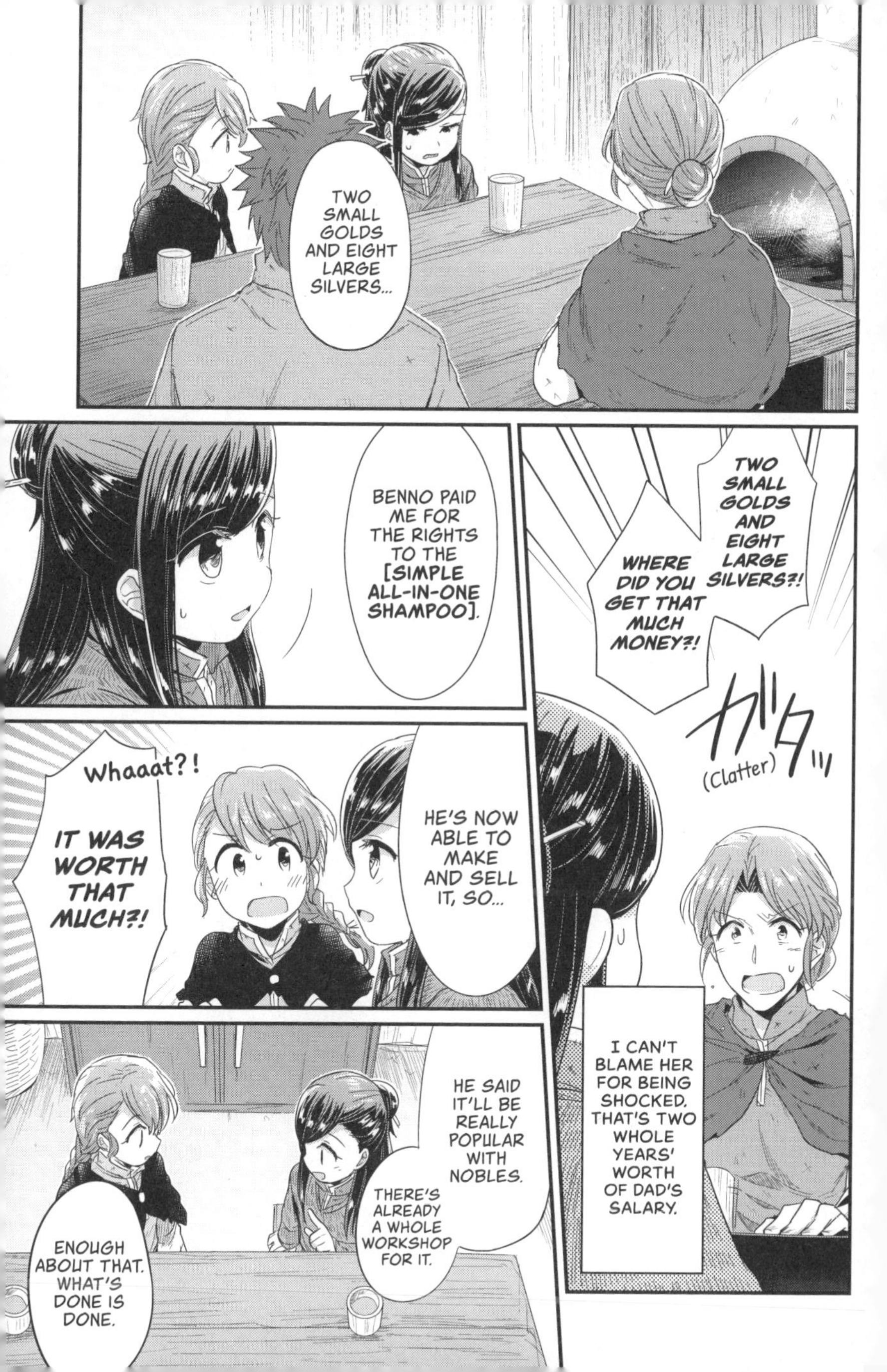

TWO SMALL GOLDS AND EIGHT LARGE SILVERS...
TWO SMALL GOLDS AND EIGHT LARGE SILVERS?!
WHERE DID YOU GET THAT MUCH MONEY?!
ガタッ
(Clatter)
I CAN'T BLAME HER FOR BEING SHOCKED. THAT'S TWO WHOLE YEARS' WORTH OF DAD'S SALARY.
BENNO PAID ME FOR THE RIGHTS TO THE [SIMPLE ALL-IN-ONE SHAMPOO].
HE'S NOW ABLE TO MAKE AND SELL IT, SO...
Whaaat?!
IT WAS WORTH THAT MUCH?!
HE SAID IT'LL BE REALLY POPULAR WITH NOBLES.
THERE'S ALREADY A WHOLE WORKSHOP FOR IT.
ENOUGH ABOUT THAT. WHAT'S DONE IS DONE.

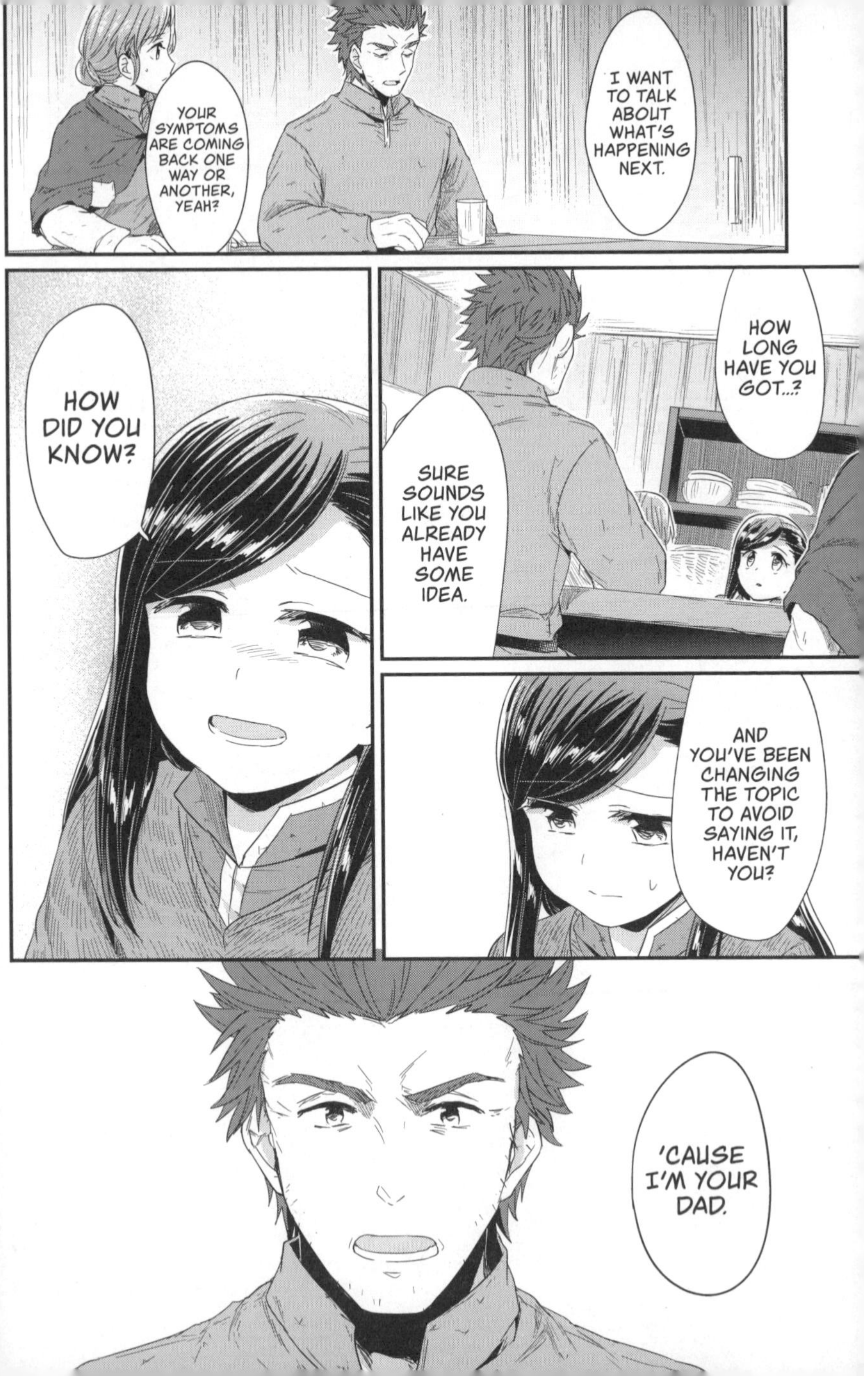
I WANT TO TALK ABOUT WHAT'S HAPPENING NEXT.
YOUR SYMPTOMS ARE COMING BACK ONE WAY OR ANOTHER, YEAH?
HOW LONG HAVE YOU GOT...?
SURE SOUNDS LIKE YOU ALREADY HAVE SOME IDEA.
AND YOU'VE BEEN CHANGING THE TOPIC TO AVOID SAYING IT, HAVEN'T YOU?
HOW DID YOU KNOW?
'CAUSE I'M YOUR DAD.

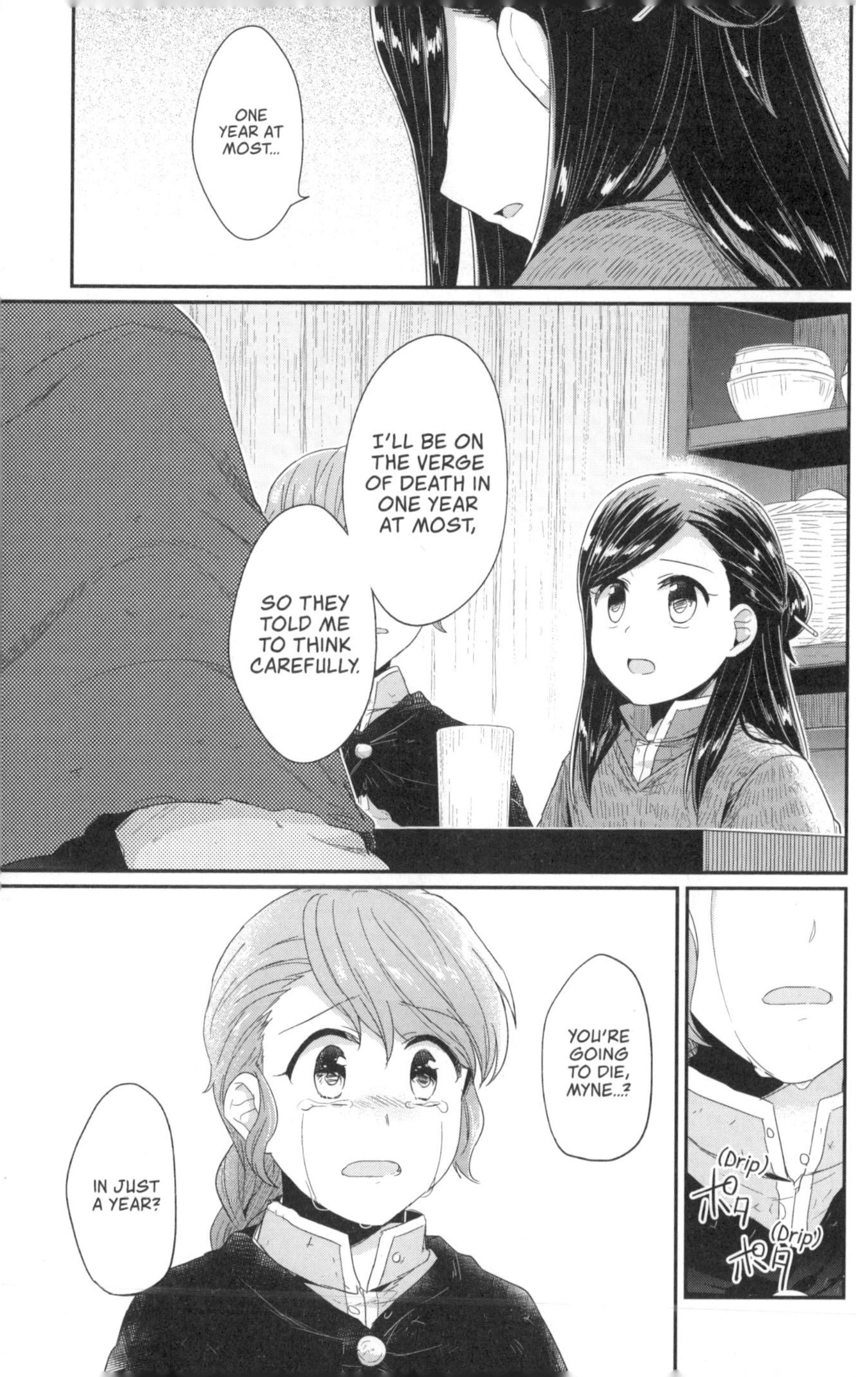
ONE YEAR AT MOST...
I'LL BE ON THE VERGE OF DEATH IN ONE YEAR AT MOST,
SO THEY TOLD ME TO THINK CAREFULLY.
(Drip)
(Drip)
YOU'RE GOING TO DIE, MYNE...?
IN JUST A YEAR?

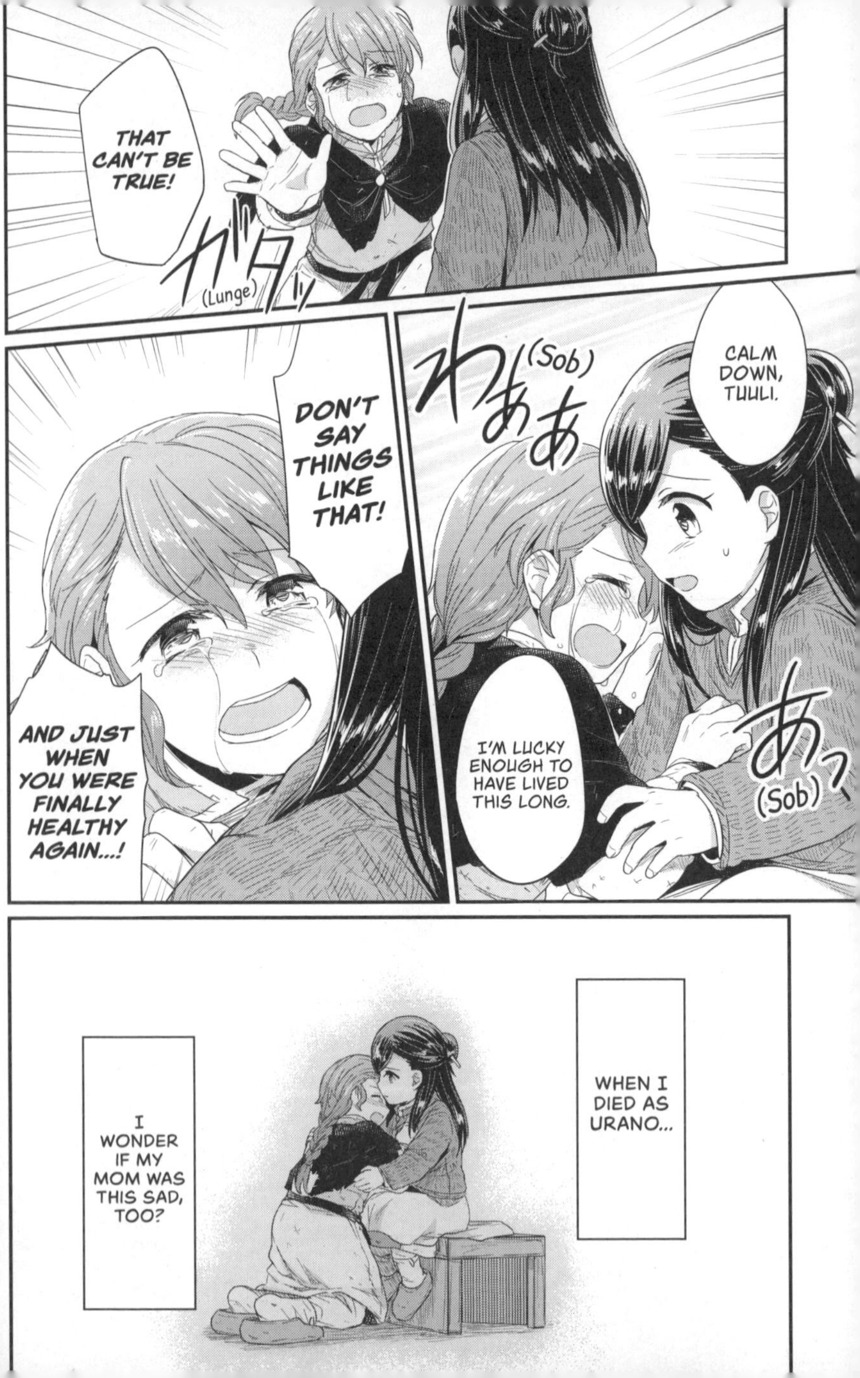
THAT CAN'T BE TRUE!
ガタッ
(Lunge)
わああ
(Sob)
CALM DOWN, TUULI.
I'M LUCKY ENOUGH TO HAVE LIVED THIS LONG.
あっ
(Sob)
DON'T SAY THINGS LIKE THAT!
AND JUST WHEN YOU WERE FINALLY HEALTHY AGAIN...!
WHEN I DIED AS URANO...
I WONDER IF MY MOM WAS THIS SAD, TOO?

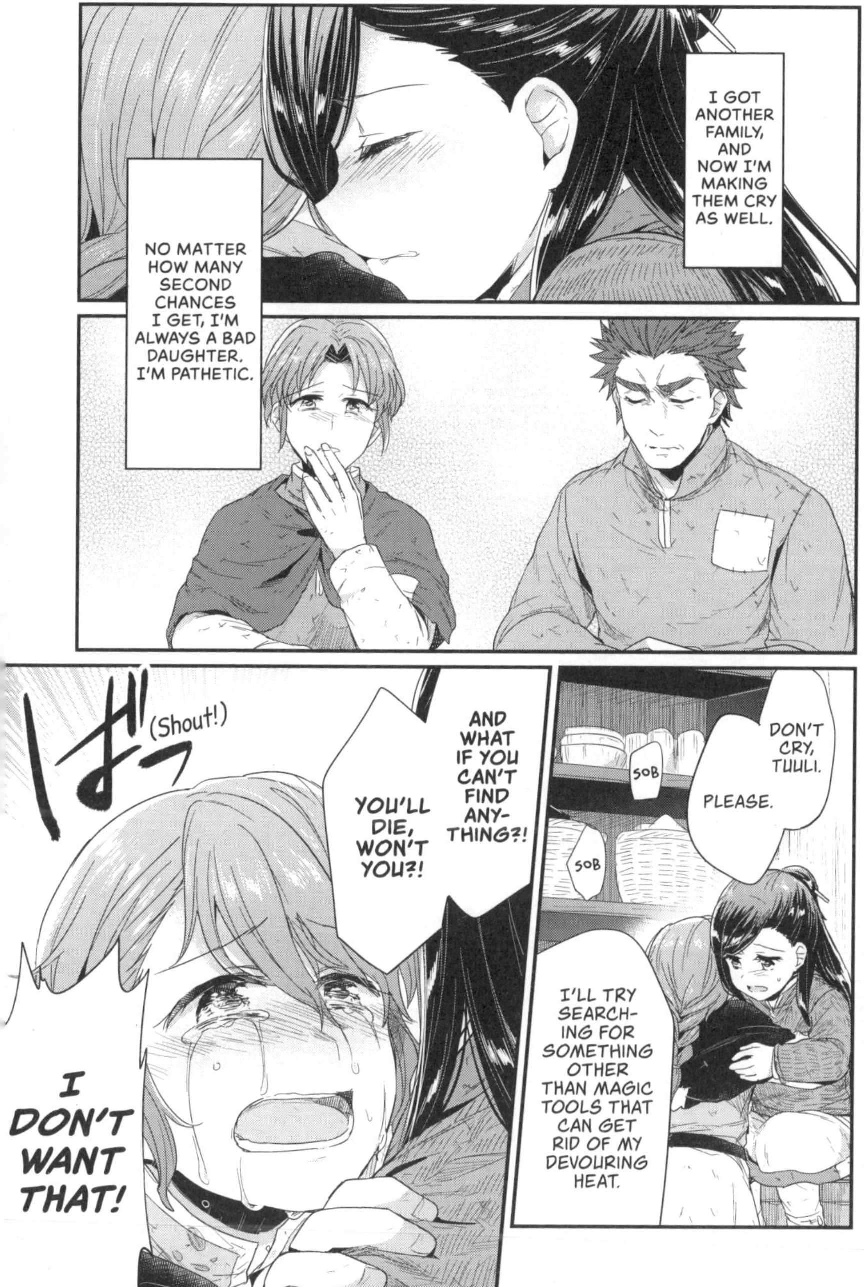
I GOT ANOTHER FAMILY, AND NOW I'M MAKING THEM CRY AS WELL.
NO MATTER HOW MANY SECOND CHANCES I GET, I'M ALWAYS A BAD DAUGHTER. I'M PATHETIC.
DON'T CRY, TUULI.
PLEASE.
SOB
SOB
I'LL TRY SEARCHING FOR SOMETHING OTHER THAN MAGIC TOOLS THAT CAN GET RID OF MY DEVOURING HEAT.
AND WHAT IF YOU CAN'T FIND ANYTHING?!
YOU'LL DIE, WON'T YOU?!
ばっ
(Shout!)
I DON'T WANT THAT!

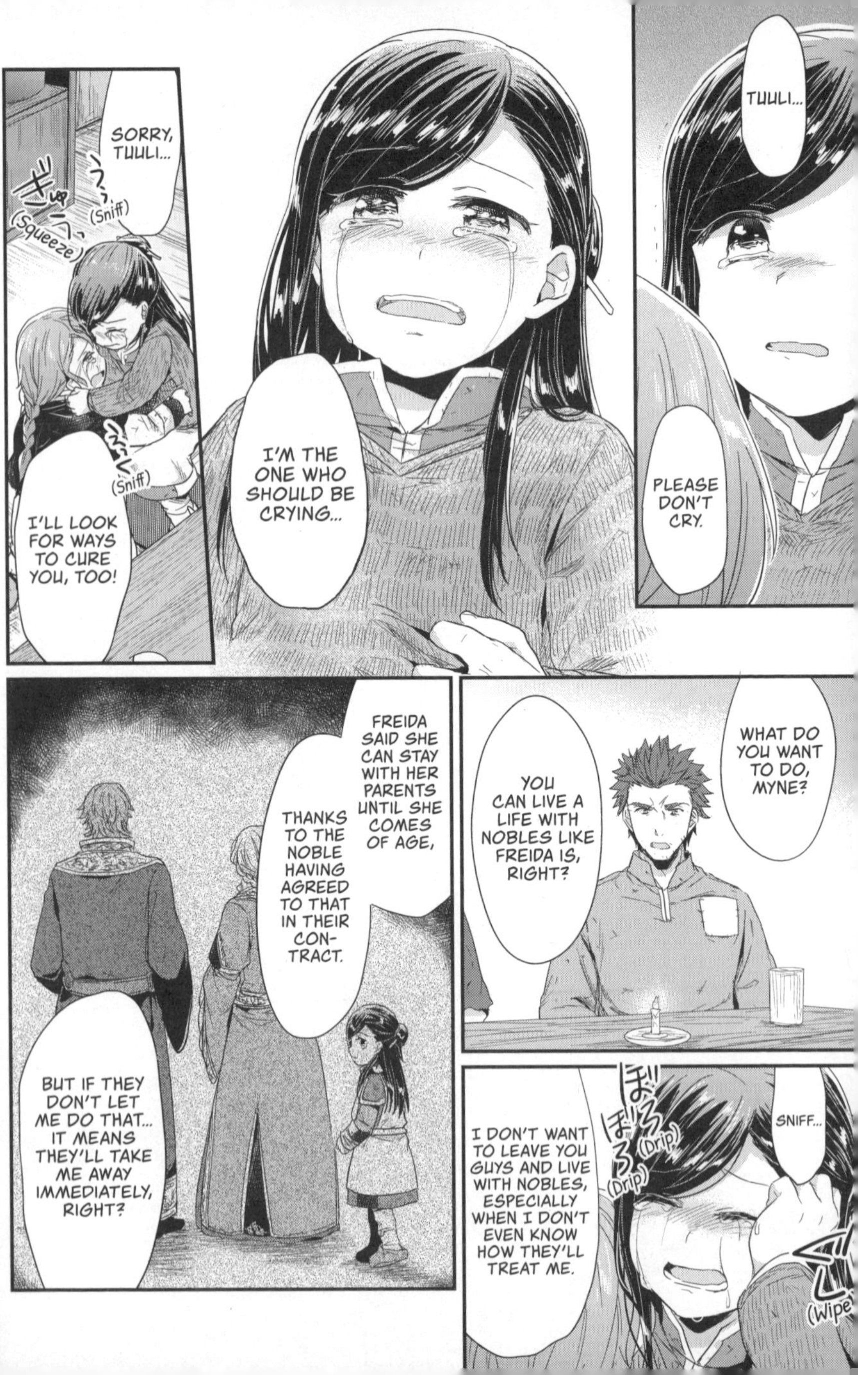
TUULI...
PLEASE DON'T CRY.
I'M THE ONE WHO SHOULD BE CRYING...
SORRY, TUULI...
(Sniff)
(Squeeze)
(Sniff)
I'LL LOOK FOR WAYS TO CURE YOU, TOO!
WHAT DO YOU WANT TO DO, MYNE?
YOU CAN LIVE A LIFE WITH NOBLES LIKE FREIDA IS, RIGHT?
SNIFF...
(Drip)
(Drip)
I DON'T WANT TO LEAVE YOU GUYS AND LIVE WITH NOBLES, ESPECIALLY WHEN I DON'T EVEN KNOW HOW THEY'LL TREAT ME.
(Wipe)
FREIDA SAID SHE CAN STAY WITH HER PARENTS UNTIL SHE COMES OF AGE,
THANKS TO THE NOBLE HAVING AGREED TO THAT IN THEIR CONTRACT.
BUT IF THEY DON'T LET ME DO THAT... IT MEANS THEY'LL TAKE ME AWAY IMMEDIATELY, RIGHT?

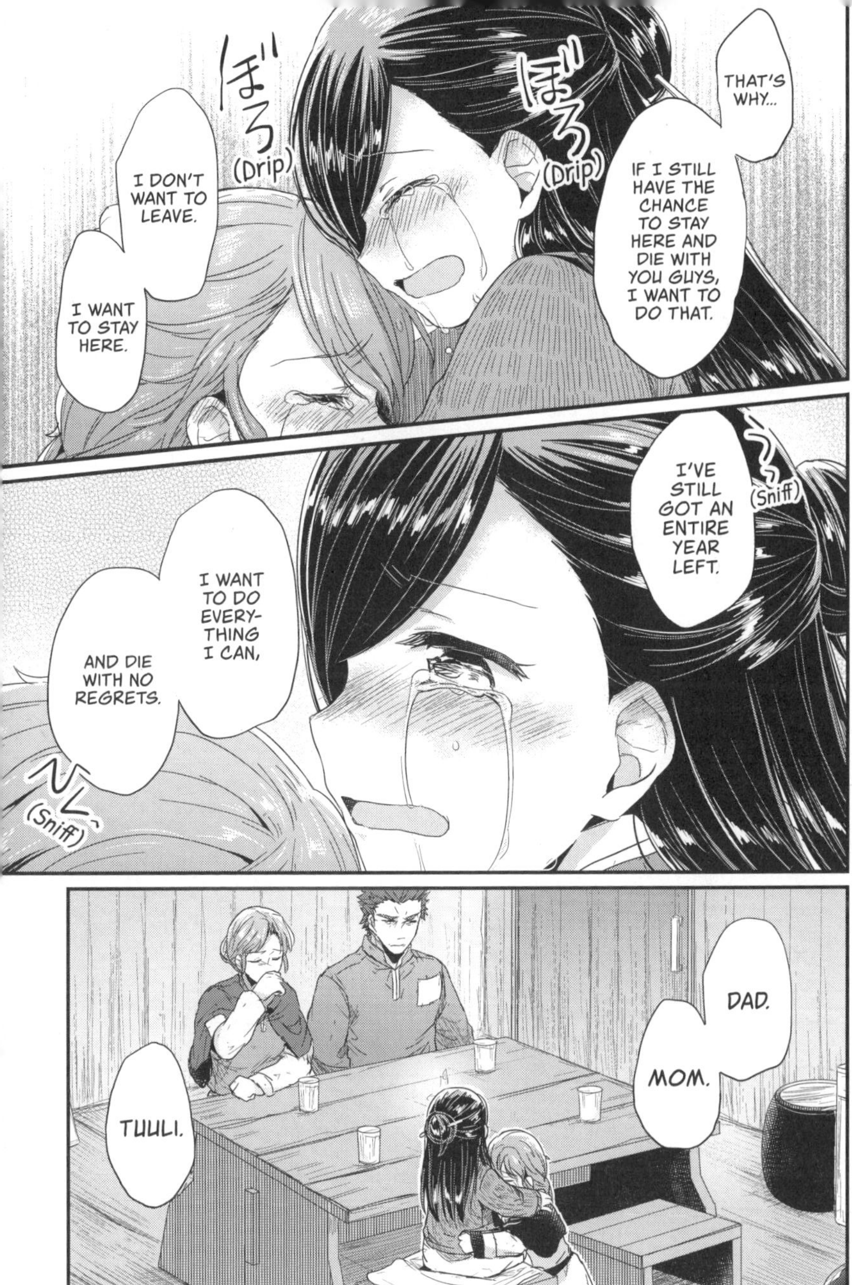
THAT'S WHY...
ぼろ (Drip)
IF I STILL HAVE THE CHANCE TO STAY HERE AND DIE WITH YOU GUYS, I WANT TO DO THAT.
ぼろ (Drip)
I DON'T WANT TO LEAVE.
I WANT TO STAY HERE.
(Sniff)
I'VE STILL GOT AN ENTIRE YEAR LEFT.
I WANT TO DO EVERY-THING I CAN,
AND DIE WITH NO REGRETS.
(Sniff)
DAD.
MOM.
TUULI.

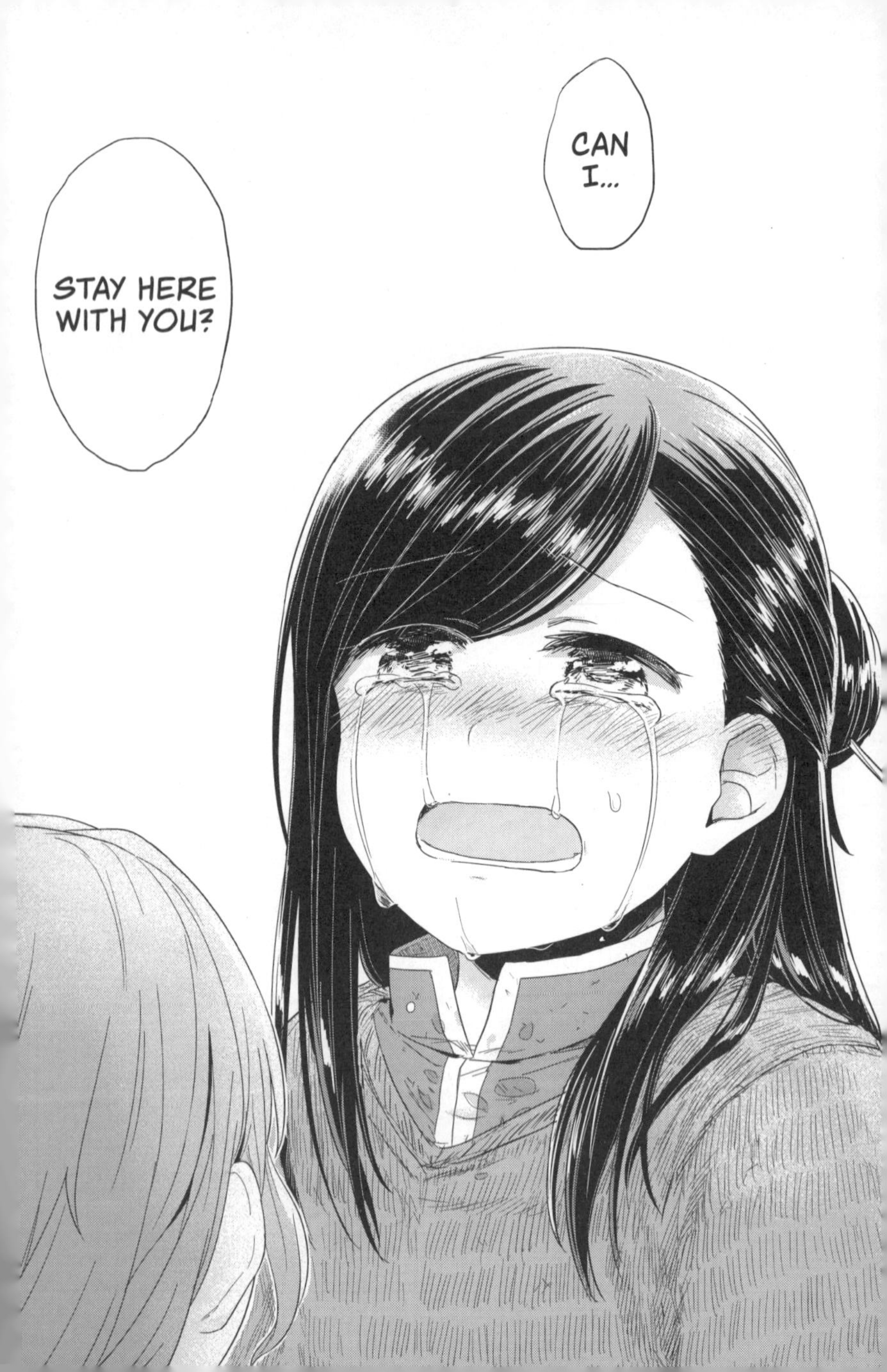
CAN I...
STAY HERE WITH YOU?

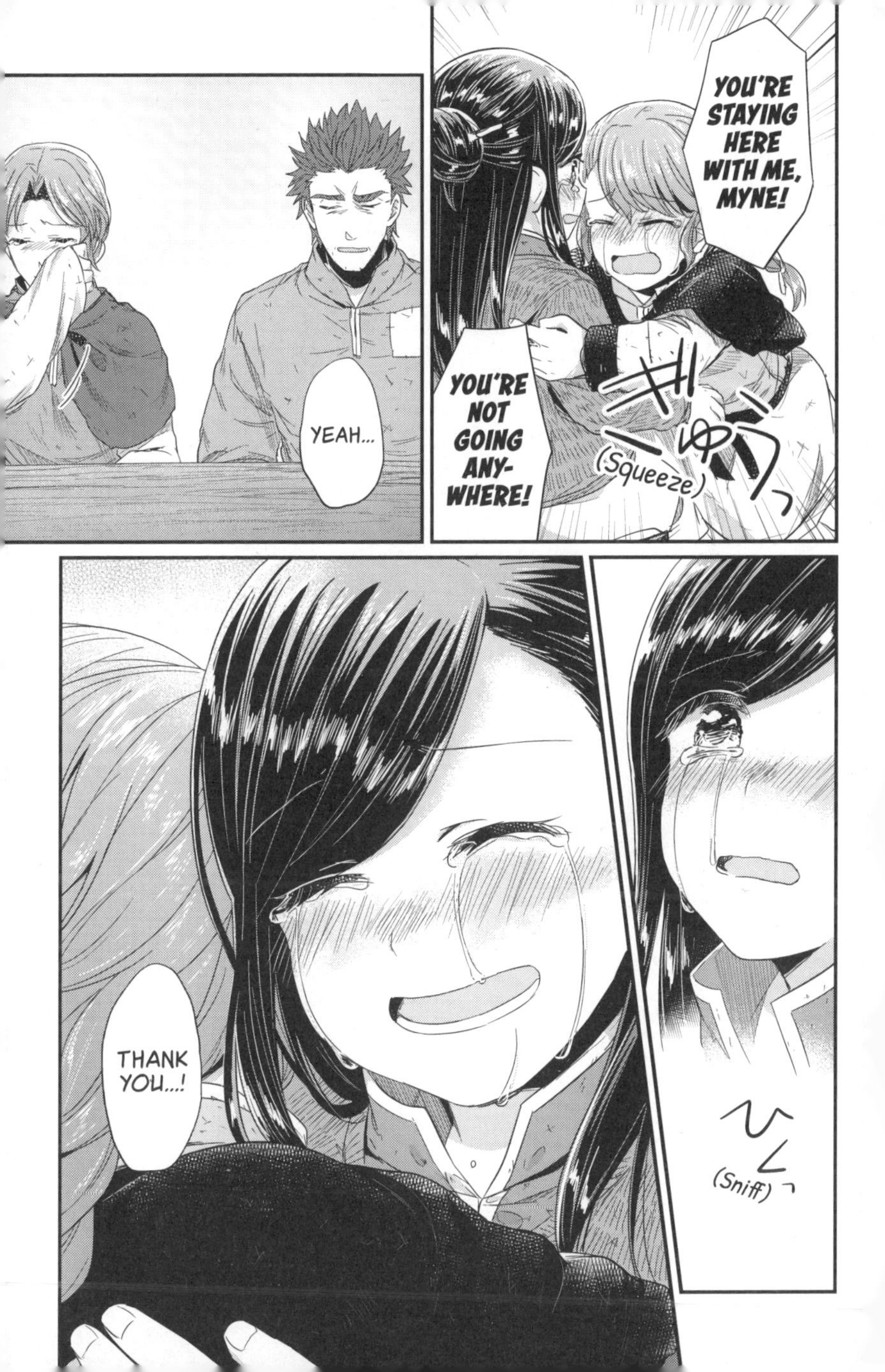
YOU'RE STAYING HERE WITH ME, MYNE!
YOU'RE NOT GOING ANY-WHERE!
(Squeeze)
YEAH...
(Sniff)
THANK YOU...!

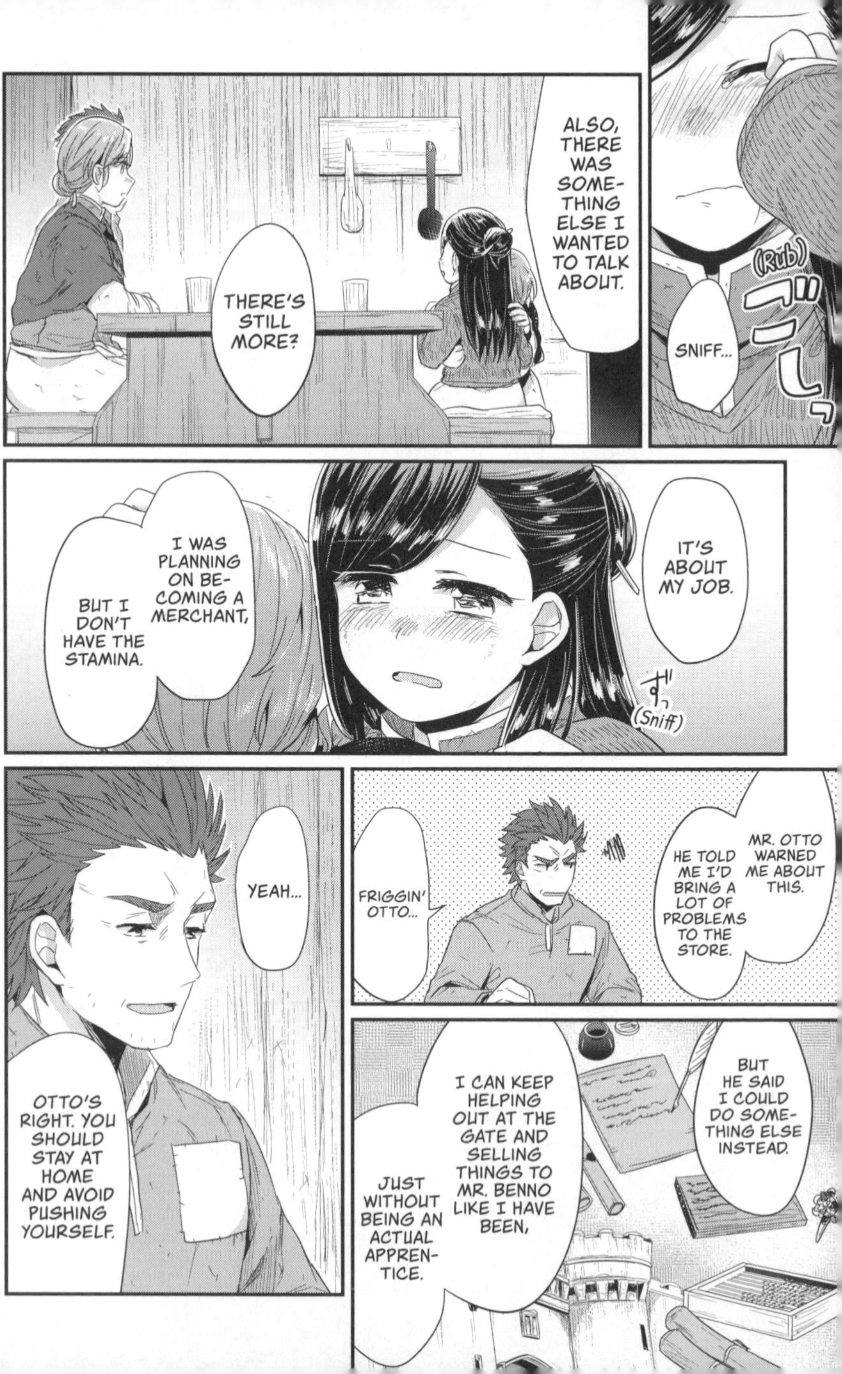
(Rub)
ごしっ
SNIFF...
ALSO, THERE WAS SOME-THING ELSE I WANTED TO TALK ABOUT.
THERE'S STILL MORE?
IT'S ABOUT MY JOB.
ずっ
(Sniff)
I WAS PLANNING ON BE-COMING A MERCHANT,
BUT I DON'T HAVE THE STAMINA.
MR. OTTO WARNED ME ABOUT THIS.
HE TOLD ME I'D BRING A LOT OF PROBLEMS TO THE STORE.
FRIGGIN' OTTO...
BUT HE SAID I COULD DO SOME-THING ELSE INSTEAD.
I CAN KEEP HELPING OUT AT THE GATE AND SELLING THINGS TO MR. BENNO LIKE I HAVE BEEN,
JUST WITHOUT BEING AN ACTUAL APPREN-TICE.
YEAH...
OTTO'S RIGHT. YOU SHOULD STAY AT HOME AND AVOID PUSHING YOURSELF.

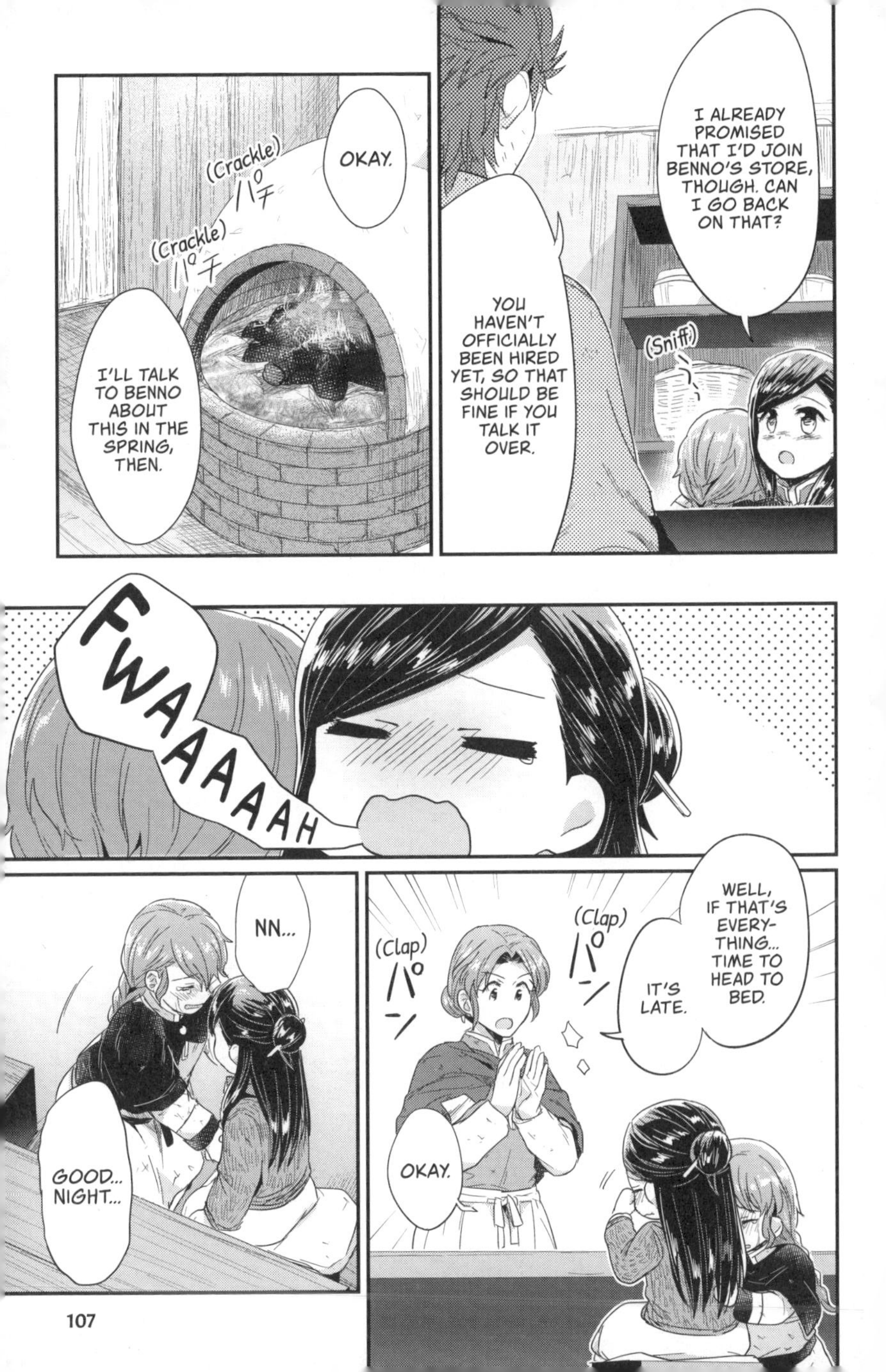
I ALREADY PROMISED THAT I'D JOIN BENNO'S STORE, THOUGH. CAN I GO BACK ON THAT?
(Sniff)
YOU HAVEN'T OFFICIALLY BEEN HIRED YET, SO THAT SHOULD BE FINE IF YOU TALK IT OVER.
OKAY.
(Crackle)
(Crackle)
I'LL TALK TO BENNO ABOUT THIS IN THE SPRING, THEN.
FWAAAAAAH
WELL, IF THAT'S EVERY-THING... TIME TO HEAD TO BED.
(Clap)
IT'S LATE.
(Clap)
OKAY.
NN...
GOOD... NIGHT...

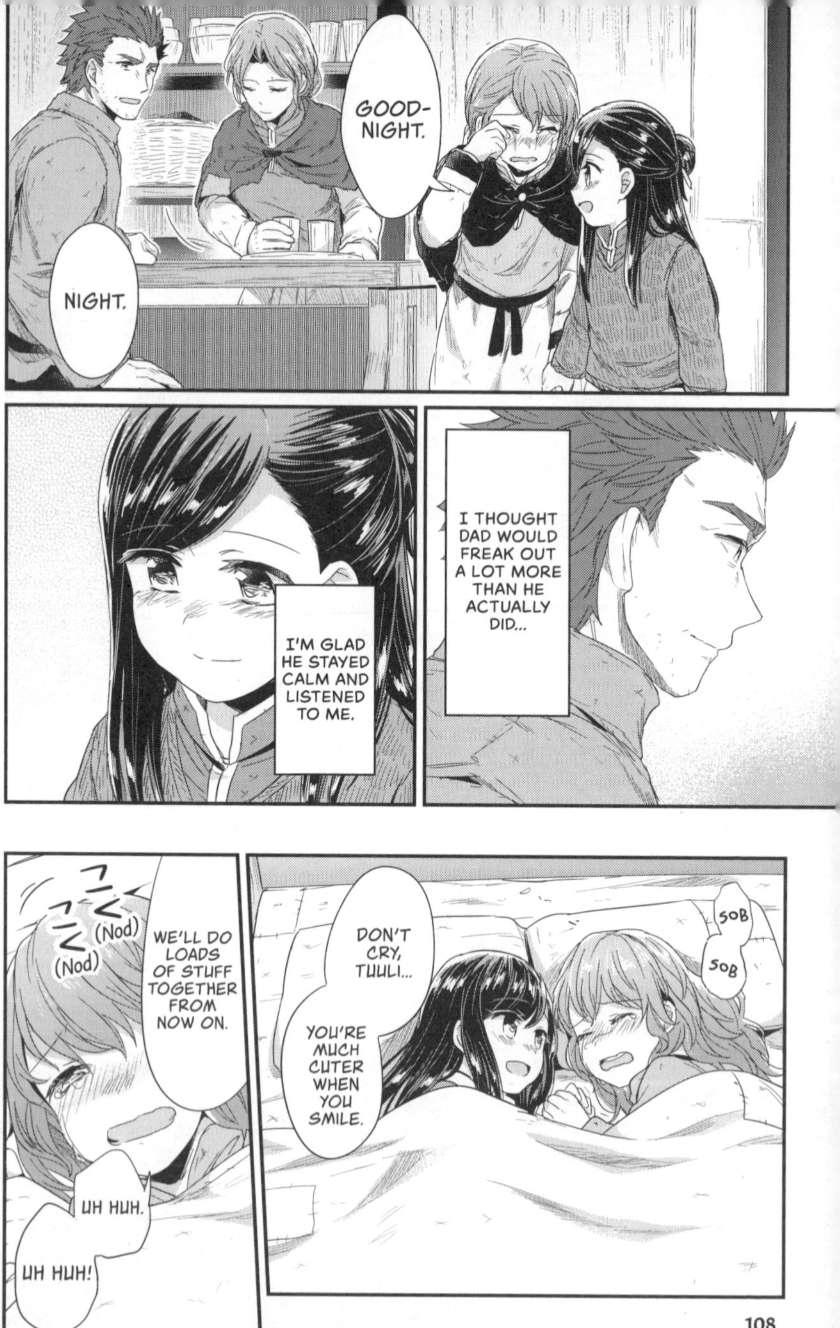
GOOD-NIGHT.
NIGHT.
I THOUGHT DAD WOULD FREAK OUT A LOT MORE THAN HE ACTUALLY DID...
I'M GLAD HE STAYED CALM AND LISTENED TO ME.
SOB
SOB
DON'T CRY, TUULI...
YOU'RE MUCH CUTER WHEN YOU SMILE.
WE'LL DO LOADS OF STUFF TOGETHER FROM NOW ON.
(Nod)
(Nod)
UH HUH.
UH HUH!

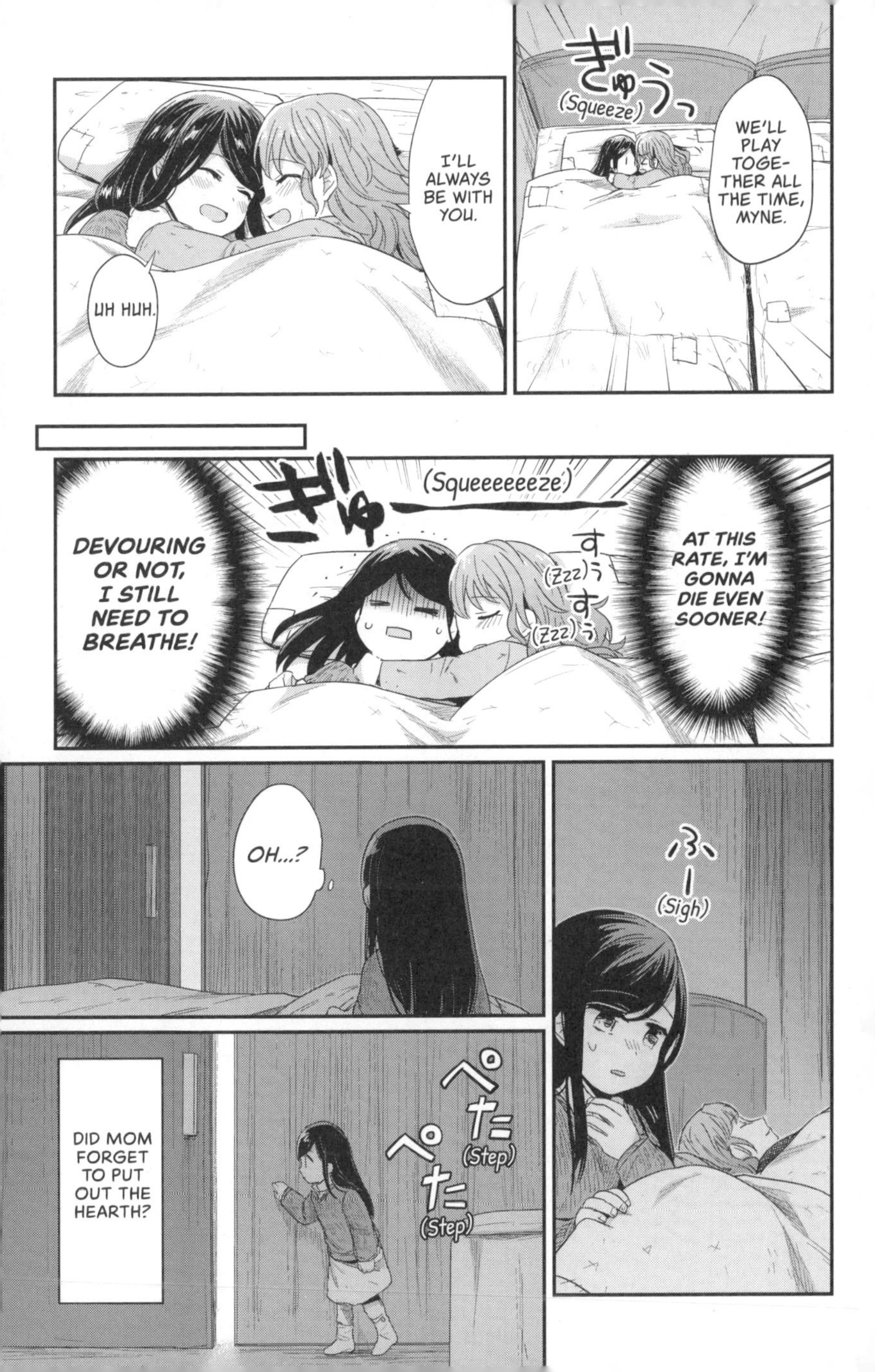

ぎゅうっ
(Squeeze)
WE'LL PLAY TOGETHER ALL THE TIME, MYNE.
I'LL ALWAYS BE WITH YOU.
UH HUH.
AT THIS RATE, I'M GONNA DIE EVEN SOONER!
ぎゅー
(Squeeeeeeeze)
すぅ (Zzz)
すぅ (Zzz)
DEVOURING OR NOT, I STILL NEED TO BREATHE!
ふー
(Sigh)
OH...?
ぺた (Step)
ぺた (Step)
DID MOM FORGET TO PUT OUT THE HEARTH?

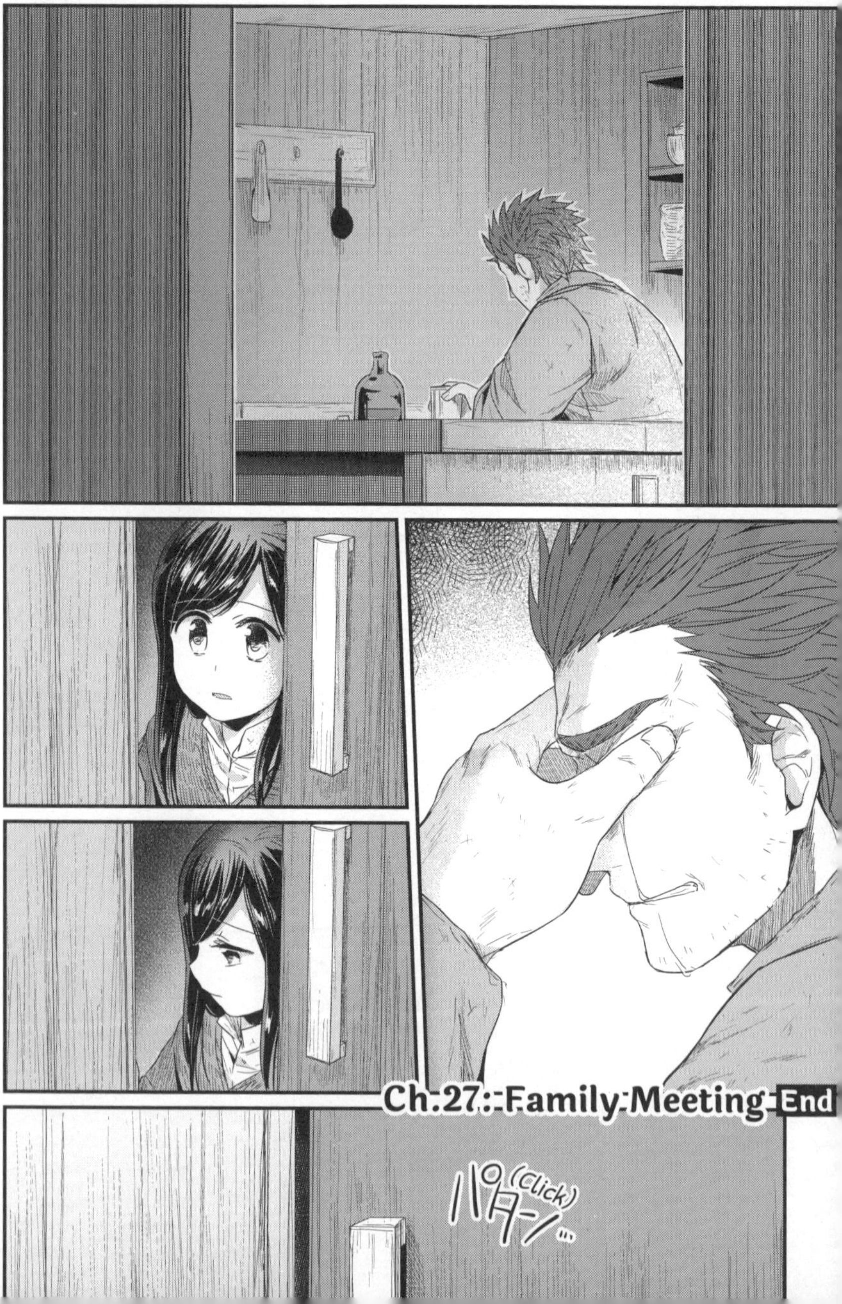
Ch.27: Family Meeting End
パタン…
(Click)

Ch.28 Resuming Paper-Making

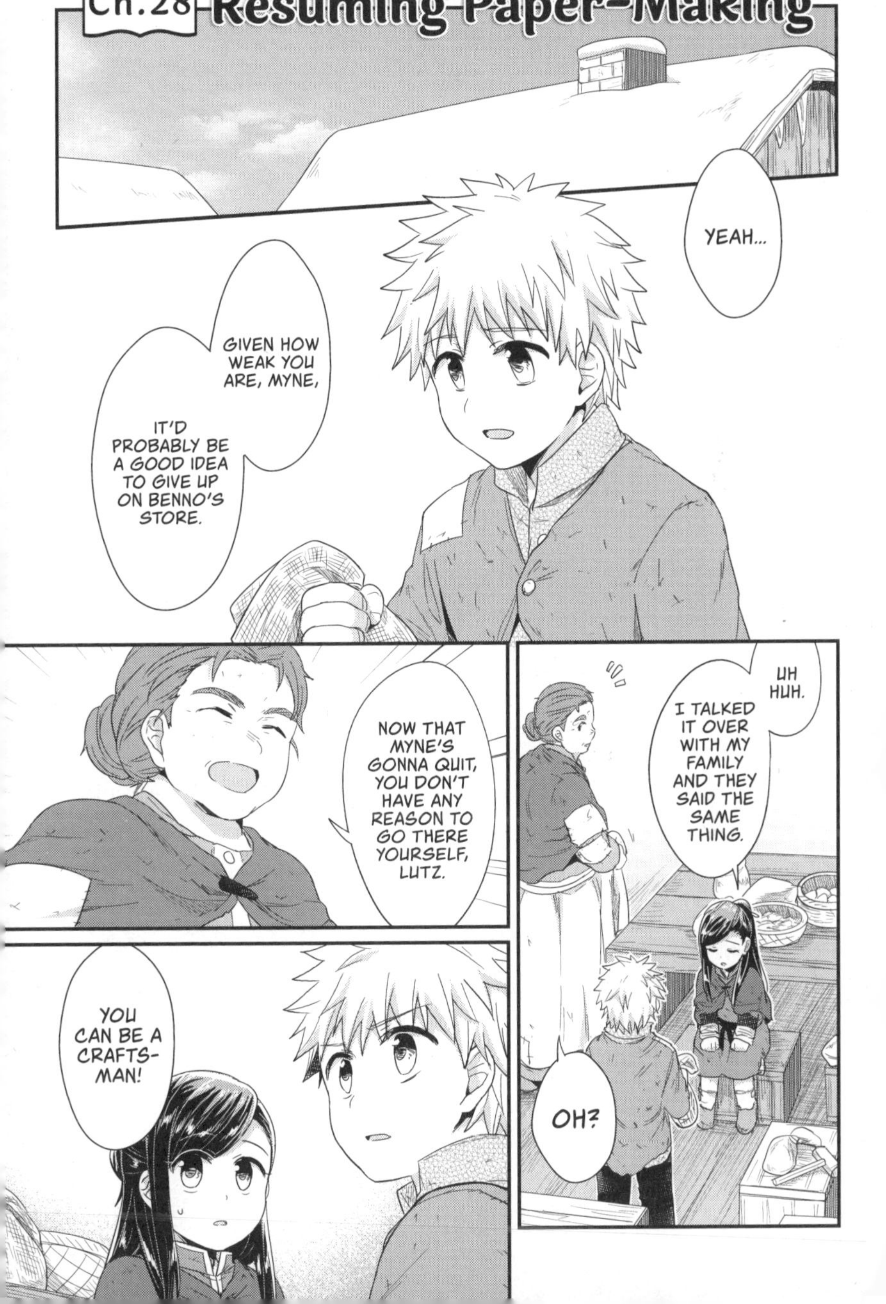
YEAH...
GIVEN HOW WEAK YOU ARE, MYNE,
IT'D PROBABLY BE A GOOD IDEA TO GIVE UP ON BENNO'S STORE.
UH HUH. I TALKED IT OVER WITH MY FAMILY AND THEY SAID THE SAME THING.
OH?
NOW THAT MYNE'S GONNA QUIT, YOU DON'T HAVE ANY REASON TO GO THERE YOURSELF, LUTZ.
YOU CAN BE A CRAFTS-MAN!

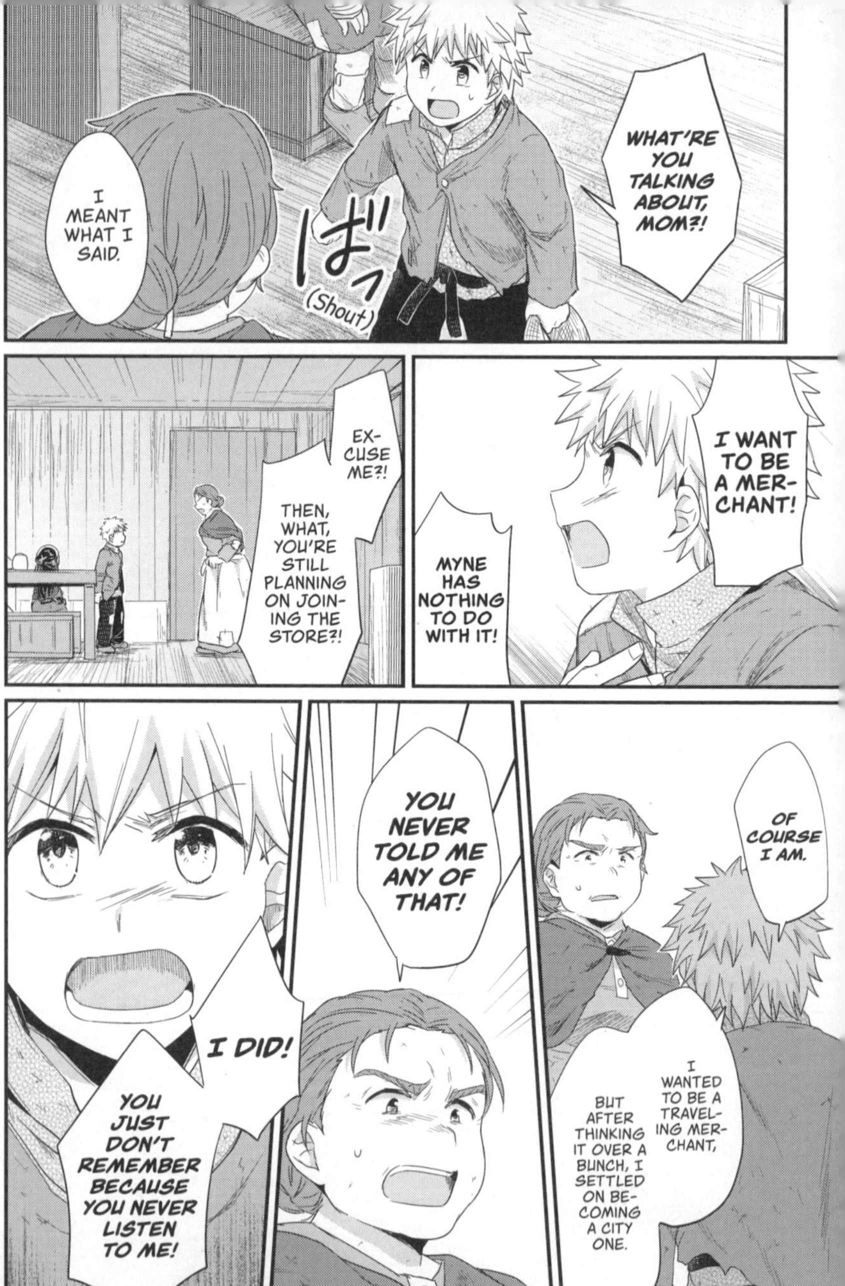
WHAT'RE YOU TALKING ABOUT, MOM?!
ばっ
(Shout)
I MEANT WHAT I SAID.
I WANT TO BE A MERCHANT!
MYNE HAS NOTHING TO DO WITH IT!
EXCUSE ME?!
THEN, WHAT, YOU'RE STILL PLANNING ON JOINING THE STORE?!
OF COURSE I AM.
I WANTED TO BE A TRAVELING MERCHANT,
BUT AFTER THINKING IT OVER A BUNCH, I SETTLED ON BECOMING A CITY ONE.
YOU NEVER TOLD ME ANY OF THAT!
I DID!
YOU JUST DON'T REMEMBER BECAUSE YOU NEVER LISTEN TO ME!

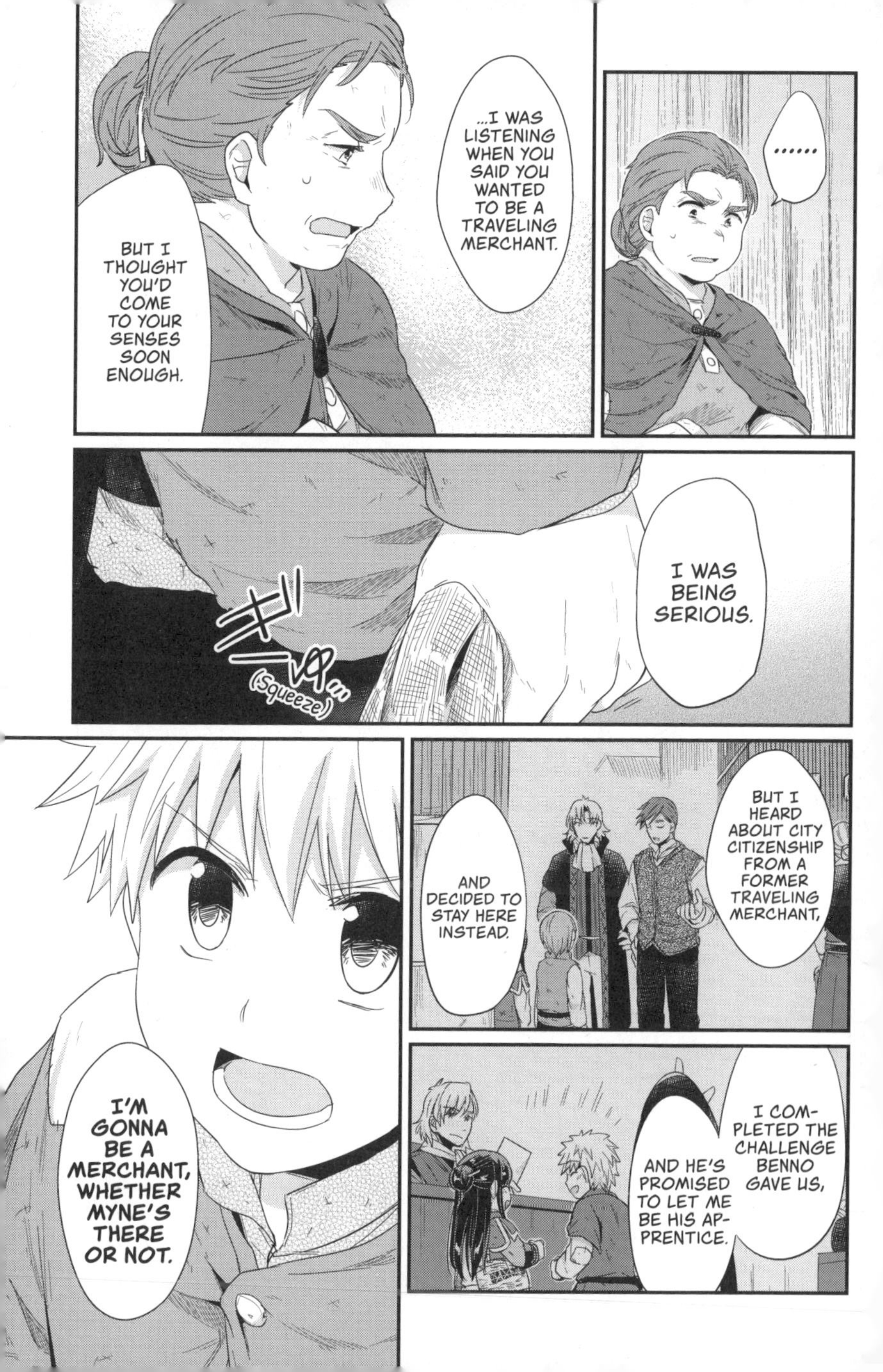
......
...I WAS LISTENING WHEN YOU SAID YOU WANTED TO BE A TRAVELING MERCHANT.
BUT I THOUGHT YOU'D COME TO YOUR SENSES SOON ENOUGH.
I WAS BEING SERIOUS.
(Squeeze)
BUT I HEARD ABOUT CITY CITIZENSHIP FROM A FORMER TRAVELING MERCHANT,
AND DECIDED TO STAY HERE INSTEAD.
I COM-PLETED THE CHALLENGE BENNO GAVE US,
AND HE'S PROMISED TO LET ME BE HIS AP-PRENTICE.
I'M GONNA BE A MERCHANT, WHETHER MYNE'S THERE OR NOT.

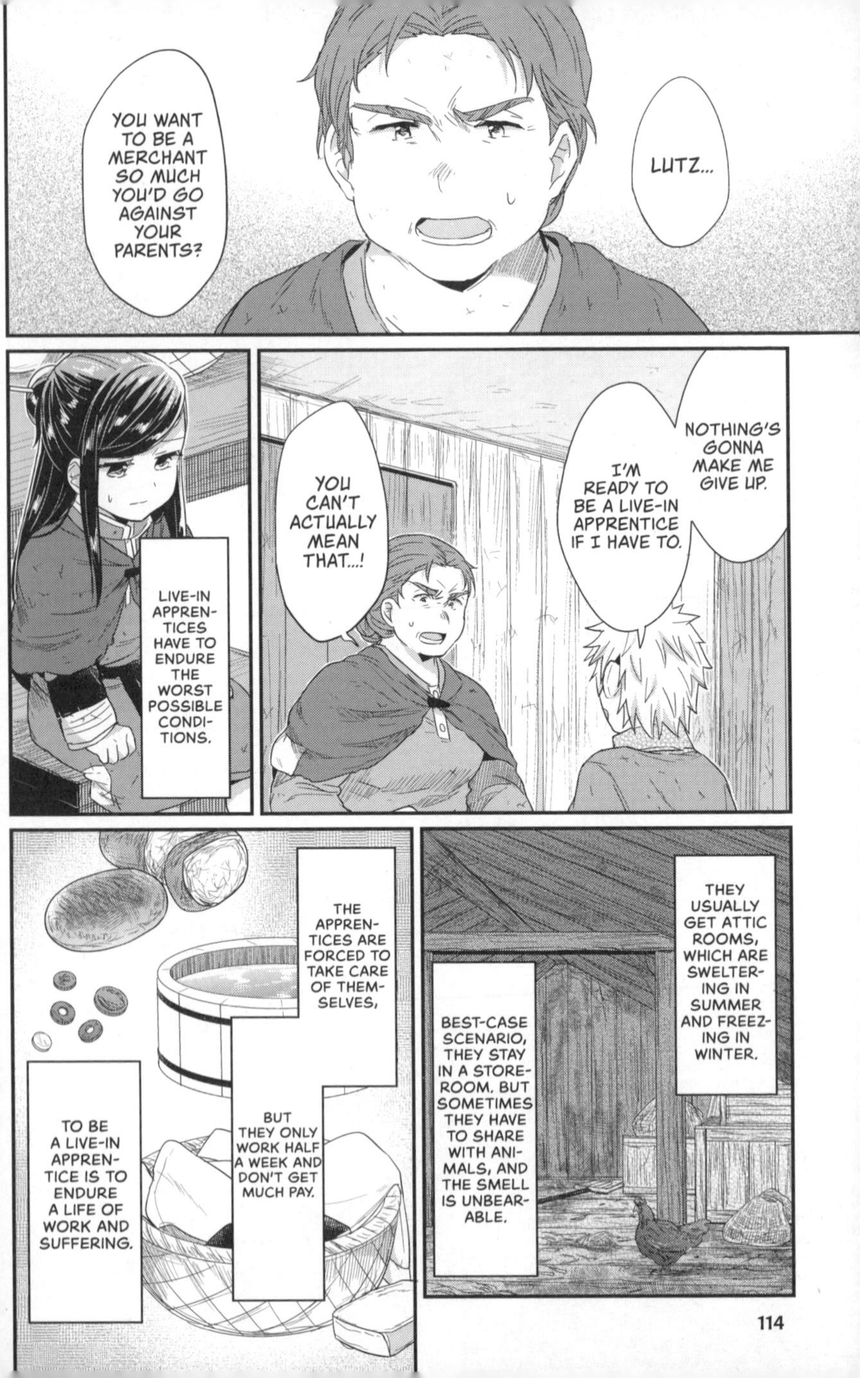
LUTZ...
YOU WANT TO BE A MERCHANT SO MUCH YOU'D GO AGAINST YOUR PARENTS?
NOTHING'S GONNA MAKE ME GIVE UP.
I'M READY TO BE A LIVE-IN APPRENTICE IF I HAVE TO.
YOU CAN'T ACTUALLY MEAN THAT...!
LIVE-IN APPREN-TICES HAVE TO ENDURE THE WORST POSSIBLE CONDI-TIONS.
THEY USUALLY GET ATTIC ROOMS, WHICH ARE SWELTER-ING IN SUMMER AND FREEZ-ING IN WINTER.
BEST-CASE SCENARIO, THEY STAY IN A STORE-ROOM. BUT SOMETIMES THEY HAVE TO SHARE WITH ANI-MALS, AND THE SMELL IS UNBEAR-ABLE.
THE APPREN-TICES ARE FORCED TO TAKE CARE OF THEM-SELVES,
BUT THEY ONLY WORK HALF A WEEK AND DON'T GET MUCH PAY.
TO BE A LIVE-IN APPREN-TICE IS TO ENDURE A LIFE OF WORK AND SUFFERING.

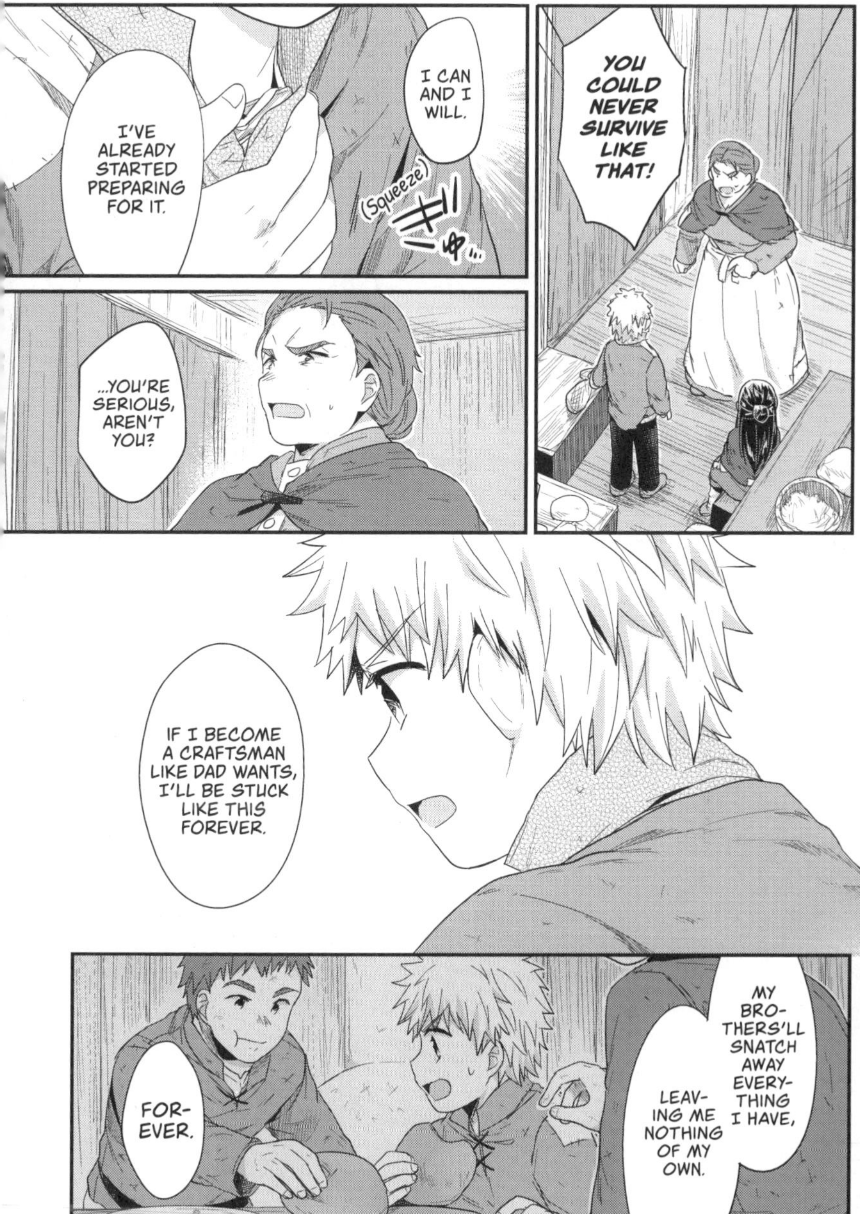
YOU COULD NEVER SURVIVE LIKE THAT!
I CAN AND I WILL.
(Squeeze)
I'VE ALREADY STARTED PREPARING FOR IT.
...YOU'RE SERIOUS, AREN'T YOU?
IF I BECOME A CRAFTSMAN LIKE DAD WANTS, I'LL BE STUCK LIKE THIS FOREVER.
MY BROTHERS'LL SNATCH AWAY EVERYTHING I HAVE,
LEAVING ME NOTHING OF MY OWN.
FOREVER.

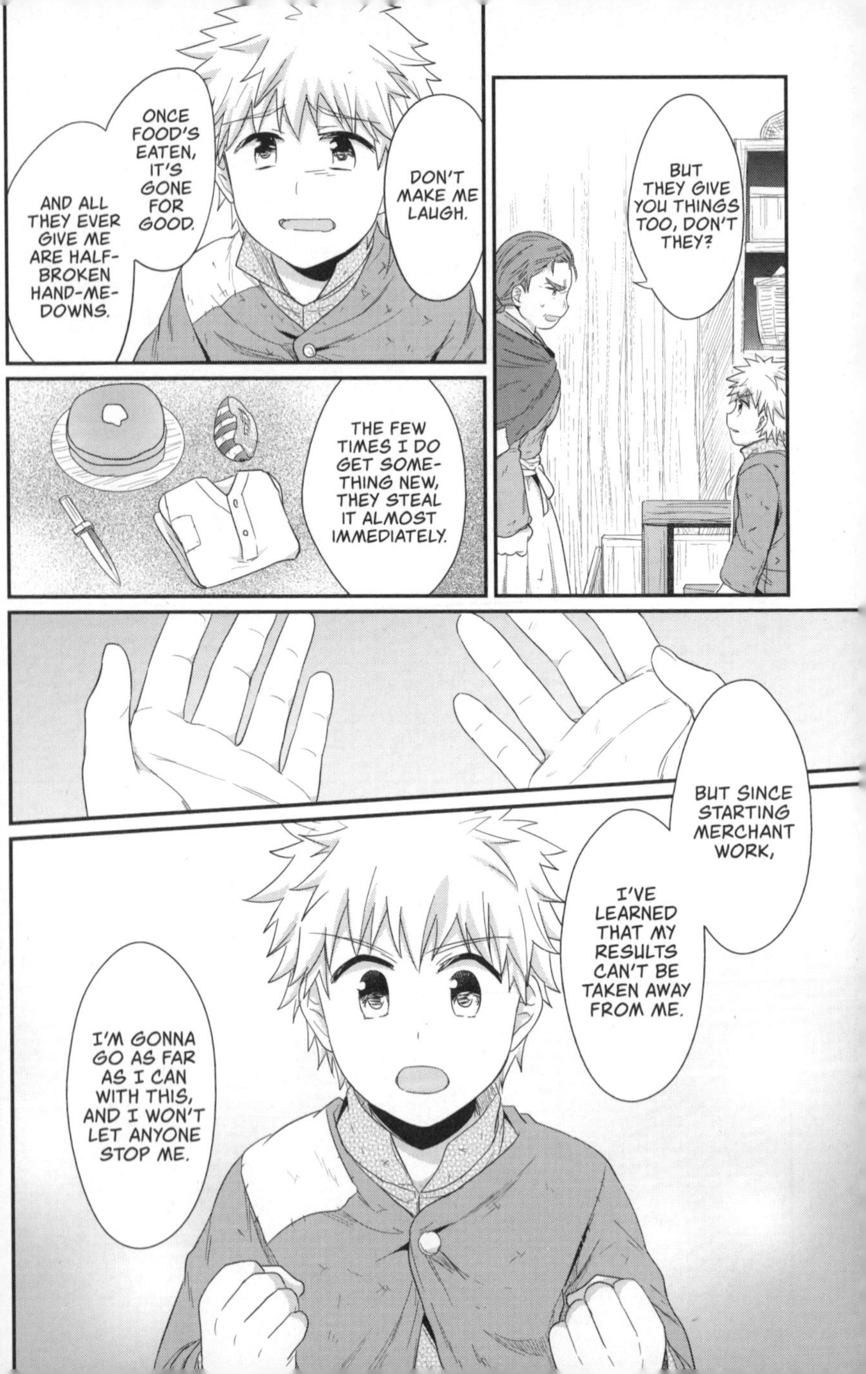
BUT THEY GIVE YOU THINGS TOO, DON'T THEY?
DON'T MAKE ME LAUGH.
ONCE FOOD'S EATEN, IT'S GONE FOR GOOD.
AND ALL THEY EVER GIVE ME ARE HALF-BROKEN HAND-ME-DOWNS.
THE FEW TIMES I DO GET SOME-THING NEW, THEY STEAL IT ALMOST IMMEDIATELY.
BUT SINCE STARTING MERCHANT WORK,
I'VE LEARNED THAT MY RESULTS CAN'T BE TAKEN AWAY FROM ME.
I'M GONNA GO AS FAR AS I CAN WITH THIS, AND I WON'T LET ANYONE STOP ME.

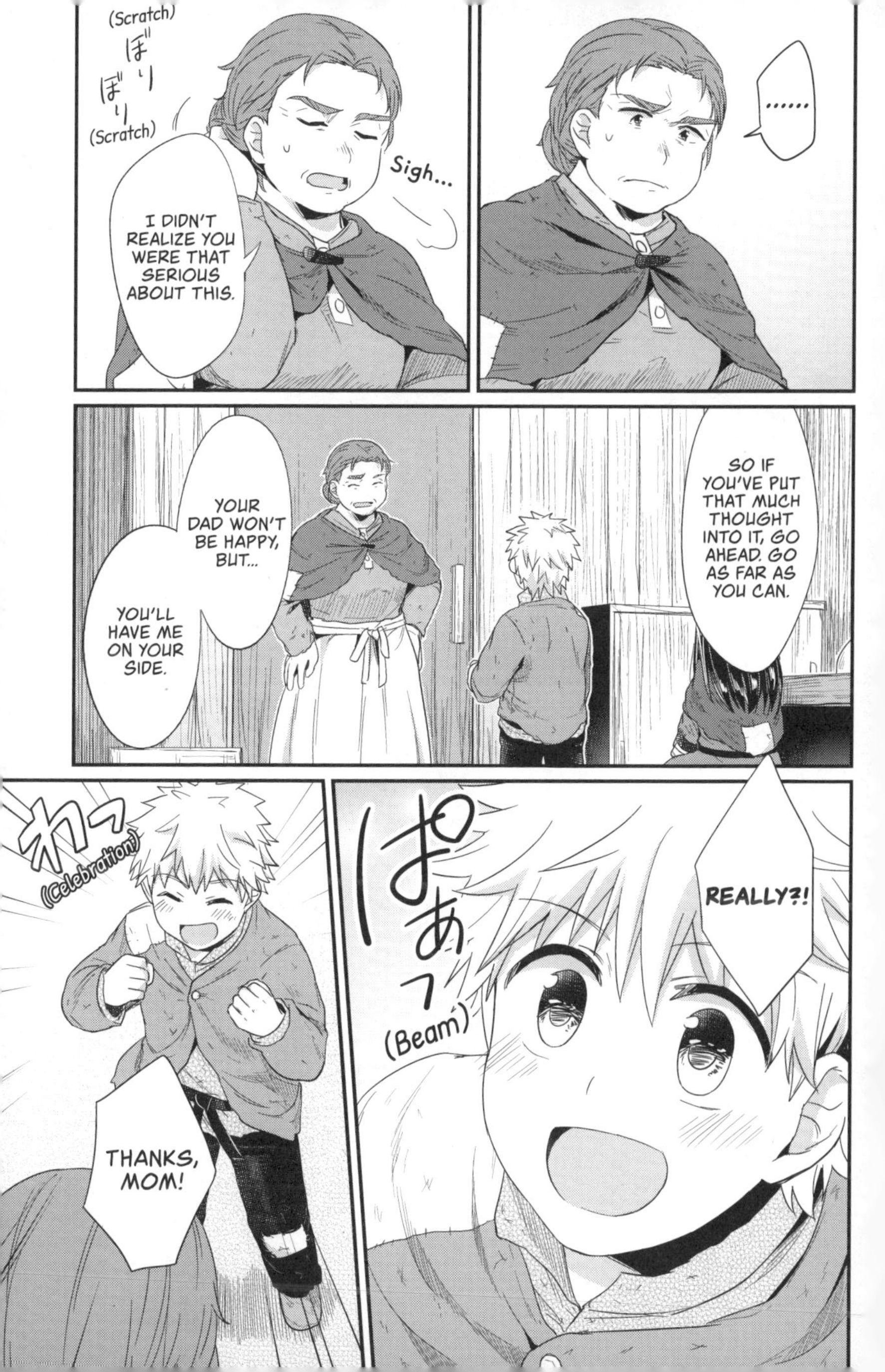
......
ぼり
(Scratch)
ぼり
(Scratch)
Sigh...
I DIDN'T REALIZE YOU WERE THAT SERIOUS ABOUT THIS.
SO IF YOU'VE PUT THAT MUCH THOUGHT INTO IT, GO AHEAD. GO AS FAR AS YOU CAN.
YOUR DAD WON'T BE HAPPY, BUT...
YOU'LL HAVE ME ON YOUR SIDE.
REALLY?!
ぱあっ
(Beam)
わっ
(Celebration)
THANKS, MOM!

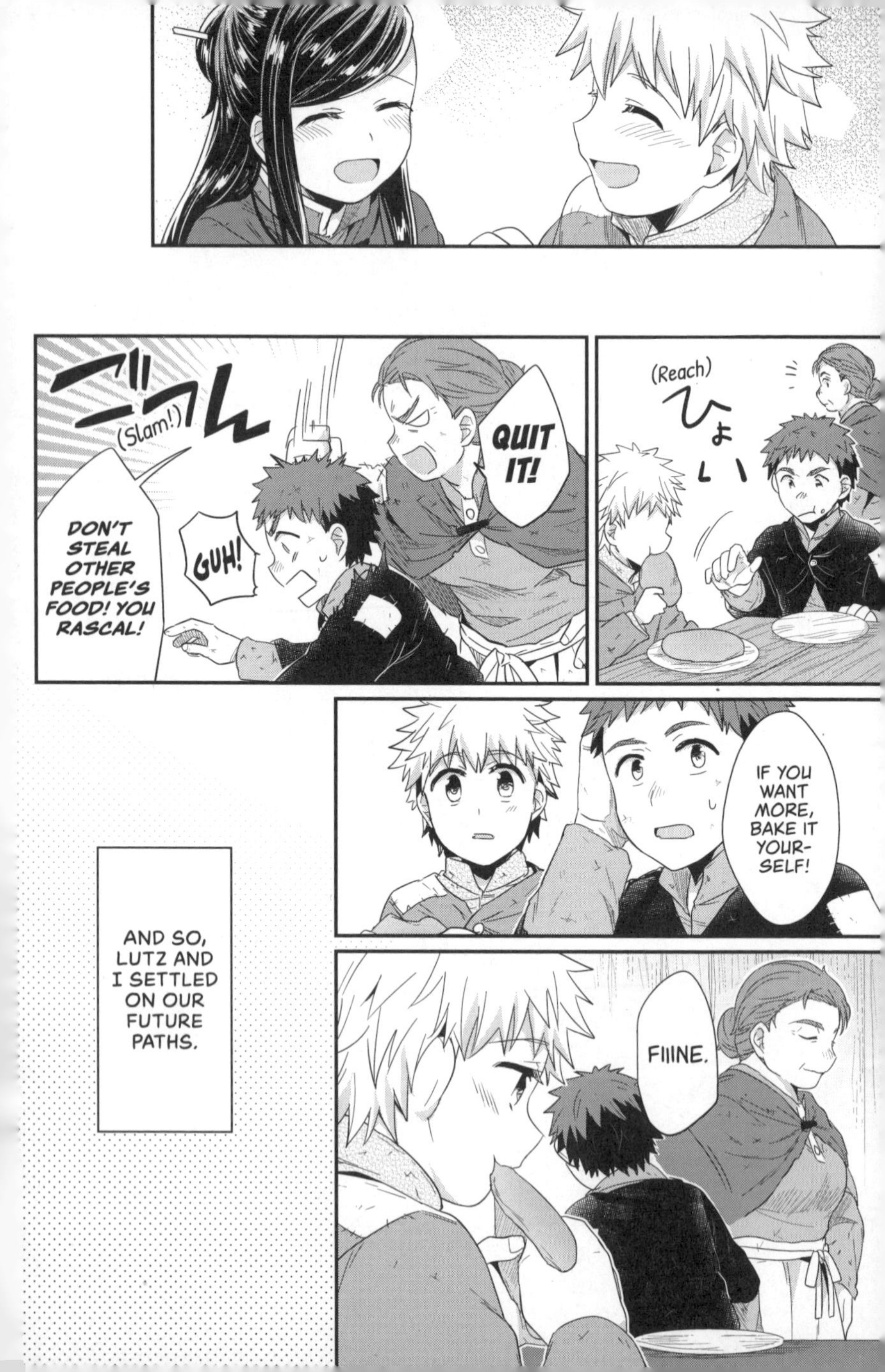
(Reach)
ひょい
QUIT IT!
(Slam!)
ゴツん
GUH!
DON'T STEAL OTHER PEOPLE'S FOOD! YOU RASCAL!
IF YOU WANT MORE, BAKE IT YOUR-SELF!
FIIINE.
AND SO, LUTZ AND I SETTLED ON OUR FUTURE PATHS.

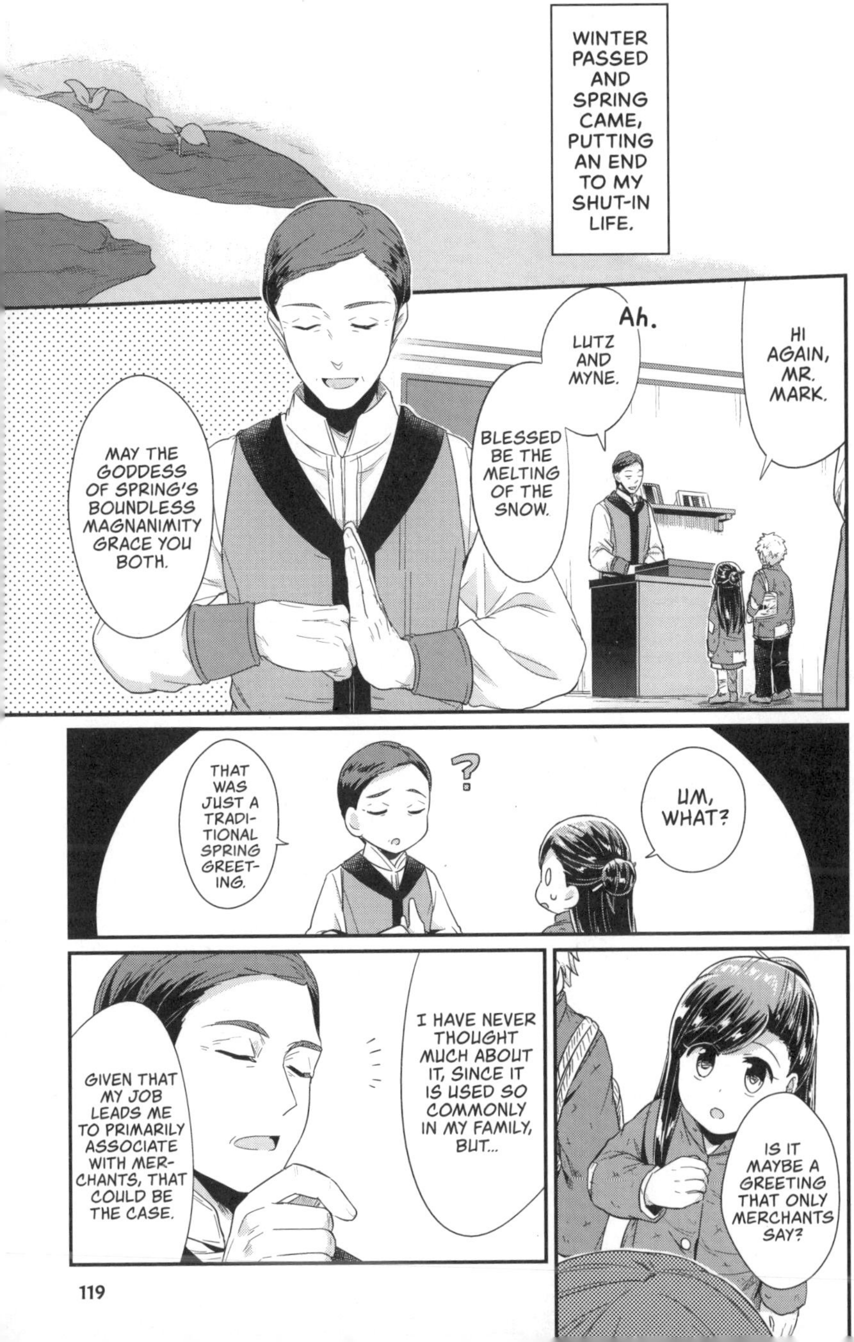
WINTER PASSED AND SPRING CAME, PUTTING AN END TO MY SHUT-IN LIFE.
HI AGAIN, MR. MARK.
Ah.
LUTZ AND MYNE.
BLESSED BE THE MELTING OF THE SNOW.
MAY THE GODDESS OF SPRING'S BOUNDLESS MAGNANIMITY GRACE YOU BOTH.
UM, WHAT?
?
THAT WAS JUST A TRADI-TIONAL SPRING GREET-ING.
IS IT MAYBE A GREETING THAT ONLY MERCHANTS SAY?
I HAVE NEVER THOUGHT MUCH ABOUT IT, SINCE IT IS USED SO COMMONLY IN MY FAMILY, BUT...
GIVEN THAT MY JOB LEADS ME TO PRIMARILY ASSOCIATE WITH MER-CHANTS, THAT COULD BE THE CASE.

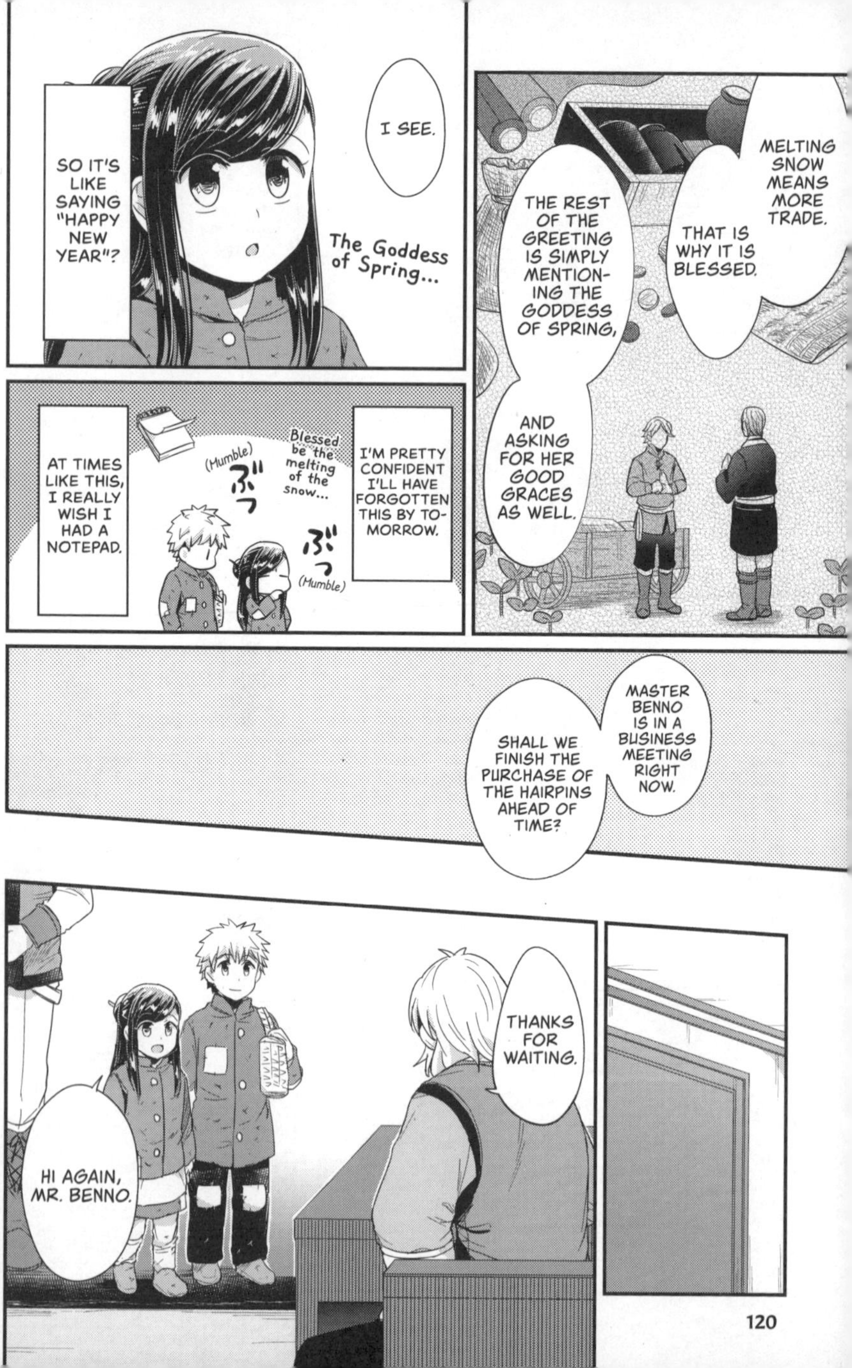
MELTING SNOW MEANS MORE TRADE.
THAT IS WHY IT IS BLESSED.
THE REST OF THE GREETING IS SIMPLY MENTIONING THE GODDESS OF SPRING,
AND ASKING FOR HER GOOD GRACES AS WELL.
I SEE.
The Goddess of Spring...
SO IT'S LIKE SAYING "HAPPY NEW YEAR"?
I'M PRETTY CONFIDENT I'LL HAVE FORGOTTEN THIS BY TO-MORROW.
ぶつ
(Humble)
Blessed be the melting of the snow...
ぶつ
(Humble)
AT TIMES LIKE THIS, I REALLY WISH I HAD A NOTEPAD.
MASTER BENNO IS IN A BUSINESS MEETING RIGHT NOW.
SHALL WE FINISH THE PURCHASE OF THE HAIRPINS AHEAD OF TIME?
THANKS FOR WAITING.
HI AGAIN, MR. BENNO.

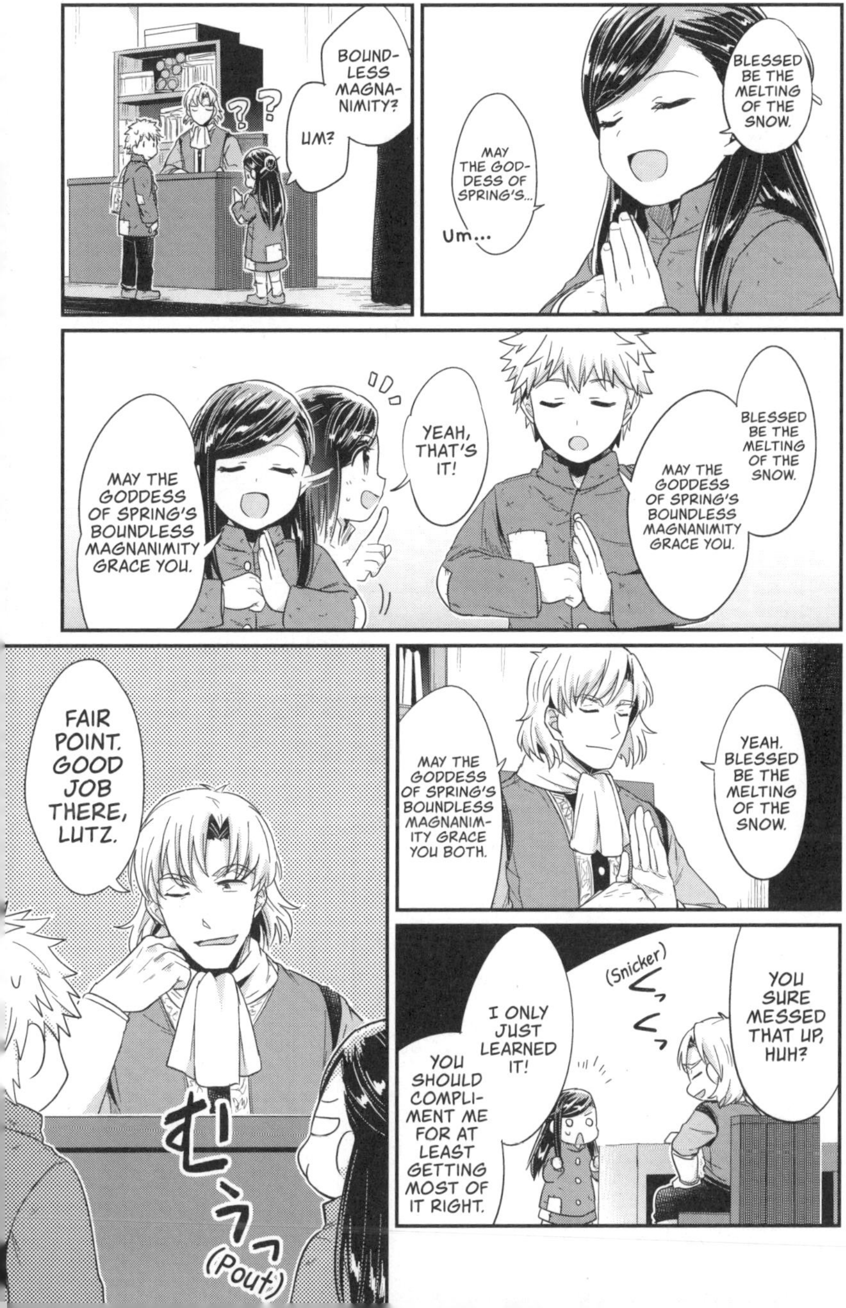
BLESSED BE THE MELTING OF THE SNOW.
MAY THE GODDESS OF SPRING'S...
Um...
BOUNDLESS MAGNANIMITY?
UM?
BLESSED BE THE MELTING OF THE SNOW.
MAY THE GODDESS OF SPRING'S BOUNDLESS MAGNANIMITY GRACE YOU.
YEAH, THAT'S IT!
MAY THE GODDESS OF SPRING'S BOUNDLESS MAGNANIMITY GRACE YOU.
YEAH. BLESSED BE THE MELTING OF THE SNOW.
MAY THE GODDESS OF SPRING'S BOUNDLESS MAGNANIMITY GRACE YOU BOTH.
YOU SURE MESSED THAT UP, HUH?
(Snicker)
I ONLY JUST LEARNED IT!
YOU SHOULD COMPLIMENT ME FOR AT LEAST GETTING MOST OF IT RIGHT.
FAIR POINT. GOOD JOB THERE, LUTZ.
(Pout)

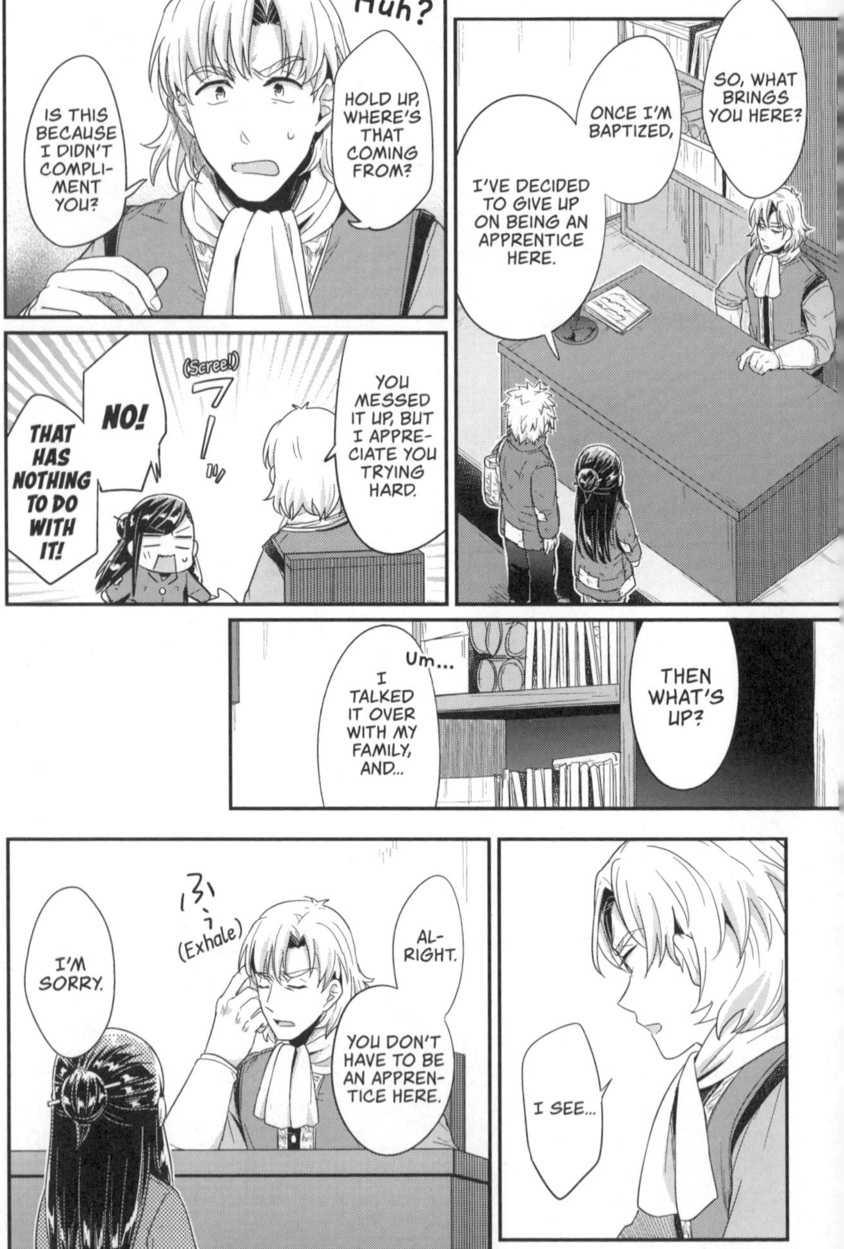
SO, WHAT BRINGS YOU HERE?
ONCE I'M BAPTIZED,
I'VE DECIDED TO GIVE UP ON BEING AN APPRENTICE HERE.
Huh?
HOLD UP, WHERE'S THAT COMING FROM?
IS THIS BECAUSE I DIDN'T COMPLIMENT YOU?
YOU MESSED IT UP, BUT I APPRECIATE YOU TRYING HARD.
(Scree!)
NO!
THAT HAS NOTHING TO DO WITH IT!
THEN WHAT'S UP?
Um...
I TALKED IT OVER WITH MY FAMILY, AND...
I SEE...
ALRIGHT.
YOU DON'T HAVE TO BE AN APPRENTICE HERE.
(Exhale)
I'M SORRY.

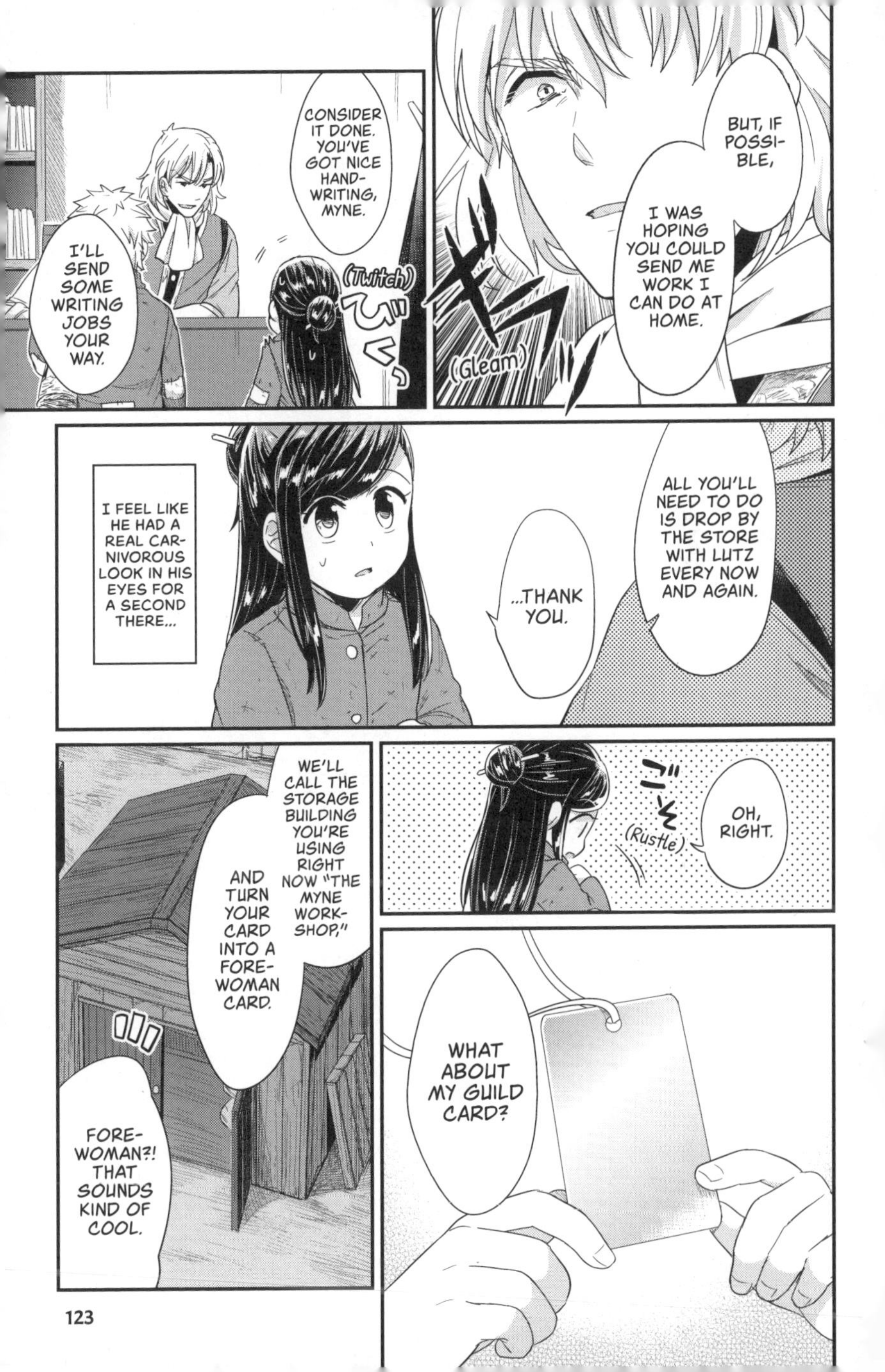
BUT, IF POSSIBLE,
I WAS HOPING YOU COULD SEND ME WORK I CAN DO AT HOME.
(Gleam)
CONSIDER IT DONE. YOU'VE GOT NICE HANDWRITING, MYNE.
(Twitch)
I'LL SEND SOME WRITING JOBS YOUR WAY.
ALL YOU'LL NEED TO DO IS DROP BY THE STORE WITH LUTZ EVERY NOW AND AGAIN.
...THANK YOU.
I FEEL LIKE HE HAD A REAL CARNIVOROUS LOOK IN HIS EYES FOR A SECOND THERE...
(Rustle)
OH, RIGHT.
WHAT ABOUT MY GUILD CARD?
WE'LL CALL THE STORAGE BUILDING YOU'RE USING RIGHT NOW "THE MYNE WORKSHOP,"
AND TURN YOUR CARD INTO A FOREWOMAN CARD.
FOREWOMAN?! THAT SOUNDS KIND OF COOL.

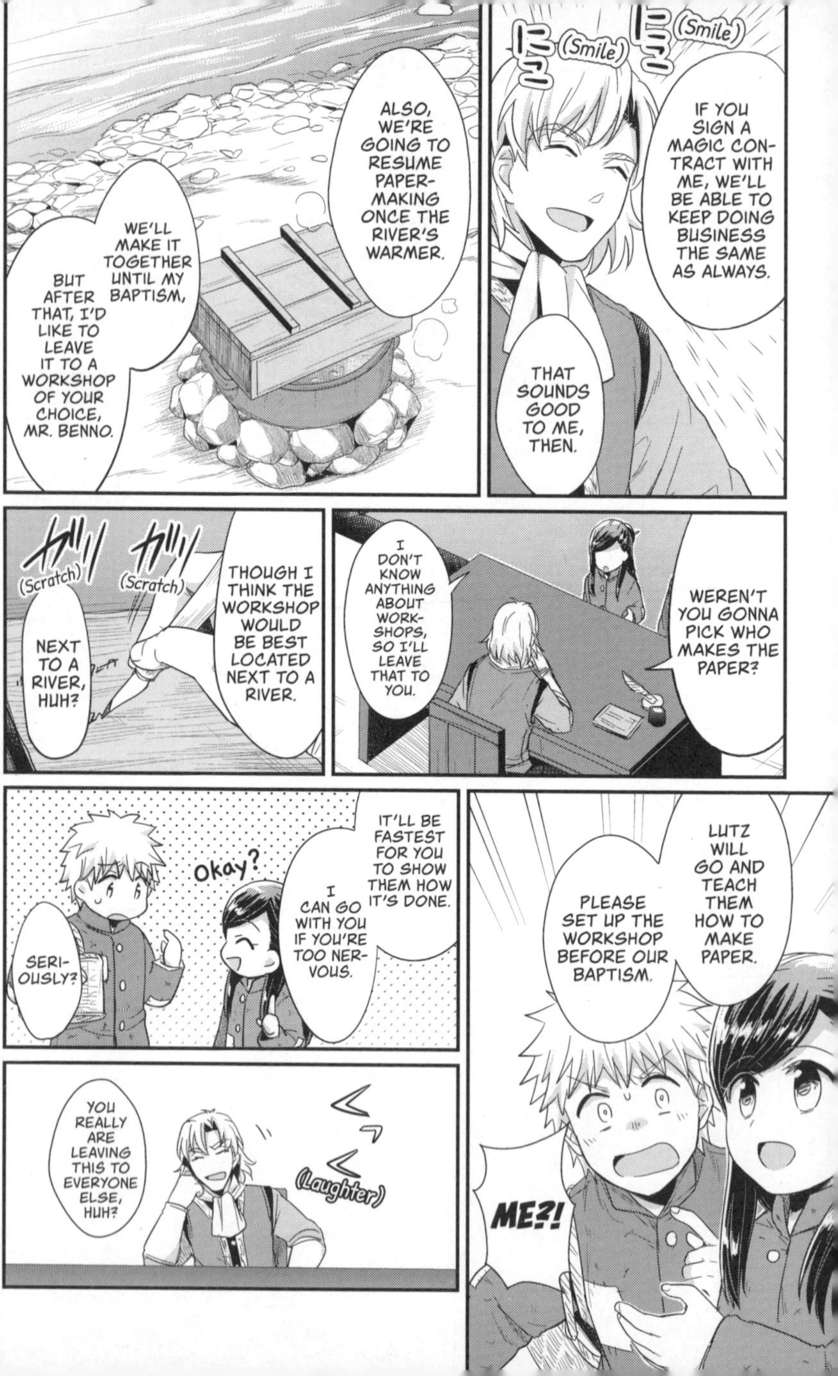
(Smile)
(Smile)
IF YOU SIGN A MAGIC CONTRACT WITH ME, WE'LL BE ABLE TO KEEP DOING BUSINESS THE SAME AS ALWAYS.
THAT SOUNDS GOOD TO ME, THEN.
ALSO, WE'RE GOING TO RESUME PAPER-MAKING ONCE THE RIVER'S WARMER.
WE'LL MAKE IT TOGETHER UNTIL MY BAPTISM, BUT AFTER THAT, I'D LIKE TO LEAVE IT TO A WORKSHOP OF YOUR CHOICE, MR. BENNO.
WEREN'T YOU GONNA PICK WHO MAKES THE PAPER?
I DON'T KNOW ANYTHING ABOUT WORKSHOPS, SO I'LL LEAVE THAT TO YOU.
THOUGH I THINK THE WORKSHOP WOULD BE BEST LOCATED NEXT TO A RIVER.
(Scratch)
(Scratch)
NEXT TO A RIVER, HUH?
LUTZ WILL GO AND TEACH THEM HOW TO MAKE PAPER.
PLEASE SET UP THE WORKSHOP BEFORE OUR BAPTISM.
ME?!
IT'LL BE FASTEST FOR YOU TO SHOW THEM HOW IT'S DONE.
I CAN GO WITH YOU IF YOU'RE TOO NERVOUS.
Okay?
SERIOUSLY?
(Laughter)
YOU REALLY ARE LEAVING THIS TO EVERYONE ELSE, HUH?

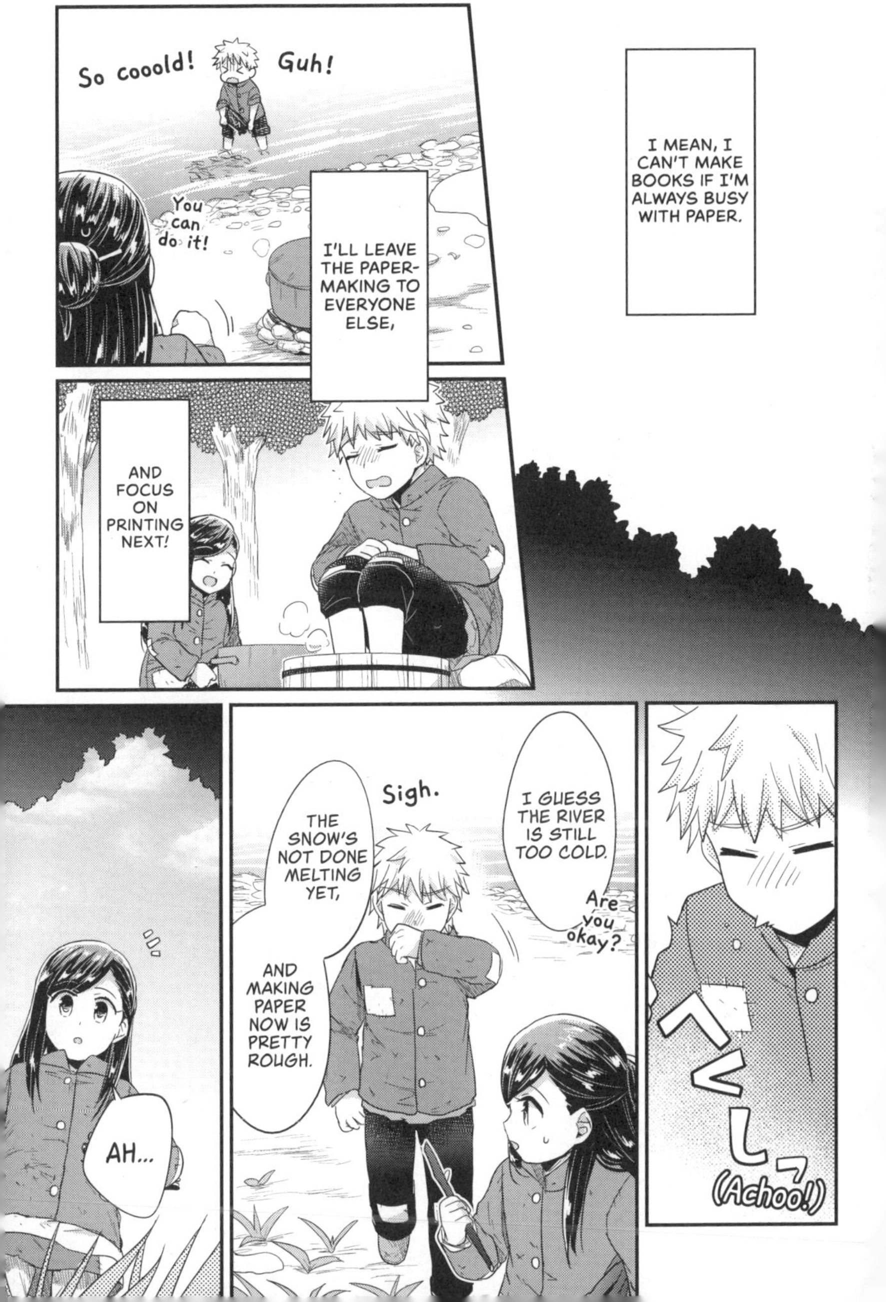
I MEAN, I CAN'T MAKE BOOKS IF I'M ALWAYS BUSY WITH PAPER.
Guh!
So cooold!
You can do it!
I'LL LEAVE THE PAPER-MAKING TO EVERYONE ELSE,
AND FOCUS ON PRINTING NEXT!
(Achoo!)
I GUESS THE RIVER IS STILL TOO COLD.
Are you okay?
Sigh.
THE SNOW'S NOT DONE MELTING YET,
AND MAKING PAPER NOW IS PRETTY ROUGH.
AH...

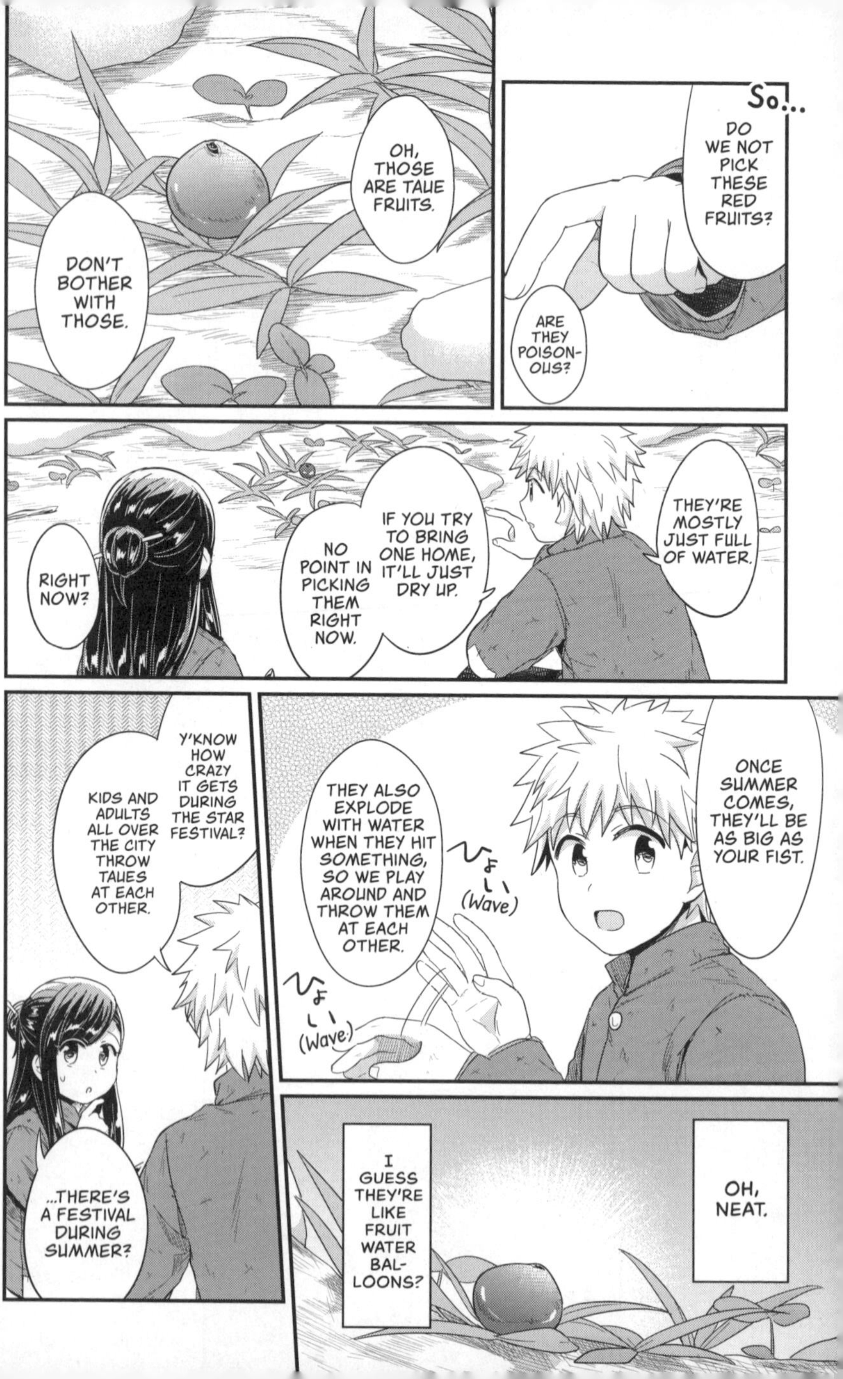
So...
DO WE NOT PICK THESE RED FRUITS?
ARE THEY POISONOUS?
OH, THOSE ARE TAUE FRUITS.
DON'T BOTHER WITH THOSE.
THEY'RE MOSTLY JUST FULL OF WATER.
IF YOU TRY TO BRING ONE HOME, IT'LL JUST DRY UP.
NO POINT IN PICKING THEM RIGHT NOW.
RIGHT NOW?
ONCE SUMMER COMES, THEY'LL BE AS BIG AS YOUR FIST.
THEY ALSO EXPLODE WITH WATER WHEN THEY HIT SOMETHING, SO WE PLAY AROUND AND THROW THEM AT EACH OTHER.
ひょい (Wave)
ひょい (Wave)
OH, NEAT.
I GUESS THEY'RE LIKE FRUIT WATER BALLOONS?
Y'KNOW HOW CRAZY IT GETS DURING THE STAR FESTIVAL?
KIDS AND ADULTS ALL OVER THE CITY THROW TAUES AT EACH OTHER.
...THERE'S A FESTIVAL DURING SUMMER?

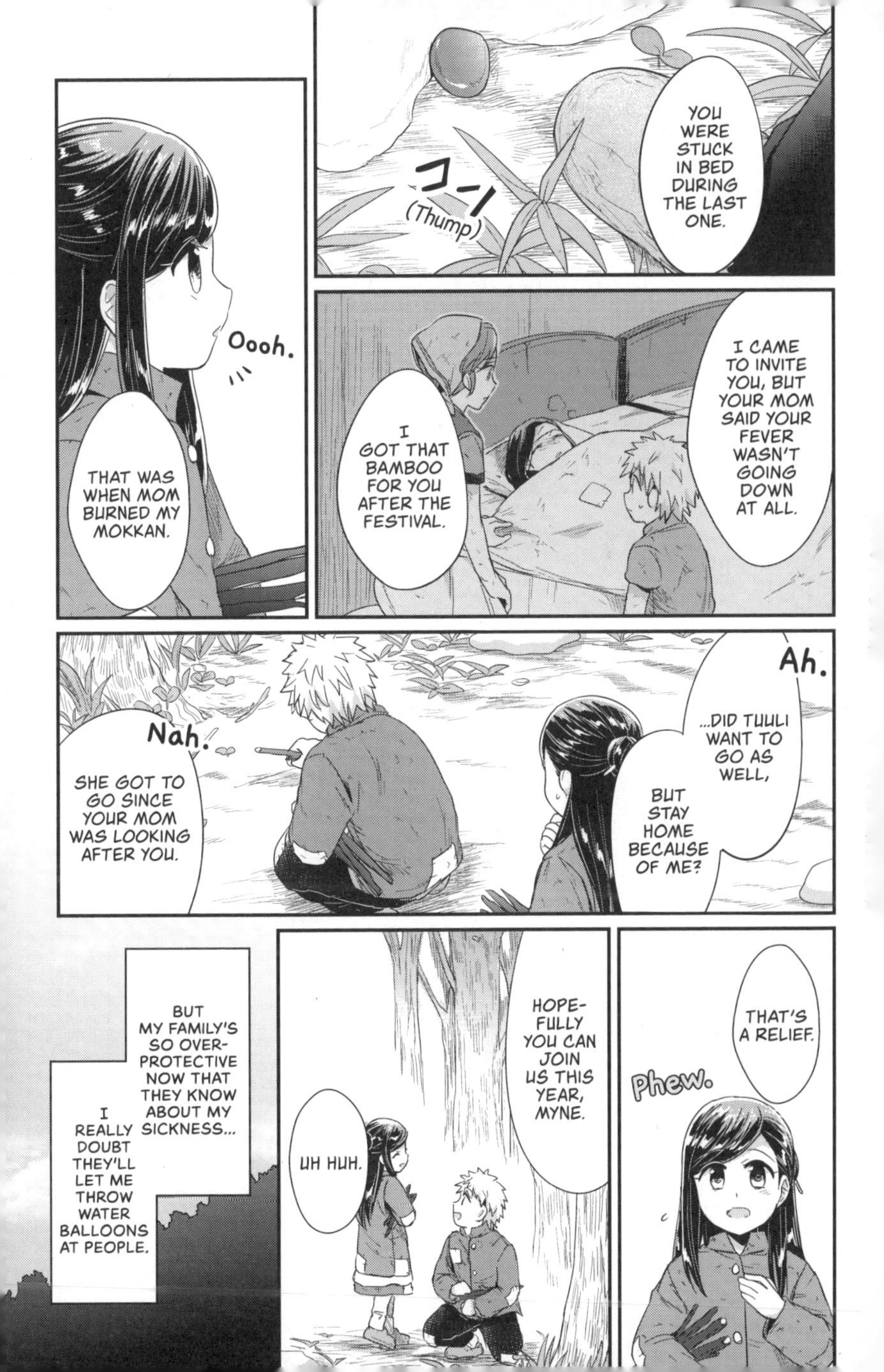
YOU WERE STUCK IN BED DURING THE LAST ONE.
コーノ
(Thump)
I CAME TO INVITE YOU, BUT YOUR MOM SAID YOUR FEVER WASN'T GOING DOWN AT ALL.
I GOT THAT BAMBOO FOR YOU AFTER THE FESTIVAL.
Oooh.
THAT WAS WHEN MOM BURNED MY MOKKAN.
Ah.
...DID TUULI WANT TO GO AS WELL,
BUT STAY HOME BECAUSE OF ME?
Nah.
SHE GOT TO GO SINCE YOUR MOM WAS LOOKING AFTER YOU.
THAT'S A RELIEF.
Phew.
HOPE-FULLY YOU CAN JOIN US THIS YEAR, MYNE.
UH HUH.
BUT MY FAMILY'S SO OVER-PROTECTIVE NOW THAT THEY KNOW ABOUT MY SICKNESS...
I REALLY DOUBT THEY'LL LET ME THROW WATER BALLOONS AT PEOPLE.

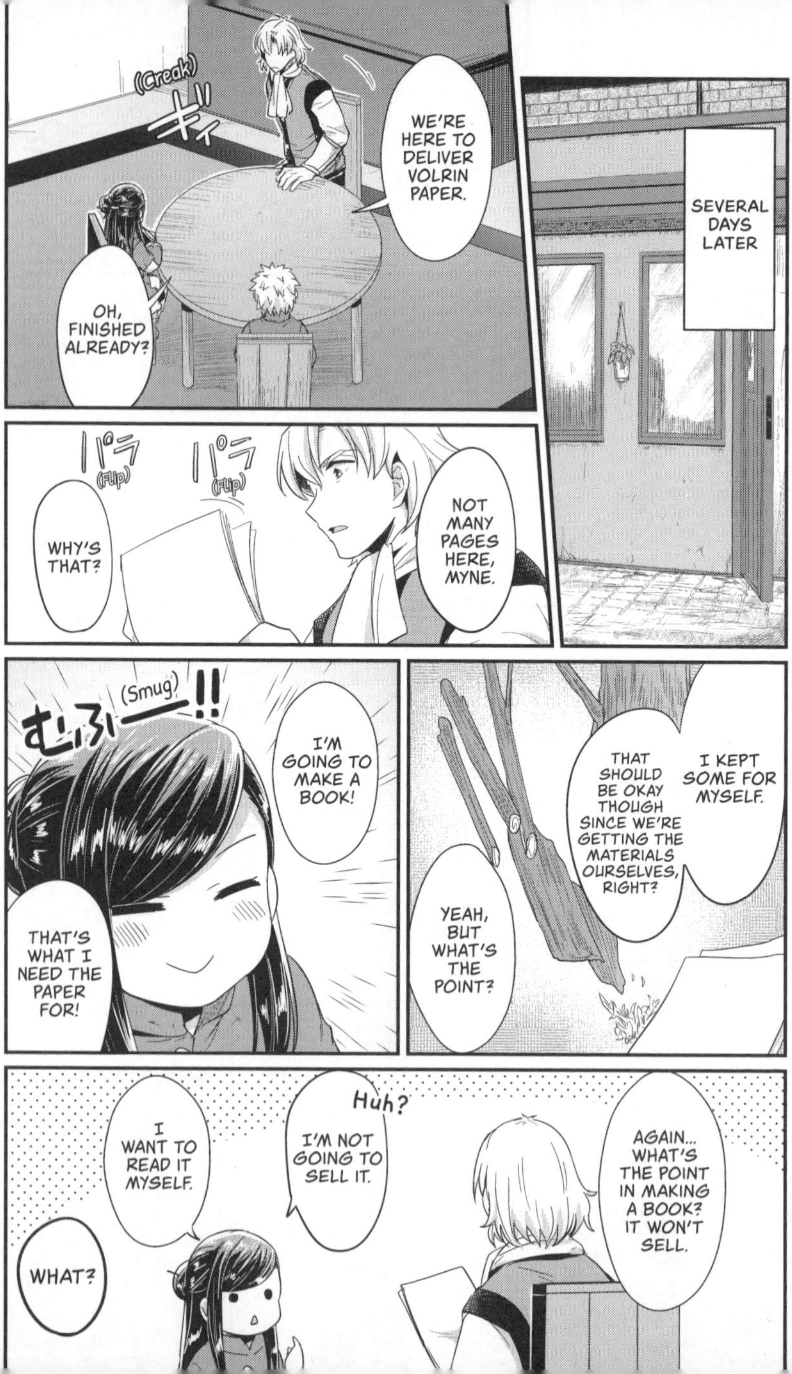
SEVERAL DAYS LATER
ギィ
(Creak)
WE'RE HERE TO DELIVER VOLRIN PAPER.
OH, FINISHED ALREADY?
パラ
(Flip)
パラ
(Flip)
NOT MANY PAGES HERE, MYNE.
WHY'S THAT?
I KEPT SOME FOR MYSELF.
THAT SHOULD BE OKAY THOUGH SINCE WE'RE GETTING THE MATERIALS OURSELVES, RIGHT?
YEAH, BUT WHAT'S THE POINT?
むふー!!
(Smug)
I'M GOING TO MAKE A BOOK!
THAT'S WHAT I NEED THE PAPER FOR!
AGAIN... WHAT'S THE POINT IN MAKING A BOOK? IT WON'T SELL.
Huh?
I'M NOT GOING TO SELL IT.
I WANT TO READ IT MYSELF.
WHAT?

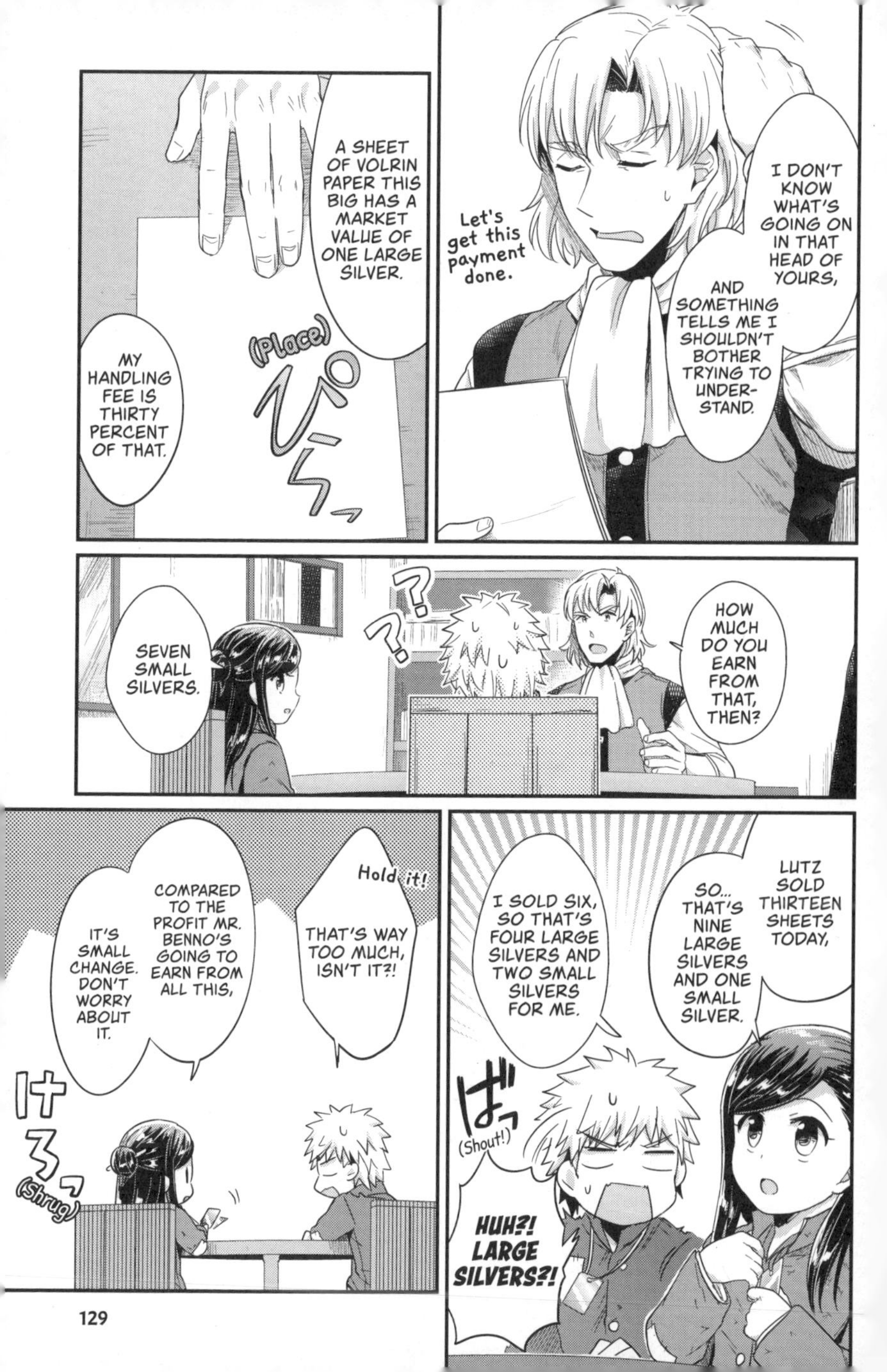
I DON'T KNOW WHAT'S GOING ON IN THAT HEAD OF YOURS,
AND SOMETHING TELLS ME I SHOULDN'T BOTHER TRYING TO UNDER-STAND.
Let's get this payment done.
A SHEET OF VOLRIN PAPER THIS BIG HAS A MARKET VALUE OF ONE LARGE SILVER.
ぴらっ
(Place)
MY HANDLING FEE IS THIRTY PERCENT OF THAT.
HOW MUCH DO YOU EARN FROM THAT, THEN?
??
SEVEN SMALL SILVERS.
LUTZ SOLD THIRTEEN SHEETS TODAY,
SO... THAT'S NINE LARGE SILVERS AND ONE SMALL SILVER.
I SOLD SIX, SO THAT'S FOUR LARGE SILVERS AND TWO SMALL SILVERS FOR ME.
ばっ
(Shout!)
HUH?! LARGE SILVERS?!
Hold it!
THAT'S WAY TOO MUCH, ISN'T IT?!
COMPARED TO THE PROFIT MR. BENNO'S GOING TO EARN FROM ALL THIS,
IT'S SMALL CHANGE. DON'T WORRY ABOUT IT.
けろっ
(Shrug)

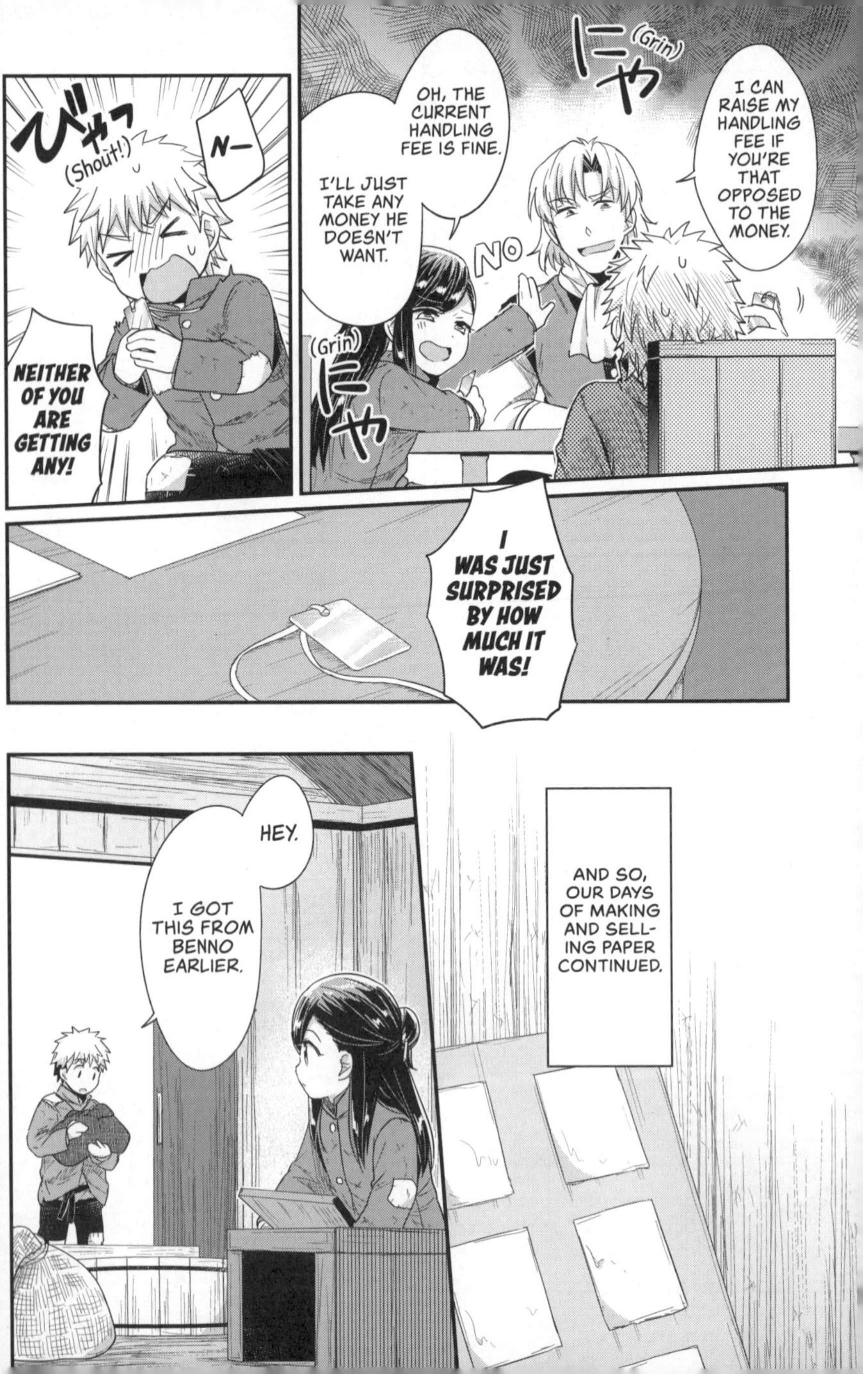
にゃ
(Grin)
I CAN RAISE MY HANDLING FEE IF YOU'RE THAT OPPOSED TO THE MONEY.
OH, THE CURRENT HANDLING FEE IS FINE.
I'LL JUST TAKE ANY MONEY HE DOESN'T WANT.
NO
(Grin)
にゃ
びゃっ
(Shout!)
N—
NEITHER OF YOU ARE GETTING ANY!
I WAS JUST SURPRISED BY HOW MUCH IT WAS!
AND SO, OUR DAYS OF MAKING AND SELL-ING PAPER CONTINUED.
HEY.
I GOT THIS FROM BENNO EARLIER.

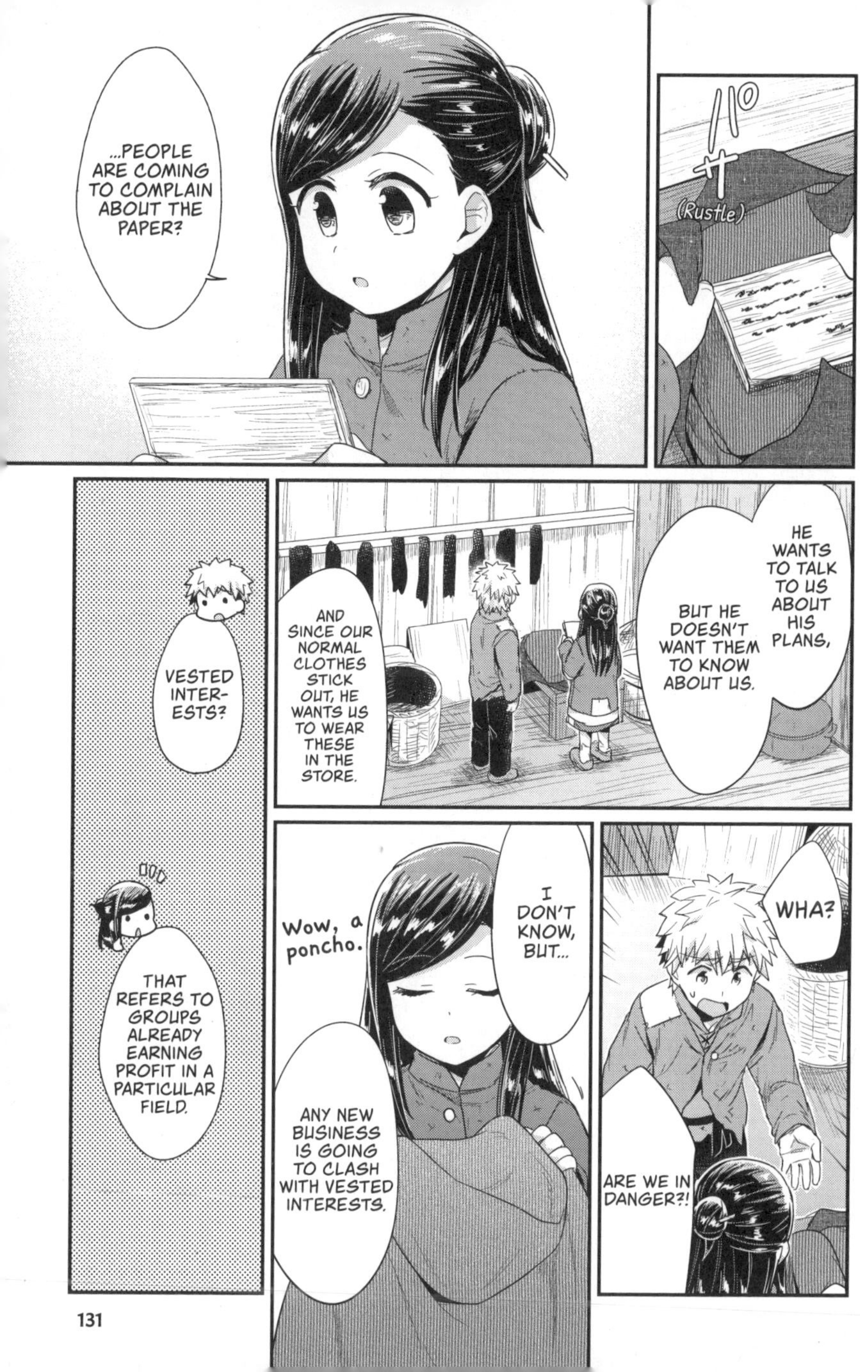
パサ
(Rustle)
...PEOPLE ARE COMING TO COMPLAIN ABOUT THE PAPER?
HE WANTS TO TALK TO US ABOUT HIS PLANS,
BUT HE DOESN'T WANT THEM TO KNOW ABOUT US.
AND SINCE OUR NORMAL CLOTHES STICK OUT, HE WANTS US TO WEAR THESE IN THE STORE.
WHA?
ARE WE IN DANGER?!
I DON'T KNOW, BUT...
Wow, a poncho.
ANY NEW BUSINESS IS GOING TO CLASH WITH VESTED INTERESTS.
VESTED INTER-ESTS?
THAT REFERS TO GROUPS ALREADY EARNING PROFIT IN A PARTICULAR FIELD.

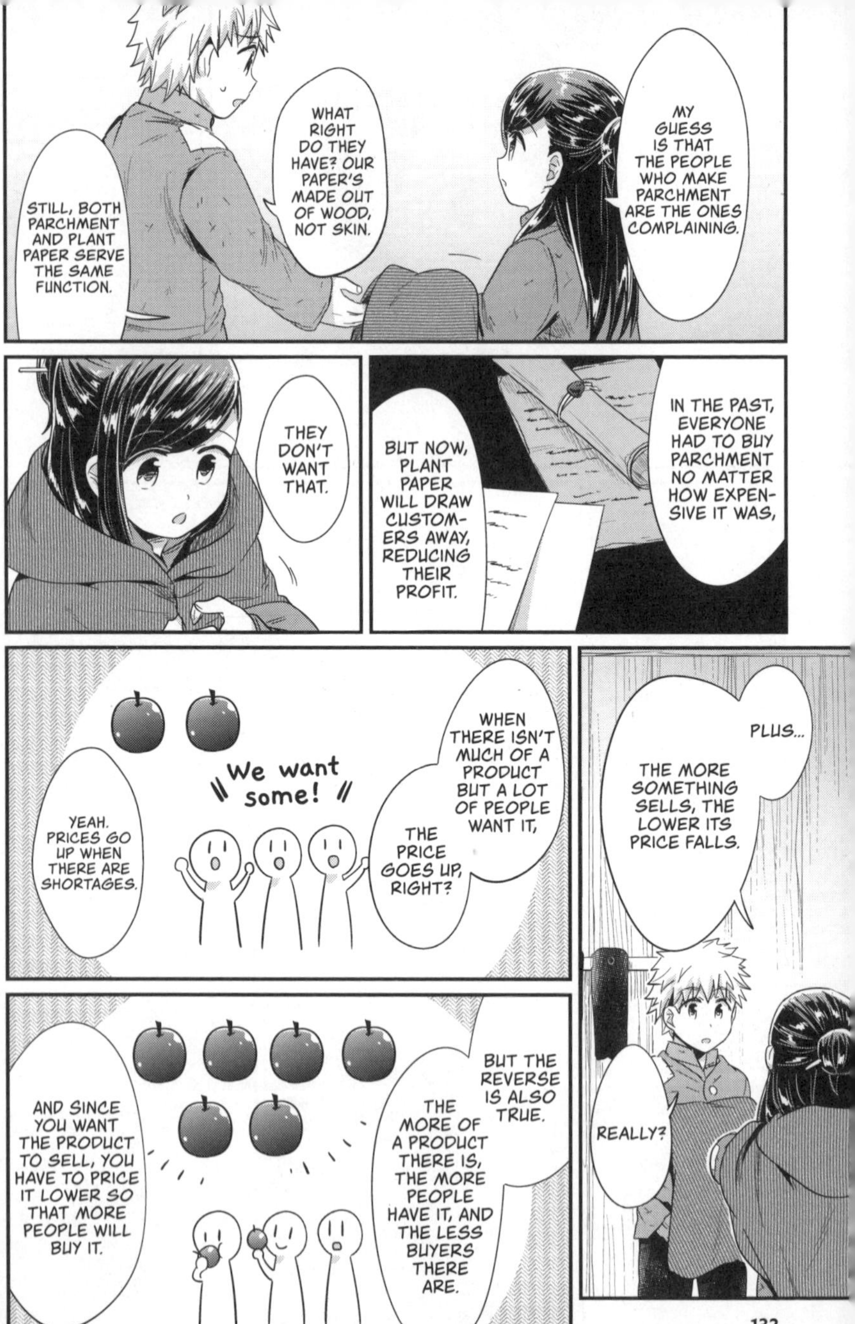
MY GUESS IS THAT THE PEOPLE WHO MAKE PARCHMENT ARE THE ONES COMPLAINING.
WHAT RIGHT DO THEY HAVE? OUR PAPER'S MADE OUT OF WOOD, NOT SKIN.
STILL, BOTH PARCHMENT AND PLANT PAPER SERVE THE SAME FUNCTION.
IN THE PAST, EVERYONE HAD TO BUY PARCHMENT NO MATTER HOW EXPEN-SIVE IT WAS,
BUT NOW, PLANT PAPER WILL DRAW CUSTOM-ERS AWAY, REDUCING THEIR PROFIT.
THEY DON'T WANT THAT.
PLUS...
THE MORE SOMETHING SELLS, THE LOWER ITS PRICE FALLS.
REALLY?
WHEN THERE ISN'T MUCH OF A PRODUCT BUT A LOT OF PEOPLE WANT IT,
THE PRICE GOES UP, RIGHT?
We want some!
YEAH. PRICES GO UP WHEN THERE ARE SHORTAGES.
BUT THE REVERSE IS ALSO TRUE.
THE MORE OF A PRODUCT THERE IS, THE MORE PEOPLE HAVE IT, AND THE LESS BUYERS THERE ARE.
AND SINCE YOU WANT THE PRODUCT TO SELL, YOU HAVE TO PRICE IT LOWER SO THAT MORE PEOPLE WILL BUY IT.

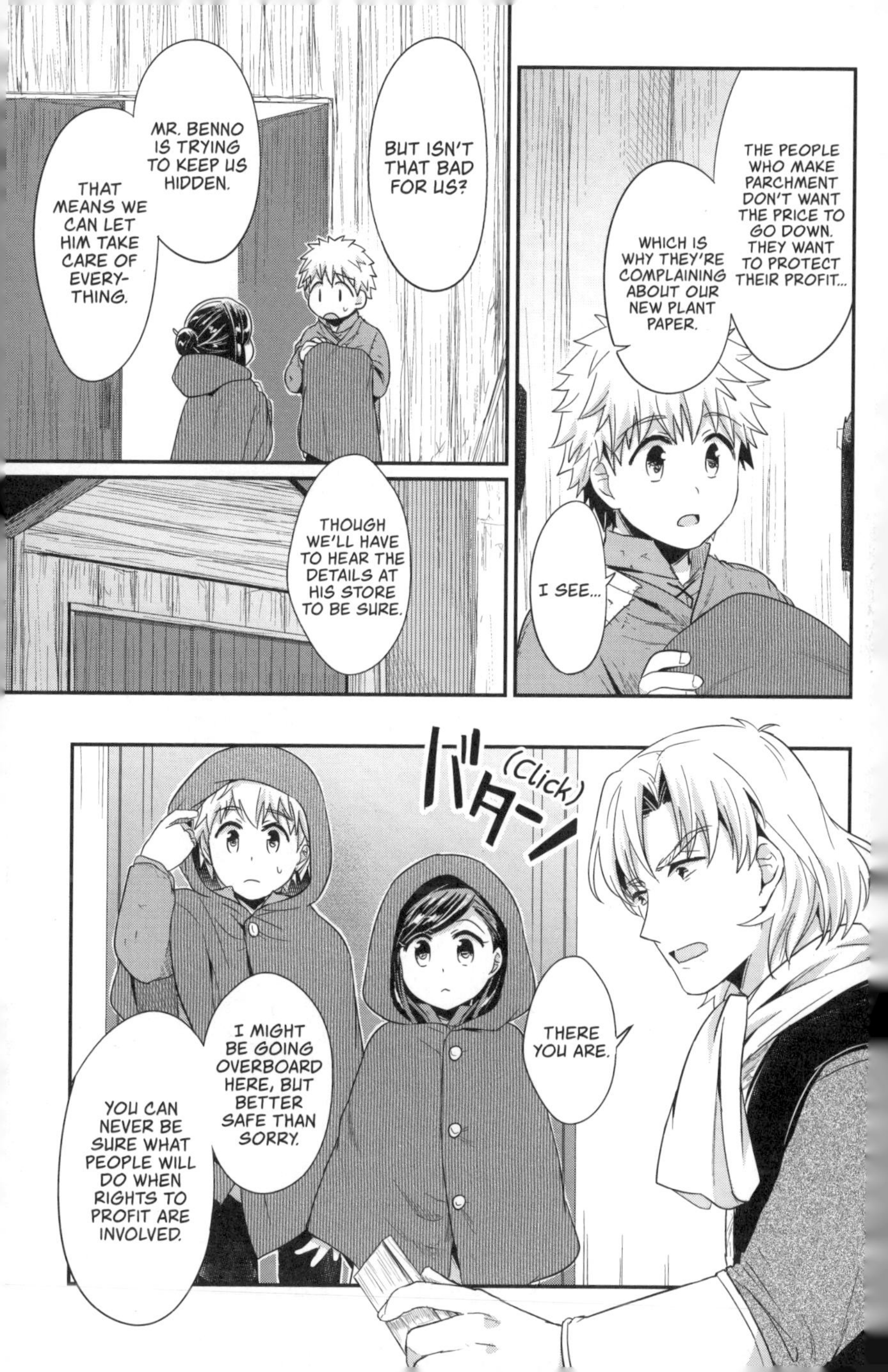
THE PEOPLE WHO MAKE PARCHMENT DON'T WANT THE PRICE TO GO DOWN. THEY WANT TO PROTECT THEIR PROFIT...
WHICH IS WHY THEY'RE COMPLAINING ABOUT OUR NEW PLANT PAPER.
I SEE...
MR. BENNO IS TRYING TO KEEP US HIDDEN.
THAT MEANS WE CAN LET HIM TAKE CARE OF EVERY-THING.
BUT ISN'T THAT BAD FOR US?
THOUGH WE'LL HAVE TO HEAR THE DETAILS AT HIS STORE TO BE SURE.
バターン
(Click)
THERE YOU ARE.
I MIGHT BE GOING OVERBOARD HERE, BUT BETTER SAFE THAN SORRY.
YOU CAN NEVER BE SURE WHAT PEOPLE WILL DO WHEN RIGHTS TO PROFIT ARE INVOLVED.

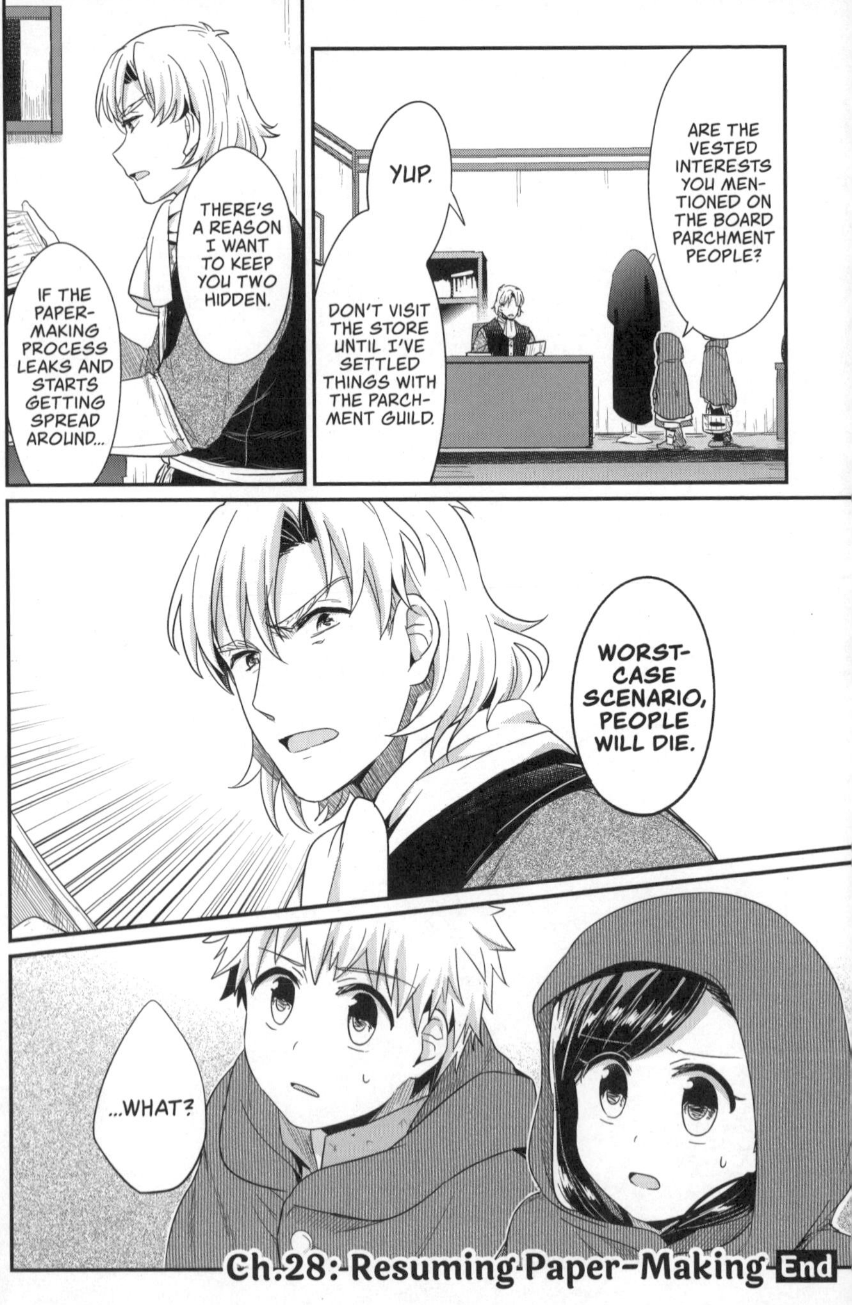
ARE THE VESTED INTERESTS YOU MENTIONED ON THE BOARD PARCHMENT PEOPLE?
YUP.
DON'T VISIT THE STORE UNTIL I'VE SETTLED THINGS WITH THE PARCHMENT GUILD.
THERE'S A REASON I WANT TO KEEP YOU TWO HIDDEN.
IF THE PAPER-MAKING PROCESS LEAKS AND STARTS GETTING SPREAD AROUND...
WORST-CASE SCENARIO, PEOPLE WILL DIE.
...WHAT?
Ch.28: Resuming Paper-Making End

Ch.29 Vested Interests

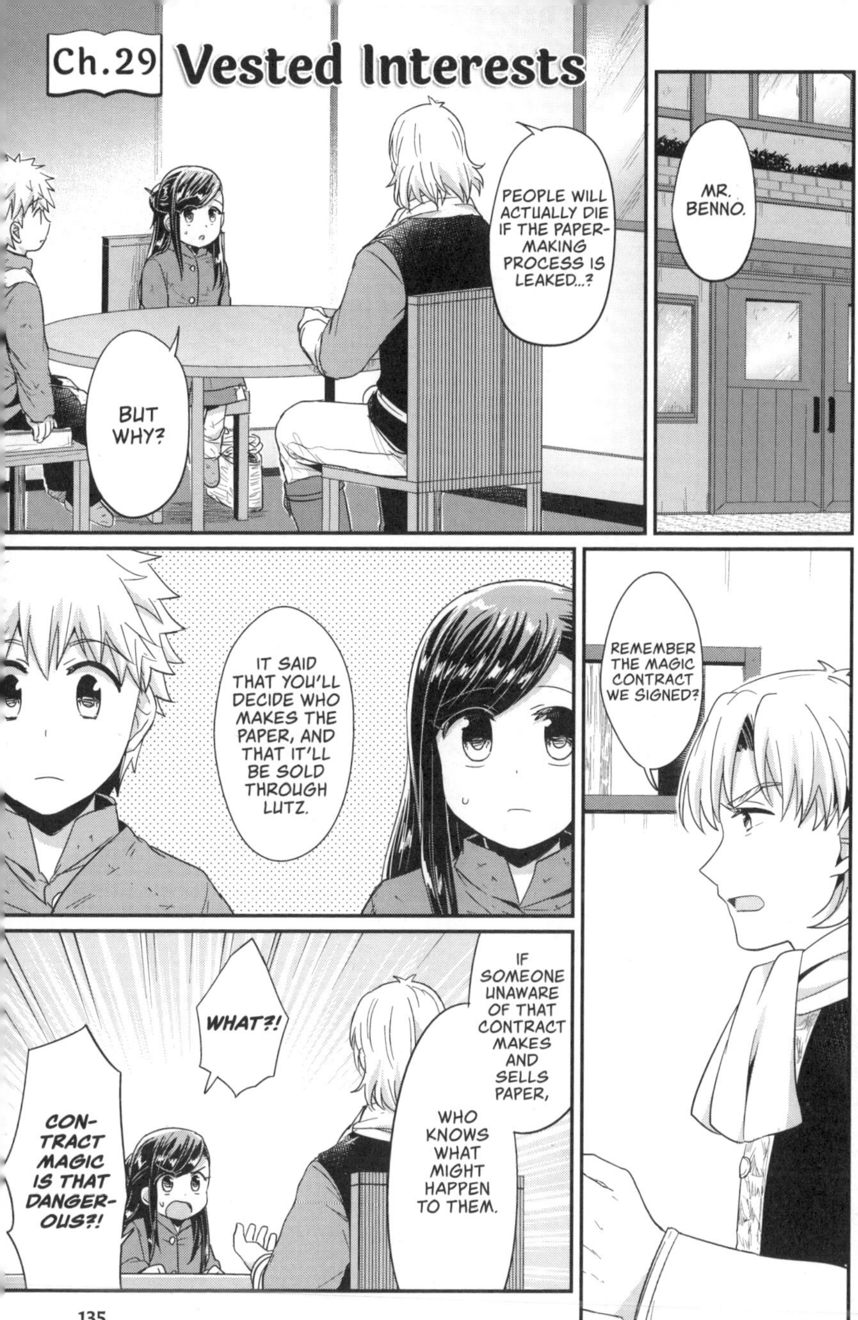
MR. BENNO.
PEOPLE WILL ACTUALLY DIE IF THE PAPER-MAKING PROCESS IS LEAKED...?
BUT WHY?
REMEMBER THE MAGIC CONTRACT WE SIGNED?
IT SAID THAT YOU'LL DECIDE WHO MAKES THE PAPER, AND THAT IT'LL BE SOLD THROUGH LUTZ.
IF SOMEONE UNAWARE OF THAT CONTRACT MAKES AND SELLS PAPER,
WHO KNOWS WHAT MIGHT HAPPEN TO THEM.
WHAT?!
CON-TRACT MAGIC IS THAT DANGER-OUS?!

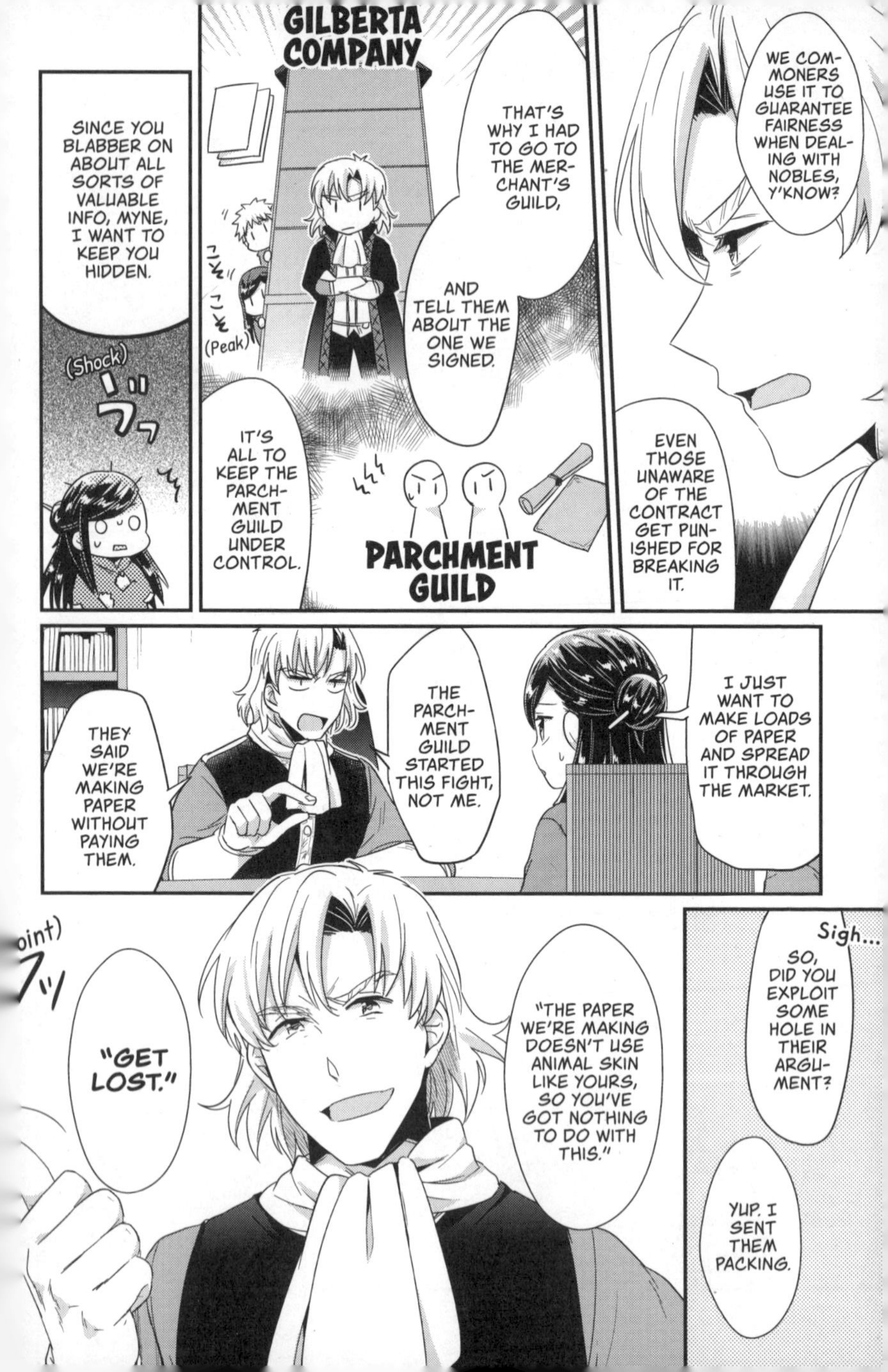
WE COMMONERS USE IT TO GUARANTEE FAIRNESS WHEN DEALING WITH NOBLES, Y'KNOW?
EVEN THOSE UNAWARE OF THE CONTRACT GET PUNISHED FOR BREAKING IT.
GILBERTA COMPANY
THAT'S WHY I HAD TO GO TO THE MERCHANT'S GUILD,
AND TELL THEM ABOUT THE ONE WE SIGNED.
(Peak)
IT'S ALL TO KEEP THE PARCHMENT GUILD UNDER CONTROL.
PARCHMENT GUILD
SINCE YOU BLABBER ON ABOUT ALL SORTS OF VALUABLE INFO, MYNE, I WANT TO KEEP YOU HIDDEN.
(Shock)
I JUST WANT TO MAKE LOADS OF PAPER AND SPREAD IT THROUGH THE MARKET.
THE PARCHMENT GUILD STARTED THIS FIGHT, NOT ME.
THEY SAID WE'RE MAKING PAPER WITHOUT PAYING THEM.
Sigh...
SO, DID YOU EXPLOIT SOME HOLE IN THEIR ARGUMENT?
YUP. I SENT THEM PACKING.
"THE PAPER WE'RE MAKING DOESN'T USE ANIMAL SKIN LIKE YOURS, SO YOU'VE GOT NOTHING TO DO WITH THIS."
"GET LOST."

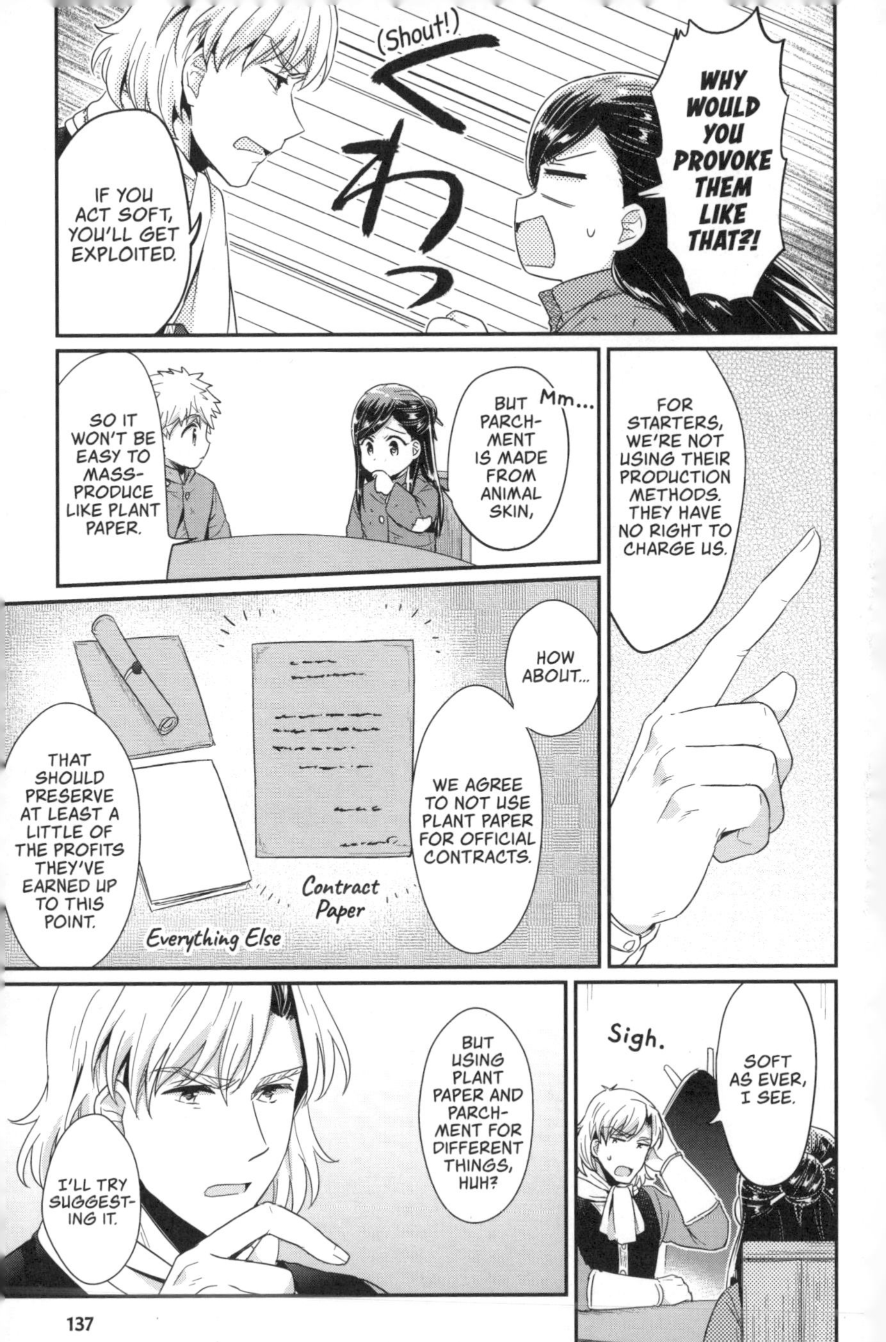
WHY WOULD YOU PROVOKE THEM LIKE THAT?!
(Shout!)
IF YOU ACT SOFT, YOU'LL GET EXPLOITED.
FOR STARTERS, WE'RE NOT USING THEIR PRODUCTION METHODS. THEY HAVE NO RIGHT TO CHARGE US.
Mm...
BUT PARCH-MENT IS MADE FROM ANIMAL SKIN,
SO IT WON'T BE EASY TO MASS-PRODUCE LIKE PLANT PAPER.
HOW ABOUT...
WE AGREE TO NOT USE PLANT PAPER FOR OFFICIAL CONTRACTS.
Contract Paper
Everything Else
THAT SHOULD PRESERVE AT LEAST A LITTLE OF THE PROFITS THEY'VE EARNED UP TO THIS POINT.
Sigh.
SOFT AS EVER, I SEE.
BUT USING PLANT PAPER AND PARCH-MENT FOR DIFFERENT THINGS, HUH?
I'LL TRY SUGGEST-ING IT.

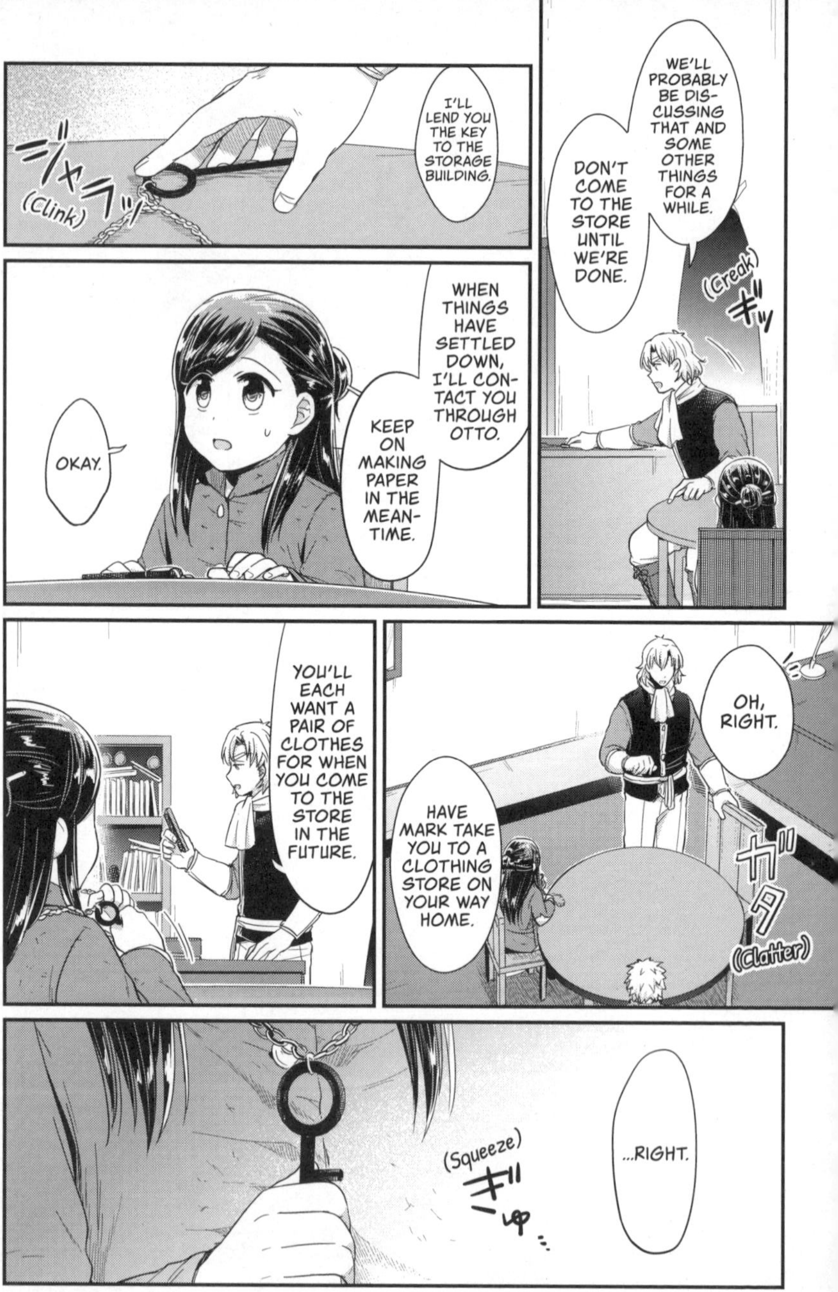
WE'LL PROBABLY BE DIS-CUSSING THAT AND SOME OTHER THINGS FOR A WHILE.
DON'T COME TO THE STORE UNTIL WE'RE DONE.
(Creak)
I'LL LEND YOU THE KEY TO THE STORAGE BUILDING.
(Clink)
WHEN THINGS HAVE SETTLED DOWN, I'LL CON-TACT YOU THROUGH OTTO.
KEEP ON MAKING PAPER IN THE MEAN-TIME.
OKAY.
OH, RIGHT.
HAVE MARK TAKE YOU TO A CLOTHING STORE ON YOUR WAY HOME.
(Clatter)
YOU'LL EACH WANT A PAIR OF CLOTHES FOR WHEN YOU COME TO THE STORE IN THE FUTURE.
...RIGHT.
(Squeeze)

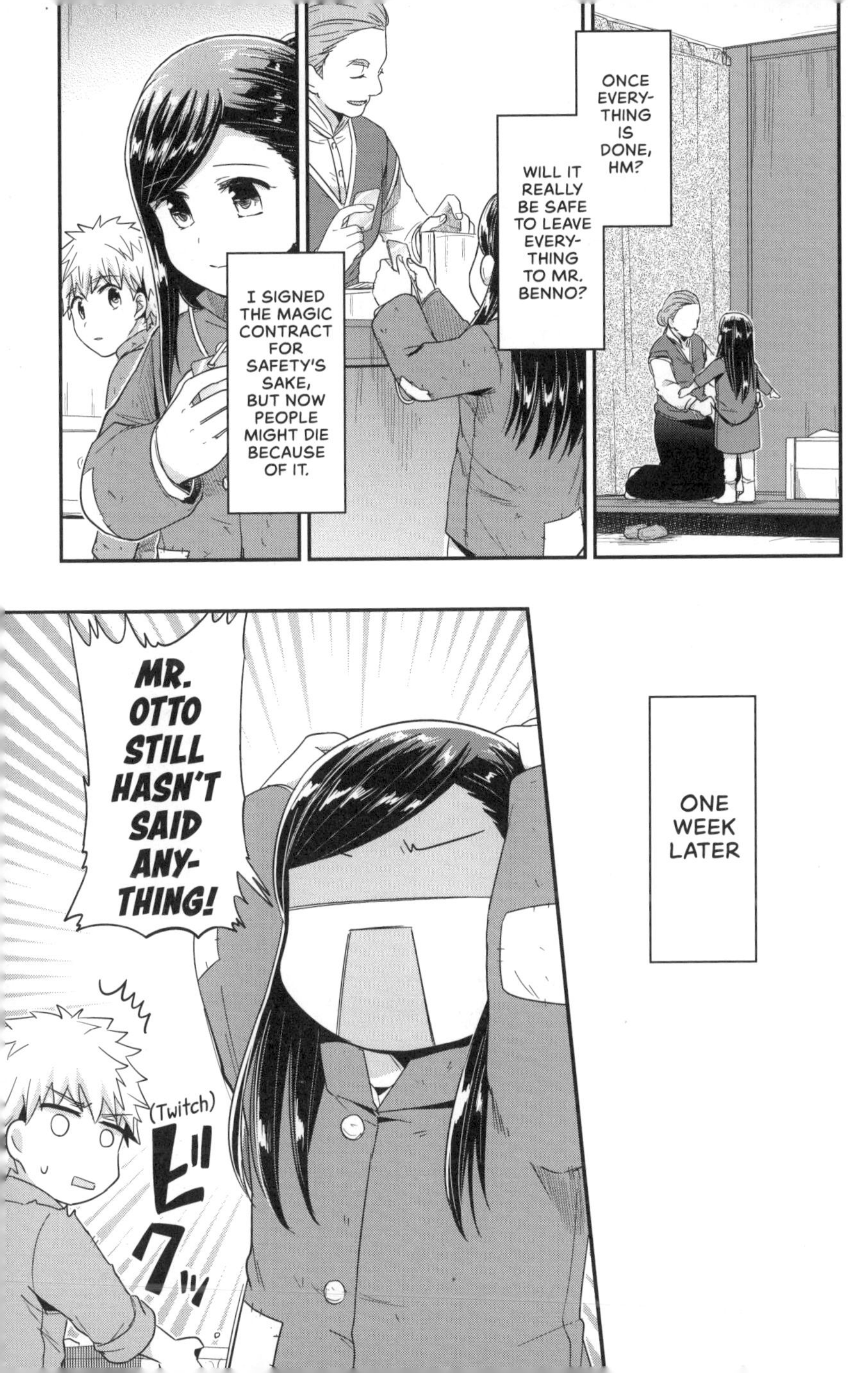
ONCE EVERYTHING IS DONE, HM?
WILL IT REALLY BE SAFE TO LEAVE EVERYTHING TO MR. BENNO?
I SIGNED THE MAGIC CONTRACT FOR SAFETY'S SAKE, BUT NOW PEOPLE MIGHT DIE BECAUSE OF IT.
ONE WEEK LATER
MR. OTTO STILL HASN'T SAID ANYTHING!
(Twitch)

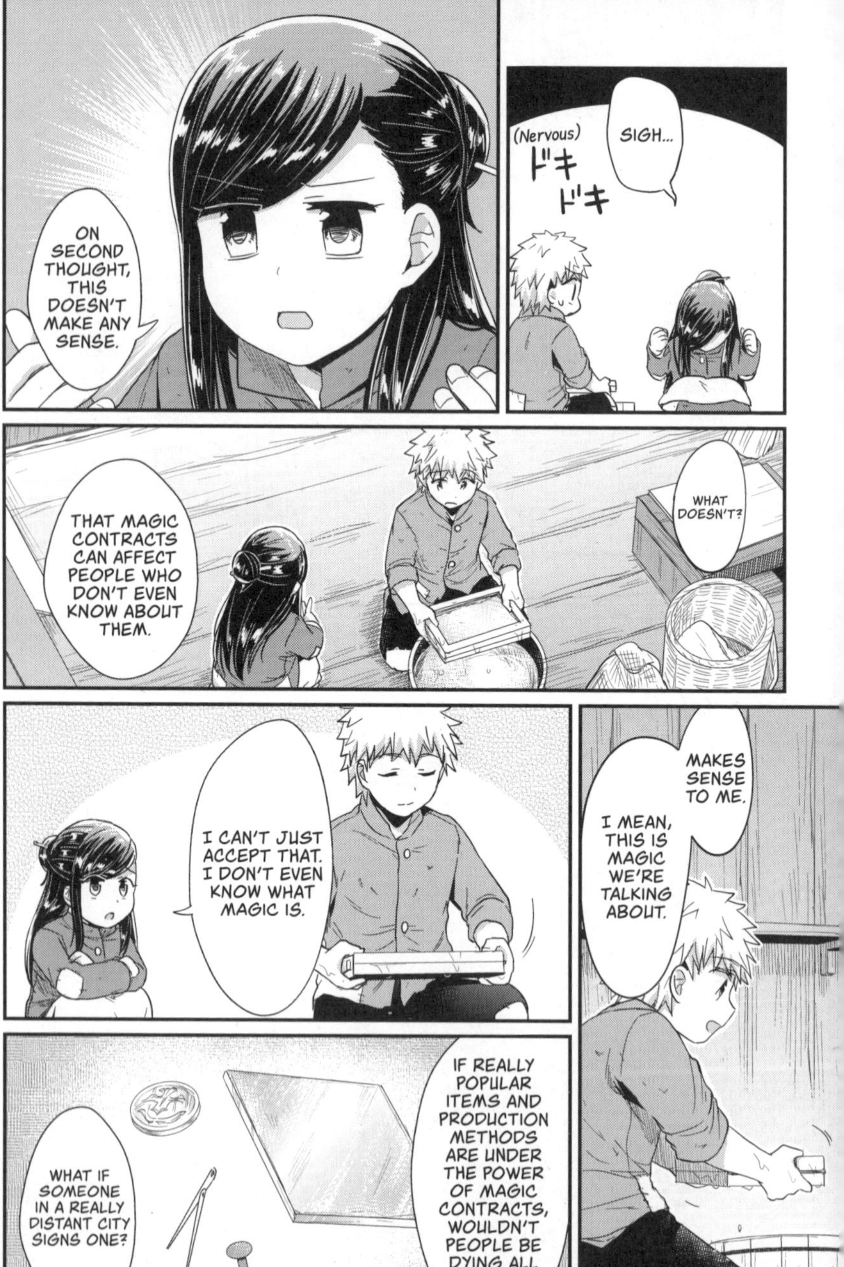
SIGH...
(Nervous) ドキドキ
ON SECOND THOUGHT, THIS DOESN'T MAKE ANY SENSE.
WHAT DOESN'T?
THAT MAGIC CONTRACTS CAN AFFECT PEOPLE WHO DON'T EVEN KNOW ABOUT THEM.
MAKES SENSE TO ME.
I MEAN, THIS IS MAGIC WE'RE TALKING ABOUT.
I CAN'T JUST ACCEPT THAT. I DON'T EVEN KNOW WHAT MAGIC IS.
IF REALLY POPULAR ITEMS AND PRODUCTION METHODS ARE UNDER THE POWER OF MAGIC CONTRACTS, WOULDN'T PEOPLE BE DYING ALL OVER THE PLACE?
WHAT IF SOMEONE IN A REALLY DISTANT CITY SIGNS ONE?

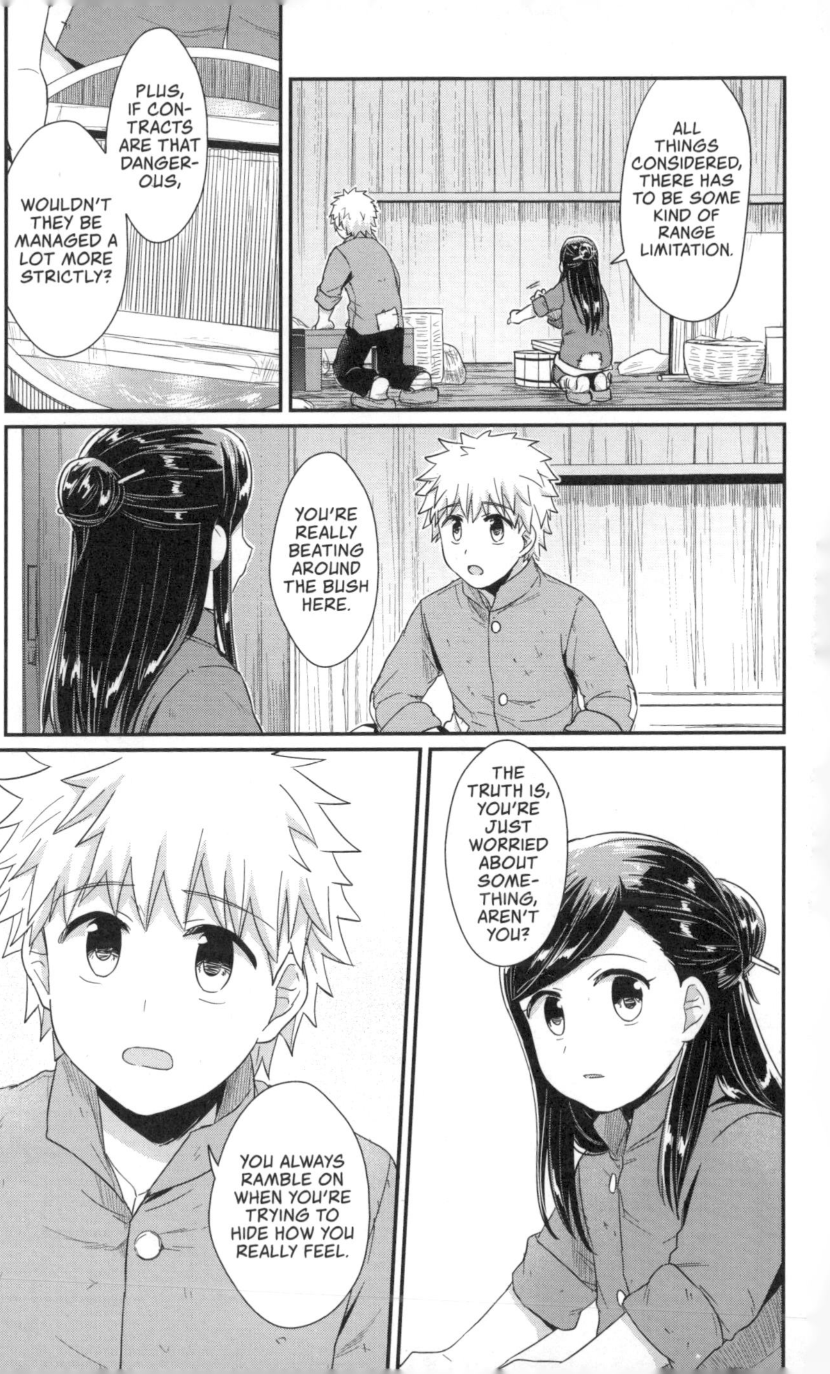

ALL THINGS CONSIDERED, THERE HAS TO BE SOME KIND OF RANGE LIMITATION.
PLUS, IF CONTRACTS ARE THAT DANGEROUS,
WOULDN'T THEY BE MANAGED A LOT MORE STRICTLY?
YOU'RE REALLY BEATING AROUND THE BUSH HERE.
THE TRUTH IS, YOU'RE JUST WORRIED ABOUT SOMETHING, AREN'T YOU?
YOU ALWAYS RAMBLE ON WHEN YOU'RE TRYING TO HIDE HOW YOU REALLY FEEL.

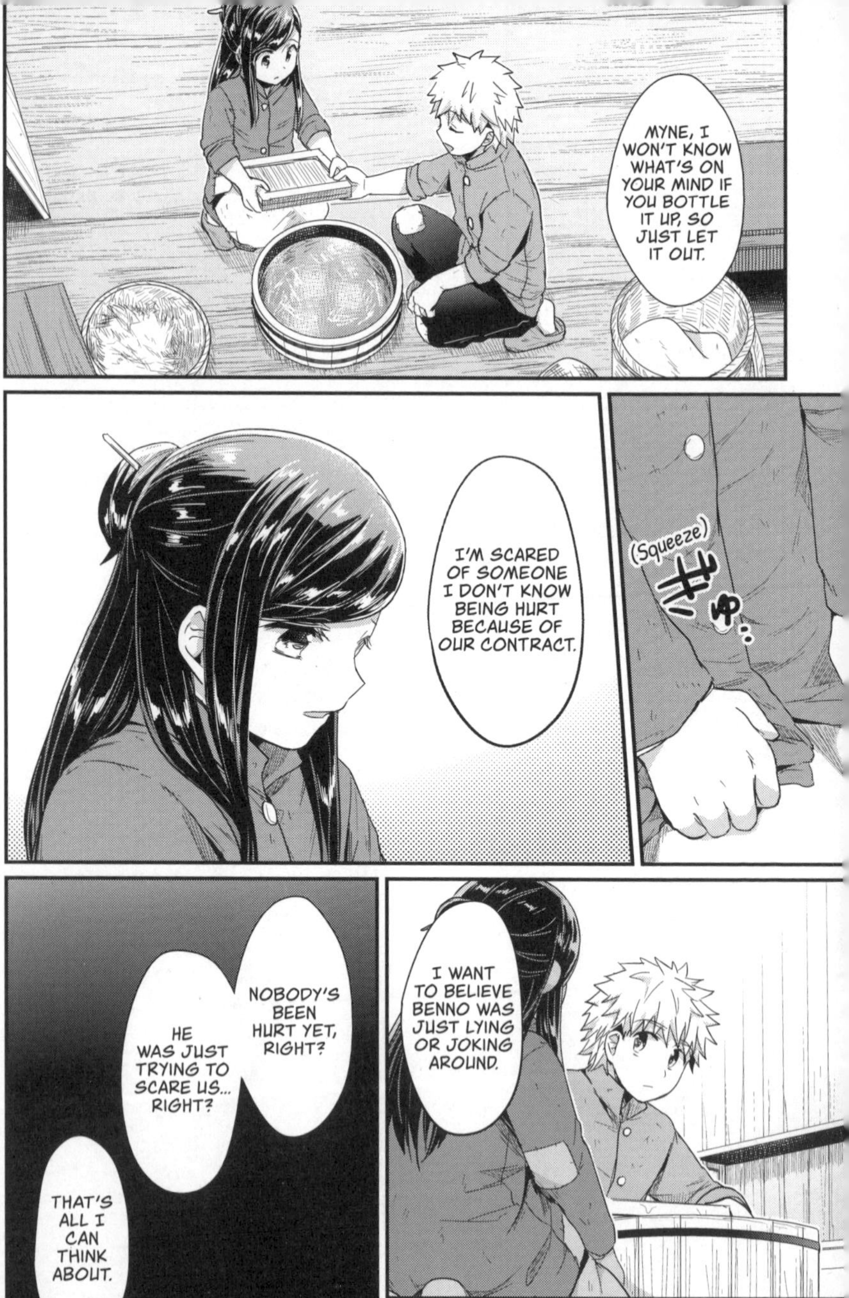
MYNE, I WON'T KNOW WHAT'S ON YOUR MIND IF YOU BOTTLE IT UP, SO JUST LET IT OUT.
(Squeeze)
ぎゅ..
I'M SCARED OF SOMEONE I DON'T KNOW BEING HURT BECAUSE OF OUR CONTRACT.
I WANT TO BELIEVE BENNO WAS JUST LYING OR JOKING AROUND.
NOBODY'S BEEN HURT YET, RIGHT?
HE WAS JUST TRYING TO SCARE US... RIGHT?
THAT'S ALL I CAN THINK ABOUT.

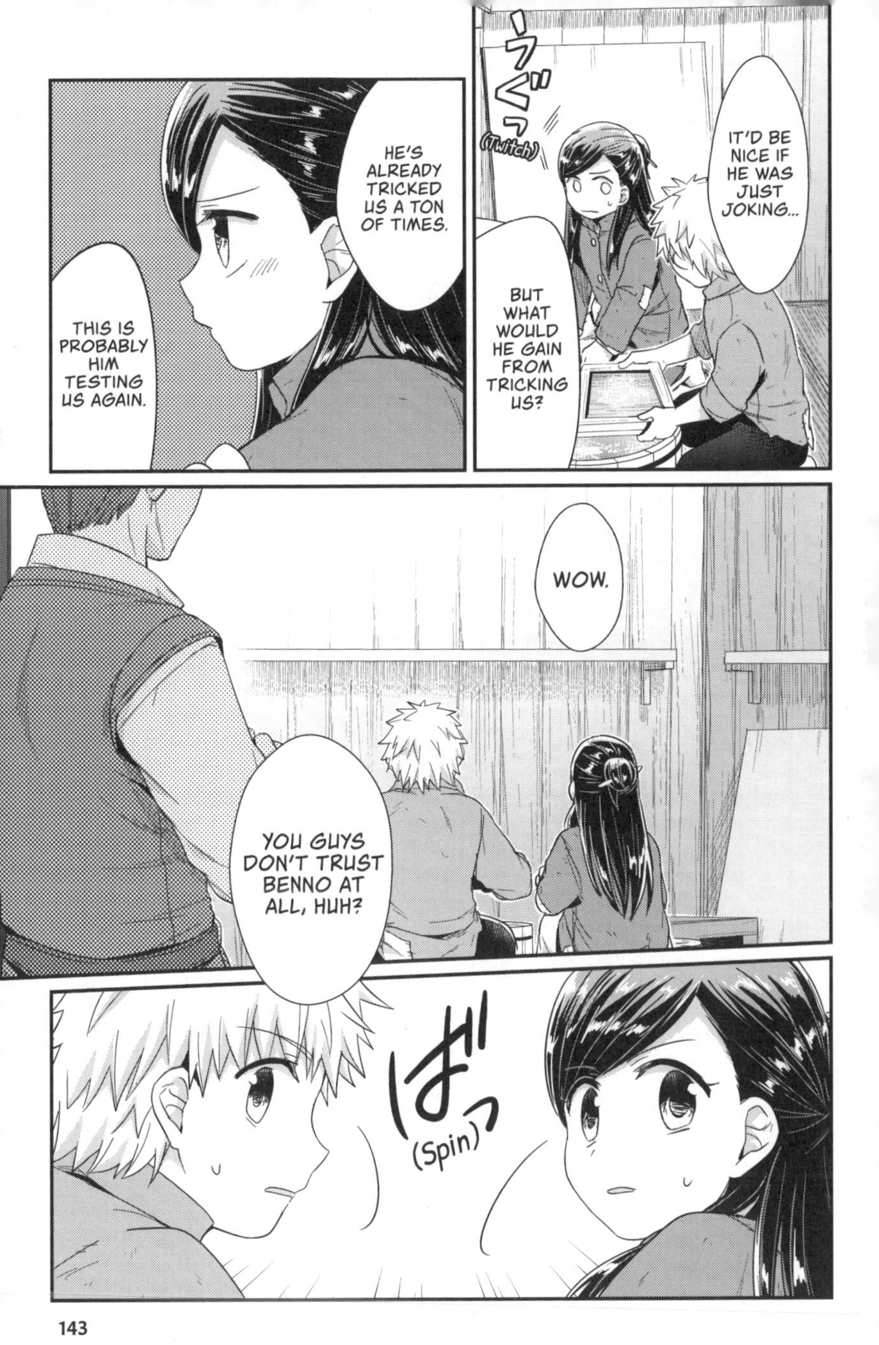
(Twitch)
IT'D BE NICE IF HE WAS JUST JOKING...
BUT WHAT WOULD HE GAIN FROM TRICKING US?
HE'S ALREADY TRICKED US A TON OF TIMES.
THIS IS PROBABLY HIM TESTING US AGAIN.
WOW.
YOU GUYS DON'T TRUST BENNO AT ALL, HUH?
ばっ
(Spin)

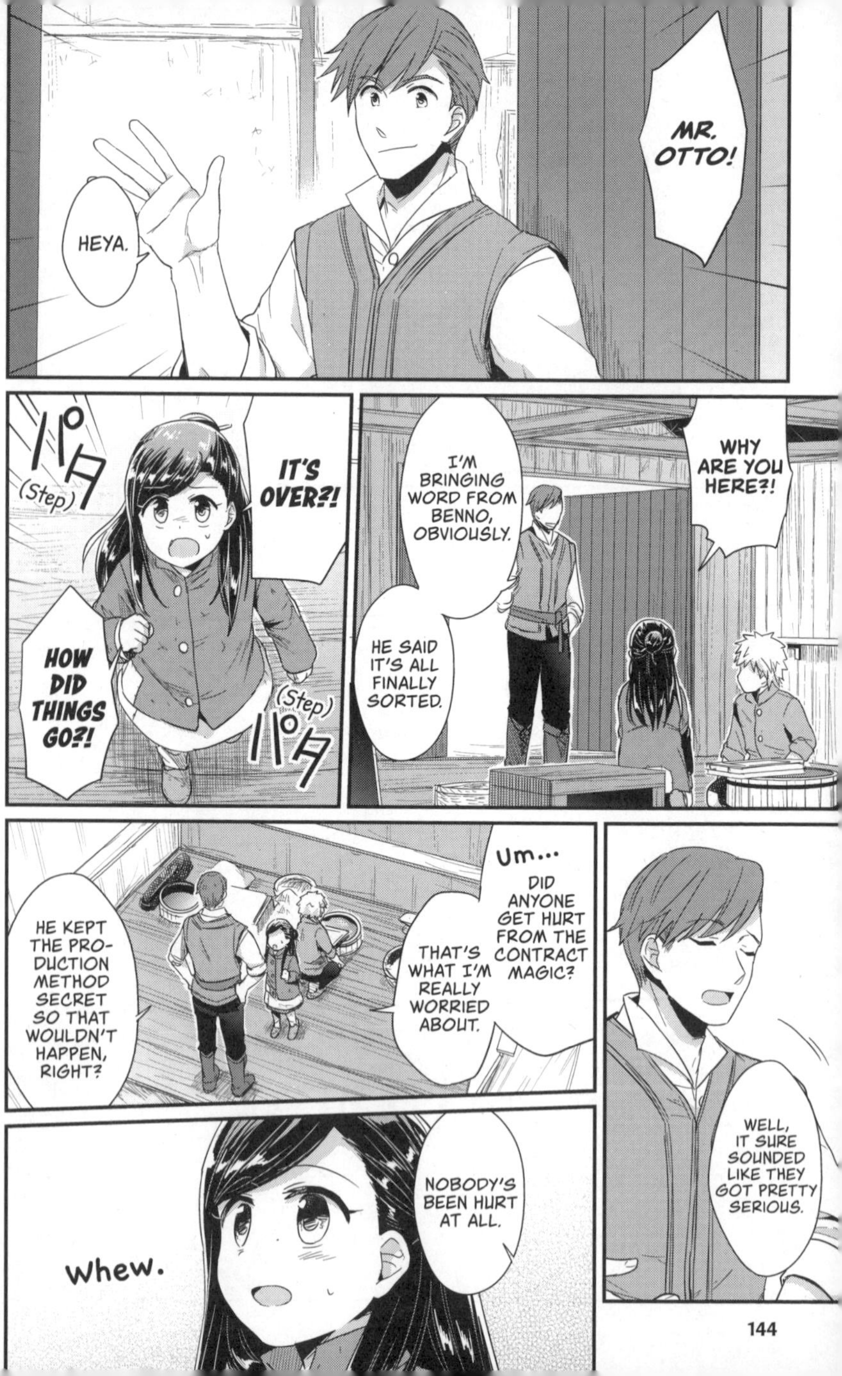
MR. OTTO!
HEYA.
WHY ARE YOU HERE?!
I'M BRINGING WORD FROM BENNO, OBVIOUSLY.
HE SAID IT'S ALL FINALLY SORTED.
IT'S OVER?!
パタ (Step)
HOW DID THINGS GO?!
パタ (Step)
WELL, IT SURE SOUNDED LIKE THEY GOT PRETTY SERIOUS.
Um...
DID ANYONE GET HURT FROM THE CONTRACT MAGIC?
THAT'S WHAT I'M REALLY WORRIED ABOUT.
HE KEPT THE PRO-DUCTION METHOD SECRET SO THAT WOULDN'T HAPPEN, RIGHT?
NOBODY'S BEEN HURT AT ALL.
Whew.

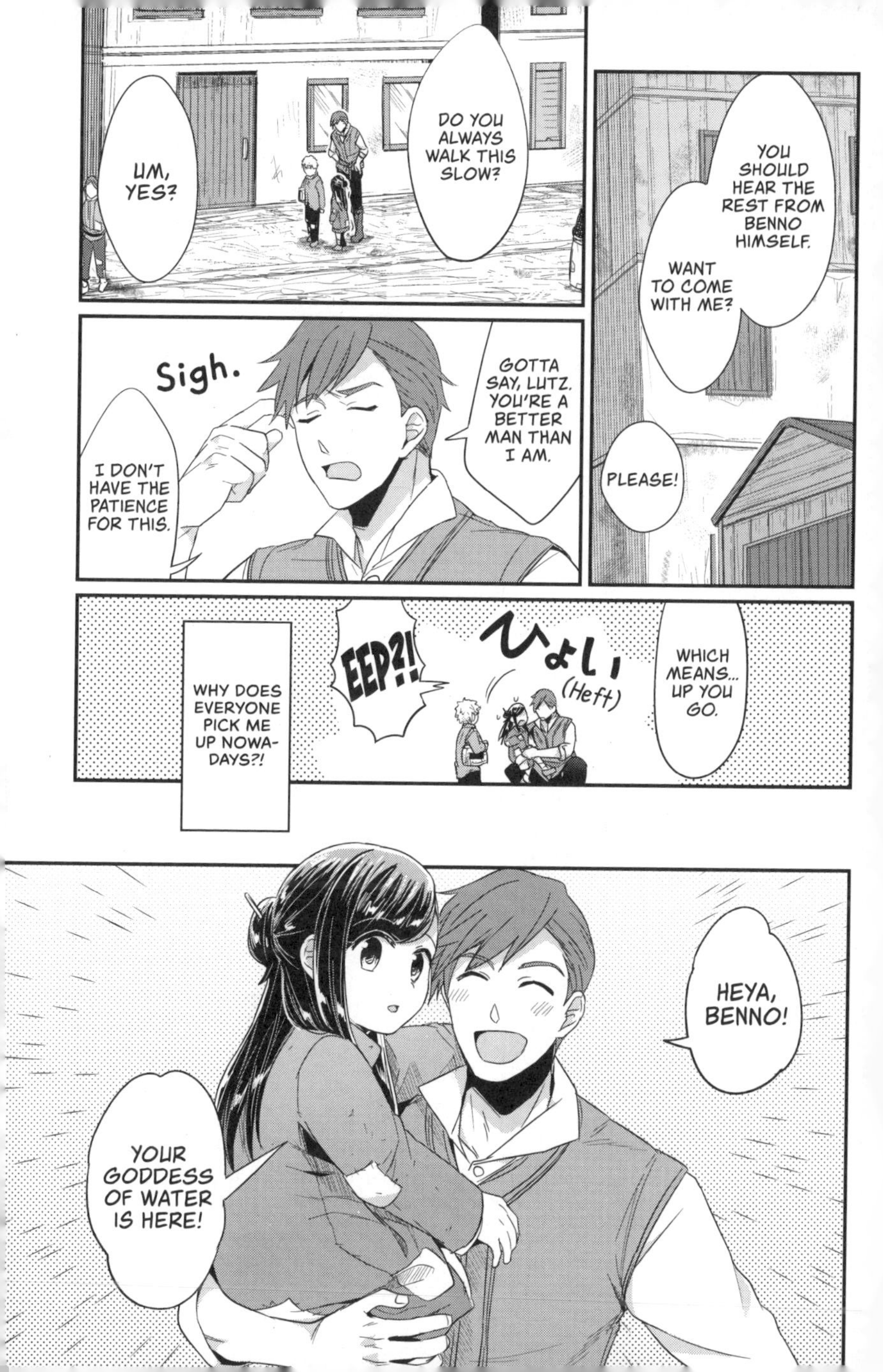
DO YOU ALWAYS WALK THIS SLOW?
UM, YES?
GOTTA SAY, LUTZ. YOU'RE A BETTER MAN THAN I AM.
Sigh.
I DON'T HAVE THE PATIENCE FOR THIS.
YOU SHOULD HEAR THE REST FROM BENNO HIMSELF.
WANT TO COME WITH ME?
PLEASE!
WHICH MEANS... UP YOU GO.
ひょい
(Heft)
EEP?!
WHY DOES EVERYONE PICK ME UP NOWADAYS?!
HEYA, BENNO!
YOUR GODDESS OF WATER IS HERE!

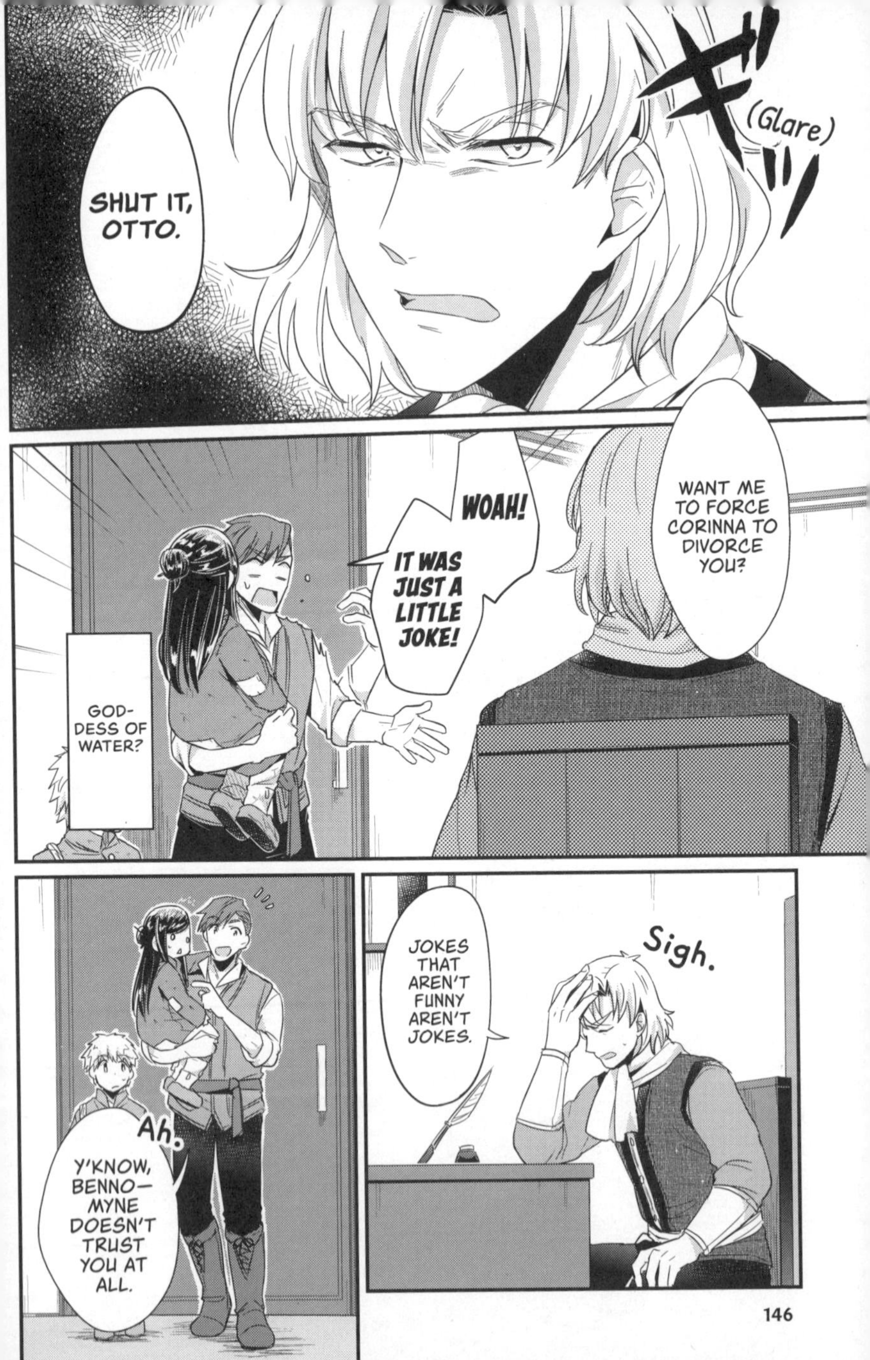

(Glare)
SHUT IT, OTTO.
WANT ME TO FORCE CORINNA TO DIVORCE YOU?
WOAH!
IT WAS JUST A LITTLE JOKE!
GOD-DESS OF WATER?
Sigh.
JOKES THAT AREN'T FUNNY AREN'T JOKES.
Ah.
Y'KNOW, BENNO—MYNE DOESN'T TRUST YOU AT ALL.

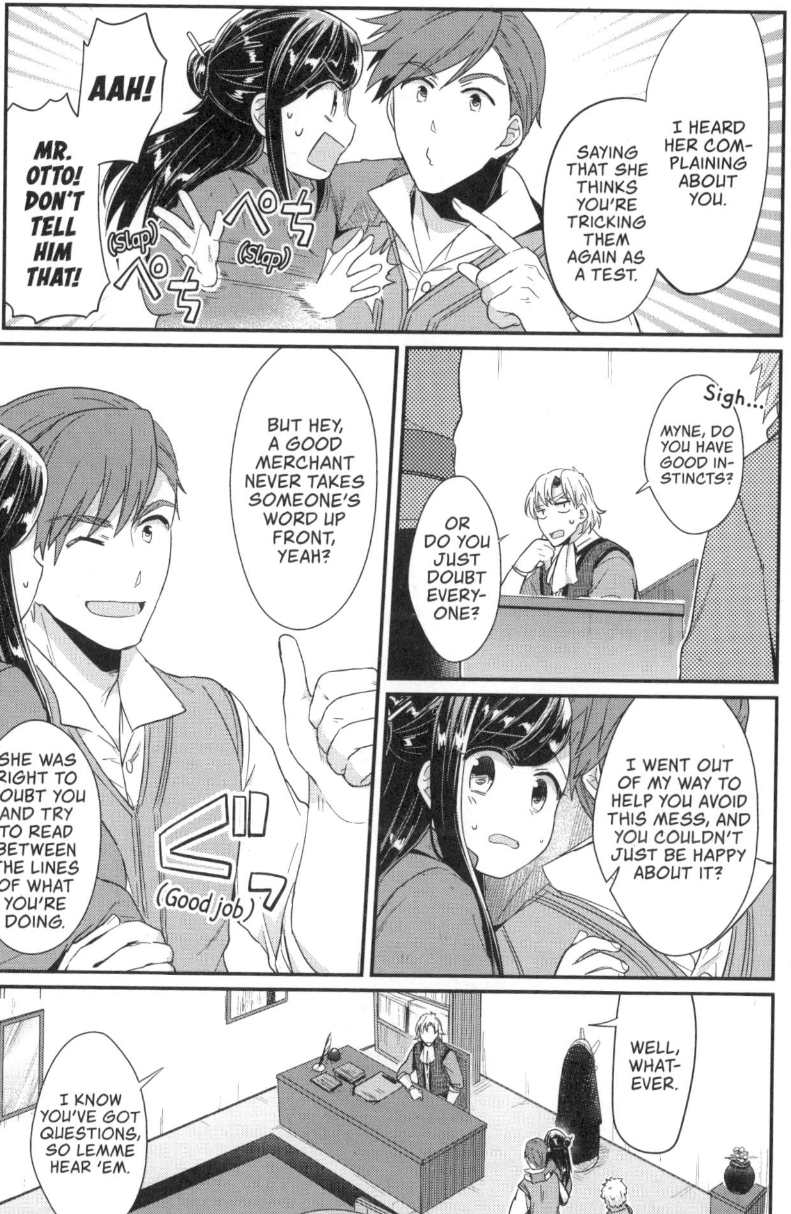
I HEARD HER COM-PLAINING ABOUT YOU.
SAYING THAT SHE THINKS YOU'RE TRICKING THEM AGAIN AS A TEST.
AAH!
MR. OTTO! DON'T TELL HIM THAT!
ぺち
(Slap)
(Slap)
ぺち
Sigh...
MYNE, DO YOU HAVE GOOD IN-STINCTS?
OR DO YOU JUST DOUBT EVERY-ONE?
I WENT OUT OF MY WAY TO HELP YOU AVOID THIS MESS, AND YOU COULDN'T JUST BE HAPPY ABOUT IT?
BUT HEY, A GOOD MERCHANT NEVER TAKES SOMEONE'S WORD UP FRONT, YEAH?
SHE WAS RIGHT TO DOUBT YOU AND TRY TO READ BETWEEN THE LINES OF WHAT YOU'RE DOING.
(Good job)
WELL, WHAT-EVER.
I KNOW YOU'VE GOT QUESTIONS, SO LEMME HEAR 'EM.

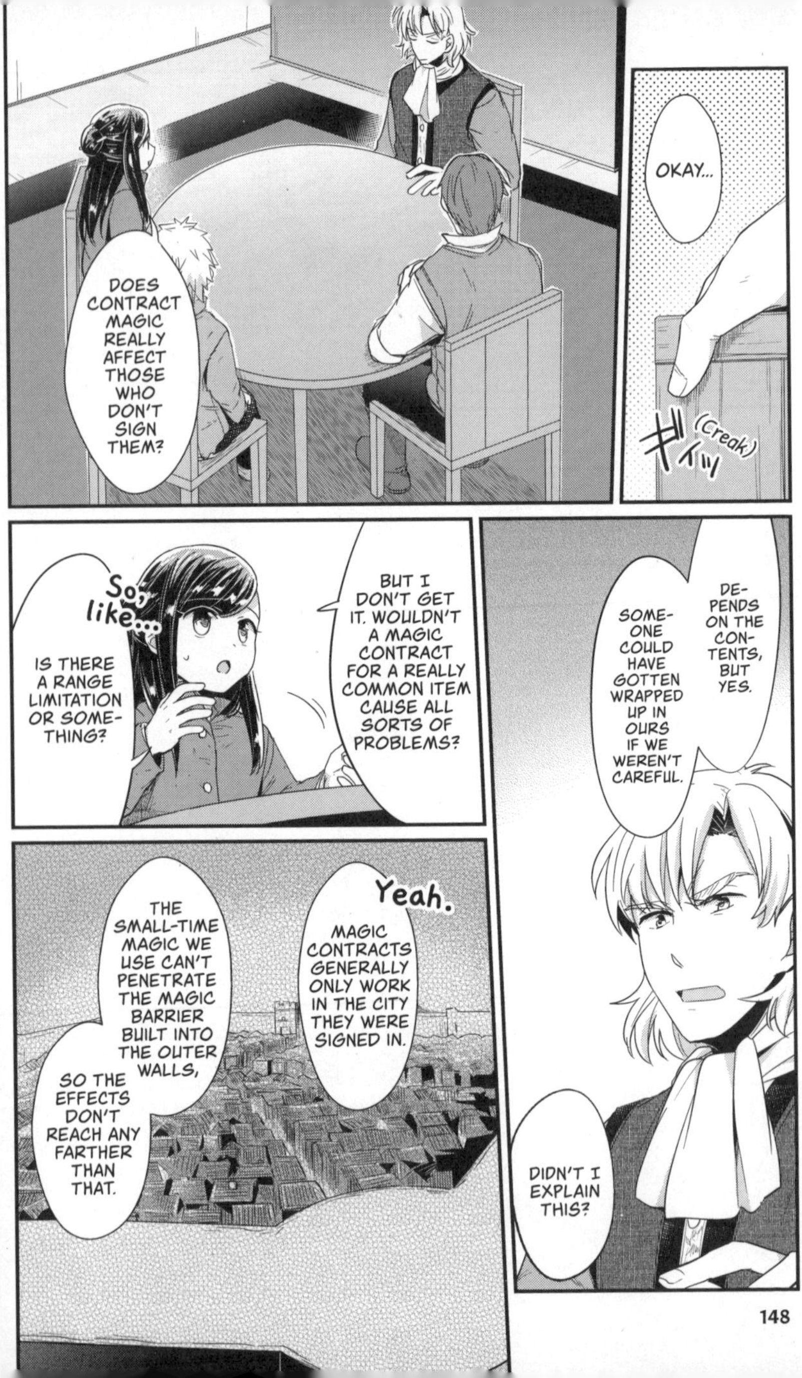
OKAY...
ギィッ (Creak)
DOES CONTRACT MAGIC REALLY AFFECT THOSE WHO DON'T SIGN THEM?
DE-PENDS ON THE CON-TENTS, BUT YES.
SOME-ONE COULD HAVE GOTTEN WRAPPED UP IN OURS IF WE WEREN'T CAREFUL.
DIDN'T I EXPLAIN THIS?
BUT I DON'T GET IT. WOULDN'T A MAGIC CONTRACT FOR A REALLY COMMON ITEM CAUSE ALL SORTS OF PROBLEMS?
So, like...
IS THERE A RANGE LIMITATION OR SOME-THING?
Yeah.
MAGIC CONTRACTS GENERALLY ONLY WORK IN THE CITY THEY WERE SIGNED IN.
THE SMALL-TIME MAGIC WE USE CAN'T PENETRATE THE MAGIC BARRIER BUILT INTO THE OUTER WALLS,
SO THE EFFECTS DON'T REACH ANY FARTHER THAN THAT.

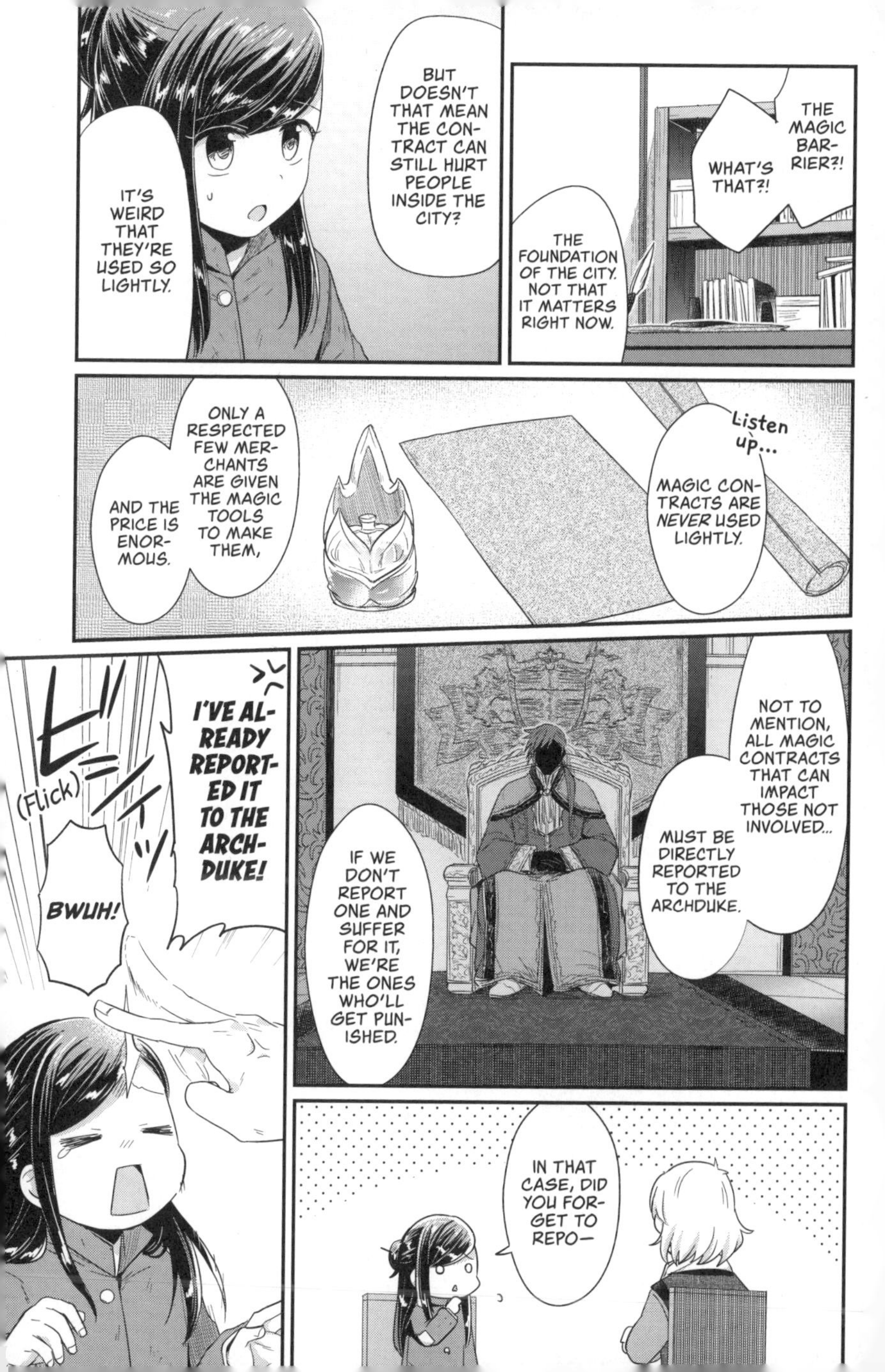
THE MAGIC BARRIER?!
WHAT'S THAT?!
THE FOUNDATION OF THE CITY. NOT THAT IT MATTERS RIGHT NOW.
BUT DOESN'T THAT MEAN THE CONTRACT CAN STILL HURT PEOPLE INSIDE THE CITY?
IT'S WEIRD THAT THEY'RE USED SO LIGHTLY.
Listen up...
MAGIC CONTRACTS ARE NEVER USED LIGHTLY.
ONLY A RESPECTED FEW MERCHANTS ARE GIVEN THE MAGIC TOOLS TO MAKE THEM,
AND THE PRICE IS ENORMOUS.
NOT TO MENTION, ALL MAGIC CONTRACTS THAT CAN IMPACT THOSE NOT INVOLVED...
MUST BE DIRECTLY REPORTED TO THE ARCHDUKE.
IF WE DON'T REPORT ONE AND SUFFER FOR IT, WE'RE THE ONES WHO'LL GET PUNISHED.
IN THAT CASE, DID YOU FORGET TO REPO—
I'VE ALREADY REPORTED IT TO THE ARCHDUKE!
(Flick)
BWUH!

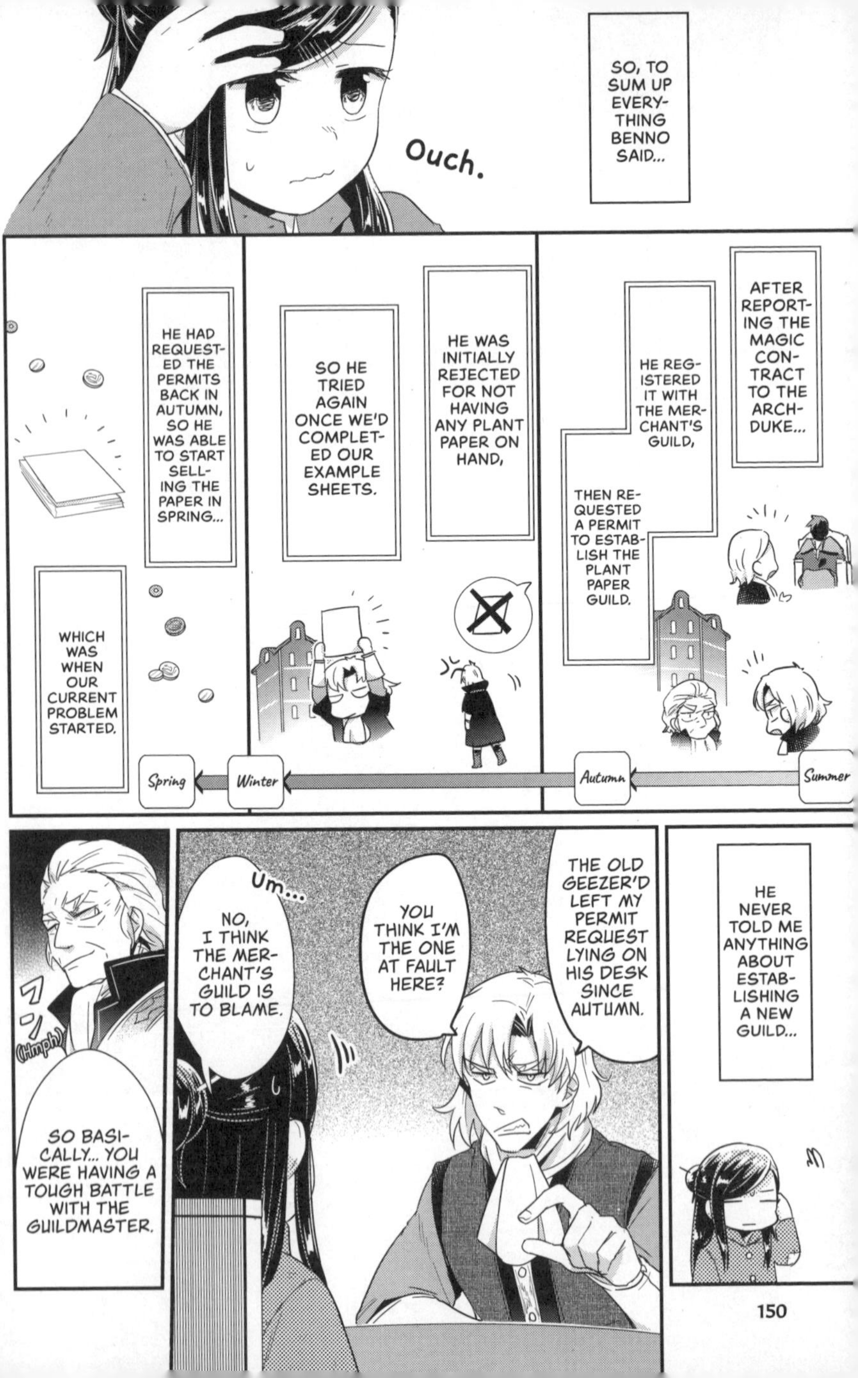
SO, TO SUM UP EVERYTHING BENNO SAID...
Ouch.
AFTER REPORTING THE MAGIC CONTRACT TO THE ARCHDUKE...
HE REGISTERED IT WITH THE MERCHANT'S GUILD,
THEN REQUESTED A PERMIT TO ESTABLISH THE PLANT PAPER GUILD.
Summer
Autumn
HE WAS INITIALLY REJECTED FOR NOT HAVING ANY PLANT PAPER ON HAND,
SO HE TRIED AGAIN ONCE WE'D COMPLETED OUR EXAMPLE SHEETS.
Winter
HE HAD REQUESTED THE PERMITS BACK IN AUTUMN, SO HE WAS ABLE TO START SELLING THE PAPER IN SPRING...
WHICH WAS WHEN OUR CURRENT PROBLEM STARTED.
Spring
HE NEVER TOLD ME ANYTHING ABOUT ESTABLISHING A NEW GUILD...
THE OLD GEEZER'D LEFT MY PERMIT REQUEST LYING ON HIS DESK SINCE AUTUMN.
YOU THINK I'M THE ONE AT FAULT HERE?
NO, I THINK THE MERCHANT'S GUILD IS TO BLAME.
Um...
(Hmph)
SO BASICALLY... YOU WERE HAVING A TOUGH BATTLE WITH THE GUILDMASTER.

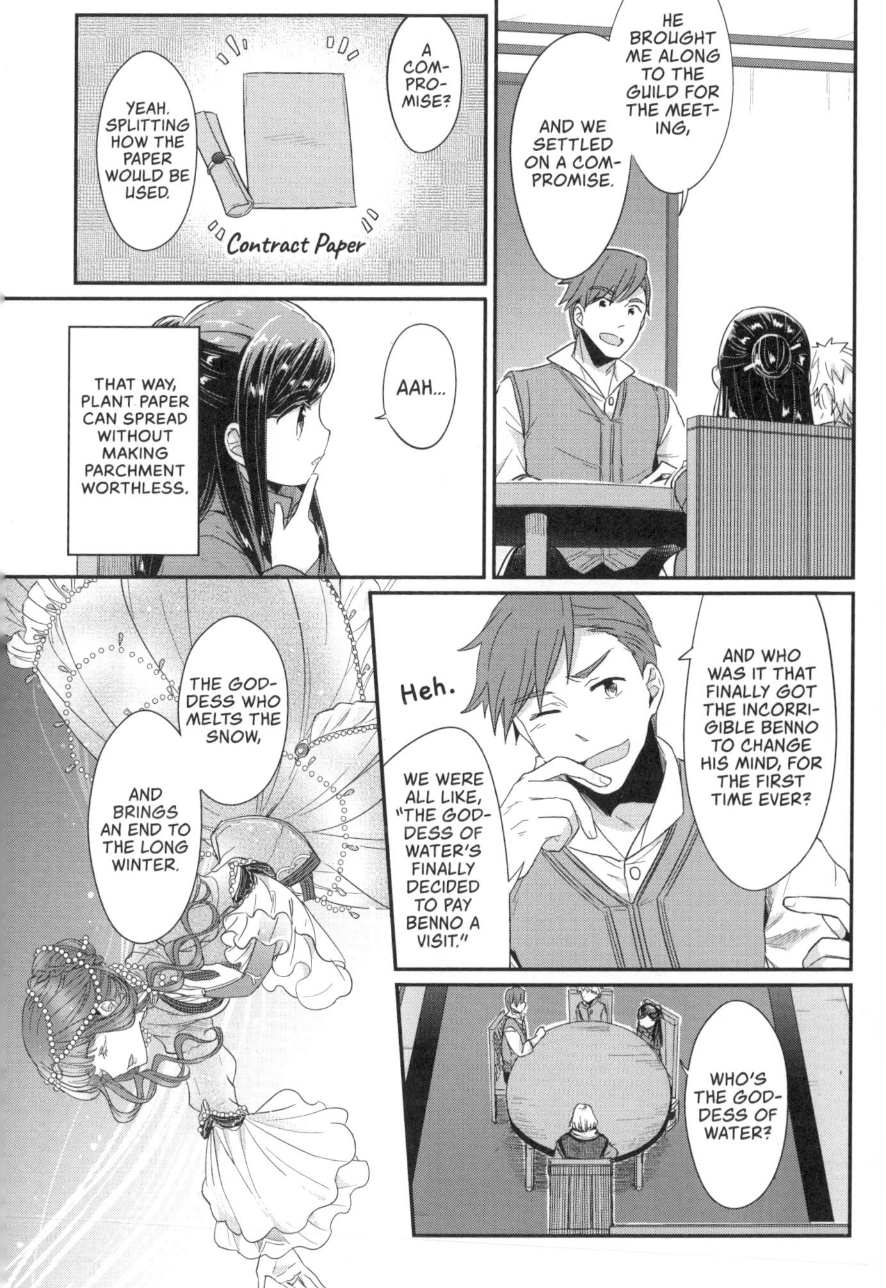
HE BROUGHT ME ALONG TO THE GUILD FOR THE MEETING,
AND WE SETTLED ON A COMPROMISE.
A COMPROMISE?
YEAH. SPLITTING HOW THE PAPER WOULD BE USED.
Contract Paper
AAH...
THAT WAY, PLANT PAPER CAN SPREAD WITHOUT MAKING PARCHMENT WORTHLESS.
AND WHO WAS IT THAT FINALLY GOT THE INCORRIGIBLE BENNO TO CHANGE HIS MIND, FOR THE FIRST TIME EVER?
Heh.
WE WERE ALL LIKE, "THE GODDESS OF WATER'S FINALLY DECIDED TO PAY BENNO A VISIT."
WHO'S THE GODDESS OF WATER?
THE GODDESS WHO MELTS THE SNOW,
AND BRINGS AN END TO THE LONG WINTER.

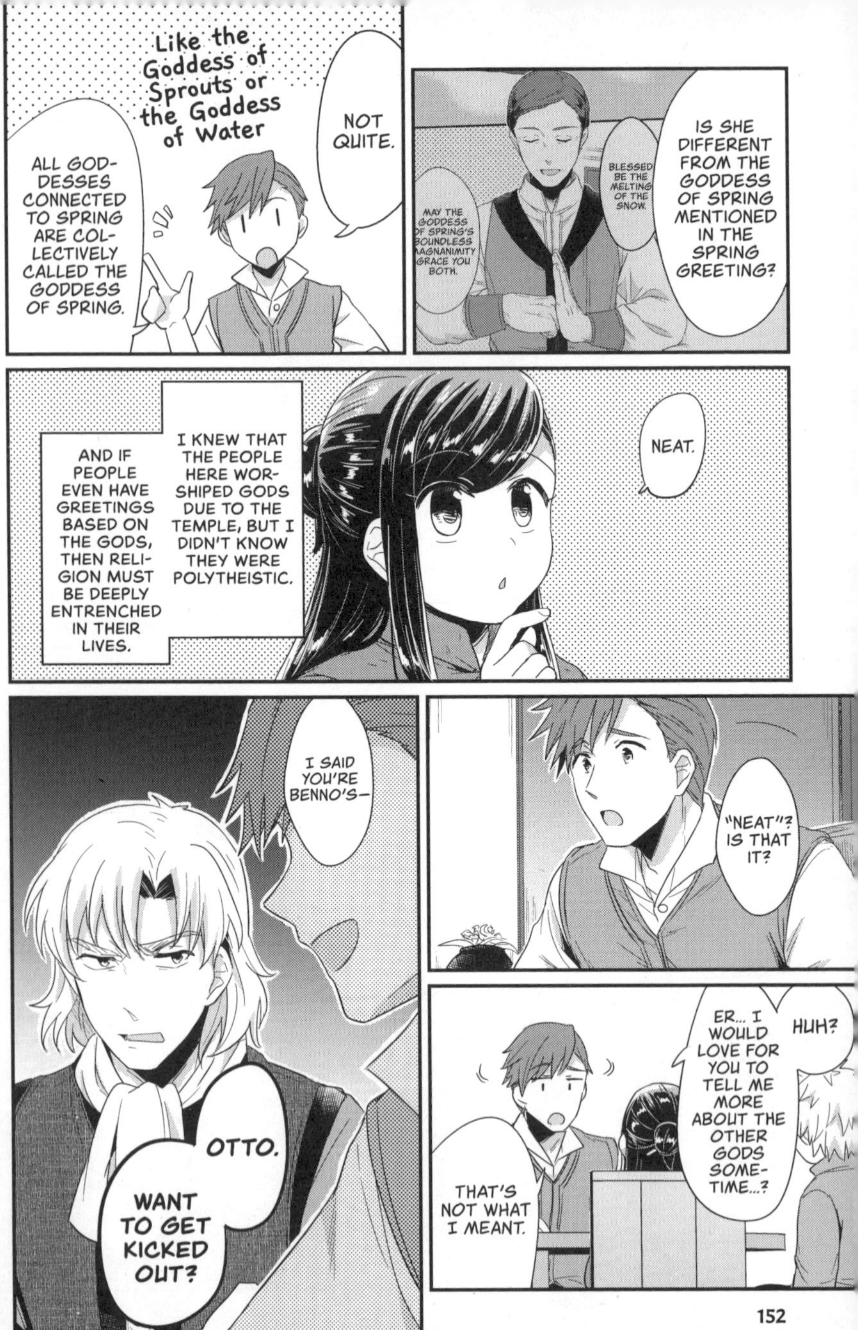
IS SHE DIFFERENT FROM THE GODDESS OF SPRING MENTIONED IN THE SPRING GREETING?
BLESSED BE THE MELTING OF THE SNOW.
MAY THE GODDESS OF SPRING'S BOUNDLESS MAGNANIMITY GRACE YOU BOTH.
NOT QUITE.
Like the Goddess of Sprouts or the Goddess of Water
ALL GODDESSES CONNECTED TO SPRING ARE COLLECTIVELY CALLED THE GODDESS OF SPRING.
NEAT.
I KNEW THAT THE PEOPLE HERE WORSHIPED GODS DUE TO THE TEMPLE, BUT I DIDN'T KNOW THEY WERE POLYTHEISTIC.
AND IF PEOPLE EVEN HAVE GREETINGS BASED ON THE GODS, THEN RELIGION MUST BE DEEPLY ENTRENCHED IN THEIR LIVES.
"NEAT"? IS THAT IT?
HUH?
ER... I WOULD LOVE FOR YOU TO TELL ME MORE ABOUT THE OTHER GODS SOMETIME...?
THAT'S NOT WHAT I MEANT.
I SAID YOU'RE BENNO'S—
OTTO.
WANT TO GET KICKED OUT?

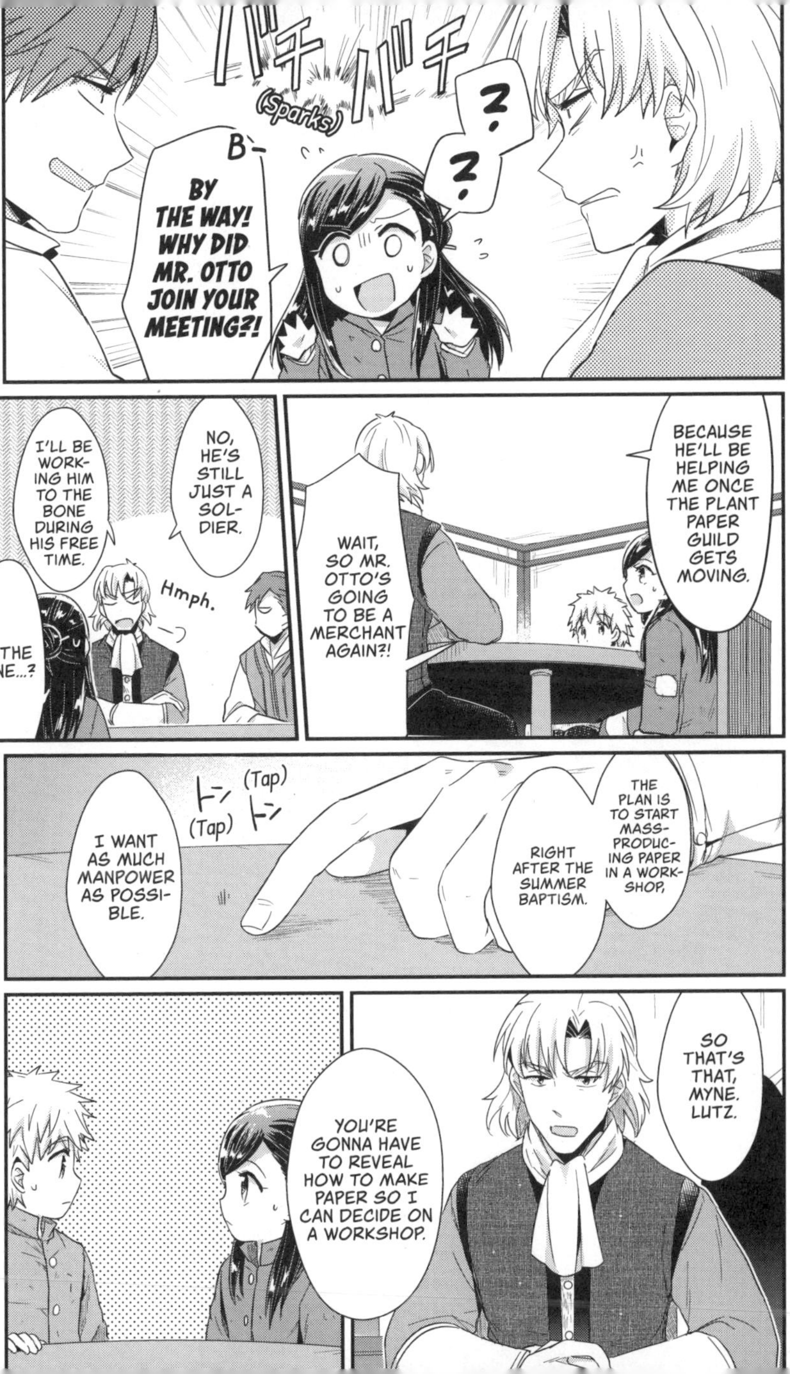
バチ バチ
(Sparks)
?
?
B-
BY THE WAY! WHY DID MR. OTTO JOIN YOUR MEETING?!
BECAUSE HE'LL BE HELPING ME ONCE THE PLANT PAPER GUILD GETS MOVING.
WAIT, SO MR. OTTO'S GOING TO BE A MERCHANT AGAIN?!
NO, HE'S STILL JUST A SOLDIER.
I'LL BE WORKING HIM TO THE BONE DURING HIS FREE TIME.
Hmph.
TO THE BONE...?
THE PLAN IS TO START MASS-PRODUCING PAPER IN A WORKSHOP,
RIGHT AFTER THE SUMMER BAPTISM.
トン (Tap)
トン (Tap)
I WANT AS MUCH MANPOWER AS POSSIBLE.
SO THAT'S THAT, MYNE. LUTZ.
YOU'RE GONNA HAVE TO REVEAL HOW TO MAKE PAPER SO I CAN DECIDE ON A WORKSHOP.

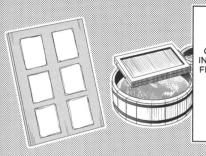

I SHOULD CHARGE AN INFORMATION FEE FOR THIS LIKE I DID WITH THE RINSHAM, RIGHT?
SINCE THE PROFITS FROM THE PLANT PAPER GUILD WON'T GO TO US,
(Rustle)
I'LL BE CHARGING AN INFORMATION FEE FOR THE PAPER-MAKING PROCESS.
SURE.
HOW MUCH DO YOU WANT?
UM...
HOW MUCH ARE YOU WILLING TO PAY?
にい
(Grin)
I'LL PAY AS MUCH AS YOU WANT.
NAME YOUR PRICE.

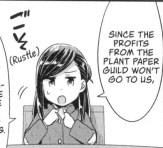

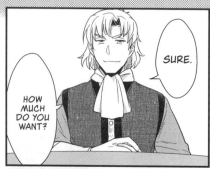

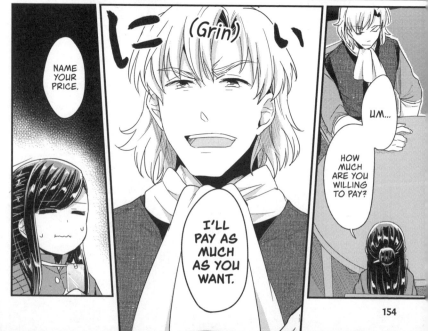

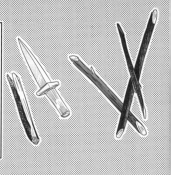

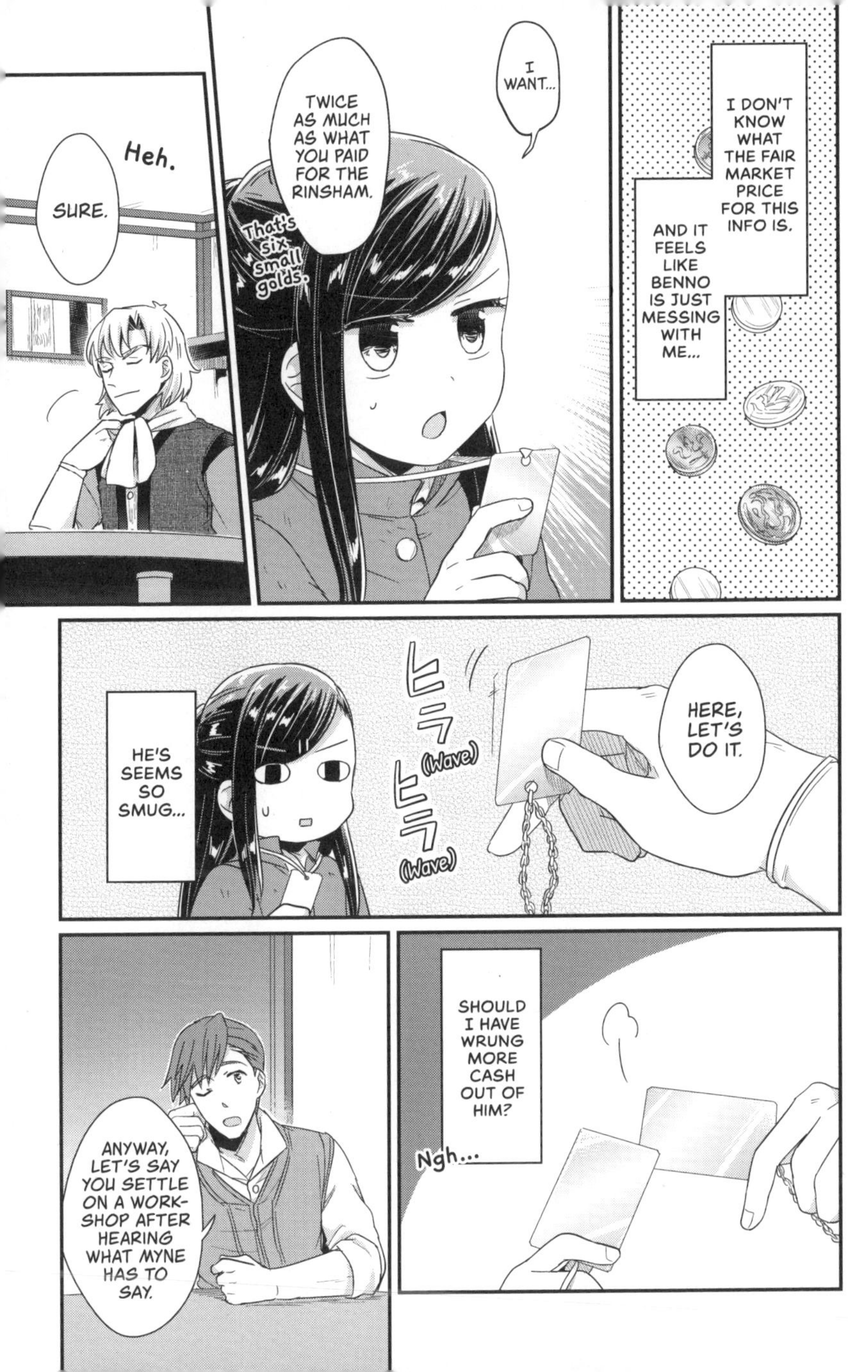
I DON'T KNOW WHAT THE FAIR MARKET PRICE FOR THIS INFO IS.
AND IT FEELS LIKE BENNO IS JUST MESSING WITH ME...
I WANT...
TWICE AS MUCH AS WHAT YOU PAID FOR THE RINSHAM.
That's six small golds.
Heh.
SURE.
HERE, LET'S DO IT.
ヒラ (Wave)
ヒラ (Wave)
HE'S SEEMS SO SMUG...
SHOULD I HAVE WRUNG MORE CASH OUT OF HIM?
Ngh...
ANYWAY, LET'S SAY YOU SETTLE ON A WORK-SHOP AFTER HEARING WHAT MYNE HAS TO SAY.

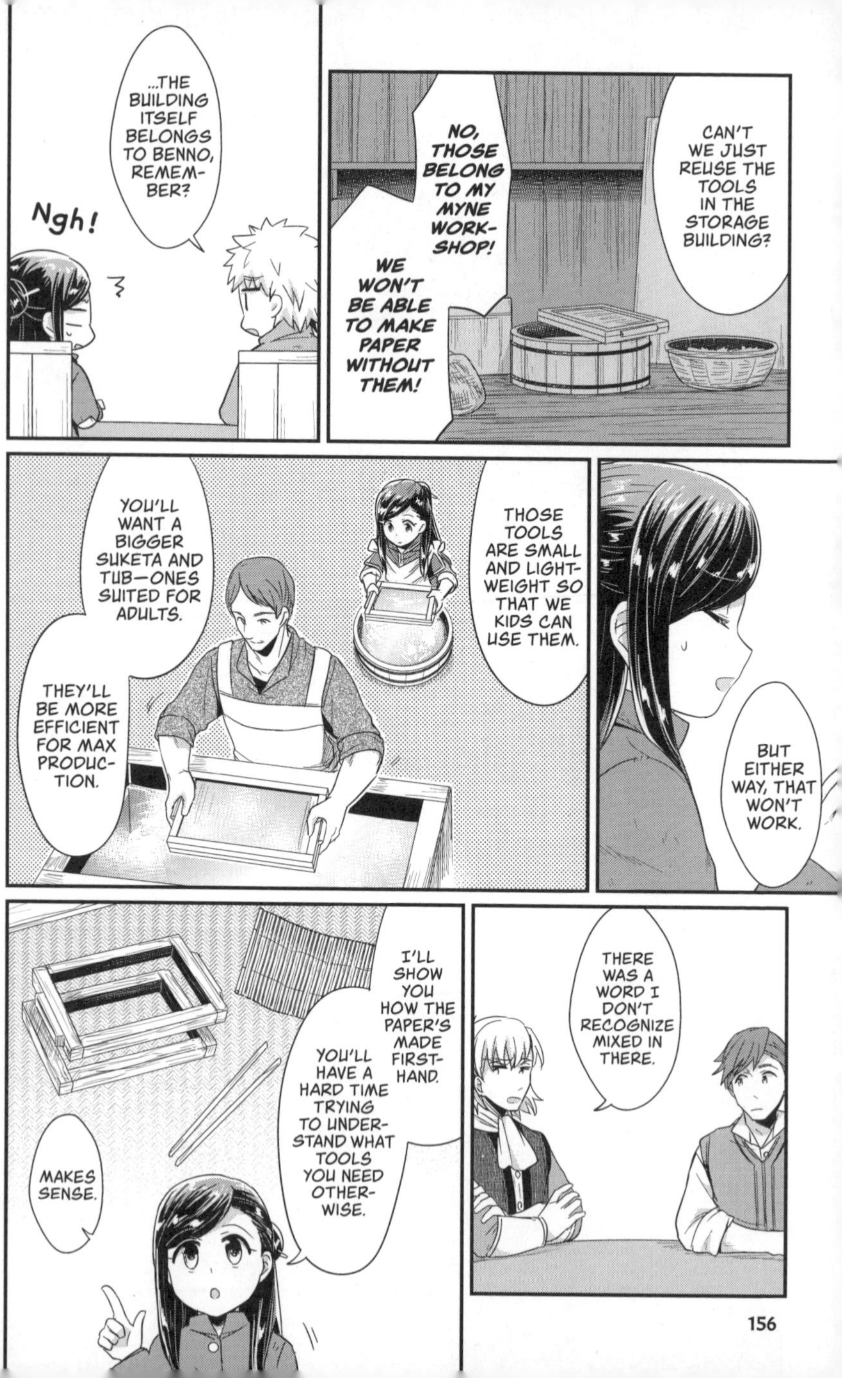
CAN'T WE JUST REUSE THE TOOLS IN THE STORAGE BUILDING?
NO, THOSE BELONG TO MY MYNE WORKSHOP!
WE WON'T BE ABLE TO MAKE PAPER WITHOUT THEM!
...THE BUILDING ITSELF BELONGS TO BENNO, REMEMBER?
Ngh!
BUT EITHER WAY, THAT WON'T WORK.
THOSE TOOLS ARE SMALL AND LIGHTWEIGHT SO THAT WE KIDS CAN USE THEM.
YOU'LL WANT A BIGGER SUKETA AND TUB—ONES SUITED FOR ADULTS.
THEY'LL BE MORE EFFICIENT FOR MAX PRODUCTION.
THERE WAS A WORD I DON'T RECOGNIZE MIXED IN THERE.
I'LL SHOW YOU HOW THE PAPER'S MADE FIRSTHAND.
YOU'LL HAVE A HARD TIME TRYING TO UNDERSTAND WHAT TOOLS YOU NEED OTHERWISE.
MAKES SENSE.

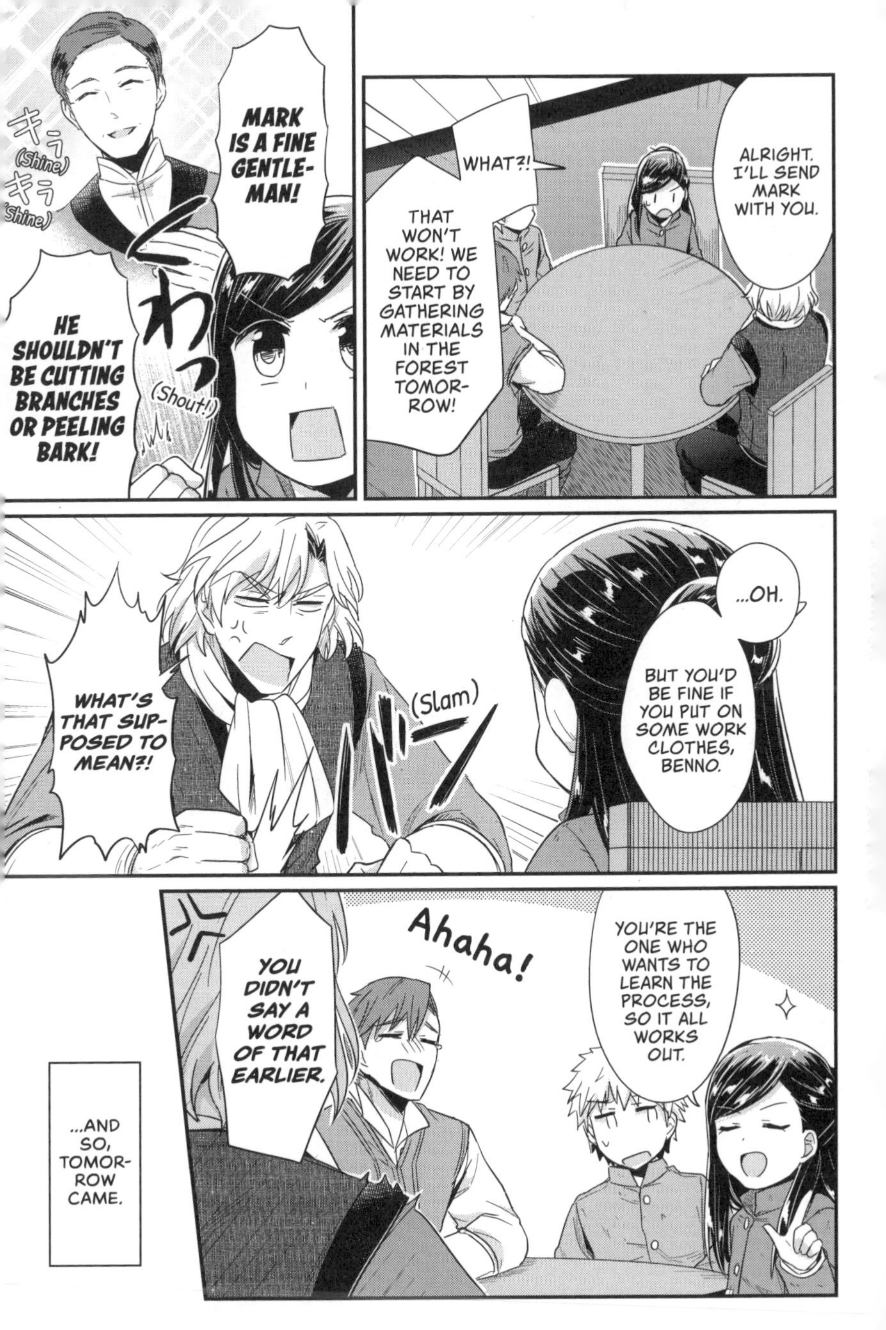
ALRIGHT. I'LL SEND MARK WITH YOU.
WHAT?!
THAT WON'T WORK! WE NEED TO START BY GATHERING MATERIALS IN THE FOREST TOMORROW!
MARK IS A FINE GENTLEMAN!
キラ (Shine) キラ (Shine)
わっ (Shout!)
HE SHOULDN'T BE CUTTING BRANCHES OR PEELING BARK!
...OH.
BUT YOU'D BE FINE IF YOU PUT ON SOME WORK CLOTHES, BENNO.
(Slam)
WHAT'S THAT SUPPOSED TO MEAN?!
YOU'RE THE ONE WHO WANTS TO LEARN THE PROCESS, SO IT ALL WORKS OUT.
Ahaha!
YOU DIDN'T SAY A WORD OF THAT EARLIER.
...AND SO, TOMORROW CAME.

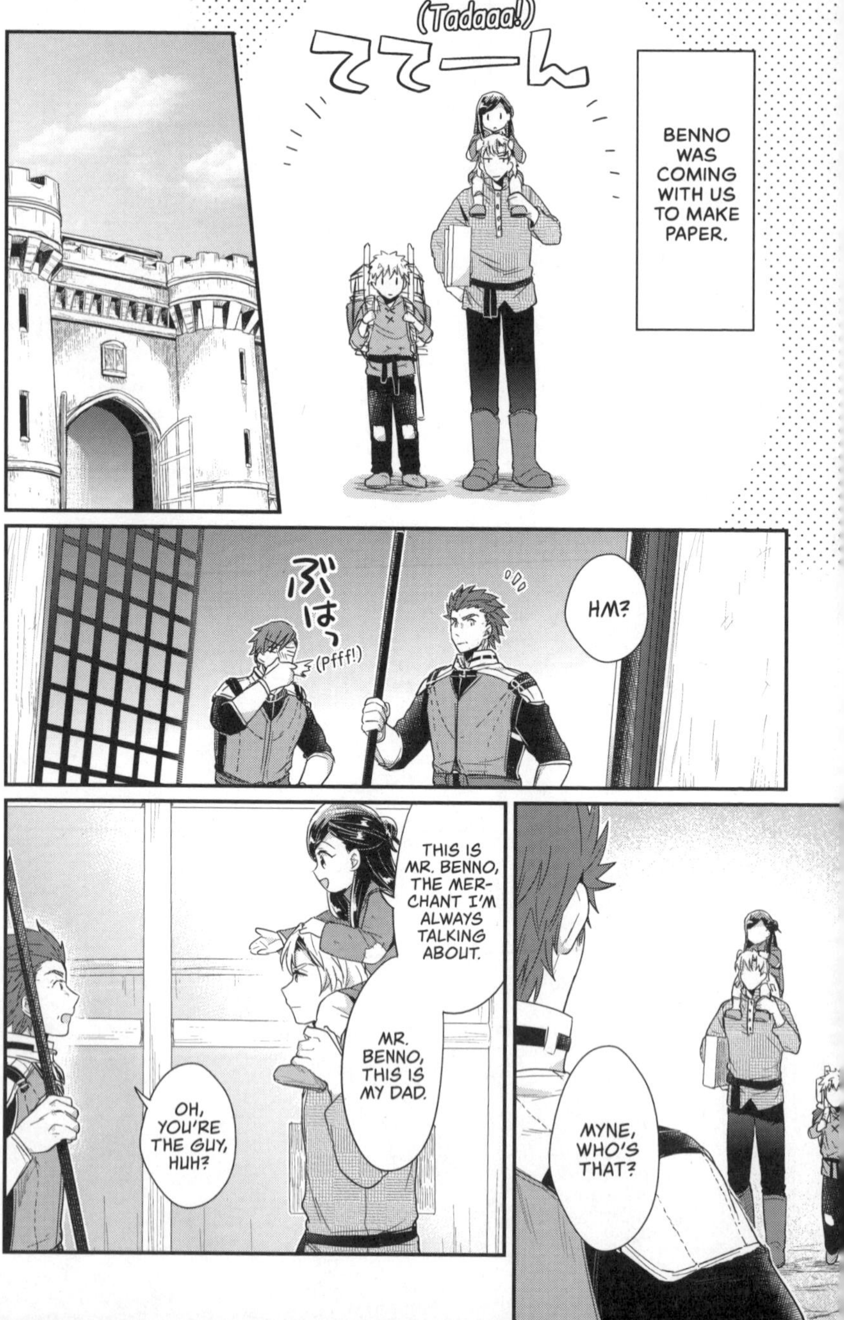
ててーん
(Tadaaa!)
BENNO WAS COMING WITH US TO MAKE PAPER.
HM?
ぶはっ
(Pfff!)
MYNE, WHO'S THAT?
THIS IS MR. BENNO, THE MER-CHANT I'M ALWAYS TALKING ABOUT.
MR. BENNO, THIS IS MY DAD.
OH, YOU'RE THE GUY, HUH?

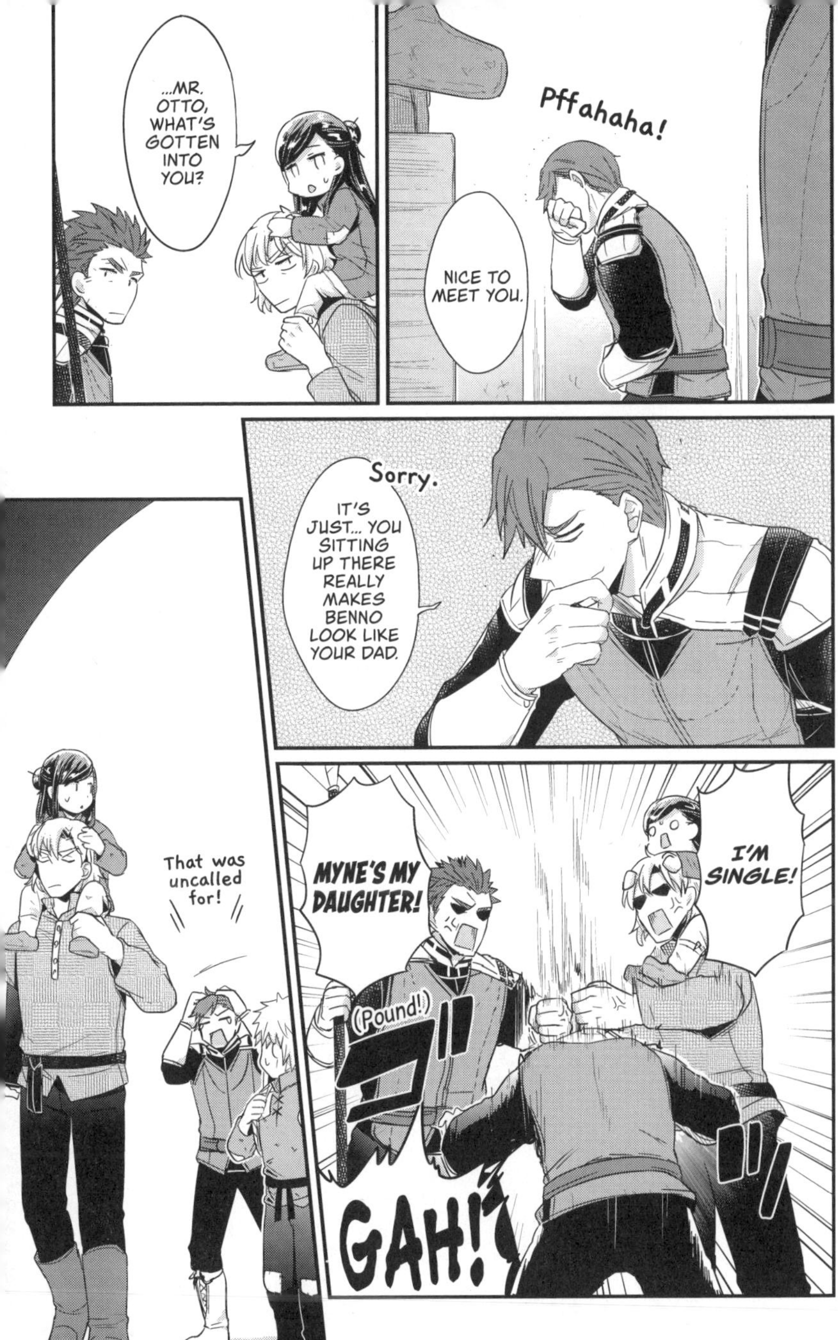
Pffahaha!
NICE TO MEET YOU.
...MR. OTTO, WHAT'S GOTTEN INTO YOU?
Sorry.
IT'S JUST... YOU SITTING UP THERE REALLY MAKES BENNO LOOK LIKE YOUR DAD.
I'M SINGLE!
MYNE'S MY DAUGHTER!
(Pound!)
GAH!
That was uncalled for!

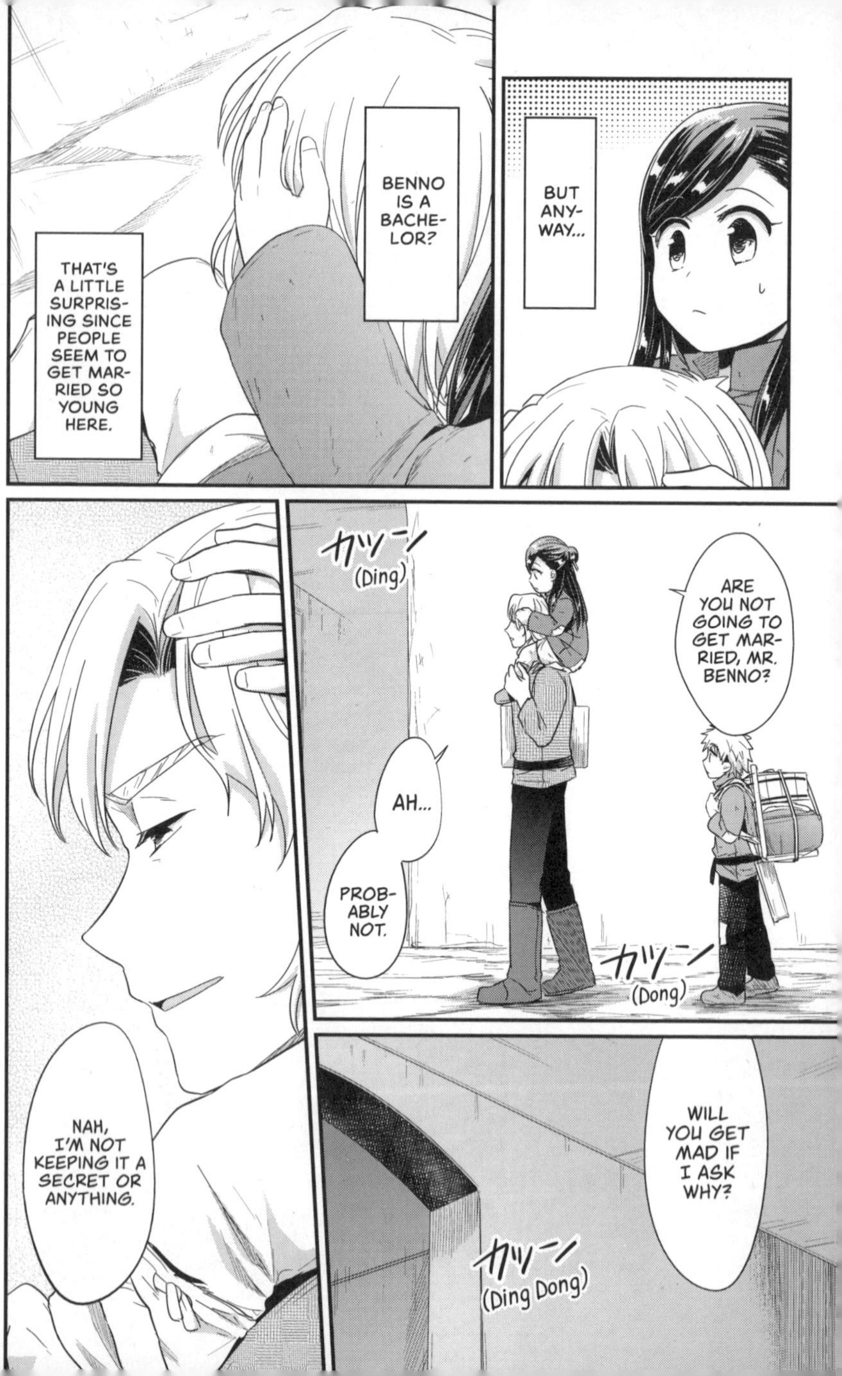
BUT ANYWAY...
BENNO IS A BACHELOR?
THAT'S A LITTLE SURPRISING SINCE PEOPLE SEEM TO GET MARRIED SO YOUNG HERE.
ARE YOU NOT GOING TO GET MARRIED, MR. BENNO?
カツーン
(Ding)
AH...
PROBABLY NOT.
カツーン
(Dong)
WILL YOU GET MAD IF I ASK WHY?
カツーン
(Ding Dong)
NAH, I'M NOT KEEPING IT A SECRET OR ANYTHING.

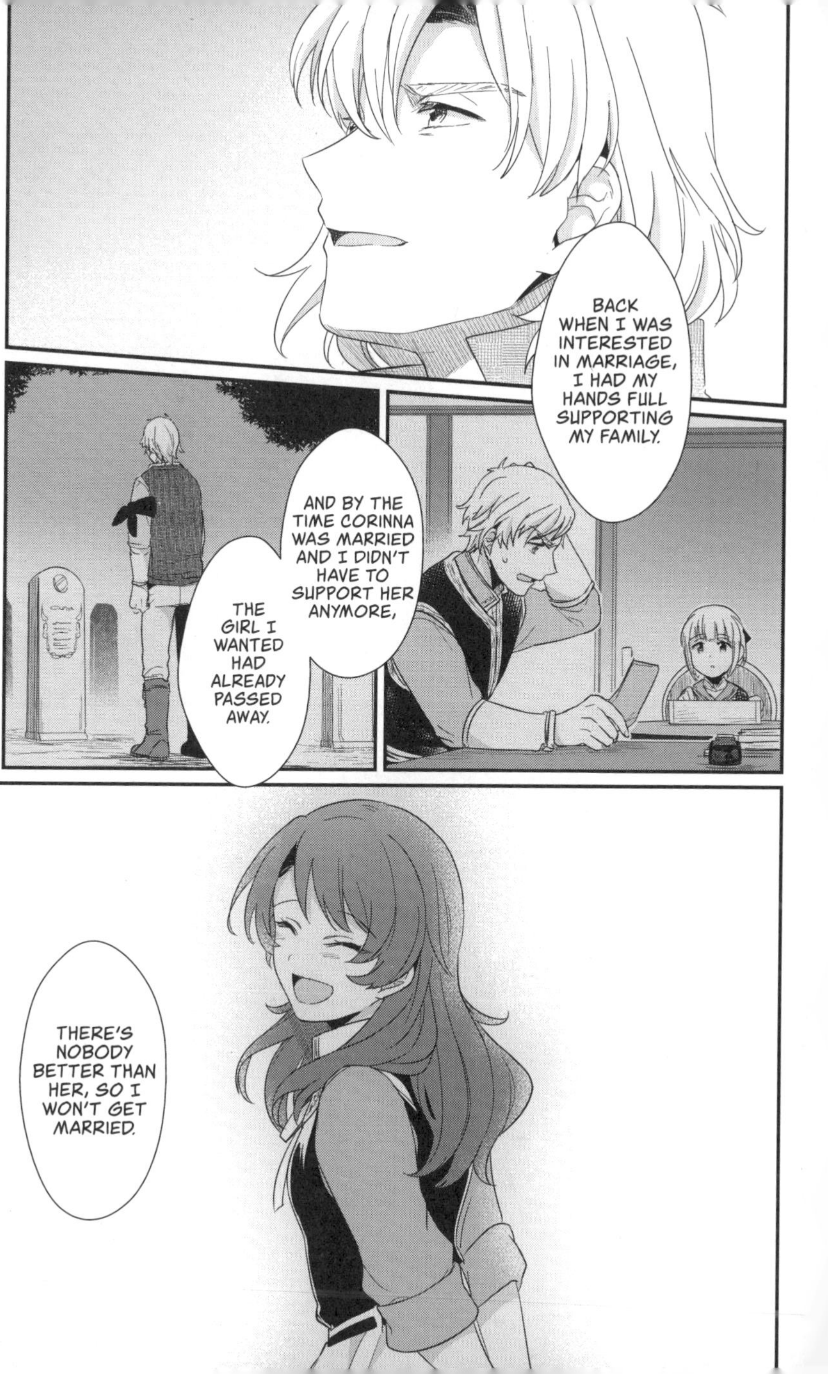
BACK WHEN I WAS INTERESTED IN MARRIAGE, I HAD MY HANDS FULL SUPPORTING MY FAMILY.
AND BY THE TIME CORINNA WAS MARRIED AND I DIDN'T HAVE TO SUPPORT HER ANYMORE,
THE GIRL I WANTED HAD ALREADY PASSED AWAY.
THERE'S NOBODY BETTER THAN HER, SO I WON'T GET MARRIED.

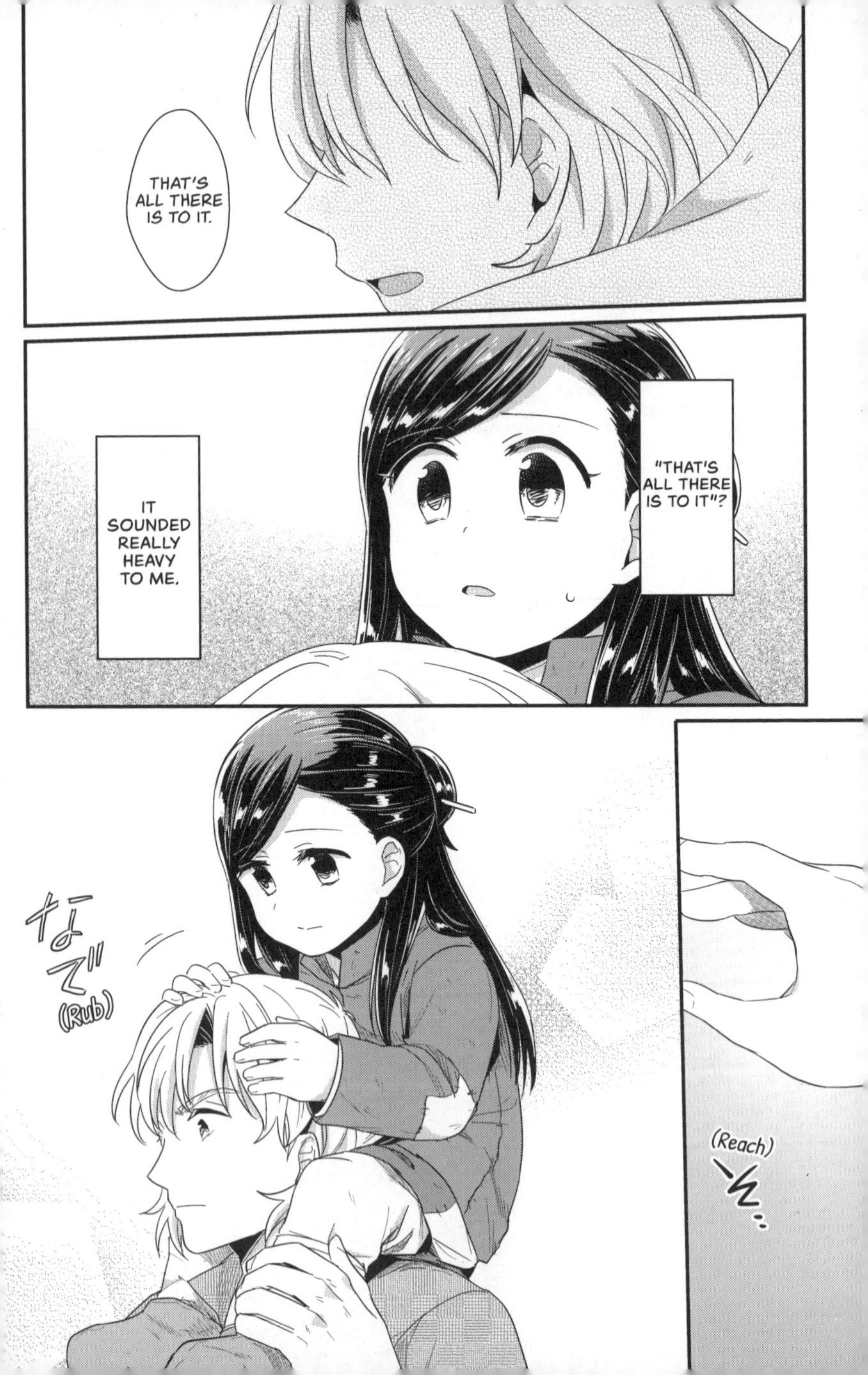
THAT'S ALL THERE IS TO IT.
"THAT'S ALL THERE IS TO IT"?
IT SOUNDED REALLY HEAVY TO ME.
(Reach)
なで
(Rub)

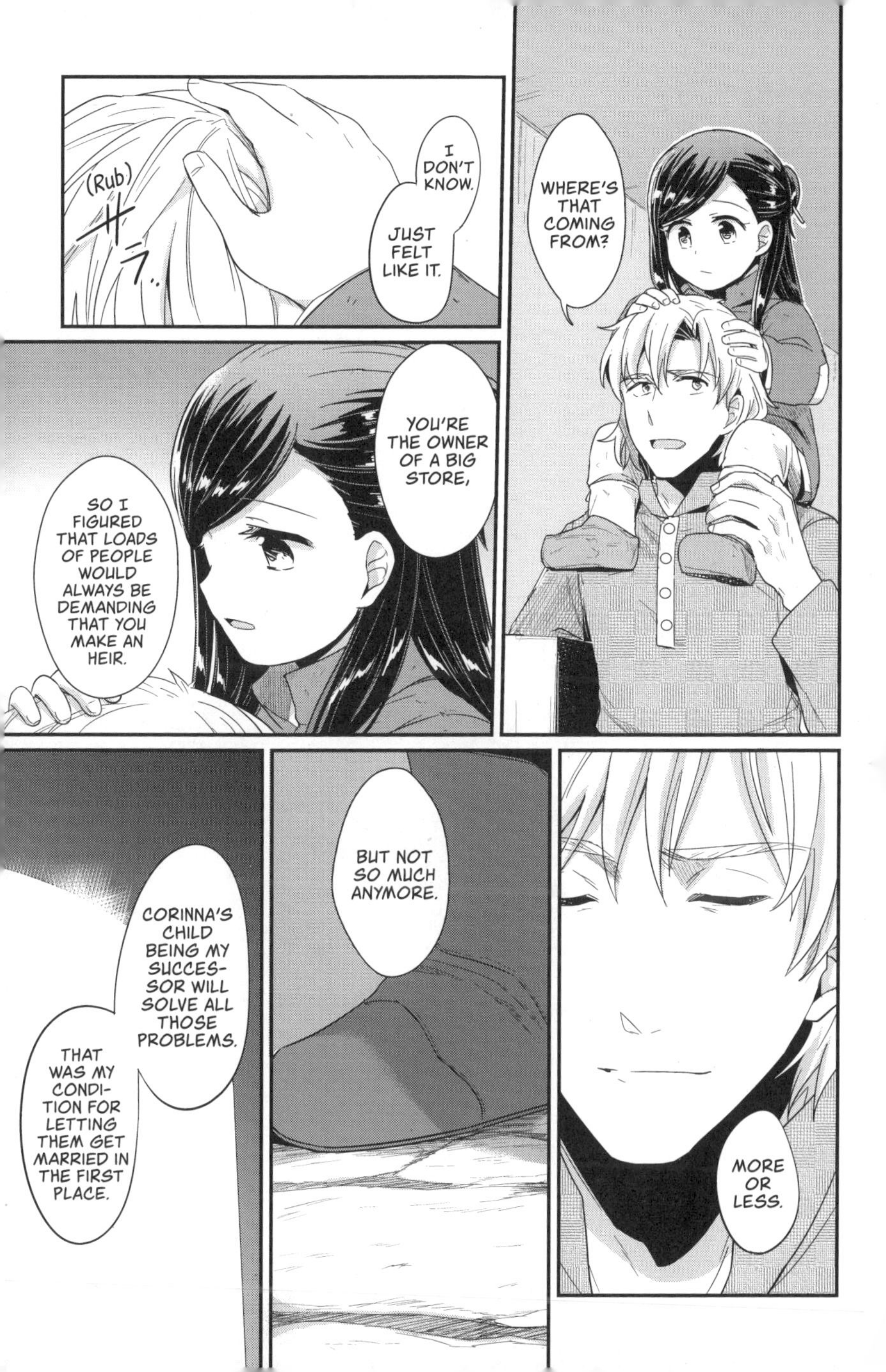
WHERE'S THAT COMING FROM?
I DON'T KNOW.
JUST FELT LIKE IT.
(Rub)
YOU'RE THE OWNER OF A BIG STORE,
SO I FIGURED THAT LOADS OF PEOPLE WOULD ALWAYS BE DEMANDING THAT YOU MAKE AN HEIR.
MORE OR LESS.
BUT NOT SO MUCH ANYMORE.
CORINNA'S CHILD BEING MY SUCCES-SOR WILL SOLVE ALL THOSE PROBLEMS.
THAT WAS MY CONDI-TION FOR LETTING THEM GET MARRIED IN THE FIRST PLACE.

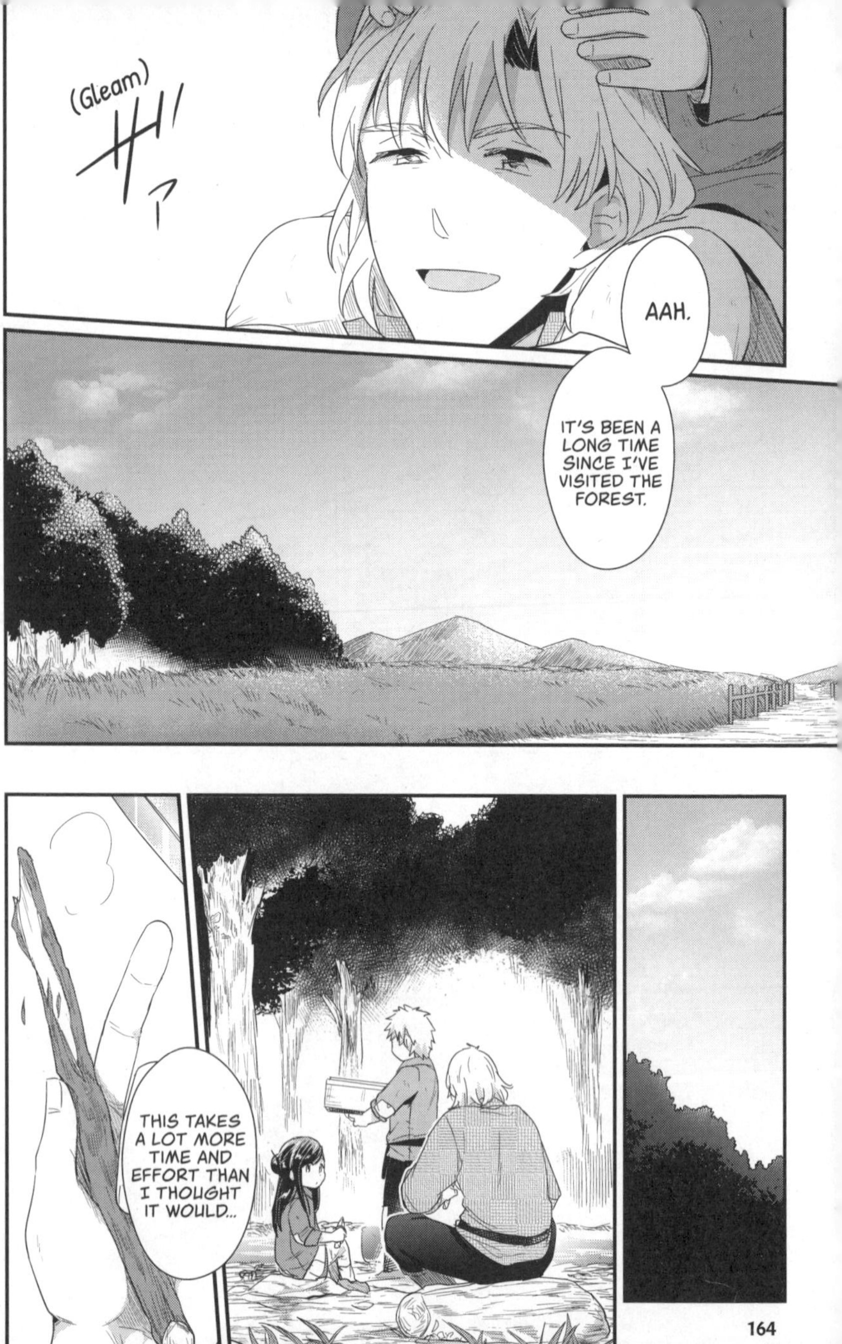
(Gleam)
AAH.
IT'S BEEN A LONG TIME SINCE I'VE VISITED THE FOREST.
THIS TAKES A LOT MORE TIME AND EFFORT THAN I THOUGHT IT WOULD...

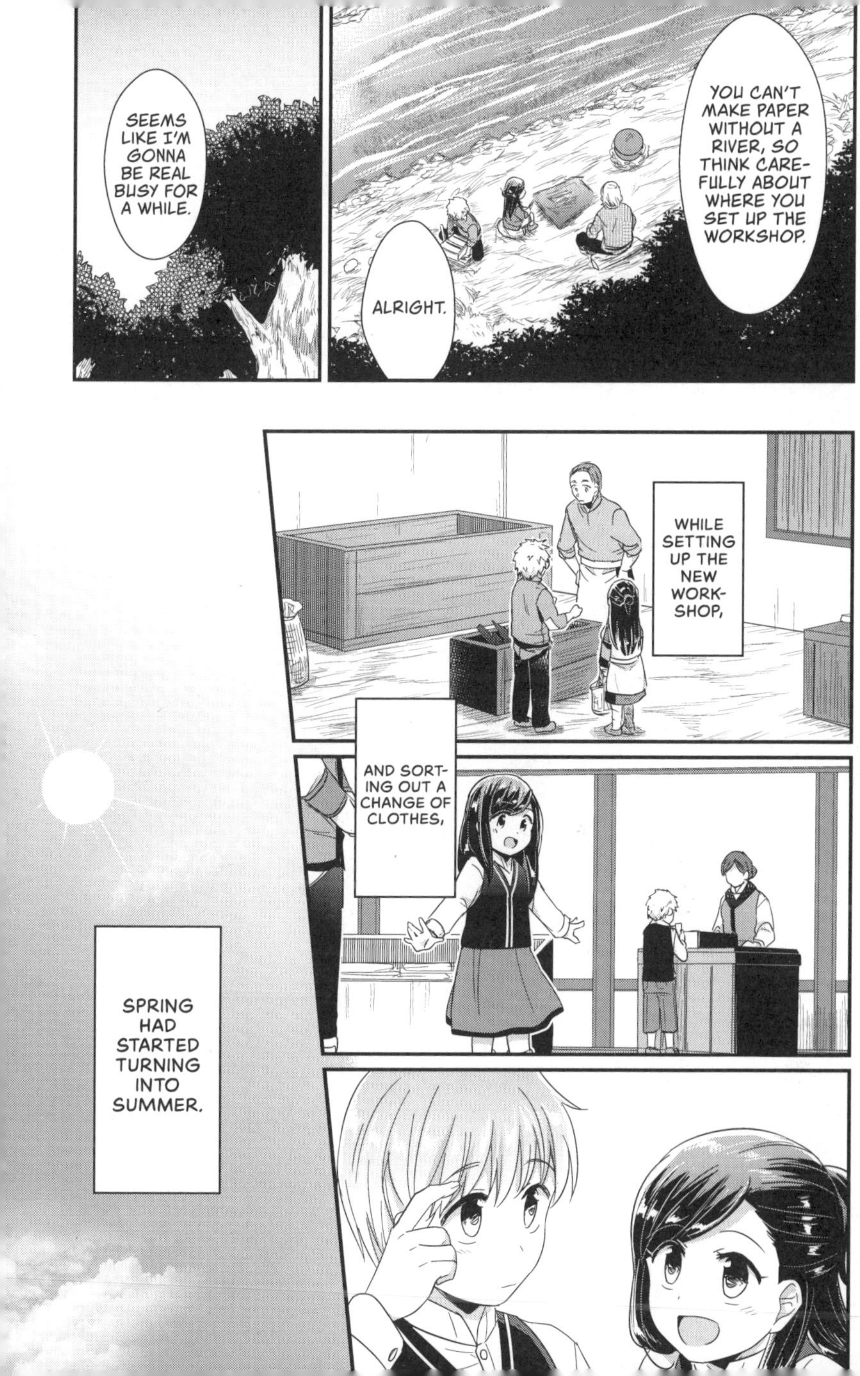

YOU CAN'T MAKE PAPER WITHOUT A RIVER, SO THINK CARE-FULLY ABOUT WHERE YOU SET UP THE WORKSHOP.
ALRIGHT.
SEEMS LIKE I'M GONNA BE REAL BUSY FOR A WHILE.
WHILE SETTING UP THE NEW WORK-SHOP,
AND SORT-ING OUT A CHANGE OF CLOTHES,
SPRING HAD STARTED TURNING INTO SUMMER.

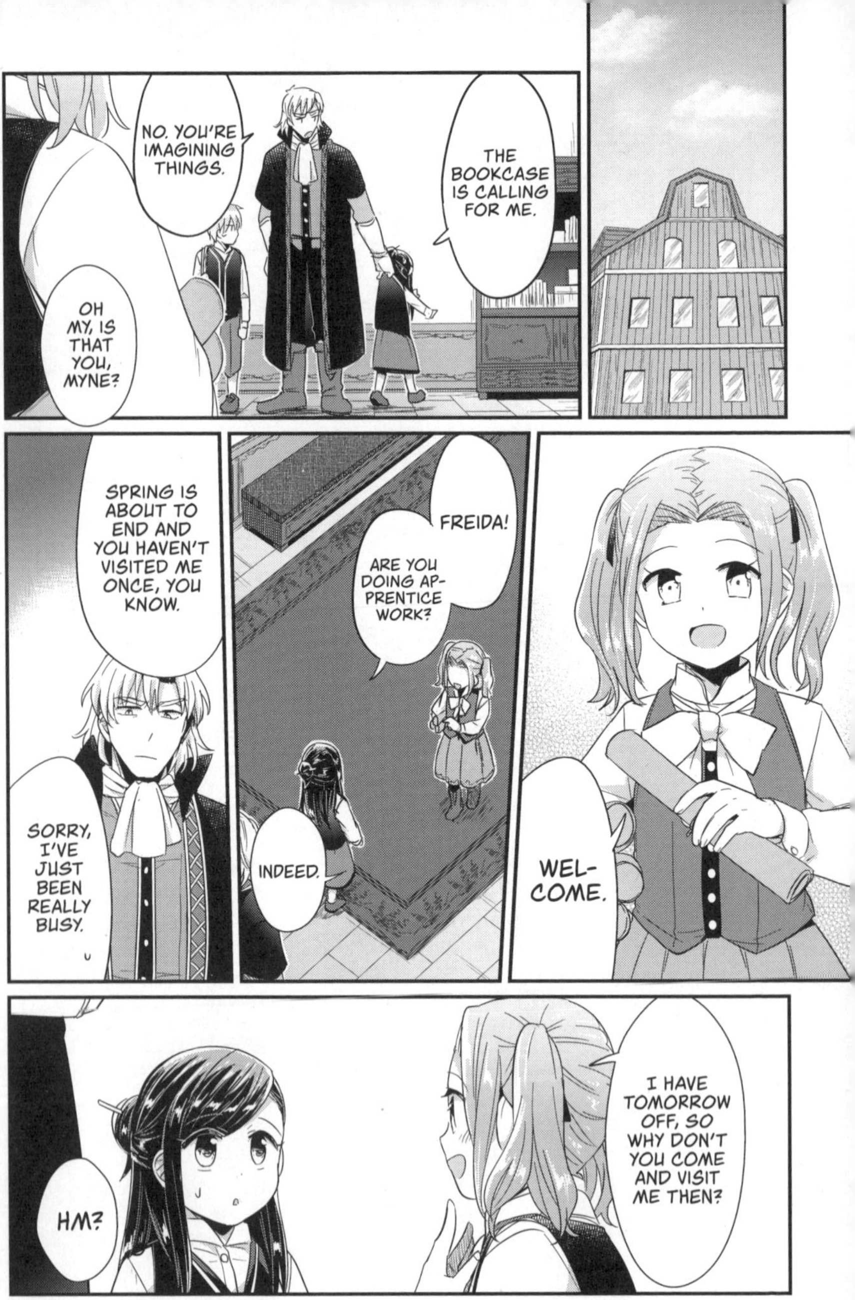
THE BOOKCASE IS CALLING FOR ME.
NO. YOU'RE IMAGINING THINGS.
OH MY, IS THAT YOU, MYNE?
WEL-COME.
FREIDA!
ARE YOU DOING AP-PRENTICE WORK?
INDEED.
SPRING IS ABOUT TO END AND YOU HAVEN'T VISITED ME ONCE, YOU KNOW.
SORRY, I'VE JUST BEEN REALLY BUSY.
I HAVE TOMORROW OFF, SO WHY DON'T YOU COME AND VISIT ME THEN?
HM?

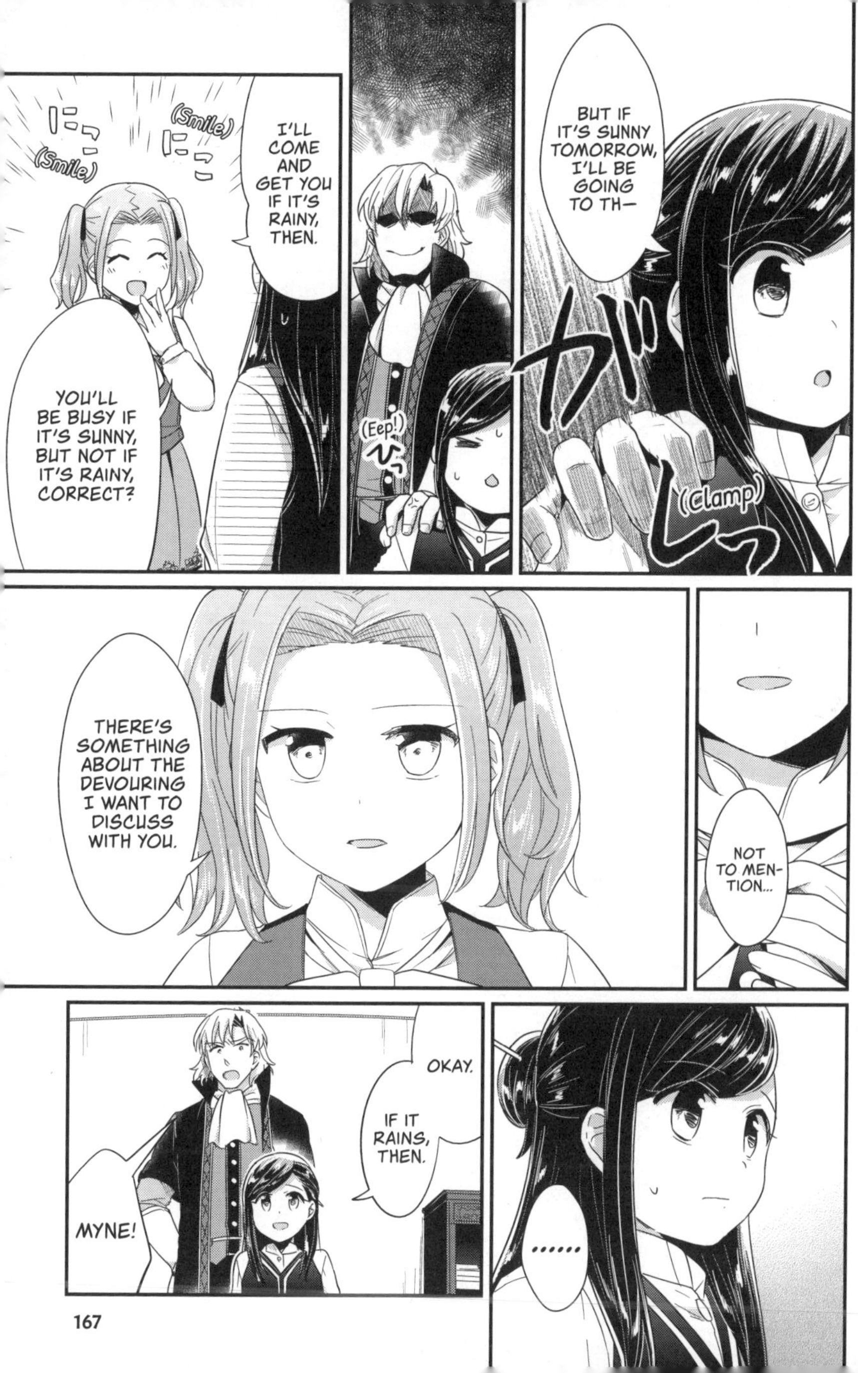
BUT IF IT'S SUNNY TOMORROW, I'LL BE GOING TO TH—
(Clamp)
(Eep!)
I'LL COME AND GET YOU IF IT'S RAINY, THEN.
(Smile)
(Smile)
YOU'LL BE BUSY IF IT'S SUNNY, BUT NOT IF IT'S RAINY, CORRECT?
NOT TO MEN-TION...
THERE'S SOMETHING ABOUT THE DEVOURING I WANT TO DISCUSS WITH YOU.
......
OKAY.
IF IT RAINS, THEN.
MYNE!

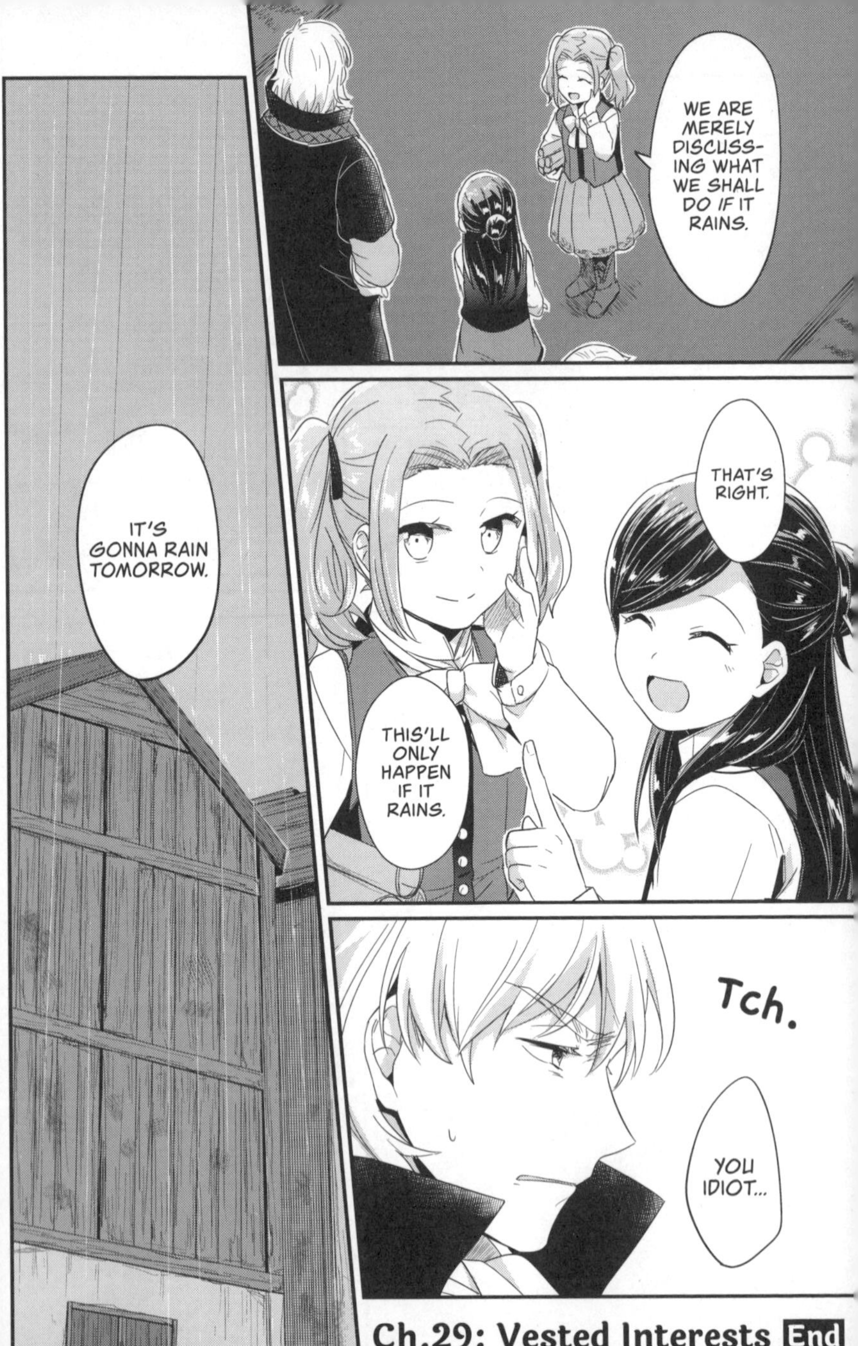
WE ARE MERELY DISCUSSING WHAT WE SHALL DO IF IT RAINS.
THAT'S RIGHT.
THIS'LL ONLY HAPPEN IF IT RAINS.
Tch.
YOU IDIOT...
IT'S GONNA RAIN TOMORROW.

Ch.29: Vested Interests **End**

ASCENDANCE
OF A
BOOKWORM
I'll do anything to
become a librarian!

Part 1 **If there aren't any
books, I'll just have
to make some!**

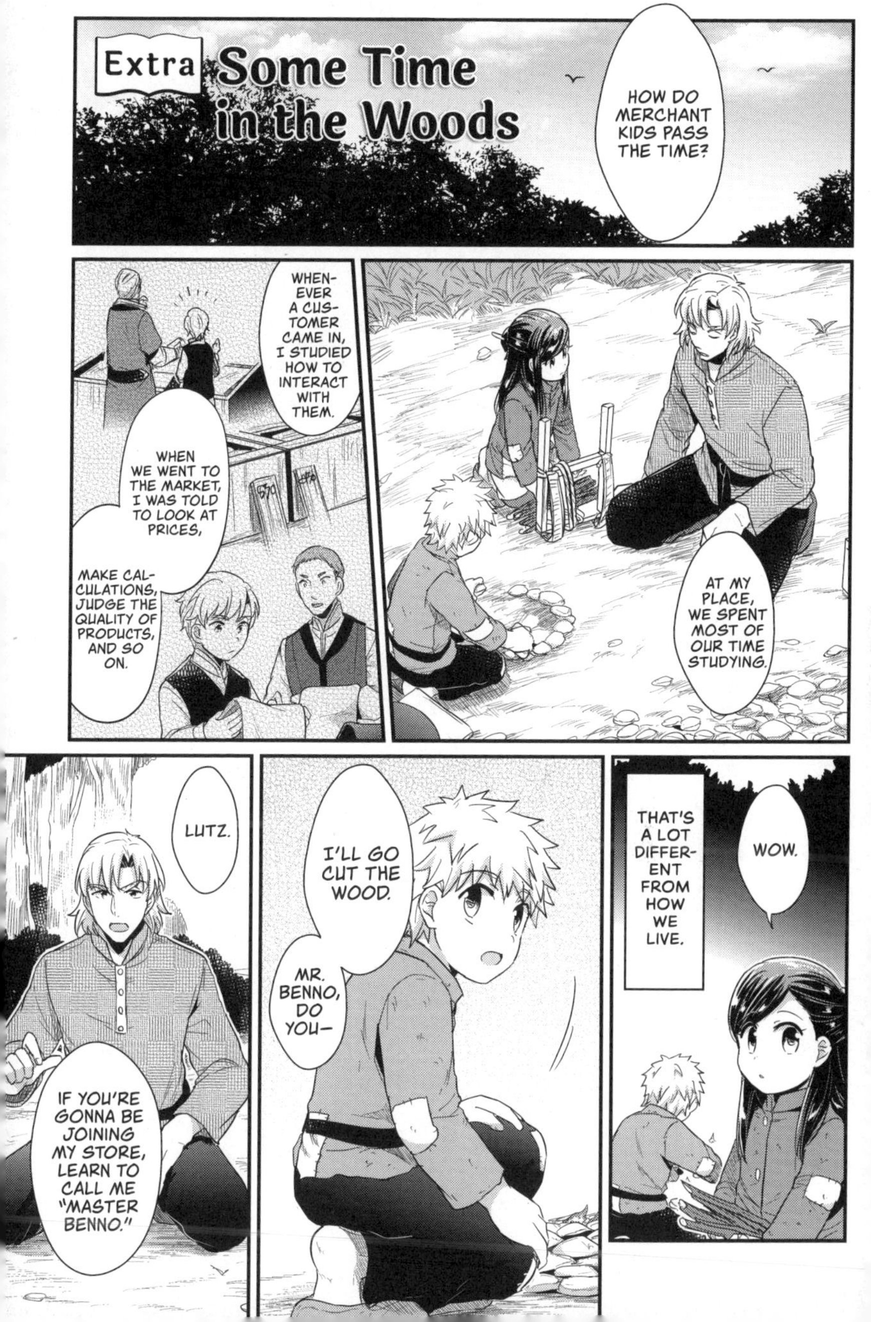
Extra Some Time in the Woods
HOW DO MERCHANT KIDS PASS THE TIME?
AT MY PLACE, WE SPENT MOST OF OUR TIME STUDYING.
WHEN-EVER A CUS-TOMER CAME IN, I STUDIED HOW TO INTERACT WITH THEM.
WHEN WE WENT TO THE MARKET, I WAS TOLD TO LOOK AT PRICES,
MAKE CAL-CULATIONS, JUDGE THE QUALITY OF PRODUCTS, AND SO ON.
WOW.
THAT'S A LOT DIFFER-ENT FROM HOW WE LIVE.
I'LL GO CUT THE WOOD.
MR. BENNO, DO YOU—
LUTZ.
IF YOU'RE GONNA BE JOINING MY STORE, LEARN TO CALL ME "MASTER BENNO."

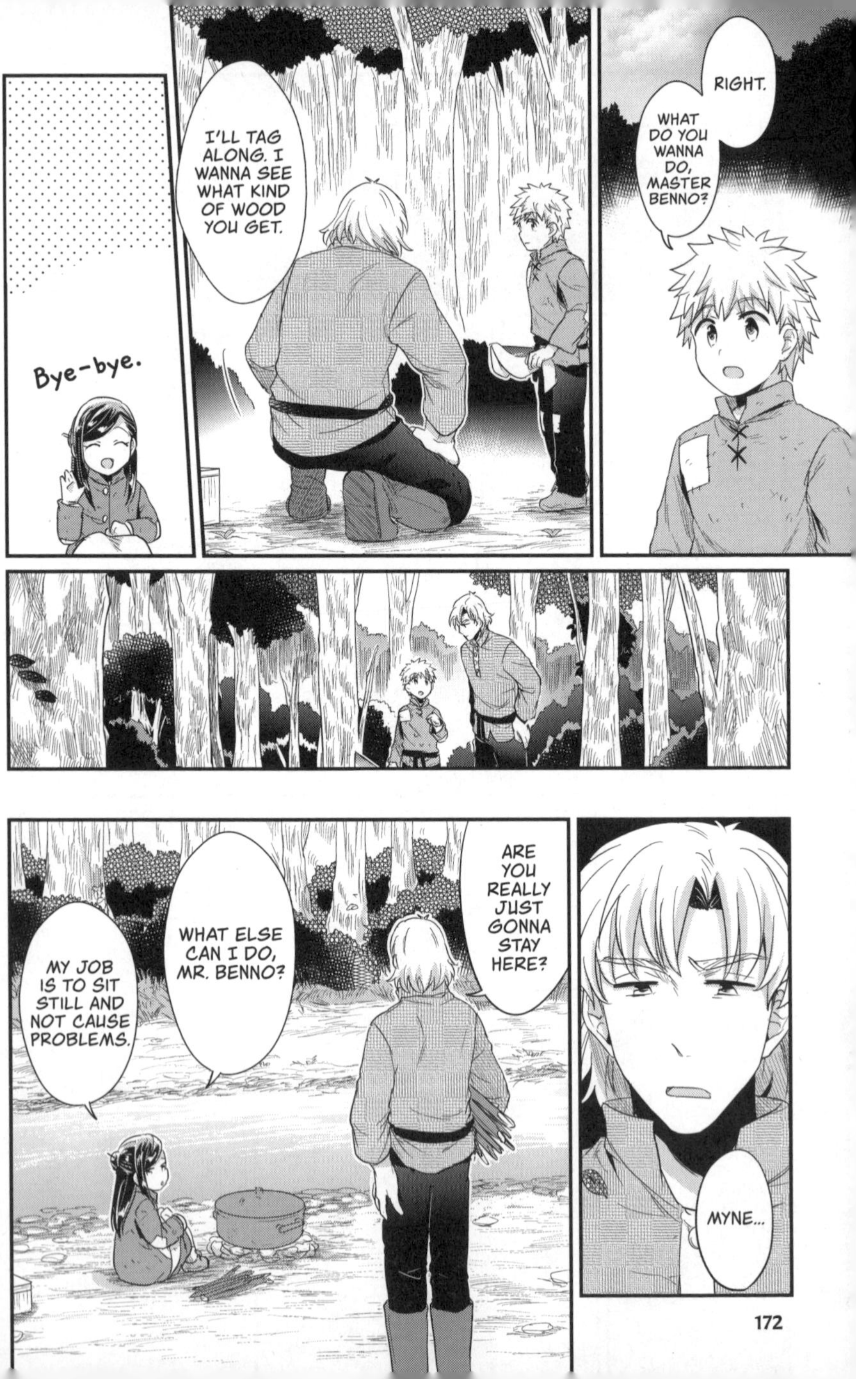
RIGHT.
WHAT DO YOU WANNA DO, MASTER BENNO?
I'LL TAG ALONG. I WANNA SEE WHAT KIND OF WOOD YOU GET.
Bye-bye.
MYNE...
ARE YOU REALLY JUST GONNA STAY HERE?
WHAT ELSE CAN I DO, MR. BENNO?
MY JOB IS TO SIT STILL AND NOT CAUSE PROBLEMS.

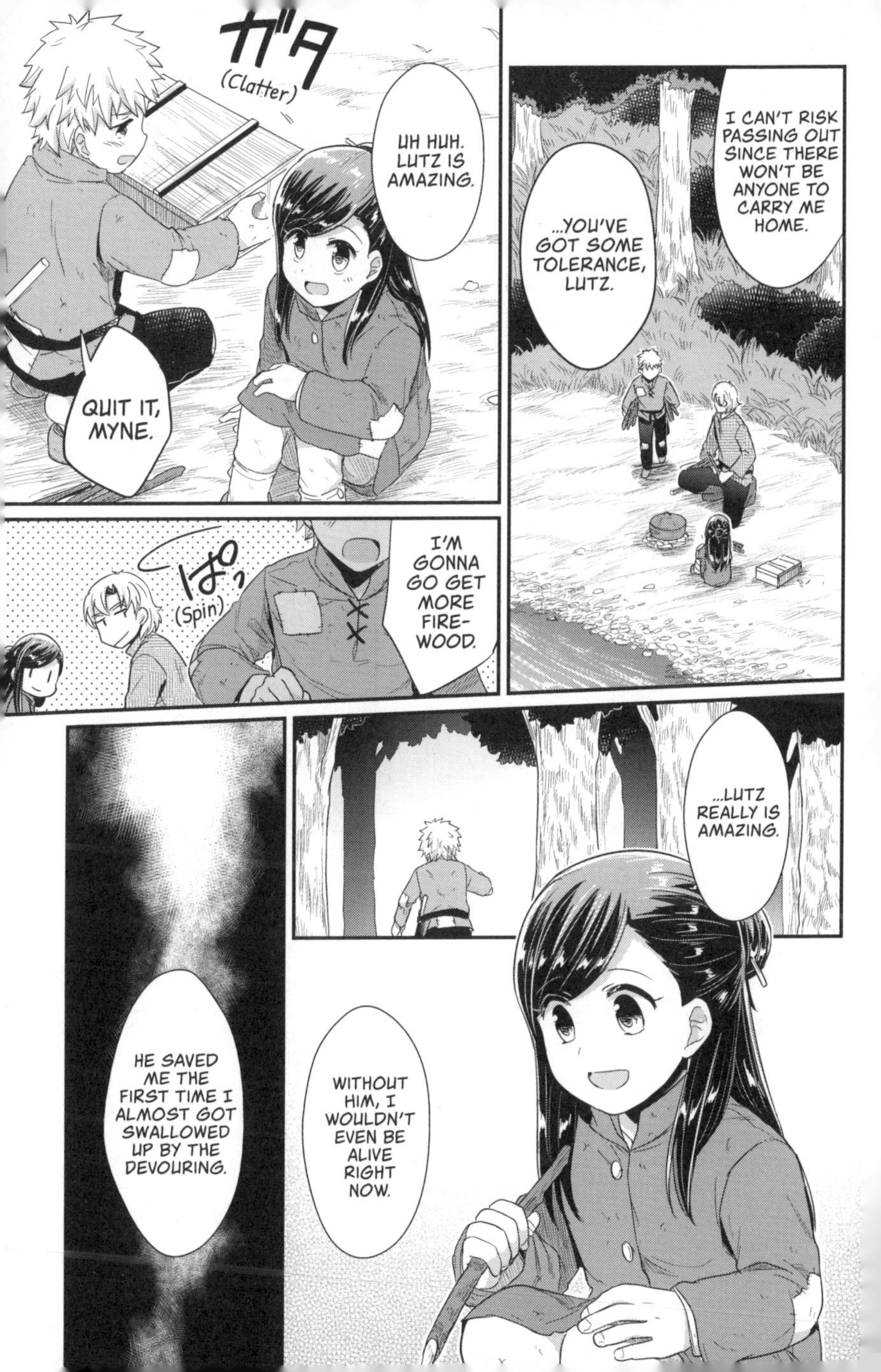
I CAN'T RISK PASSING OUT SINCE THERE WON'T BE ANYONE TO CARRY ME HOME.
...YOU'VE GOT SOME TOLERANCE, LUTZ.
ガタ
(Clatter)
UH HUH. LUTZ IS AMAZING.
QUIT IT, MYNE.
I'M GONNA GO GET MORE FIRE-WOOD.
ぱっ
(Spin)
...LUTZ REALLY IS AMAZING.
WITHOUT HIM, I WOULDN'T EVEN BE ALIVE RIGHT NOW.
HE SAVED ME THE FIRST TIME I ALMOST GOT SWALLOWED UP BY THE DEVOURING.

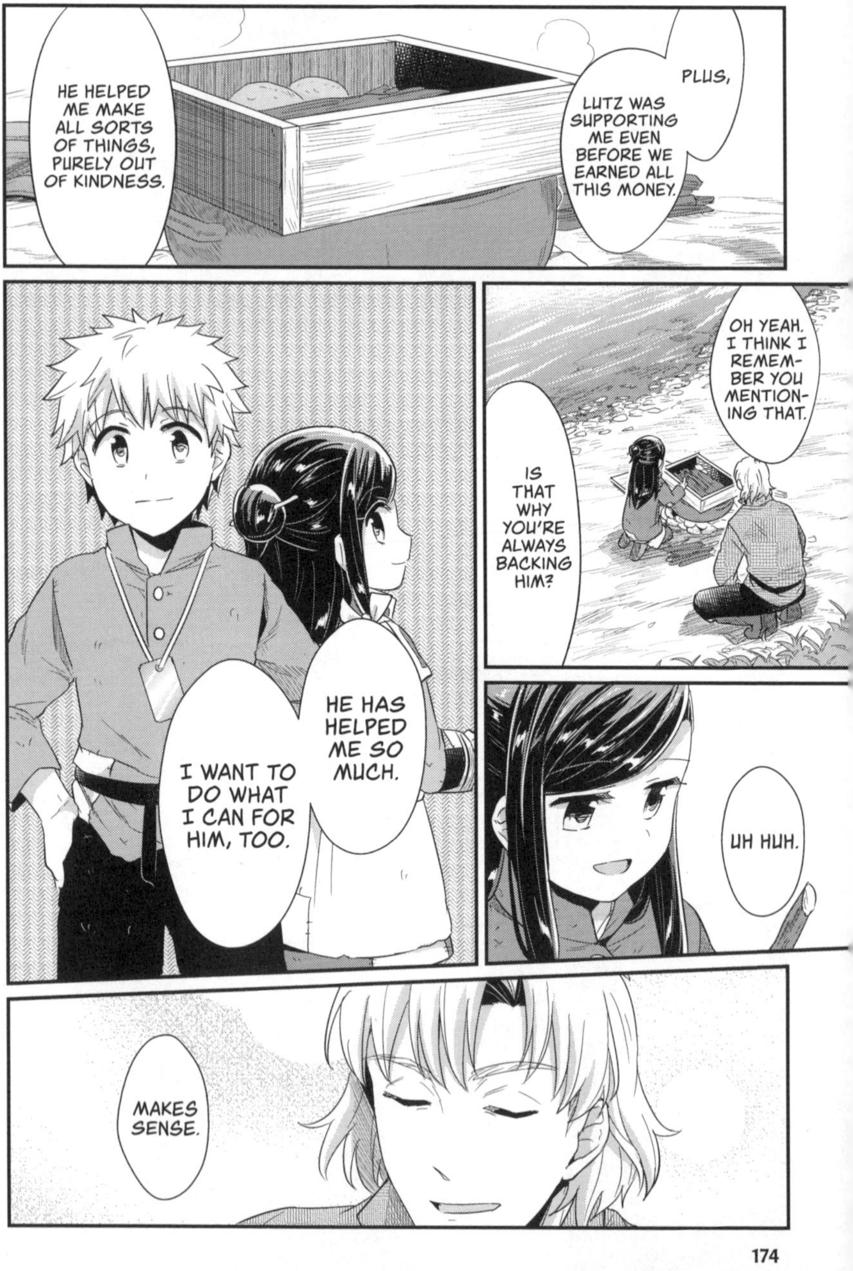
PLUS, LUTZ WAS SUPPORTING ME EVEN BEFORE WE EARNED ALL THIS MONEY.
HE HELPED ME MAKE ALL SORTS OF THINGS, PURELY OUT OF KINDNESS.
OH YEAH. I THINK I REMEMBER YOU MENTIONING THAT.
IS THAT WHY YOU'RE ALWAYS BACKING HIM?
UH HUH.
HE HAS HELPED ME SO MUCH.
I WANT TO DO WHAT I CAN FOR HIM, TOO.
MAKES SENSE.

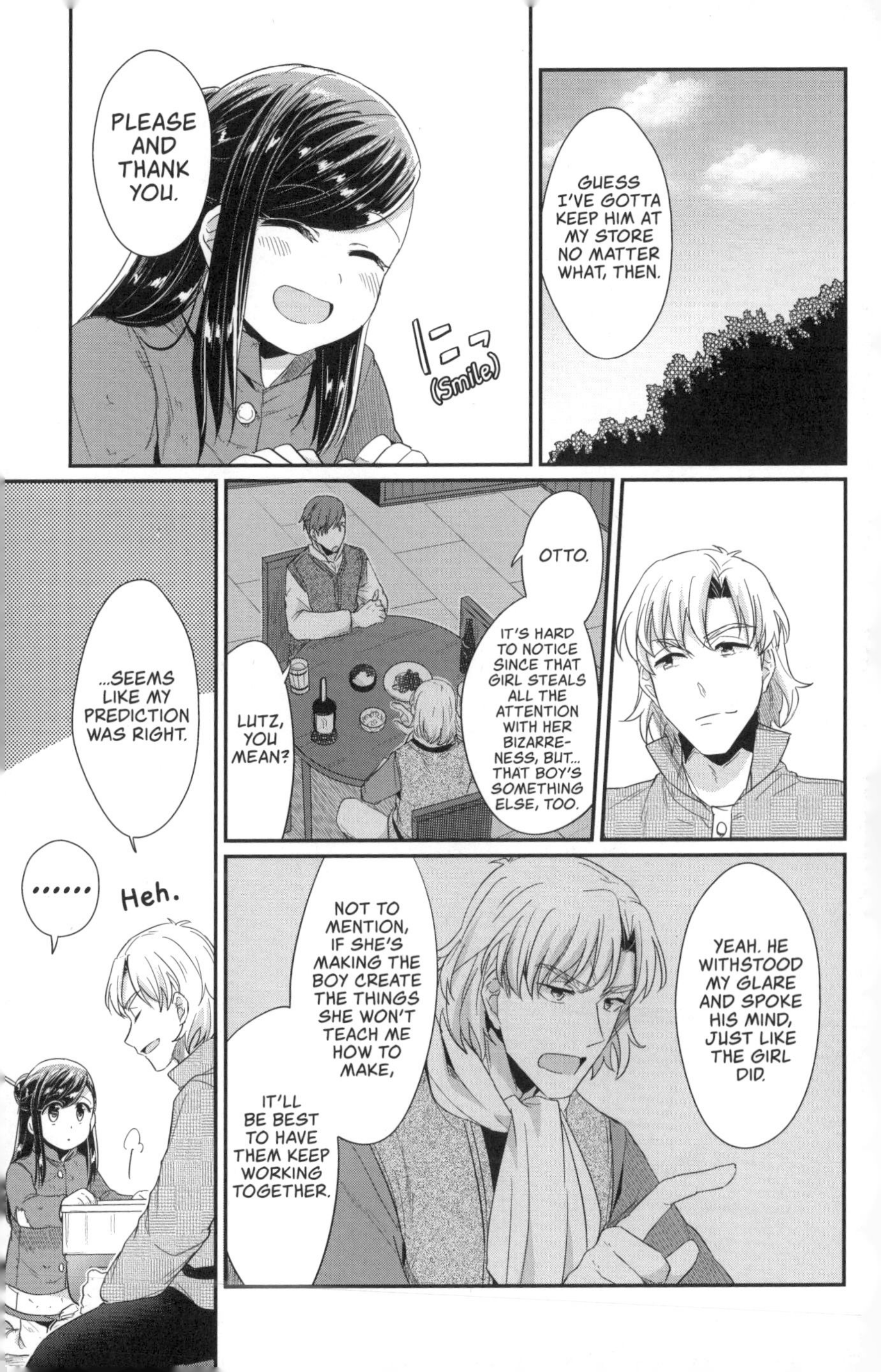
GUESS I'VE GOTTA KEEP HIM AT MY STORE NO MATTER WHAT, THEN.
PLEASE AND THANK YOU.
(Smile)
OTTO.
IT'S HARD TO NOTICE SINCE THAT GIRL STEALS ALL THE ATTENTION WITH HER BIZARRE-NESS, BUT... THAT BOY'S SOMETHING ELSE, TOO.
LUTZ, YOU MEAN?
YEAH. HE WITHSTOOD MY GLARE AND SPOKE HIS MIND, JUST LIKE THE GIRL DID.
NOT TO MENTION, IF SHE'S MAKING THE BOY CREATE THE THINGS SHE WON'T TEACH ME HOW TO MAKE,
IT'LL BE BEST TO HAVE THEM KEEP WORKING TOGETHER.
...SEEMS LIKE MY PREDICTION WAS RIGHT.
......
Heh.

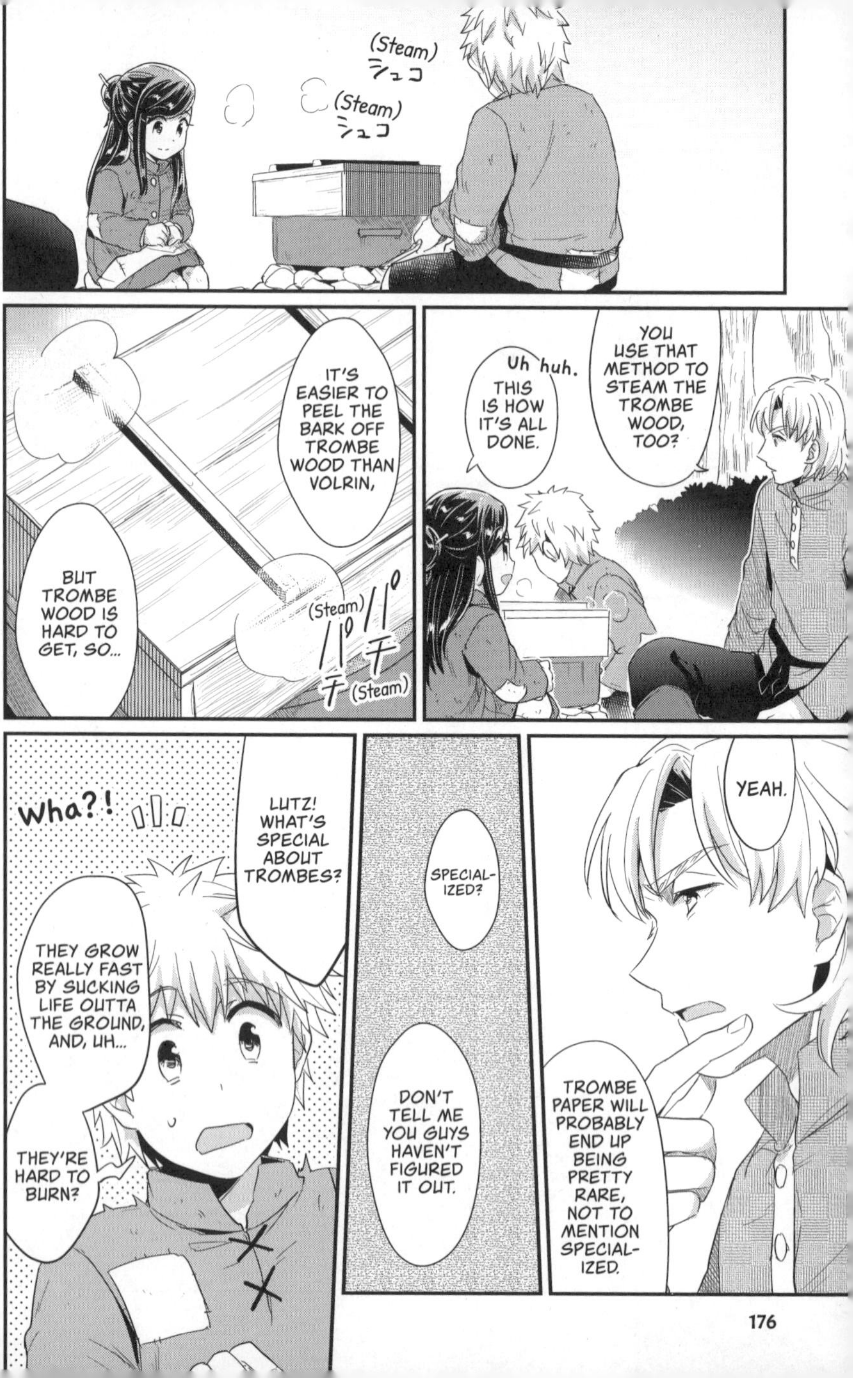
(Steam) シュコ
(Steam) シュコ
YOU USE THAT METHOD TO STEAM THE TROMBE WOOD, TOO?
Uh huh.
THIS IS HOW IT'S ALL DONE.
IT'S EASIER TO PEEL THE BARK OFF TROMBE WOOD THAN VOLRIN,
BUT TROMBE WOOD IS HARD TO GET, SO...
(Steam) パチ
(Steam) パチ
YEAH.
TROMBE PAPER WILL PROBABLY END UP BEING PRETTY RARE, NOT TO MENTION SPECIAL-IZED.
SPECIAL-IZED?
DON'T TELL ME YOU GUYS HAVEN'T FIGURED IT OUT.
LUTZ! WHAT'S SPECIAL ABOUT TROMBES?
Wha?!
THEY GROW REALLY FAST BY SUCKING LIFE OUTTA THE GROUND, AND, UH...
THEY'RE HARD TO BURN?

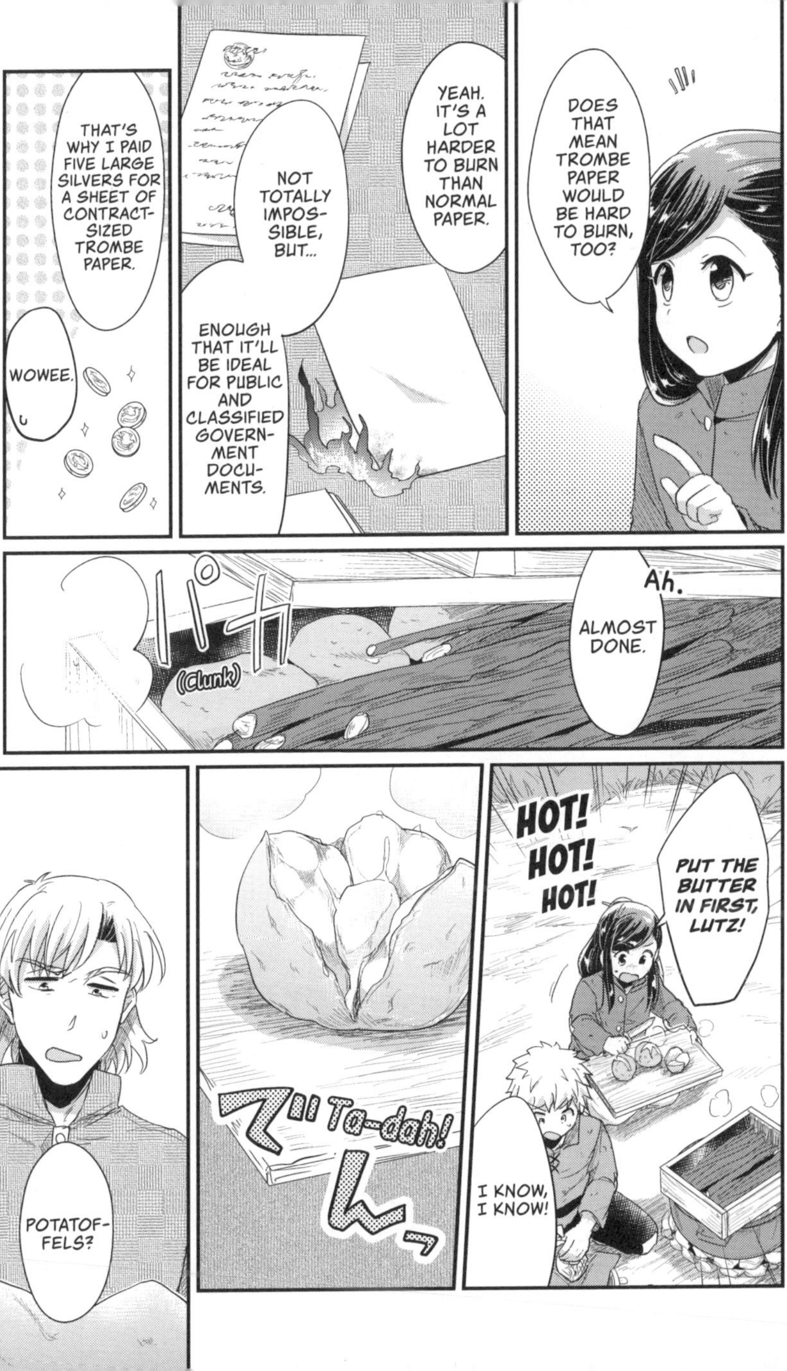
DOES THAT MEAN TROMBE PAPER WOULD BE HARD TO BURN, TOO?
YEAH. IT'S A LOT HARDER TO BURN THAN NORMAL PAPER.
NOT TOTALLY IMPOSSIBLE, BUT...
ENOUGH THAT IT'LL BE IDEAL FOR PUBLIC AND CLASSIFIED GOVERNMENT DOCUMENTS.
THAT'S WHY I PAID FIVE LARGE SILVERS FOR A SHEET OF CONTRACT-SIZED TROMBE PAPER.
WOWEE.
Ah.
ALMOST DONE.
パカ
(Clunk)
HOT! HOT! HOT!
PUT THE BUTTER IN FIRST, LUTZ!
I KNOW, I KNOW!
でーん
Ta-dah!
POTATOFFELS?

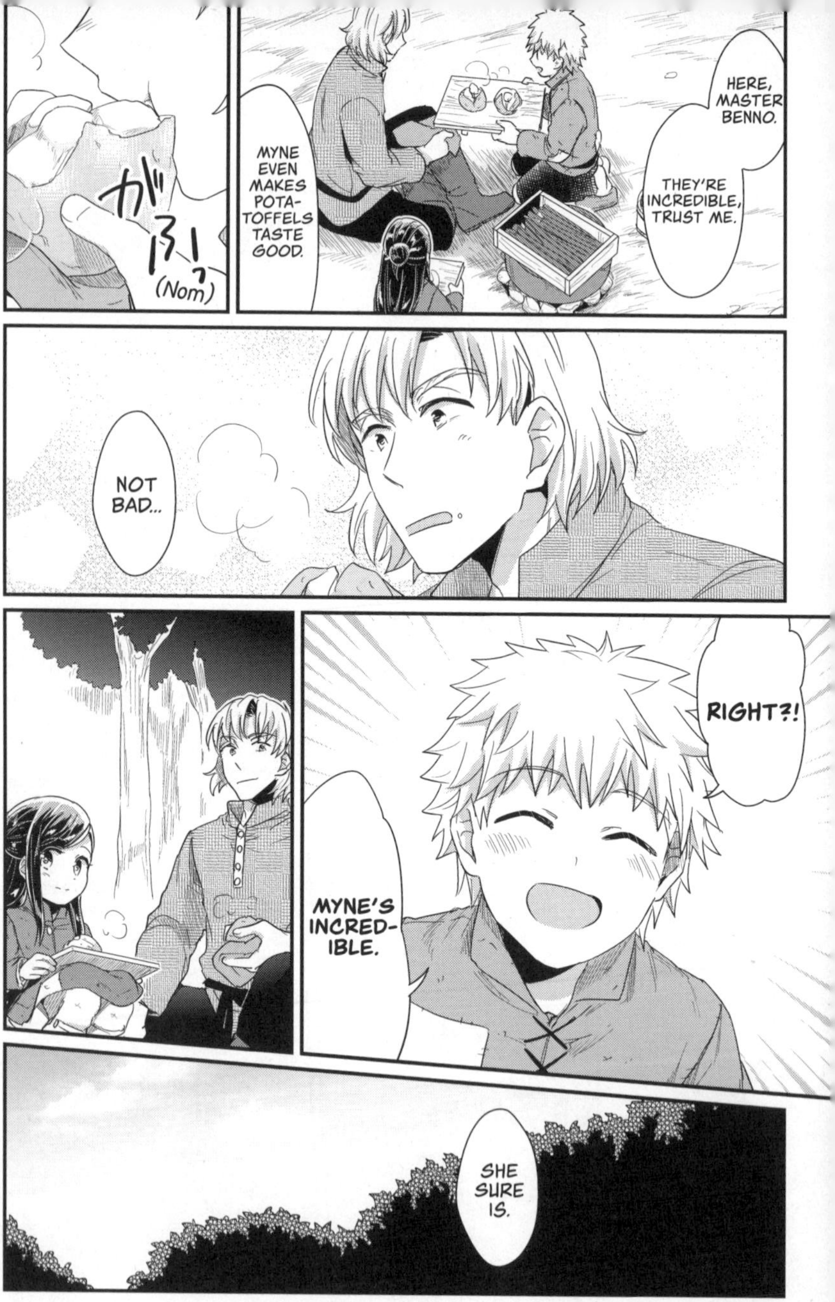
HERE, MASTER BENNO.
THEY'RE INCREDIBLE, TRUST ME.
MYNE EVEN MAKES POTA-TOFFELS TASTE GOOD.
がぶっ
(Nom)
NOT BAD...
RIGHT?!
MYNE'S INCRED-IBLE.
SHE SURE IS.

ASCENDANCE OF A BOOKWORM

OF A

BOOKWORM

I'll do anything to become a librarian!

Part 1 If there aren't any books, I'll just have to make some!

Peeling Bark

(Scratch)
(Scratch)
MR. BENNO...
YOU'RE NOT VERY GOOD WITH YOUR HANDS, ARE YOU?
LAY OFF!

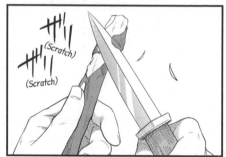

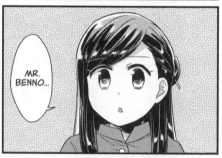

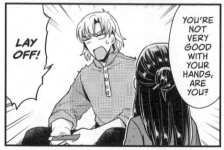

A Long-Awaited Reunion

A Long-Awaited Reunion

"Myne isn't visiting me, Leise," I said aloud, turning to my chef and pursing my lips as she walked around giving orders for the upcoming dinner. It had been ten days since Myne returned home after collapsing in the Gilberta Company, yet she had still not come to visit me.

Leise glanced my way, taking out salt and seasonal herbs from a cabinet. "She lives in the south, doesn't she? The people down there are busy preparing for winter at this time of year. Unlike the rich folk in the north of the city, the poor have to prepare everything by themselves."

I was surprised to learn that Lutz and Myne had to gather their own firewood, make their own candles, and even preserve their own food. At the Othmar Company, we performed winter preparations with all of our leherls, which meant we had a lot of people working together all at once. But even then, we simply bought most of what we needed.

"I see. Even though we both call them 'winter preparations,' those words mean something very different based on where you live."

"Not to mention, the snow's already begun to fall. People have started hunkering down in their homes. And Myne's weak enough that, even without the Devouring to worry about, she could barely even last through dinner, remember? She said that she wouldn't be able to come until spring, so you're just gonna have to wait until then."

"That's true, but..." I began, before quickly trailing off.

I had told Myne what happened to those with the Devouring—how long they had to live and how to survive—so that she could talk things over with her family. Her life was on the line here. Negotiations with nobles would go a lot smoother if she had more time to live, so the faster she made her move, the better.

"I hope she comes soon. If my family can turn her wisdom into money, she'll have more bargaining power to secure better terms in her contract," I said.

The Othmar Company's noble connections would be crucial for Myne's negotiations. The Gilberta Company, on the other hand, had only recently been recognized as a large store and started trade with nobles, meaning they did not yet have any connections that would prove useful. If she wanted to live as comfortable of a life as possible, the Gilberta Company's influence would be insufficient.

"The longer she remains indecisive, the less time she will have to negotiate. Surely she understands something so simple. What's more, we became such good friends in such a short time span. I cannot believe that her family would want her to die, so... What? Does she truly not intend to come until spring?" I mused aloud, before letting out a sigh and biting into one of the pound cakes that Leise had improved upon herself. "...Your pound cakes truly are delicious now, Leise. I would love for Myne to try one."

"I know how you feel. I'd like for her to try one too," Leise replied, setting some meat that a servant had brought over onto a cutting board and beginning to salt it. Once that was done, she started rubbing the salt into the meat.

"I really would like to go to the Noble's Quarter with Myne," I murmured as I watched Leise.

"Even if you did, you'd be living in different estates unless you got the same master. That said, I only know how things work from a servant's perspective. I couldn't tell you where children with the Devouring end up, but I can guess that someone signed to be a mistress and allowed to live alone in a separate building won't be treated the same as a normal Devouring kid."

Even though Leise was a chef, I spoke to her quite frequently; she had previously worked in the Noble's Quarter, and so knew more than most about how the people who went there from the lower city lived. At Grandfather's orders, Leise would either be moving with me to the Noble's Quarter when I came of age, or, in the case that there was an age-related problem with that, training a successor to accompany me.

"But even that's better than death, no? Furthermore, if Myne is willing to sell her knowledge to us, we will be able to support her in full."

"Yeah, but didn't she mention that some store or another was keeping her knowledge all to themselves?"

"Ah, that's it! That's the source of all our problems!" I exclaimed, clapping my hands together. But my excitement soon turned to anger. "Myne is no doubt desperate to come and visit me, but that Benno is getting in her way... Those with the Devouring need to sign with nobles to survive, but he refuses to allow her to see me. What a cruel man he is!"

Leise raised an eyebrow as she continued working salt into the meat. "Try to keep your delusions in check, milady. If things really were that bad, Myne would be asking for our help. Like you said, she's not an idiot. She'll come and visit in the spring."

"...You're right."

"I want to see her too, especially now that my pound cakes taste so good. Plus I'm sure she knows lots more recipes that nobody else does," Leise said, narrowing her green eyes as she started massaging herbs into the meat. The only time Leise had spent with Myne was when we were making the pound cake together, and yet she seemed so confident in that assertion. It didn't quite make sense to me.

"Why do you think that, Leise?"

"I can tell because she doesn't always eat her food. I'd assumed she never ate the soup because she didn't like vegetables, but she had vegetables in other meals. She must know some secret to make soup taste better."

I hadn't been aware that Myne was leaving food during meals. "If she knows more recipes, I would like for her to visit even sooner. They would help her to sign with a better noble for sure."

If only she would come soon. But the winter has only just begun... I thought sadly.

Blizzard season was over, and sunny days were slowly starting to return. By the time I was more comfortable going outside, it was time for the spring baptism ceremony.

The clinking sound of gold coins filled my brightly lit room. That would normally be enough to make my heart dance with joy, but right now, I couldn't focus on them at all.

"It's rare for you to lose focus like this, Freida. Is something wrong?" Grandfather asked, looking over from his conversation with Cosimo.

"Spring is here, but Myne still hasn't come to visit me, Grandfather." I set down my gold coins and moved to the window.

The snow outside had melted, and the once white streets were now visible again. Anyone could tell that spring had returned, and yet, Myne was not coming to visit me.

"You've certainly taken a liking to Myne, haven't you?" Grandfather asked.

I gave big nod. "I think it's wonderful to spend time with a fellow child who is going to be in the same position as me when we grow up. Before her... I only ever thought about how I will one day be separated from everyone."

The only way I could survive my Devouring was by signing a contract with a noble, which meant I would need to move to the Noble's Quarter once I came of age. I was personally being permitted to stay in the lower city until then, but this did not change the reality that I would one day have to say goodbye to my entire life here—my family, friends, the home I was raised in, and even my daily habits. But rather than facing my fate alone, there was now a chance that I would have a friend by my side—a friend who understood my struggle.

"Hmm, I see..." Grandfather replied, before leaning back in his chair and letting out a sigh. He fell into thought for a moment, then grinned as though he had come up with an excellent idea. "Then perhaps I should adopt Myne...?"

"Grandfather?!"

"Master Gustav, what are you saying?!"

His statement came so out of nowhere that even Cosimo, his right-hand man, let out a cry of shock. Who could blame him? Grandfather's idea would have far too many ramifications, especially as one that he had come up with on the spot.

"According to Leise, Myne knows many more recipes than she is letting on. What if, in return for them, I were to propose an adoption? It would be easier for us to assist in her negotiations, and she might even be able to sign with someone on good terms with Lord Henrik, the noble you have signed with."

It was true that adopting Myne would make it easier for the Othmar Company to support her during negotiations. I would be able to assist her not as a friend, but as a sister.

...What a wonderful idea!

But while I was overjoyed, Cosimo looked none too pleased. "Master Gustav, if you were to adopt her, it would have an impact on the line of succession. Please do not suggest such things."

"Myne will have no such impact if she is going to be signing with a noble and moving to the Noble's Quarter. Even if someone tries to protest, I will merely silence them using the assistance that I have provided them in the past. Furthermore... were I to have one of my sons adopt her, it would potentially be harder to separate her from the Othmar Company. I, on the other hand, am already retired, so this will minimize the impact on the store."

Grandfather was no longer seen as a member of the Othmar Company, since he had retired to become guildmaster of the Merchant's Guild. At the moment, everyone viewed him solely as the guildmaster.

"I will make the necessary preparations. But either way, nothing can begin unless Myne comes and asks us for assistance."

"That's true."

If Myne didn't ask the Othmar Company for help, we couldn't just up and adopt her out of nowhere.

"That said, there is no need for you to worry. I will instruct those in the Guild to inform me whenever Myne arrives, and I will send probes through Benno to get updates on her status.

You should worry about yourself rather than her, Freida. Have you gotten used to your apprentice work in the Guild yet?"

"Yes, Grandfather. There's so much to learn that I'm enjoying myself each and every day. My supervisors praise me for my work as well," I replied. I had to study hard if I wanted to survive in the Noble's Quarter.

Feeling a little relieved, I picked the gold coins back up.

The snow had completely melted, and various plants were growing once again. Flowers bloomed amid the expanse of green. A soft breeze accompanied the warm sunlight, and before I knew it, that light turned from warm to hot. The summer baptism ceremony was just around the corner.

And yet, I had not seen Myne once. She was registered with the Merchant's Guild and so would normally be sent on chores like bringing paperwork to the front desk, but no. Neither she nor Lutz had showed up at the Guild even once.

...She only has half a year left before the Devouring consumes her! The fact that she has not visited me after all this time has to be the work of Benno!

At this point, perhaps my only option was to directly interfere with the Gilberta Company. No matter how displeased Benno might be about that, Myne's life was more important.

I suppose I'll have to think up some kind of excuse to visit the Gilberta Company... I thought while doing my apprentice work behind the counter. But that was when I heard a familiar voice.

"The bookcase is calling for me."

"No. You're imagining things."

I turned around in surprise, and there I found Benno, Myne, and Lutz heading for the counter. In stark contrast to when she had been brought to my store, Myne looked healthy; she was walking on her own two feet and even talking back to Benno. When I saw her last, just bathing or making sweets was enough for her to fall ill, but now she was well enough to have walked all the way to the Merchant's Guild.

Finally, we meet again!

I had been waiting so long that just seeing Myne made me happy, but it didn't seem that she had noticed my presence. I quickly finished the work in front of me and asked my supervisor to inform the guildmaster that Myne had arrived.

...I won't miss this opportunity, no matter what. I will *defeat Benno!*

I took a deep breath, then headed to the counter and called out Myne's name, putting a firm hand on my hip and pursing my lips to make her feel bad about not visiting me.

"Oh my, is that you, Myne? Spring is about to end and you haven't visited me once, you know."

The End.

AFTERWORD

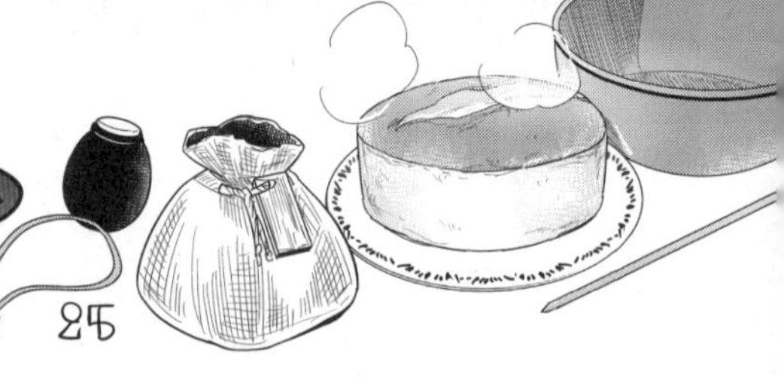

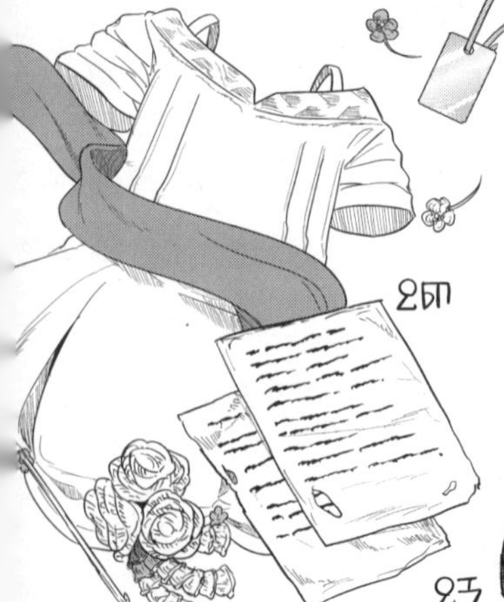

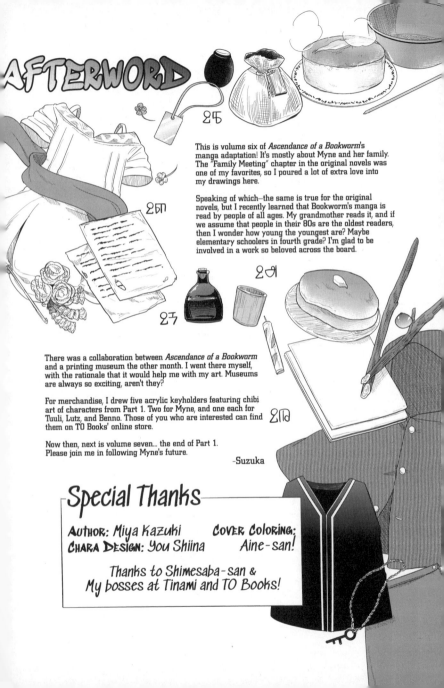

This is volume six of *Ascendance of a Bookworm*'s manga adaptation! It's mostly about Myne and her family. The "Family Meeting" chapter in the original novels was one of my favorites, so I poured a lot of extra love into my drawings here.

Speaking of which—the same is true for the original novels, but I recently learned that Bookworm's manga is read by people of all ages. My grandmother reads it, and if we assume that people in their 80s are the oldest readers, then I wonder how young the youngest are? Maybe elementary schoolers in fourth grade? I'm glad to be involved in a work so beloved across the board.

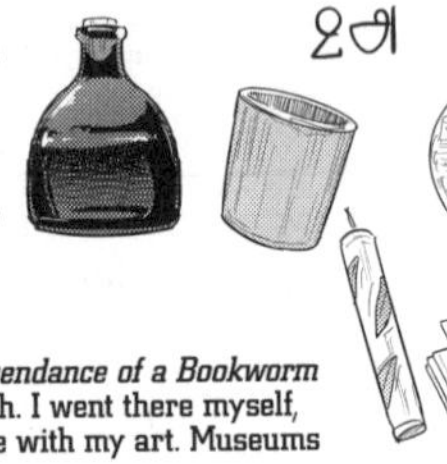

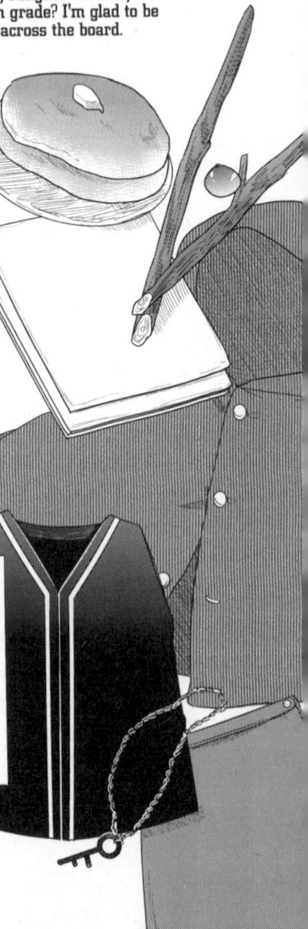

There was a collaboration between *Ascendance of a Bookworm* and a printing museum the other month. I went there myself, with the rationale that it would help me with my art. Museums are always so exciting, aren't they?

For merchandise, I drew five acrylic keyholders featuring chibi art of characters from Part 1. Two for Myne, and one each for Tuuli, Lutz, and Benno. Those of you who are interested can find them on TO Books' online store.

Now then, next is volume seven... the end of Part 1. Please join me in following Myne's future.

-Suzuka

Special Thanks

Author: Miya Kazuki
Chara Design: You Shiina
Cover Coloring: Aine-san!

Thanks to Shimesaba-san &
My bosses at Tinami and TO Books!

Afterword

To both those who are new to *Bookworm* and those who read the web novel or light novel: Thank you very much for reading Volume 6 of *Ascendance of a Bookworm*'s manga adaptation.

Myne's life was extended thanks to one of the magic tools that had been purchased for Freida's sake, but she was told that she only has one year before she'll be on death's door again. What will she do next? She struggles to break this news to her family, but it's a very important matter for them to discuss. When she eventually does tell her family, Myne decides that she's going to continue living with them, putting her all into doing what she wants. And so, Myne will be dedicating herself to making paper, living in accordance with her own ideals.

The most important part of this volume is the family meeting, and I cried when I saw how Suzuka-sama depicted it. Each character is so expressive, and you can really feel that Gunther's a good father.

Another thing to talk about is Myne's baptism clothes. Many people who read the light novels have told me that the exact alterations made to Tuuli's baptism outfit were hard to understand, but I think the manga has depicted them in a way that's a lot easier to understand. The embroidery was especially fantastic, and the outfit ends up looking a lot fancier than when it was worn by Tuuli. Myne's hairpin adds a lot too, and all the details are drawn really well. Another thing I was personally looking forward to was Benno's deceased lover, Liz. She wasn't important enough of a character to get an illustration in the light novels, so here, Suzuka-sama had a chance to design her. She asked whether this was how I imagined her, and the answer was a resounding yes. Suzuka-sama, it's perfect.

Now then, let's talk about the poundcake that Myne made. In French, it's known as a "quatre-quarts," which means "four quarters." This is because you add equal amounts of sugar, flour, butter, and eggs to make it. I've actually made one myself, though I was using an electric mixer and an electric oven. Leise is pretty impressive.

The short story for this volume was written at Suzuka-sama's request, since she wanted to see Freida agonizing over Myne not coming to visit even when spring came. Freida never lost faith that Myne would come and see her, Leise kept practicing to make her poundcakes taste even better, and the guildmaster started making unnecessary plans to make his beloved granddaughter happy. I hope you enjoyed seeing their antics!

On one last note, I would like to recommend the acrylic keyholders that are being sold on TO Books' online store. Myne, Tuuli, Lutz, and Benno are available, and they all look very cute.

Miya Kazuki

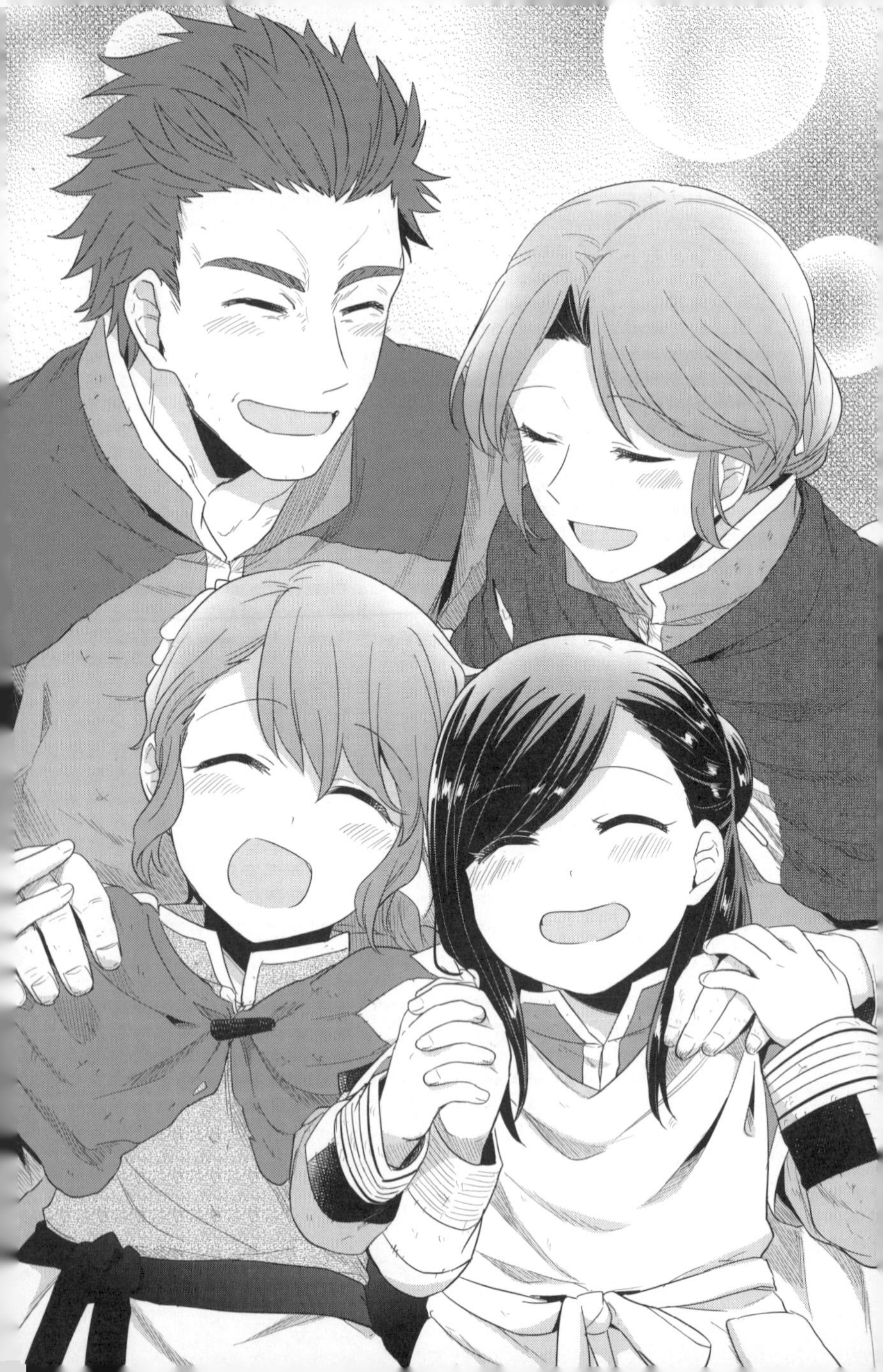

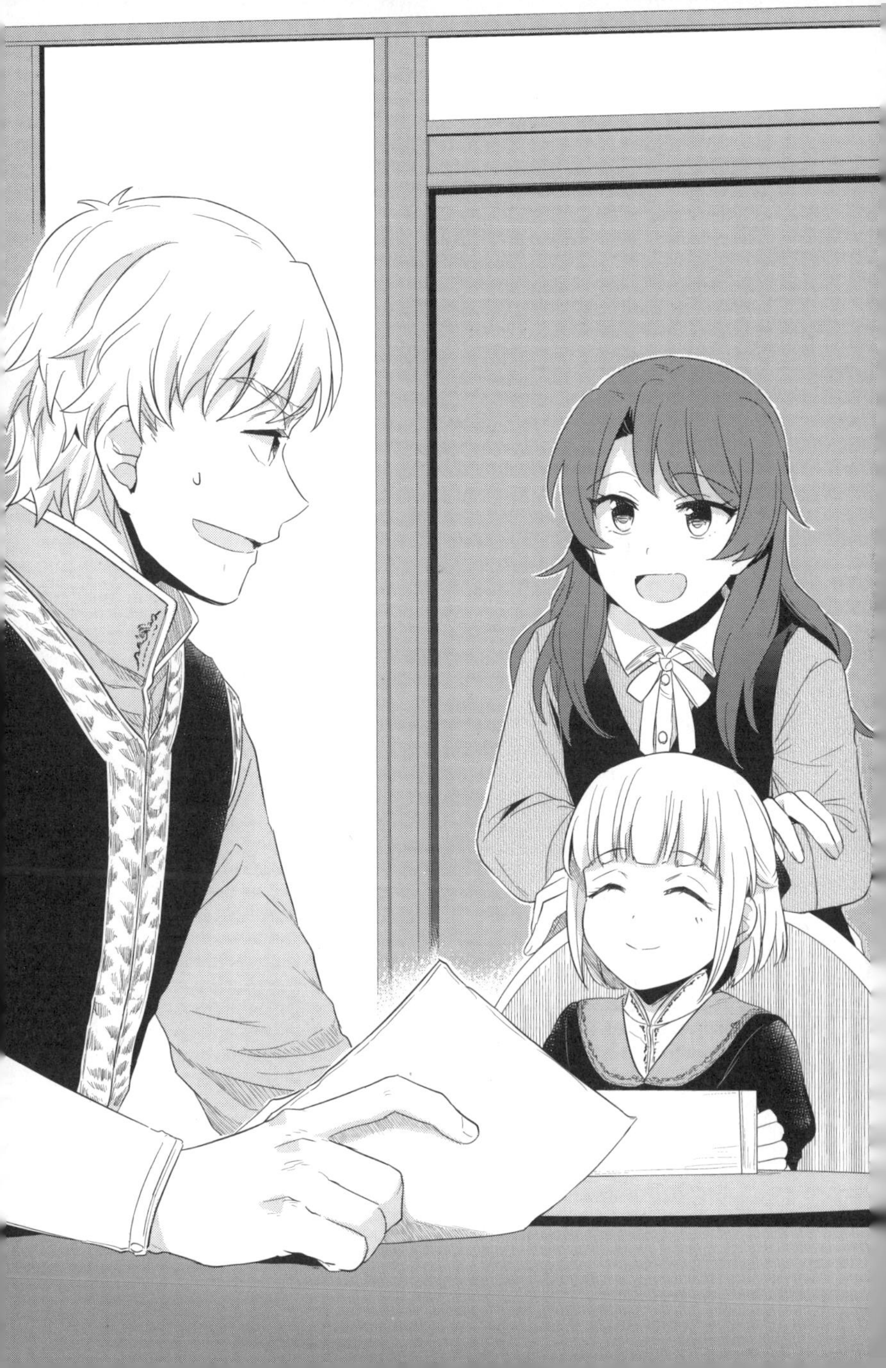

ASCENDANCE OF A BOOKWORM (MANGA)VOLUME 6
by Miya Kazuki (story) and Suzuka (artwork)
Original character designs by You Shiina

Translated by Carter "Quof" Collins
Edited by Kieran Redgewell
Lettered by Meiru

First published in Japan in 2018 by TO Books, Tokyo.
Publication rights for this English edition arranged through TO Books, Tokyo.

Find more books like this one at www.j-novel.club!

President and Publisher: Samuel Pinansky
Managing Editor (Manga): J. Collis
Managing Translator: Kristi Fernandez
QA Manager: Hannah N. Carter
Marketing Manager: Stephanie Hii

ISBN: 978-1-7183-7255-9
First Printing: July 2021
Printed in Korea
10 9 8 7 6 5 4 3 2 1

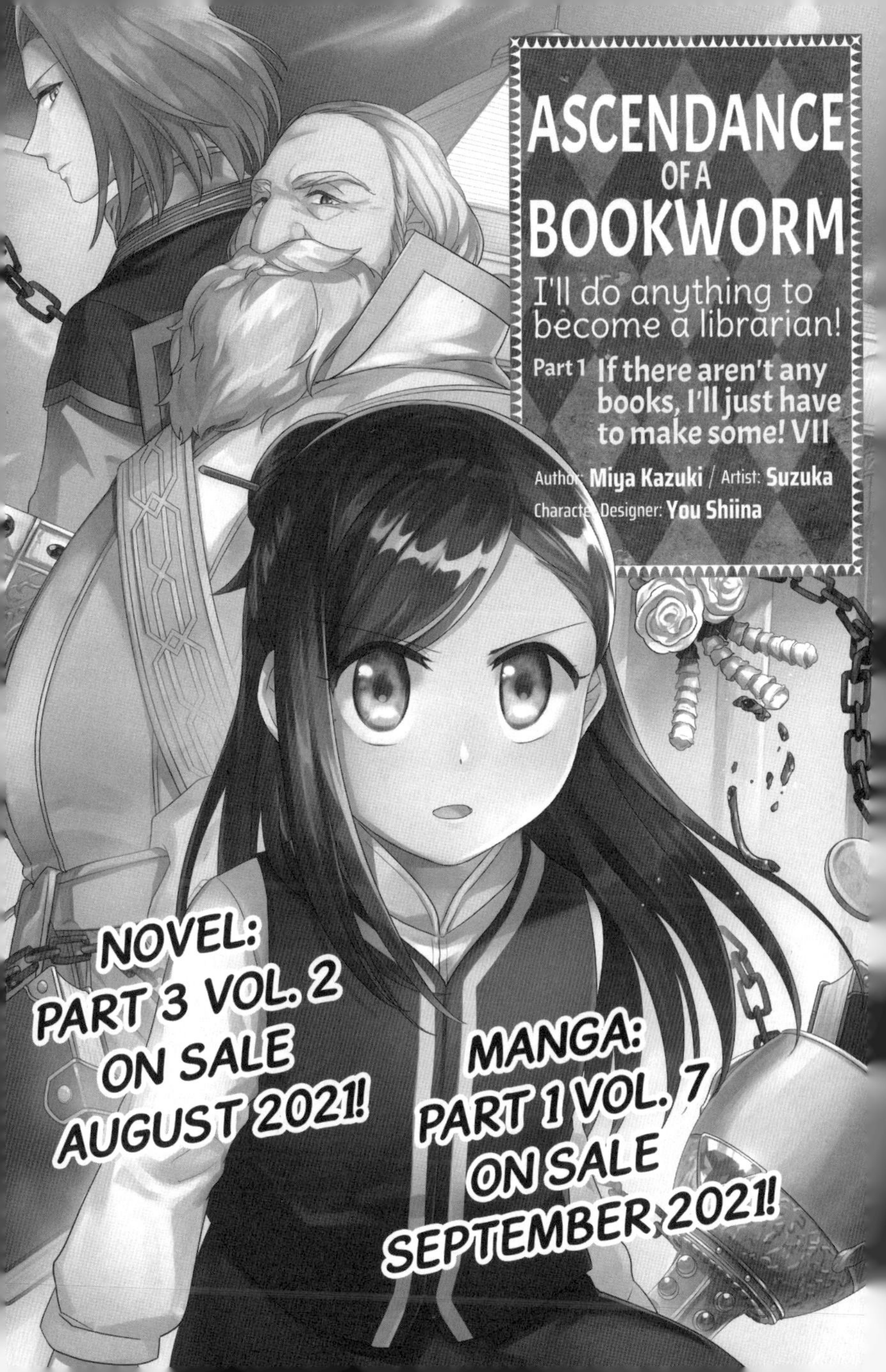

ASCENDANCE OF A BOOKWORM
I'll do anything to become a librarian!
Part 1 If there aren't any books, I'll just have to make some! VII
Author: Miya Kazuki / Artist: Suzuka
Character Designer: You Shiina
NOVEL: PART 3 VOL. 2 ON SALE AUGUST 2021!
MANGA: PART 1 VOL. 7 ON SALE SEPTEMBER 2021!

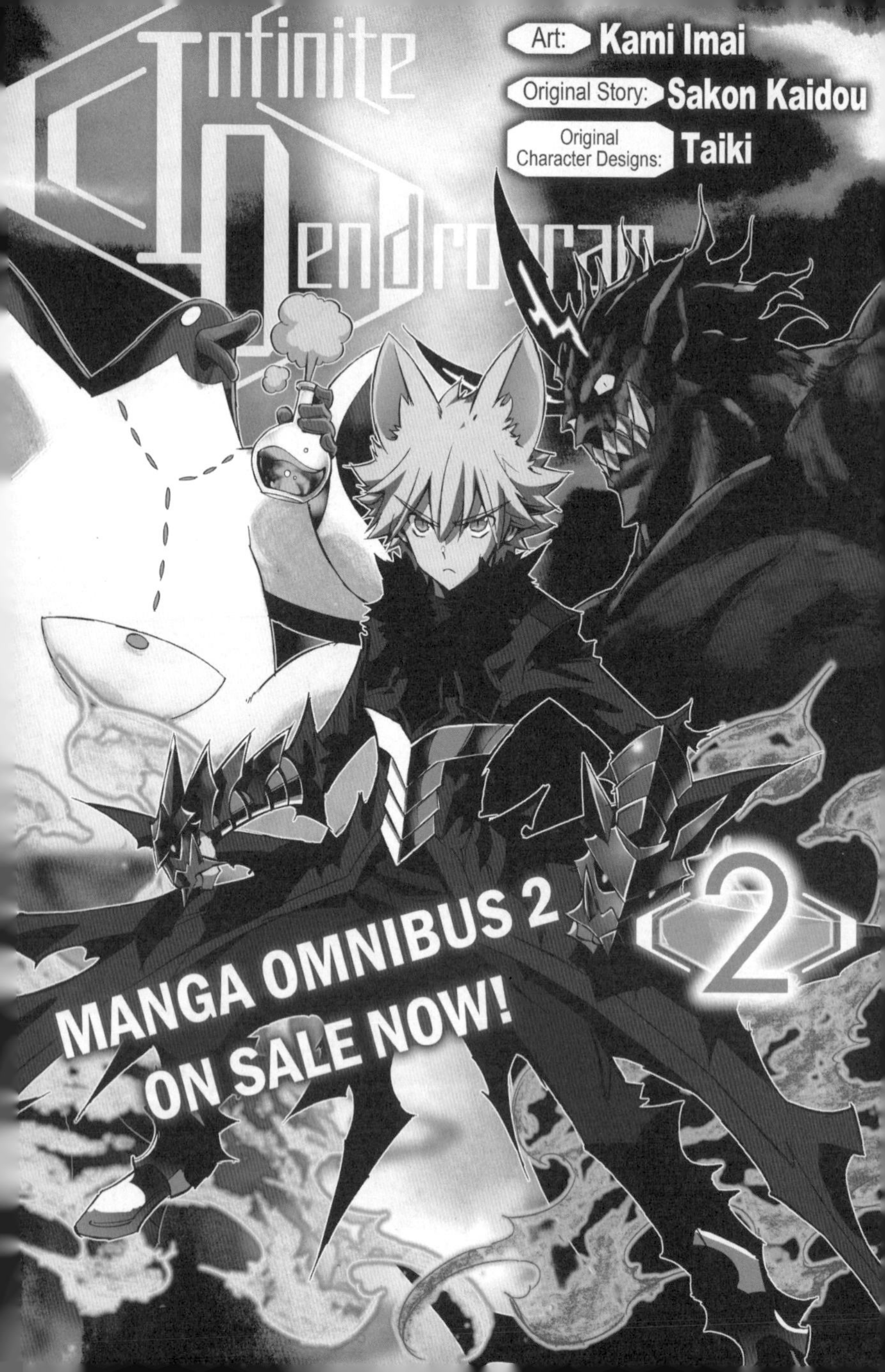

Infinite Dendrogram
Art: Kami Imai
Original Story: Sakon Kaidou
Original Character Designs: Taiki
2
MANGA OMNIBUS 2
ON SALE NOW!

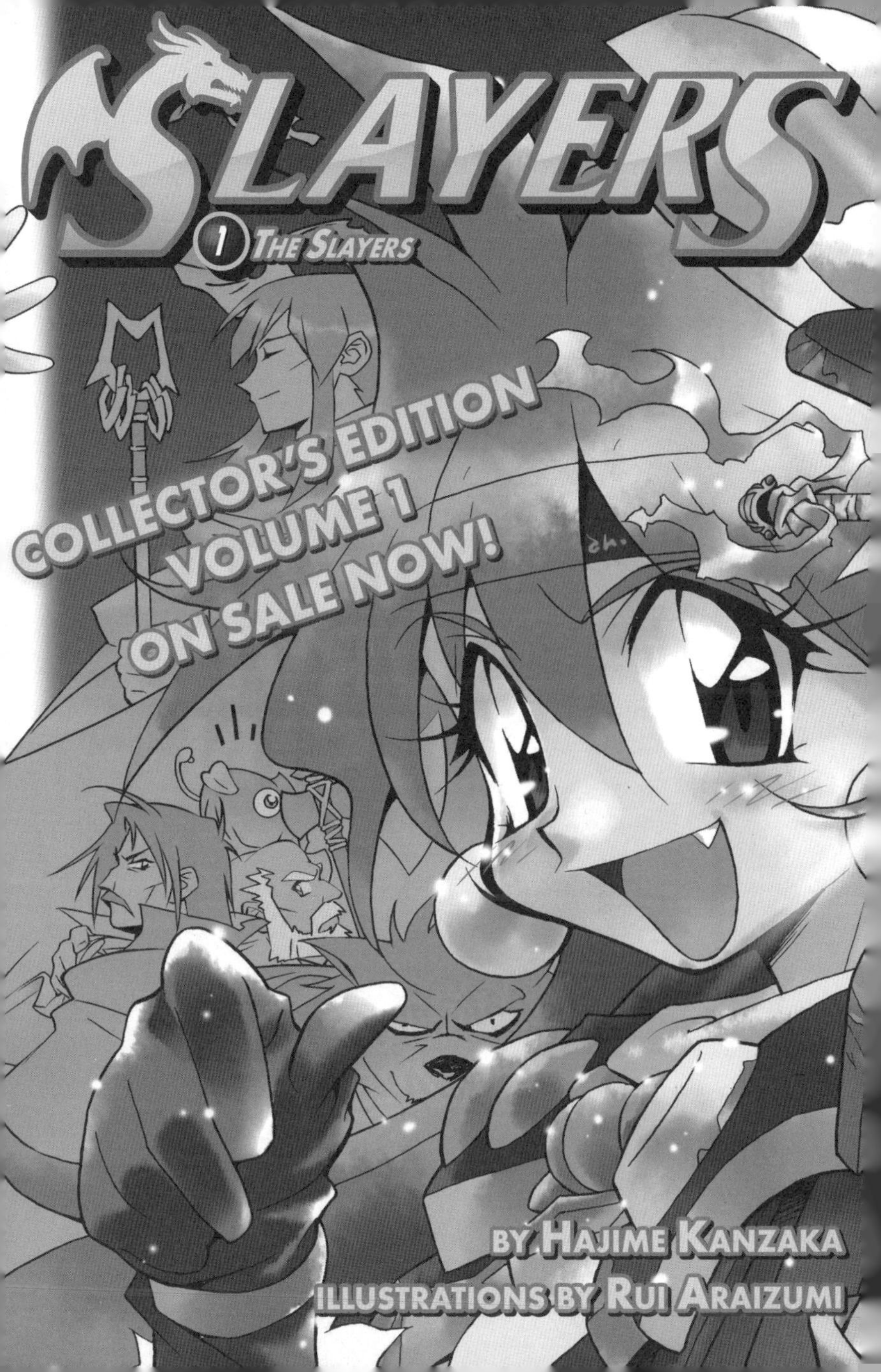

SLAYERS
1 THE SLAYERS
COLLECTOR'S EDITION
VOLUME 1
ON SALE NOW!
BY HAJIME KANZAKA
ILLUSTRATIONS BY RUI ARAIZUMI

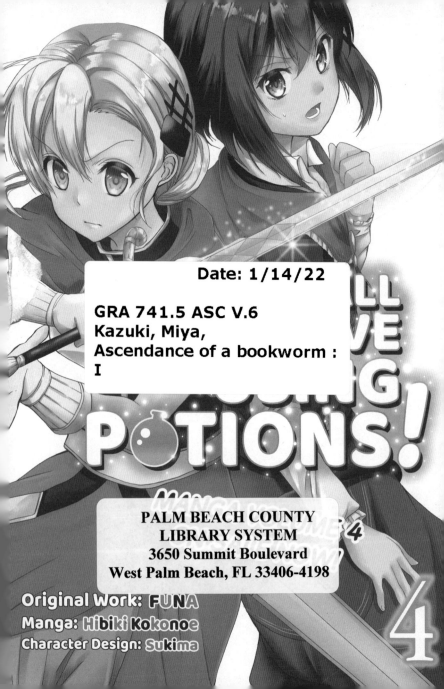

Original Work: FUNA
Manga: Hibiki Kokonoe
Character Design: Sukima

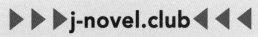

J-Novel Club Lineup

Ebook Releases Series List

A Lily Blooms in Another World
A Very Fairy Apartment**
A Wild Last Boss Appeared!
Altina the Sword Princess
Amagi Brilliant Park
An Archdemon's Dilemma:
    How to Love Your Elf Bride**
Animetal!**
The Apothecary Diaries
Are You Okay With a Slightly Older
    Girlfriend?
Arifureta: From Commonplace
    to World's Strongest
Arifureta Zero
Ascendance of a Bookworm*
Banner of the Stars
Beatless
Bibliophile Princess*
Black Summoner*
The Bloodline
By the Grace of the Gods
Campfire Cooking in Another
    World with My Absurd Skill*
Can Someone Please Explain
    What's Going On?!
The Combat Baker and Automaton
    Waitress
Cooking with Wild Game*
Deathbound Duke's Daughter
Demon King Daimaou
Demon Lord, Retry!*
Der Werwolf: The Annals of Veight*
Discommunication**
Dungeon Busters
The Economics of Prophecy
The Epic Tale of the Reincarnated
    Prince Herscherik
The Extraordinary, the Ordinary,
    and SOAP!
The Faraway Paladin*
From Truant to Anime Screenwriter:
    My Path to "Anohana" and "The
    Anthem of the Heart"
Full Metal Panic!
Fushi no Kami: Rebuilding
    Civilization Starts With a Village
The Great Cleric
The Greatest Magicmaster's
    Retirement Plan
Girls Kingdom
Grimgar of Fantasy and Ash
Her Majesty's Swarm

Holmes of Kyoto
The Holy Knight's Dark Road
How a Realist Hero Rebuilt the
    Kingdom*
How NOT to Summon a Demon
    Lord
I Love Yuri and I Got Bodyswapped
    with a Fujoshi!**
I Refuse to Be Your Enemy!
I Saved Too Many Girls and Caused
    the Apocalypse
I Shall Survive Using Potions!*
I'll Never Set Foot in That House
    Again!
The Ideal Sponger Life
If It's for My Daughter, I'd Even
    Defeat a Demon Lord
In Another World With My
    Smartphone
Infinite Dendrogram*
Infinite Stratos
Invaders of the Rokujouma!?
Isekai Rebuilding Project
JK Haru is a Sex Worker in Another
    World
Kobold King
Kokoro Connect
Last and First Idol
Lazy Dungeon Master
The Magic in this Other World is
    Too Far Behind!*
The Magician Who Rose From
    Failure
Mapping: The Trash-Tier Skill That
    Got Me Into a Top-Tier Party*
Marginal Operation**
The Master of Ragnarok & Blesser
    of Einherjar*
Middle-Aged Businessman, Arise in
    Another World!
Mixed Bathing in Another
    Dimension
Monster Tamer
My Big Sister Lives in a Fantasy
    World
My Friend's Little Sister Has It
    In For Me!
My Instant Death Ability is So
    Overpowered, No One in This
    Other World Stands a Chance
    Against Me!

My Next Life as a Villainess: All
    Routes Lead to Doom!
Our Crappy Social Game Club Is
    Gonna Make the Most Epic
    Game
Otherside Picnic
Outbreak Company
Outer Ragna
Record of Wortenia War*
Seirei Gensouki: Spirit Chronicles*
Sexiled: My Sexist Party Leader
    Kicked Me Out, So I Teamed Up
    With a Mythical Sorceress!
She's the Cutest... But We're
    Just Friends!
Slayers
The Sorcerer's Receptionist
Sorcerous Stabber Orphen*
Sweet Reincarnation**
The Tales of Marielle Clarac*
Tearmoon Empire
Teogonia
The Underdog of the Eight Greater
    Tribes
The Unwanted Undead
    Adventurer*
WATARU!!! The Hot-Blooded
    Fighting Teen & His Epic
    Adventures After Stopping a
    Truck with His Bare Hands!!
Welcome to Japan, Ms. Elf!*
When the Clock Strikes Z
The White Cat's Revenge as
    Plotted from the Dragon King's
    Lap
Wild Times with a Fake Fake
    Princess
The World's Least Interesting
    Master Swordsman
Yume Nikki: I Am Not in
    Your Dream

* Novel and Manga Editions
** Manga Only

Keep an eye out at j-novel.club
    for further new title
    announcements!